Outsourcing Management Information Systems

Marc J. Schniederjans, University of Nebraska - Lincoln, USA

Ashlyn M. Schniederjans, Johns Hopkins University, USA

Dara G. Schniederjans, University of Minnesota - Twin Cities, USA

T0325224

IDEA GROUP PUBLISHING

Hershey • London • Melbourne • Singapore

Acquisitions Editor: Michelle Potter
Development Editor: Kristin Roth
Senior Managing Editor: Jennifer Neidig
Managing Editor: Sara Reed
Copy Editor: April Schmidt and Evelyn Maitens
Typesetter: Jessie Weik
Cover Design: Lisa Tosheff
Printed at: Integrated Book Technology

Published in the United States of America by
    Idea Group Publishing (an imprint of Idea Group Inc.)
    701 E. Chocolate Avenue
    Hershey PA 17033
    Tel: 717-533-8845
    Fax: 717-533-8661
    E-mail: cust@idea-group.com
    Web site: http://www.idea-group.com

and in the United Kingdom by
    Idea Group Publishing (an imprint of Idea Group Inc.)
    3 Henrietta Street
    Covent Garden
    London WC2E 8LU
    Tel: 44 20 7240 0856
    Fax: 44 20 7379 0609
    Web site: http://www.eurospanonline.com

Library of Congress Cataloging-in-Publication   Data

Outsourcing management information systems / Marc Schniederjans, Ashlyn M. Schniederjans and Dara G. Schniederjans, editors.
    p. cm.
  Summary: "This book balances the positive outcomes of outsourcing, which have made it a popular management strategy with the negative to provide a more inclusive decision; it explores risk factors that have not yet been widely associated with this strategy. It focuses on the conceptual "what", "why", and "where" aspects of outsourcing as well as the methodological "how" aspects"--Provided by publisher.
  ISBN 1-59904-195-2 (hardcover) -- ISBN 1-59904-196-0 (softcover) -- ISBN 1-59904-197-9 (ebook)
  1. Information technology--Management. 2. Contracting out. 3. Offshore outsourcing. I. Schniederjans, Marc J. II. Schniederjans, Ashlyn M. III. Schniederjans, Dara G.
  HD30.2.O88 2007
  004.068'4--dc22
                    2006019118

British Cataloguing in Publication Data
A Cataloguing in Publication record for this book is available from the British Library.

Outsourcing Management Information Systems

Table of Contents

Preface vii

Section I: Fundamental Issues in Information System Outsourcing

Chapter I
Conceptual Evolution of Business Organizations into Outsourcing-Insourcing Alliance Networks 1
Ashlyn M. Schniederjans, Johns Hopkins University, USA
Dara G. Schniederjans, University of Minnesota - Twin Cities, USA

Chapter II
Why, When, and What to Outsource 17
Donald A. Carpenter, Mesa State College, USA
Vijay K. Agrawal, University of Nebraska - Kearney, USA

Chapter III
Planning for Information Systems Outsourcing 43
Vijay K. Agrawal, University of Nebraska - Kearney, USA
Donald A. Carpenter, Mesa State College, USA

Chapter IV
Strategic and Tactical Planning of Outsourcing in MIS 63
Jeanette Nasem Morgan, Duquesne University, USA

Section II: Decision-Making Issues in Management Information Systems Outsourcing

Chapter V
Establishing Performance Metrics for Managing the Outsourced
MIS Project 94
    Jeanette Nasem Morgan, Duquesne University, USA

Chapter VI
The Case for Centralized IT Contract Management: A Four Force
Model 125
    Anthony Briggs, Best Buy, USA
    Eric Walden, Texas Tech University, USA
    James J. Hoffman, Texas Tech University, USA

Chapter VII
Decision-Making Methods in MIS Outsourcing: Case Studies of
Successes and Failures 134
    Jeanette Nasem Morgan, Duquesne University, USA

Chapter VIII
Lessons Learned from Successes and Failures in Information
Systems Outsourcing 153
    Kathryn M. Zuckweiler, University of Nebraska - Kearney, USA

Chapter IX
Information System Outsourcing Decision: Case Study on the
Automotive Industry 176
    Rafael Lapiedra, University Jaume I, Spain
    Joaquin Alegre, University of Valencia, Spain
    Ricardo Chiva, University Jaume I, Spain
    Steve Smithson, London School of Economics and Political Science, UK

Chapter X
Outsourcing Information Technology: The Role of Social Capital 190
    James J. Hoffman, Texas Tech University, USA
    Eric A. Walden, Texas Tech University, USA
    Mark L. Hoelscher, Illinois State University, USA

Chapter XI
Outsourcing of Services by Service Firms: An Empirical
Investigation 200
  Masaaki Kotabe, Temple University, USA
  Janet Y. Murray, University of Missouri - St. Louis, USA
  Maneesh Chandra, ZS Associates, USA

Section III: Risk Issues in Management
Information Systems Outsourcing

Chapter XII
Outsourcing and Information Systems Development: How
Complementary Corporate Cultures Minimize the Risks of
Outsourced Systems Projects 225
  Julie E. Kendall, Rutgers University, USA
  Kenneth E. Kendall, Rutgers University, USA

Chapter XIII
Managing Risks of IT Outsourcing 242
  Leonardo Legorreta, California State University, USA
  Rajneesh Goyal, California State University, USA

Chapter XIV
A Framework for Evaluating Outsourcing Risk 270
  Merrill Warkentin, Mississippi State University, USA
  April M. Adams, Mississippi State University, USA

Section IV: Quantitative Methods in Management
Information System Outsourcing

Chapter XV
A Goal Programming Model for Evaluating Outsourcing Partners
on a Global Scale 283
  James J. Hoffman, Texas Tech University, USA
  Eric Walden, Texas Tech University, USA
  Francisco Delgadillo Jr., Texas Tech University, USA
  Ronald Bremer, Texas Tech University, USA

Chapter XVI
Real Option Appraisal in R&D Outsourcing 299
  Qing Cao, University of Missouri - Kansas City, USA
  Karyl B. Leggio, University of Missouri - Kansas City, USA

Chapter XVII
The Application of Real Options to the R&D Outsourcing
Decision 312
    Qing Cao, University of Missouri - Kansas City, USA
    David N. Ford, Texas A&M University, USA
    Karyl B. Leggio, University of Missouri - Kansas City, USA

Chapter XVIII
An Application of Multi-Criteria Decision-Making Model to
Strategic Outsourcing for Effective Supply-Chain Linkages 324
    N. K. Kwak, Saint Louis University, USA
    Chang Won Lee, Jinju National University, Korea

Chapter XIX
Is the Business Model Broken? A Model of the Difference
Between Pay-Now and Pay-Later Contracts in IT Outsourcing 344
    Eric Walden, Texas Tech University, USA
    Param Vir Singh, University of Washington, USA

About the Authors 369

Index 378

Preface

Overview of Outsourcing

Outsourcing is defined as being one of allocating or reallocating business activities from an internal source to an external source (Schniederjans, Schniederjans, & Schniederjans, 2005, p. 3). Any business activity can be outsourced. All or part of any of the unique business activities in a functional area, like management information systems, which have been historically insourced can be outsourced today. Outsourcing, however, requires an agreement with an external organization. If a contract can be written to define any type of business activity between a client organization and its potential outsource provider, then that business activity can be outsourced.

Outsourcing is not a new concept according to James and Weidenbaum (1993, p. 42) but can find its origins in the practice of *subcontracting* production activities. For example, the use of external lawyers or information technology consultants can be viewed as outsourced services. Indeed, the classic "buy-or-make" decisions on service products, processes, and facilities, which companies have been making for many decades, are examples of outsourcing from external organizations (Russell & Taylor, 2003, p. 126). Regardless of its origin, outsourcing is not a revolution but an evolution of change in business organizations and the way they conduct business activities.

Outsourcing is viewed as one of the most important management strategies of our time. In a business survey of executives the most important reasons for outsourcing include among many items, cost savings, to gain outside expertise, to improve services, focus on core competencies and to gain access to technology (Goldsmith, 2003). The survey sought to ascertain the future outsourcing general trends by asking executives what outsourcing they planned to undertake in the future. A total of 35% of the executives said they would continue or expand outsourcing, 40% said they would continue but alter their outsourcing arrangements to better favor themselves, and 25% said they would reduce outsourcing or choose to insource their work. These last two percentages reveal that the majority of their experiences in outsourcing did not completely satisfy the executives, requiring a need for a change in their future outsourcing strategy. Yet other research on outsourcing reveals significant expansion trends. According to Gartner, Inc. outsourcing will account for 53% of the total worldwide *information technology* (IT) service market, and is estimated to make up 56% of the market by 2007 (IT outsourcing likely to grow, 2004).

Outsourcing and Management Information Systems

Of the primary functional areas within any firm mentioned by Goldsmith (2003), the most commonly outsourced functional area is *information technology* (IT) which included all aspects of management information systems. Lackow's (2001) survey of the IT outsourcing industry revealed IT provider service categories included user support, voice network management, disaster recovery, software development, data network management, software maintenance, data center operations, IT strategy and planning, support services, application hosting, and business processes. The survey predicted IT outsourcing would continue and grow in importance. This prediction was confirmed by a later follow-up survey by Goldsmith (2003). This latter survey confirmed the prediction by estimating 79% of the U.S. firms outsourced IT and the current outsourcing industry provides a full range of services from small-scale projects to complete business process solutions. Other research by Lee, Huynh, and Kwok (2003) confirms clients continue to benefit from outsourcing IT. With projections of U.S. firms saving almost $21 billion in IT expenses by offshoring from 2003 to 2008, it is difficult to argue against the potential cost savings reasoning for outsourcing IT (McDougall, 2004). This recurring theme is obvious in other IT outsourcing literature as well (Offshore outsourcing poised, 2004). What is new and only now beginning to surface is the recognition of including risk elements in the decision process (Bhattacharya, Behara, & Gundersen, 2003; "Discover Weighs the Risk", 2004; Offshore outsourcing poised, 2004; Negotiating the Contract, 2004). Indeed, the IT outsourcing clients in the industry are now starting to recognize that outsourcing risks can cause failed projects with greater costs and poorer quality than expected (Challenges to consider, 2004; Natovich, 2003; Offshoring call centers, 2004; Soliman & Chen, 2003).

Problems with MIS Outsourcing

While the general trend for outsourcing is ever increasing (Offshore outsourcing boosts, 2004) there are other observed trends (e.g., government anti-outsourcing legislation, the need to revise existing outsourcing arrangements, or *backsourcing* by experienced outsourcers, etc.) that indicate the current practice of outsourcing needs improvement if it is to be more than just a "make-or-buy" decision process.

With growth, there are always problems. As the outsourcing industry grows every year, there is an increased need to be more knowledgeable about this new industry, how it can benefit management of information systems, and improve business operations in general. There is an urgent need to be educated on issues, concepts, philosophies, procedures, methodologies, and practices of outsourcing. As noted in a report by Hall (2003), half of all outsourcing agreements fail because firms run risks by not performing appropriate analyses. For example, some organizations consider outsourcing as a means of migrating risk (e.g., the outsource provider takes on the risks of investing in human resources, technology, etc., while the client firm avoids those risks and simply pays a fee for the services). Yet Natovich (2003) reports that while some risks are absorbed by the outsource provider, the client assumes the set of risks inherent in the outsourcing arrangement in addition to most of the outsource provider assumed risks. Greaver (1999, pp. 37-58), Chorafas (2003, pp. 49-70), and Kern and Willcocks (2001, pp. 39-80) report dozens of differing types of risk and the possible range of concern managers should be wary of in undertaking outsourcing projects, while recognizing that some risks are valid and some are not depending on differing situations (Bahli & Rivard, 2005).

A careful and comprehensive analysis of outsourcing decisions and decision making is simply not being performed prior to many outsourcing ventures. Meisler (2004) reports international outsourcing fails 50% of the time because organizations have not considered the risky nature of this type of international business decision. After the fact, some firms today are reversing their international outsourcing decision, bringing it back to the country of origin (Metz, 2004). This is partially due to the perceived failure of outsourcing to achieve the expected gains. When managers set outsourcing goals of 75% cost reduction (Meisler, 2004), and then receive a 30% or 40% reduction, they undoubtedly view the outsourcing strategy as a failure, when in fact it may be a successful strategy for a client firm. It should be noted that in the previously Goldsmith (2003) survey of executives, the top five challenges for off-shore outsourcing include understanding cultural differences and dealing with political uncertainty (rated the top reason), evaluating contract performance, client firm's ignorance of what the outsource provider is doing for them, accountability, and the expenses of travel. These reasons, which find their basis in poor analysis and understanding of outsourcing, represent a substantial barrier to growth in outsourcing. The same survey reveals that while 52% of the respondents are not even considering offshore outsourcing, 27% are planning on international outsourcing of some kind in the next three years.

Of all the reasons given for outsourcing failures, the one consistent reason is a lack of analyses of the outsourcing decision (Meisler, 2004). Specifically, client firms may fail to perform adequate analyses because their approach to the outsourcing decision lacks relevant quantitative analysis, despite the fact there have been many outsourcing books published in last decade. Most of these books treat the outsourcing decision as a conceptual process, rather than a quantitative analysis (Chorafas, 2003; Cullen & Willcocks, 2003; Gouge, 2003). Unlike quantitative methods, conceptual methods tend to focus on a more limited singular variable at one time (e.g., just cost, ignoring quality or other relevant variables). This can cause the analysis to possibly miss variable changes in dynamic relationship in the analysis. Outsourcing is clearly a dynamic, highly interrelated process of business activities involving many variables and requiring consideration of many factors. In a comprehensive review of the current literature Dibbern et al. (2004) revealed a substantial body of outsourcing literature but that problems remain unsolved. There is a clear need for both more qualitative as well as quantitative approaches to outsourcing to better improve the success rate of this important strategy for business performance success.

Organization of the Book

This book is organized into four sections, containing a total of 19 chapters. There are four chapters in **Section I**, entitled "Fundamental Issues in Information System Outsourcing." The purpose of this section is to provide some of the basics in understanding where the outsourcing industry has come from, how it works, and how organizations incorporate outsourcing into their planning processes.

Chapter I focuses on how the outsourcing industry has evolved and where its organizational structure is taking it in an effort to support business operations. As the industry of outsourcing evolves, it impacts how business organizations are structured. This chapter reviews current literature and proposes two possible evolutions of how businesses motivate organizations to incorporate outsourcing as an integral strategy for success. The resulting trends show an evolution that may lead hierarchal business structures to incorporate temporary outsourcing alliance networks in the same way that general contractors in the construction industry have operated for years.

Chapter II presents an overview of the outsourcing phenomenon, focusing on the question of why, when, and what to outsource. It provides an extensive set of guidelines for business students to understand the nature of outsourcing. Drawing extensively on recent scholarly literature, this chapter presents a wide range of concepts, including causes that might lead a company to a decision to outsource and factors that contribute to an environment that is conducive to outsourcing. The question of what to outsource is answered by examining core competencies and critical success factors. The chapter also presents information about trends in outsourcing in specific countries and industries to help the reader understand what is possible.

Chapter III presents an overview of planning aspects for the outsourcing of information systems projects. The first major section of the chapter presents an historical perspective on the evolution of information systems outsourcing practices so the reader can understand subsequent sections of the chapter in context. It next deals with the need to examine goals, strategies, core competencies, and critical success factors as well as presenting all the functional areas of information systems that are candidates to be outsourced. Also included are discussions of the need to perform cost/benefits analysis and to consider cultural and other factors. The concluding section deals with all the factors that should be examined in preparing and administering outsourcing contracts.

Chapter IV lays out a set of steps for organizations to traverse in considering and crafting an outsourcing strategy for the firm. In general, outsourcing may include business process support, customer support, providing technology infrastructure, or software development services. Outsourcing deals may be even done by local or rural service providers in the same country as the client organization. Other arrangements may be negotiated with near-shore of offshore providers in different time zones. This chapter proceeds through the steps of strategic and tactical planning, addressing particular issues at each level, and concludes with operational level planning for outsourcing projects. Lessons learned from good techniques for integrating planning across the firm are included. Best practice methods and decision models for outsourcing are crafted from both outsourcing success stories as well as numerous failures, and are covered in subsequent chapters. This chapter includes suggestions for how to address and consider the option of outsourcing MIS projects as part of an overall Strategic Plan. Project management considerations in this decision are included. Ethical considerations such as humanitarian consequences and theological considerations are addressed.

In the next section of this book, **Section II**, entitled "Decision-Making Issues in Management Information System Outsourcing," seven chapters are presented. The purpose of this section is to focus on the various decision-making situations found in outsourcing MIS and to identify the types of decisions, how best to measure and make them, and what to avoid. Both theorectical and empirical results are presented in this section.

Chapter V presents the tactics and metrics an organization applies after having made a decision to use outsource providers. Tactics are used to define the nature and specifics of the outsourcing arrangement, as well as to select the contractual basis of the agreement. For these purposes, it is critical to align measures of performance compliance in the form of metrics on each MIS outsourcing relationship. When negotiating and establishing the terms of the outsourcing arrangement, management should ensure that appropriate performance metrics are identified and included, and that flexibility for change is built in to the contract. This chapter addresses some of the methods, as well as some of the metrics that might be used in such contract agreements. The use of contracts and service level agreements are discussed, as well as in-depth techniques for conducting validation and background checks on outsource suppliers. Sample outlines for service level agreement preparation and performance specifications are included for the practitioner.

Chapter VI develops a model that describes four forces that move organizations toward centralized IT contract management. Specifically, the model illustrates how centralizing IT contract management enhances organizational performance in four areas. First, centralizing IT contract management allows for a corporate level view of technology, which supports not only interoperability, but also optimizes software license inventory. Second, it combats vendor opportunism by creating a set of contract negotiators who have as much knowledge as the vendor's contract negotiators. Third, it enhances information retrieval by locating the physical contracts in a central location, which allows the legal department, project managers, and senior managers to quickly and reliably locate contract details. Fourth, it provides the proper motivation to project managers and contract negotiators by rewarding each job separately rather than by lumping the rewards for timely project completion together with the rewards for efficient contract negotiation.

Chapter VII starts with a discussion of corporate and government decision-making processes and management sciences that support development of decisions. Special decision-making considerations, trade-offs analyses, and cost-benefit studies all figure into decisions that result in outsourcing. Models of trade-offs and evaluation criteria are drawn from the management sciences. Some of these are management approaches, and models are used to justify MIS outsourcing decisions. Technologies that support different methods of decision-making include data warehouses and data mining, rules-based logic, heuristical processes, fuzzy logic and expert-based reasoning. These technologies are presented in the context of corporate planning processes that consider the ethics, payback, and rationales for outsourcing of MIS. This chapter also presents case studies that use these decision-making constructs to evaluate outsourcing for MIS projects or for ongoing information services. Current and evolving technologies are presented and discussed in the context of managing and controlling outsourced MIS. Case studies are presented as a means to illustrate both good decision-making techniques as well as poor or inappropriate decisions that resulted in outsourced project failures.

Chapter VIII presents a process map of information systems outsourcing decisions and factors which influence the outcome of the outsourcing project at each decision point. The authors take a broad view of outsourcing projects and examine IS outsourcing successes and failures in context of project phase. Brief examples are provided to illustrate various outcomes of the decisions faced by both outsourcing vendor and client. The chapter also presents a summary of lessons learned about information systems outsourcing and recommendations for future research.

Chapter IX examines outsourcing decisions in information technology (IT) research that have yielded contradictory findings and recommendations when outsourcing all or some of their information systems (IS) activities. This chapter examines the potential problems a company may face when reconsidering the outsourcing decision. For this purpose, we conducted an empirical study in a European car manufacturing company that has followed the outsourcing alternative. The case analysed offers insights about the outsourcing decision process and the difficulties the company faced when trying to adapt the software developed to the new business requirements. The problems that came out pushed the company to move back to the internalisation of the IS functions. The case shows a greater involvement of users on in-house developed projects. Our findings indicate that outsourcing is a good alternative when the IS activity is a technical one which does not require specific knowledge of the company.

Chapter X explores the role that one factor, social capital, may have on the success of IT outsourcing. It extends current understanding of outsourcing success and failure by examining the effect of social capital on outsourcing success. In the chapter it is proposed that social capital has a potential impact on information technology (IT) outsourcing success. Specifically, it is theorized that social capital has an inverted "U" shape relationship with outsourcing success.

Chapter XI examines why the traditional "make-or-buy" decision (i.e., in-house sourcing or outsourcing) has been widely studied in the context of the theory of the firm and vertical integration. One of the most popular frameworks for examining this strategic decision has been the transaction cost analysis (TCA) framework. However, much of past research has focused on the make-or-buy decisions of product manufacturing activities, to the neglect of services. The make-or-buy decisions of services and service activities, due to their inherent characteristics (i.e., intangibility, inseparability, heterogeneity, and perishability) and the unique nature of their "production" and "delivery," necessitate modifying and revamping the existing framework. The authors develop and empirically test a conceptual framework that examines factors influencing a firm's decision to use outsourcing or in-house sourcing for a service (service activity).

In the next section of this book, **Section III**, entitled "Risk Issues in Management Information System Outsourcing," three chapters are presented. The purpose of this section is to focus on the critical and often overlooked issue of risk in outsourcing MIS. How risk can be identified, managed, and evaluated are topics covered in this section.

Chapter XII examines the metaphors found in the language of client corporations and outsourcing partners and explain how to look for compatibility when designing various types of information systems including traditional MIS, decision support systems, expert systems and AI, executive information systems, cooperative systems, and competitive systems. Many firms outsource creation of program code for management information systems, but not all experiences are successful. Although some researchers and practitioners are quick to blame failures on differing country cultures, this does not appear to be the reason. Rather it is the compatibility or differences in corporate cultures between the client company and the outsourcing partner that may help or hinder the development of quality systems. We explain how the development of certain types of systems can benefit from situations where more positive metaphors exist and offer some guidelines for the MIS practitioner, thereby minimizing risk and increasing the likelihood of a more successful client company-outsourcing partner relationship.

Chapter XIII examines risks in outsourcing IT operations. The fact that firms are turning to outside vendors in increasing numbers in order to meet their needs does not mean that outsourcing is without problems. Firms often enter outsourcing deals without considering risks or assuming that all risks lay with the external service provider. In this chapter, we provide an overview of IT outsourcing, its risks, and a model for managing those risks. We identify different firm–vendor configurations for sustaining long-term relationships aimed at diversifying risk over time and discuss the need for psychological contracts to manage such outsourcing relationships.

Chapter XIV provides a framework for evaluating and mitigating the risks associated with IT outsourcing projects. Outsourcing projects have been met with successes and many failures. The causes of such failures must be systematically investigated in order to provide managers guidance to avoid future risks from outsourcing projects. This chapter discusses the outsourcing relationship, highlighting the primary causes of project successes and failures, then offers a framework for evaluating vendor relationships to avoid contingencies that may lead to failure. This framework will serve as a guide for managers of firms seeking to outsource various IT functions, as well as managers of vendor firms who seek success in these relationships.

In the last section of this book, **Section IV**, entitled "Quantitative Methods in Management Information System Outsourcing," five chapters are presented. The purpose of this section is to examine a variety of new and creative collection of quantitative methods that can be used to guide and plan outsourcing MIS.

Chapter XV examines the evaluation process on a global scale of potential outsourcing partners. In order for outsourcing to be successful, corporations must identify outsourcing partners that offer a good fit with the firm's overall outsourcing strategy. Unfortunately, little has been written to aid corporations in making complex decisions involving the evaluation of potential outsourcing partners. This chapter presents a goal programming model that combines the concepts of global outsourcing, the management science technique of goal programming, and microcomputer technology to provide managers with a more effective and efficient method for evaluating potential IT outsourcing partners. The chapter extends the existing literature on outsourcing by applying a computer optimization model to outsourcing partner selection in a way that has not been done before.

Chapter XVI will stress MIS's strides in R&D outsourcing, and will detail the risks and uncertainty associated with the process of outsourcing core areas of the business such as R&D. Moreover, this chapter will propose the use of real option analysis to assist in deciding: Why should a firm outsource R&D? and How does a company select a viable vendor using a two-stage process? This chapter includes a discussion of the cutting edge usage of outsourcing for R&D; and, to alleviate the R&D outsourcing risks, we will explore the two-stage vendor selection approach in information technology outsourcing using real options analysis.

Chapter XVII provides two real-world case studies of the application of real options to answer the question: "How do practicing planners and managers use and value flexibility in development projects?" The first case study we develop is based on the outsourcing decision-making process, more specifically, a two-stage vendor selection approach (applying real options theory) to adopting a supply chain management (SCM) system in a Shanghai-based transportation company. In the second case study, we use the example of the National Ignition Facility (NIF) to illustrate how decision-makers identify uncertainty and value flexibility in project analysis, and by deliberate decision, increase their optionality and thereby project value.

Chapter XVIII illustrates the development of outsourcing and supply-chain planning strategy needs to be based on compromised and more objective decision-making procedures. Although factors affecting business performance in manufacturing firms have been explored in the past, focuses are on financial performance and measurement, and neglecting intangible and nonfinancial factors in the decision-making planning process. This study presents development of an integrated multicriteria decision-making (MCDM) model. This model aids in allocating outsourcing and supply-chain resources pertinent to strategic planning by providing a satisfying solution. The model was developed based on the data obtained from a business firm producing intelligent home system devices. This developed model will reinforce a firm's ongoing outsourcing strategies to meet defined requirements while positioning the supply-chain system to respond to a new growth and innovation.

Chapter XIX seeks to evaluate the dominant IT outsourcing contracts model (pay-later) as compared to an alternative model (pay-now) in light of changing economic conditions. We integrate practitioner observations in the spirit of mathematical transaction cost problems to develop a conceptual economic model to compare these two types of contracts. We uncover three very important facts which suggest that pay-now contracts are always at least as good as pay-later contracts, and pay-now contracts are better than pay-later contracts when the economy is volatile. These findings provide a rich insight into the problem of failing IT outsourcing contracts since the prevailing poor state of the economy. We further discuss the implications of our findings and suggest that simply shifting the contract from a pay-later to a pay-now will fix the IT outsourcing business model.

References

Bahli, B., & Rivard, S. (2005). Validating measures of information technology outsourcing risk factors. *Omega, 33*(2), 175-187.

Bhattacharya, S., Behara, R. S., & Gundersen, D. E. (2003). Business risk perspectives on information systems outsourcing. *International Journal of Accounting Information Systems, 4*(1), 75-94.

Challenges to consider. (2004, September 19-26). *Outsourcing Intelligence Bulletin: FSO Magazine, 11*(1). Retrieved from editor @fsoutsourcing.com

Chorafas, D. N. (2003). *Outsourcing, insourcing and IT for enterprise management.* Houndmills, UK: Palgrave/MacMillan.

Cullen, S., & Willcocks, L. (2003). *Intelligent IT outsourcing.* London: Butterworth-Heinemann.

Discover weights the risk. (2004, September 19-26). *Outsourcing Intelligence Bulletin: FSO Magazine, 11*(1). Retrieved from editor @fsoutsourcing.com

Goldsmith, N. M. (2003). *Outsourcing trends.* New York: The Conference Board.

Gouge, I. (2003). *Shaping the IT organization.* London: Springer.

Greaver, M. F. (1999). *Strategic outsourcing*. New York: American Management Association.

Hall, M. (2003). Outsourcing deals fail half the time. *Computerworld, 37*(44), 10.

IT outsourcing likely to grow, says Gartner. (2004, May 23-30). *Outsourcing Intelligence Bulletin: FSO Magazine, 4*(7). Retrieved from editor @fsoutsourcing.com

James, H. S., & Weidenbaum, M. (1993). *When businesses cross international borders*. Westport, CT: Preager.

Kern, T., & Willcocks, L. P. (2001). *The relationship advantage: Information technologies, sourcing, and management*. Oxford: Oxford University Press.

Lackow, H. M. (2001). *IT outsourcing trends*. New York: The Conference Board.

Lee, J.-N., Huynh, M. Q., & Kwok, R. C.-W. (2003). IT outsourcing evolution: Past, present, and future. *Communications of the ACM, 46*(5), 84-90.

McDougall, P. (2004, September 6). The offshore equation: Is offshoring worth the heat? The financials are compelling, and the benefits may well ripple throughout the economy. *InformationWeek*. Retrieved March 16, 2006, from http://www.informationweek.com/story/showArticle.jhtml?articleID= 46800044&tid=16008

Meisler, A. (2004). Think globally, act rationally. *Workforce Management, 83*(1), 40-45.

Metz, C. (2004, February 17). Tech support coming home? *PC Magazine, 23*(3), 20.

Natovich, J. (2003). Vendor related risks in IT development: A chronology of an outsourced project failure. *Technology Analysis & Strategic Management, 15*(4), 409-420.

Negotiating the contract: Best practices in mitigating the risks of changing business needs, evolving technology, rising costs and more. (2004, June 13-20). *Outsourcing Intelligence Bulletin: FSO Magazine, 5*(2). Retrieved from editor@fsoutsourcing.com

Offshore outsourcing boosts IT service market in 2003, says Gartner. (2004, June 27-July 4). *Outsourcing Intelligence Bulletin: FSO Magazine, 9*(2).

Offshore outsourcing poised for double-digit growth. (2004, November 5). *Outsourcing Intelligence Bulletin: FSO Magazine, 14*(1). Retrieved from editor@fsoutsourcing.com

Offshoring call centers. (2004, September 19-26). *Outsourcing Intelligence Bulletin: FSO Magazine, 11*(1). Retrieved from editor@fsoutsourcing.com

Schniederjans, M. J., Schniederjans, A. M., & Schniederjans, D. G. (2005). *Outsourcing and insourcing in an international context.* Armonk, NY: M. E. Sharpe.

Soliman, K. S., & Chen, L.-D. (2003). APS: Do they work? *Information Systems Management, 20*(4), 50-58.

Acknowledgments

The authors wish to thank the many people who have helped make this book a reality. We thank the many authors whose timely contributions to this book and to the literature in general are greatly appreciated. While unnamed, we wish to thank the many reviewers who, under harsh time constraints, were able to do their job and do it well. We also thank the editorial staff at Idea Group, Inc., particularly Kristin Roth, our managing editor for their professionalism and responsiveness. It was a joy to work with them all. Finally, we wish to thank Jill Schniederjans, wife and mother, who helped edit the final chapters into the required APA form and style requirements. She has made a significant contribution to this book.

While many people have had a hand in the preparation of this book, its accuracy and completeness are the responsibility of our editing efforts. For all the errors that this book may contain we apologize for them in advance.

Marc J. Schniederjans
Ashlyn M. Schniederjans
Dara G. Schniederjans

Section I

Fundamental Issues in Information System Outsourcing

Chapter I

Conceptual Evolution of Business Organizations into Outsourcing-Insourcing Alliance Networks

Ashlyn M. Schniederjans, Johns Hopkins University, USA

Dara G. Schniederjans, University of Minnesota - Twin Cities, USA

Abstract

Most business organizations have recognized the importance of outsourcing information systems and related business processes. As the industry of outsourcing evolves it impacts how business organizations are structured. This chapter reviews current literature and proposes two possible evolutions of how businesses motivate organizations to incorporate outsourcing as an integral strategy for success. The resulting trends show an evolution that may lead hierarchal business structures to incorporate temporary outsourcing alliance networks in the same way that general contractors in the construction industry have operated for years.

Introduction

One of the underlying principles of "game theory" is that all business organizations will act in rational ways for their own economic best interest (Render & Stair, 2000, p. 22). This is a reasonable assumption in that any organization capable of identifying a winning strategy for business success will adopt that strategy to the best of their abilities.

The literature on outsourcing has shown it to be a winning strategy for business success. A research study by Goldsmith (2003) revealed 79% of the U.S. companies surveyed outsourced information systems (IS) processes. Research on IS outsourcing worldwide confirm the growing importance and use of the outsourcing strategy (Barthélemy & Geyer, 2005). Yet, as Hall (2003) and others have pointed out, outsourcing fails as often as it has been successful.

Learning from these early failures, the outsourcing industry is changing to improve its ability to provide useful decision making information to all types of business organizations. Outsourcing support organizations like *Financial Services Outsourcing* (www.fsoutsourcing.com) provide information and service access making it easy for any organization to take best advantage of the outsourcing strategy. Even the industry of outsourcing is becoming more institutionalized to provider better service. For example support organizations like the *Outsourcing Benchmarking Association* (www.obenchmarking.com) provide detailed benchmarks on various functional area business performance parameters. These benchmarks can be used by "client firms" to evaluate "outsource providers" and outsourcing decisions.

Despite the changes in the outsourcing industry, there are basic aspects of the process of outsourcing that do not change over time. When two separate businesses, a client firm and a provider firm, temporarily join their resources together, it is an alliance (O'Brien & Marakas, 2006, p. 43). For some, the process of outsourcing is considered a temporary "alliance" (Milgate, 2001; Schniederjans, Schniederjans, & Schniederjans, 2006). For others outsourcing is viewed as a long-term strategic alliance (Willcocks & Choi, 1995). Regardless of the context in which outsourcing is viewed, the important point is that it is consistently viewed as a type of alliance.

As the industry of outsourcing evolves to meet the needs of client firms, so do the client firm's organizations to utilize outsource provider services (Kotabe & Murray, 2004). The purpose of this chapter is to explore possible changes in typical business organizational structures brought by their use of outsourcing strategies. A literature review provides the basis of the suggested changes and what we suggest will become the eventual "outsourcing-insourcing alliance networks" organization structure of the future.

Trends in the Outsourcing Industry

There are five trends in the outsourcing industry in this chapter that are impacting and causing client firm organizations to change. These trends are: (1) growth of the outsourcing industry worldwide, (2) growth in the size of outsource providers, (3) increased range of services by outsource providers, (4) recognition of risk and failure in outsourcing business processes, and (5) governmental actions restricting outsourcing.

Growth in the Outsourcing Industry Worldwide

Current literature supports substantial economic growth in the outsourcing industry (Bangladesh to provide outsourcing, 2004; Dubai has business process, 2004). Some outsourcing industry sectors, like business process outsourcing (BPO) in India, are growing at almost 60% to 70% per annum (India is the leading outsourcing, 2004). The *Meta Group* has forecast growth in the off-shore outsourcing sector of IS to increase at a yearly rate of 20% and predicts that by the year 2009 the average enterprise will outsource 60% of its IS application work off-shore (Offshore outsourcing market, 2004). China, Russia, and almost every nation are now actively developing their own respective outsourcing industries (Diddi, 2004). While more providers in the industry might be helpful in increasing competition, they might also cause economic disruptions, leading to providers going out of the business.

Growth in the Size of Outsource Providers

The outsourcing industry is experiencing an industry trend toward integration and consolidation (Adler, 2003). As the industry consolidates, it moves from a pure competition environment to an oligopolistic environment. It appears to be a *differentiated oligopoly* (Wilson & Clark, 1998, p. 212) with the unique feature of ease of entry for smaller firms. This industry structure is similar to what Finkel (1997) has observed in the construction industry of the U.S. The consequences for this type of economic movement in the industry will eventually mean higher fees, and therefore, less expansion than many experts are now forecasting for industry growth. Indeed, the resulting larger firms will attract more and better talent, thus creating barriers of entry for medium-sized outsource provider organizations. For the talented entrepreneur who plans on running a smaller niche firm, this barrier will have no impact. Zhao and Calantone (2003) observed the trend that large outsourcing firms like those specializing in research and development (R&D), are attracting the very best human resource talent available, worldwide. Adler (2003) has also shown that select industry smaller niche-sized firms continue to grow in numbers and importance.

Outsourcing Firms Provide an Increased Range of Services

Adler (2003) has observed that segments of the outsourcing industry have been moving from single process (e.g., help desk services) providers to full range, multiprocess providers. This means a single outsource provider now offers many possible services or processes within a functional area, like IS. Others in the industry have noted outsourcing firms have to grow to meet the needs of ever larger outsourcing projects (Large IT outsourcing deals on the rise, 2004). Goldsmith's (2003) survey revealed most client firms currently use an average of three or more providers. This may lead client firms to reduce the number of outsource providers they use, while providing better integration and communication possibilities a single provider service offers. This will result in a "one-stop" service that can perform a complete BPO, where all of the processes that make up a functional area can be handled by a single, multiprocess provider.

Recognition of Risk and Failure in Outsourcing Business Processes

A new trend is the recognition of including risk in the basic outsource decision process (Bahli & Rivard, 2005; Schniederjans et al., 2006). Indeed, the IS outsourcing clients are now starting to recognize outsourcing risks can cause failed projects with greater costs and poorer quality than expected (Challenges to consider, 2004; MacInnis, 2003; Natovich, 2003; Soliman & Chen, 2003). Natovich (2003) suggests a lack of trust is at the heart of many failed outsourcing decisions, which explains the 50% failure rate of outsourcing reported by Hall (2003). In the *Conference Board* survey on IS outsourcing by Lackow (2001) all the firms surveyed said they would continue or increase their use of outsourcing. Only two years later Goldsmith (2003) reported using a similar question showing that 25% of the respondents were going to decrease or eliminate their use of outsourcing. This suggests a downward trend in the use of the outsourcing strategy.

Governmental Actions Restricting Outsourcing

A total of 36 U.S. states have drafted over 100 legislative bills seeking to restrict and even punish companies that outsource off-shore (U.S. federal anti-outsourcing, 2004). Some state governments restrict all international outsourcing of jobs to U.S. labor by limiting bidding on state contracts to companies with employees operating within the state or national borders (Arizona governor stops, 2004). Members of the U.S. Senate have introduced the *Keep American Jobs at Home Act* to eliminate tax deductions for businesses that ship U.S. jobs to foreign countries (U.S. senator introduces, 2004). U.S. firms respond by seeking to avoid the political backlash by setting up their own development centers (either solely owned or an equity joint venture with a provider) in the same foreign countries or "off-shoring" (U.S. firms set up, 2004). As Lok (2005) points out, such legislation does substantially inhibit growth and development in the outsourcing industry. This multioutsourcing legislation may cause a future decline in the outsourcing industry.

While there is great growth in the outsourcing industry presently, this may inhibit future growth. While there is success for some client firms, there is an equal number of failures. In such conflicting situations, the only certainty is change. This change will impact the outsource provider industry and the client firms they serve.

Evolution of Business Organizations into Outsourcing-Insourcing Alliance Networks

One Possible Evolution

The organizational structural changes in business firms suggested in this chapter employ economic logic and game theory. The evolution is based in part on what is being observed in the literature for the last decade and will not be embraced by all business organizations.

A typical base-line, functionally divided, hierarchical business organization is presented in Figure 1. Commonly, boards of directors make the outsourcing decision which is implemented by the chief executive officer or president of the firm. The chief marketing officer (CMO), chief accounting officer (CAO), chief finance officer (CFO), chief operations officer (COO), and chief information

Figure 1. Typical functional vision, hierarchical business organization structure

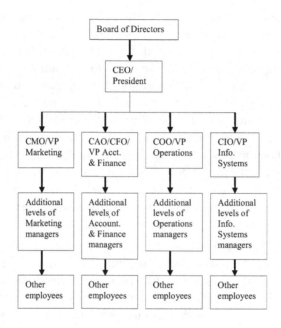

officer (CIO) are designated here as vice presidents, followed by multiple levels of other managers and the employees. We will assume other functional areas (like human resources) are equally impacted by the changes.

Outsourcing begins when a noncore competitive business activity or process is identified for outsourcing (see Gottfredson, 2005; Schniederjans et al, 2006, pp. 1-15). The decision to undertake outsourcing is usually made by the board and CEO, and passed onto the vice presidents to implement. For most organizations that are not aware of outsourcing, they may begin with a limited application of some business tasks or even an entire process. For example, a firm might find their computer help desk service (i.e., the process) is a noncore process that is competitively inefficient and in need of improvement through outsourcing. To cover all of the computer help desk services, the client firm may hire a couple of outsource providers, as depicted in Figure 2. Goldsmith (2003) has shown the typical client firm utilizes multiple outsource providers. Note the firm continues to insource the remaining IS processes. There is an inevitable integration problem when some of the business processes are insourced while others are outsourced. More than most areas, IS requires considerable integration of business activities between the various processes that make up the functional area of IS.

Figure 2. Introduction of shared outsourcing/insourcing in IS function structure

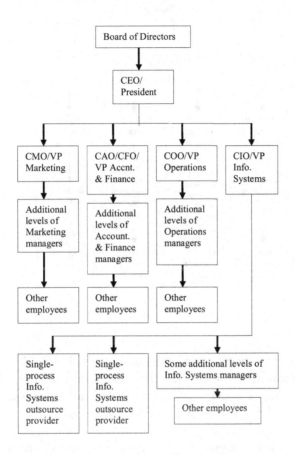

Now consider two factors: the outsourcing industry trend toward providers offering client firms full service on all processes and the economies-to-scale that might benefit the provider from doing more of the IS processes simultaneously because of better integration control. This will exert considerable economic pressure from the provider to the client to allow all of a particular functional area to be covered by a single, multiprocess outsource provider as presented in Figure 3. The cost advantages of allowing the outsource provider to handle the work will become so great, that unless the remaining processes constitute a very clear competitive advantage for the client, the provider will eventually capture all of the processes within a particular functional area.

Figure 3. Single, multiprocess outsource provider of IS function structure

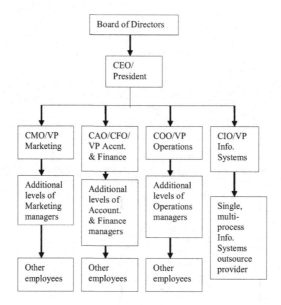

Allowing time for continued growth of outsource providers, will allow providers to erode most of the functional areas in a firm. As the outsourcing industry grows in size, it will become the main source of jobs for all businesses, worldwide because outsourced jobs tend to be at the lower and middle levels of business organizations, where the majority of the employees in a firm find employment. Moreover, it is typical for provider firms to hire existing employees in client firms, thus acquiring staff whose employment is under the control of the provider firm. From these acquisitions of employees outsource providers will be in a unique position to pick the best employees to keep in their firms. As this outsourcing labor market develops, it is expected to attract the best talent from all industries. Indeed, provider firms, which have the luxury of a high degree of specialization, will most likely become the industry leaders in the areas they function in and since they function in all areas of business, outsource providers will become the competitive edge for human resources, technology, and systems knowledge. Outsource providers will eventually be offering client firms leading-edge core competencies since they will possess the best talent in the industry. This eventuality might result in an organizational structure similar to that in Figure 4. By having a single, multiprocess provider service for each individual functional area, these outsource providers can provide improved integration within the functional areas, better utilizing their specialized skills and leading-edge abilities.

Figure 4. Individual functional areas outsourced to functionally different single providers structure

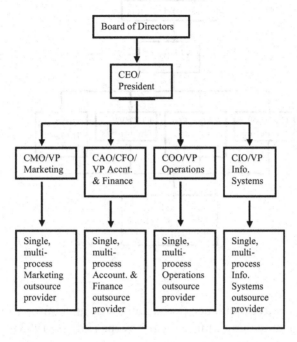

As client firms turn more of their operations over to outsource providers, they inevitably limit their own opportunities to develop new core competencies. Many outsource providers who start in one functional area within a client firm, learn how to best market their additional services to encompass further areas in the firm. This process of an outsourcing firm using internal information to takeover the client firm's business is referred to by Adler (2003) as *spillover risk*.

Observing the outsourcing industry trends of provider firms increasingly offering a range of services across functional areas, the efficiency of integration will undoubtedly motivate client firms to merge providers firms in Figure 4 into one single, multifunction provider as shown in Figure 5. Of course, when any client organization reaches the Figure 5 organizational point they will be vulnerable for takeover. In free markets, it is highly likely that this evolution will lead to outsource providers taking over corporations who follow this type of economic illogic. This type of situation has happened along product lines. One case occurred in the 1980s when General Electric (GE) outsourced microwave oven production to a then small Korean firm, Samsung. Samsung was able to produce microwaves ovens less expensively and with higher quality than GE's U.S. plants. Within a few years GE shifted all of its production to Samsung in Korea. Shortly afterwards, GE ended

Figure 5. Single outsource provider for all functional areas structure

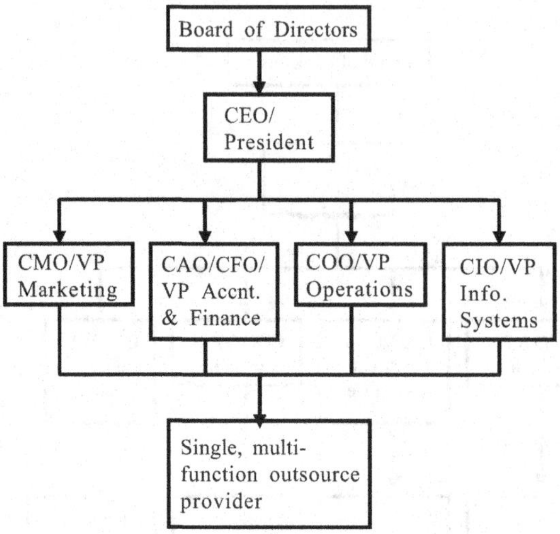

```
                    ┌──────────────────────┐
                    │  Board of Directors  │
                    └──────────┬───────────┘
                               │
                               ▼
                    ┌──────────────────┐
                    │      CEO/         │
                    │    President      │
                    └──────────────────┘
         ┌────────────┬──────────┴──────────┬────────────┐
         ▼            ▼                      ▼            ▼
  ┌───────────┐ ┌───────────┐      ┌───────────┐ ┌───────────┐
  │ CMO/VP    │ │ CAO/CFO/  │      │ COO/VP    │ │ CIO/VP    │
  │ Marketing │ │ VP Accnt. │      │ Operations│ │ Info.     │
  │           │ │ & Finance │      │           │ │ Systems   │
  └─────┬─────┘ └─────┬─────┘      └─────┬─────┘ └─────┬─────┘
        └─────────────┴──────────┬───────┴─────────────┘
                                 ▼
                    ┌──────────────────────┐
                    │ Single, multi-       │
                    │ function outsource   │
                    │ provider             │
                    └──────────────────────┘
```

all domestic microwave appliance production, leaving Samsung to become the world's largest manufacturer of microwave ovens (Jarillo, 1993).

Fortunately most firms have the common sense not to outsource their core-competencies. On the other hand, there are many instances in the history of the business that parallel outsourcing industry and might explain its eventual evolution and impact on business organizations. One commonly related industry to outsourcing is the U.S. construction industry (Finkel, 1997). Both industries are service industries organized to provide a variety of specialized services to client organizations. A client firm hires a provider in the outsourcing industry to provide a specialized task. A general contractor hires a subcontractor in the construction industry to provide a specialized task. An outsource provider is a subcontractor to a client firm. It has been a logical evolution that many smaller subcontractors eventually become general contractors as they learn how to do more tasks as well as or better than the general contractor that hires them. Similarly many outsource providers may also decide to become firms that mimic or replace their former client firms.

An Alternative Possible Evolution

The trends in the outsourcing industry show that client firms are starting to realize the risks to using an outsourcing strategy. The realization and consideration of the nature of risks firms are currently taking in outsourcing will motivate an approach to utilizing the outsourcing strategy similar to that experienced in the U.S. construction industry. From the current trends our research suggests the following events will take place.

The Outsourcing Industry will Experience a Decline in Rapid Growth Rates

The maturing reduction in growth will be caused by a number of factors including multioutsourcing legislation, political pressures, and a realistic view of the limits of outsourcing. The recognition of risks and the less-than-expected rewards of outsourcing will become more defined and noticeable to potential adopters, reducing the overall demand of outsourcing services, worldwide. Most firms will be obligated to retain a portion of their internal processes to be handled by insourcing. Current logic dictates that core competencies are retained for insourcing and as firms recognize the potential threat of takeover by a provider, increasing steps to restrict outsourcing practices will emerge. Though some growth will continue, new major providers, particularly those from China will easily absorb the new industry growth, leaving providers in other countries fighting for a lessening market share of the industry. A reduction in growth typically causes industry leaders to merge and acquire competitors to maintain the appearance of growth, resulting in a more oligopolistic market for the outsourcing industry leaders (Schiller, 2000, pp. 217-229).

Based on Economic Theory of Industry Behavior in a Nongrowth Markets, the Outsourcing Industry will Experience Mergers and Acquisitions

Current trends indicate larger outsource providers are absorbing successful medium sized firms. Yet, the entrepreneurial nature of outsourcing and the lack of barriers of entry encourage small niche providers to enter the market in all countries. The result will be a two-tier industry. The top-tier will command the majority of the business and will consist of large outsource providers, most will offer "one-stop" services to their clients either in a single functional area or in several functional areas. The other tier will be small niche outsource providers who can offer highly specialized skills focused on providing the most efficient services in their limited domains of operation. This divergence of few large dominating providers and many smaller outsource providers will create a primary and secondary market for outsourcing. The larger outsourcing firms will able to command large contracts and higher prices consistent with known economic behavior in oligopolies (Schiller, 2000, p. 217). To maintain their profits while funding larger bureaucracies, the larger outsource providers will in turn subcontract or outsource to other less overhead-intensive smaller niche outsource providers whose specialization and lesser costs will provide the economies necessary to make the outsourcing arrangements profitable for all parties.

Figure 6. Outsourcing-insourcing alliance network organizational structure for IS functional area

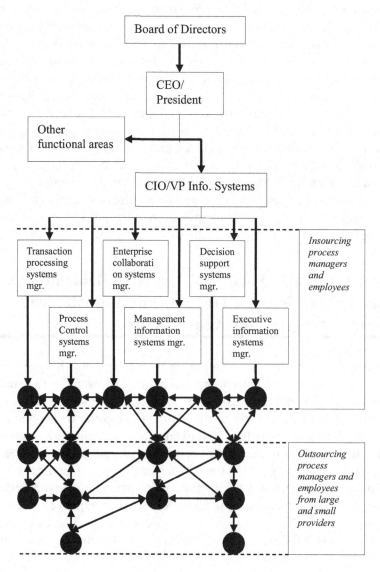

Therefore, large providers will be outsourcing work to smaller providers. The result will organizationally be a network of outsourcers working under various alliances to accomplish a variety of different process requirements for the client firm. In Figure 6, the envisioned outsourcing-insourcing alliance network organizational structure is presented. The example in Figure 6 is only for the basic divisions of an IS department as defined by O'Brien and Marakas (2006, p. 12). The horizontal and diagonal arrows represent the inactions between the various outsourcing and insourcing partners.

The justification for the conceptual organization in Figure 6 is based on over a hundred years of experience in the construction industry in the U.S. Suppose we have a large general contractor hired to build a large building. Even if the general contractor is large, it will usually farm-out smaller portions (i.e., processes like electrical work) of the building project to smaller construction contractors. This is because of the economies. A smaller, more specialized subcontractor can offer the larger bureaucratic organization of the general contractor. A great deal of joint planning and integration of actions is necessary when using multiple subcontractors in a building project in order to meet timing requirements. This necessitates considerable interaction between the general contractor and many subcontractors. Similar to the outsourcing industry in Figure 6, larger outsource providers will have to work with the available insource providers to handle required contracted outsourcing work. The large outsource providers will also farmout smaller portions of their contracted work to more focused, efficient, and less expensive outsource providers. This practice of farming-out the outsourcing work is new and will grow as the outsourcing industry experiences the oligopolistic trends. The outsourcers, like the construction companies, must be highly integrated to share the various different types of information and tasks to achieve their client's needs. With the availability of telecommunication and Web technology today, the active flow of information between insourcing employees, large outsource partners, and smaller subcontracted outsource partners, will look like a network of agents who are temporarily brought together in alliances to accomplish a specific set of tasks.

In the final analysis, outsourcing and subcontracting are the same basic process. No general contractor completely subcontracts all the construction work for a project, just as no client firm should outsource all of their processes to providers. The percentage of the processes outsourced by client firms will depend on the uniqueness of the client firm's core competencies and the degree of client firm's willingness to trust and work within the alliances established with outsourcing firms to the advantage of all. Unlike "matrix organizations" that are internalized arrangements of organization processes, possessing ownership and authority structures for compliance, the Figure 6 outsourcing-insourcing alliance network is partially an external organizational structure that must be managed with temporary alliances and mutual advantage. Moreover, the inevitable increase in the cost to client firms for outsourcing will follow the move to an oligopolistic outsourcing market. These costs will reduce the outsourcing value to potential client firms, thus preventing the providers from taking over many of the client companies as alluded to in Figure 5.

Conclusion

While future expectations of the evolution of industry outsourcing are cited in the literature (Lee, Huynh & Kwok, 2003), they have not addressed the impact of outsourcing on organizational structures. This chapter proposed possible organizational structural impacts on a typical hierarchical business. No one knows how outsourcing will end up shaping modern business organizations. The conceptual suggestions in this chapter are based on trends in the current literature and on the logic of a similar industry, the construction industry. Just as there are natural limits to the size of general contractors in the construction industry, there are natural limits on the size, use, and growth of the outsourcing industry as it matures. In much the same way that other management paradigms (like management-by-objectives, MBO or just-in-time management, JIT) have made a change in the way business is conducted and become less significant in popularity, so too will outsourcing make its mark and find its proper role in the way business is conducted. Outsourcing is a "bend in the river" of business history, not a major event in that history of business that some fear and seek to undermine.

References

Arizona governor stops state's outsourcing. (2004, April 18-25). *Outsourcing Intelligence Bulletin: FSO Magazine, 4*. Retrieved March 13, 2006, from http://www.fsoutsourcing.com

Bahli, B., & Rivard, S. (2005). Validating measures of information technology outsourcing risk factors. *Omega, 33*(2), 175-188.

Bangladesh to provide outsourcing services to U.S. financial firms. (2004, August 8-15). *Outsourcing Intelligence Bulletin: FSO Magazine, 4*. Retrieved March 13, 2006, from http://www.fsoutsourcing.com

Barthélemy, J., & Geyer, D. (2005). An empirical investigation of IT outsourcing versus quasi-outsourcing in France and Germany. *Information & Management, 42*(4), 533-542.

Challenges to consider. (2004, September 19-26). *Outsourcing Intelligence Bulletin: FSO Magazine, 4*. Retrieved March 13, 2006, from http://www.fsoutsourcing.com

Diddi, R. (2004, May 2-9). The rebuttal: FSU and East Europe prepare for a rebuttal to Indian outsourcing and BPO capability. *Outsourcing Intelligence Bulletin: FSO Magazine, 4*. Retrieved March 13, 2006, from http://www.fsoutsourcing.com

Dubai has business process outsourcing (BPO) growth potential. (2004, May 9-16). *Outsourcing Intelligence Bulletin: FSO Magazine, 4*. Retrieved March 13, 2006, from http://www.fsoutsourcing.com

Finkel, G. (1997). *The economics of the construction industry*. Armonk, NY: M. E. Sharpe, Inc.

Goldsmith, N. M. (2003). *Outsourcing trends*. New York: The Conference Board.

Gottfredson, M. (2005, February 14). Keep the core? No more! *Computerworld, 39*(7), 40.

India is the leading outsourcing destination among competitors. (2004, May 30-June 6). *Outsourcing Intelligence Bulletin: FSO Magazine, 4*. Retrieved March 13, 2006, from http://www.fsoutsourcing.com

Jarillo, J. C. (1993). *Strategic networks: Creating the borderless organisation*. Oxford: Butterworth-Heinemann.

Kotabe, M., & Murray, J. Y. (2004). Global sourcing strategy and sustainable competitive advantage. *Industrial Marketing Management, 33*(1), 7-15.

Large IT outsourcing deals on the rise says TPI study. (2004, October 24-31). *Outsourcing Intelligence Bulletin: FSO Magazine, 4*. Retrieved March 13, 2006, from http://www.fsoutsourcing.com

Lee, J.-N., Huynh, M. Q., & Kwok, R. C.-W. (2003). IT outsourcing evolution — past, present, and future. *Communications of the ACM, 46*(5), 84-90.

Lok, C. (2005). Two sides of outsourcing. *Technology Review, 108*(2), 33.

MacInnis, P. (2003). Warped expectations lead to outsourcing failures. *Computing Canada, 29*(7), 1-2.

Milgate, M. (2001). *Alliances, outsourcing, and the lean organization*. Westport, CT: Quorum Books.

Natovich, J. (2003). Vendor related risks in IT development: A chronology of an outsourced project failure. *Technology Analysis & Strategic Management, 15*(4), 409-420.

O'Brien, J. A., & Marakas, G. M. (2006). *Management information systems* (7th ed.). Boston: McGraw-Hill/Irwin.

Offshore outsourcing market to grow 20% annually through 2008. (2004, November 5). *Outsourcing Intelligence Bulletin: FSO Magazine, 14.* Retrieved March 13, 2006, from http://www.fsoutsourcing.com

Render, B., & Stair, R. M. (2000). *Quantitative analysis for management* (7th ed.). Upper Saddle River, NJ: Prentice Hall.

Schiller, B. R. (2000). *The micro economy today* (8th ed.). Boston: Irwin/ McGraw-Hill.

Schniederjans, M. J., Schniederjans, A. M., & Schniederjans, D. G. (2006). *Outsourcing and insourcing in an international context.* Armonk, NJ: M. E. Sharpe, Inc.

Soliman, K. S., & Chen, L.-D. (2003). APS: Do they work? *Information Systems Management, 20*(4), 50-58.

U.S. federal anti-outsourcing laws violate anti-protectionist trade rules. (2004, April 18-25). *Outsourcing Intelligence Bulletin: FSO Magazine, 4.* Retrieved March 13, 2006, from http://www.fsoutsourcing.com

U.S. firms set up offshoring units in India. (2004, May 9-16). *Outsourcing Intelligence Bulletin: FSO Magazine, 4.* Retrieved March 13, 2006, from http://www.fsoutsourcing.com

U.S. senator introduces anti-outsourcing bill. (2004, June 27-July 4). *Outsourcing Intelligence Bulletin: FSO Magazine, 4.* Retrieved March 13, 2006, from http://www.fsoutsourcing.com

Willcocks, L., & Choi, C. J. (1995). Co-operative partnerships and total IT outsourcing: From contractual obligation to strategic alliance. *European Management Journal, 13*(1), 67-78.

Wilson, J. H., & Clark, J. R. (1988). *Economics: The science of cost, benefit, and choice* (2nd ed.). Cincinnati, OH: South-Western Publishing.

Zhao, Y., & Calantone R. J. (2003). The trend toward outsourcing in new product development: Case studies in six firms. *International Journal of Innovation Management, 7*(1), 51-66.

Chapter II

Why, When, and What to Outsource

Donald A. Carpenter, Mesa State College, USA

Vijay K. Agrawal, University of Nebraska - Kearney, USA

Abstract

This chapter presents an overview of the outsourcing phenomenon, focusing on the question of why, when, and what to outsource. It provides an extensive set of guidelines for a business student to understand the nature of outsourcing. Drawing extensively on recent scholarly literature, the chapter presents a wide range of concepts. There are many causes that might lead a company to a decision to outsource. Similarly, there are many factors that contribute to an environment that is conducive to outsourcing. The question of what to outsource is answered by examining core competencies and critical success factors. The chapter also presents trends in outsourcing in specific countries and industries to help the reader understand what is possible.

Introduction

Today's business environmental, organizational, and technological factors require businesses to operate efficiently and effectively in order to be competitive. Toward those goals, managers employ many strategies to improve productivity, including standardization, automation, and business process reengineering. Additionally, they restructure the business organizations to be lean and flat so that they can become flexible in responding quickly to changes in environment and customers' needs.

Outsourcing is another valuable strategy managers use to achieve the above goals. Whenever a business procures resources purely from an external source to accomplish business objectives, it engages in outsourcing (Gartner, 1997). Hence, the term "outsourcing" is one that can be used to describe any external up-line function in a supply chain. When a manufacturer acquires raw materials from a supplier, it engages in outsourcing. When a wholesale company contracts with an external delivery firm, it engages in outsourcing. When a firm hires a computer consultant, it engages in outsourcing.

Outsourcing has taken on a new emphasis in today's business environment. In the interest of either efficiency or effectiveness, a modern organization often contracts out entire business functions to other companies that are specialists in their specific fields. A firm might turn over to external suppliers its human resource functions, its information technology functions, its shipping functions, or any other functions for which an external supplier is more efficient and effective than is the host company. While such outsourcing is not a new strategy — businesses have used outside consultants for as long as there have been businesses — it has gained more attention and usage in recent years.

Outsourcing has also received unprecedented attention from politicians and the press in recent elections. Some candidates and journalists have painted outsourcing as an evil to be avoided as economically undesirable to a country's economy. Those reports often confuse outsourcing with one or two of its logical extensions, namely *near-shore outsourcing* and *off-shore outsourcing,* also known as *off-shoring*. A distinction between those two is that the former typically refers to outsourcing to a country that is on the country of origin's same continent, for example, a U.S. company outsourcing to one in Mexico; the latter refers to outsourcing to a country across an ocean, for example, a U.S. company outsourcing to a supplier in India. Collectively, both are known as off-shore outsourcing and off-shoring and will be referred to in this chapter as such.

Business managers see off-shore outsourcing to lower-wage countries such as China, India, Ireland, and the Philippines in the same light as reducing labor cost by automation or technology. Conversely, politicians, the press, and a large proportion of the general population view off-shoring as a threat to local economies. Regardless of one's perspective, in the absence of government regulation to the contrary, outsourcing and off-shoring, in particular, will grow steadily (Robinson & Kalakota, 2005, p. 16)

Historical Perspective

The predominant supply chain model for several decades was vertically integrated. Each member of a supply chain was considered to be part of the same industry. Automobile manufacturers purchased parts from automotive parts manufacturers, and then sold completed cars to automobile dealers. All the ancillary activities that support the supply chain directly or indirectly were included within the automobile manufacturer. Steadily, products became complex and the scale of operations increased and management of entire operations within one corporation became less feasible. This resulted in the increasingly popular use of outsourcing and has resulted in vertical disintegration of corporations and supply chains. As travel and communication became easier in the 1970s and 1980s, as trade restrictions increased, and as the gap in wages between developed and developing countries increased, outsourcing began to move off-shore.

Arguably, the advanced industrialized economies of the United States, Japan, and Europe are the principal candidates for origination of outsourcing transactions (Koveos & Tang, 2004, p. 52). For decades, U.S. industry has outsourced blue-collar jobs to the lower wage countries. That trend now includes white-collar jobs as well. Economic development in Japan and Europe in the past couple decades has generated an environment that has fostered outsourcing practices. In addition, some developed Asian economies have both the experience and the location advantage in outsourcing to China and India. Taiwan and Korea are such examples. In 2002, for instance, India had 90% of U.S. organizations' information technology (IT) off-shore business. However, many Fortune 500 companies that have outsourced to India are looking to diversify the risk associated with dependence on one country (Gupta, 2002). China looms as India's biggest competitor, although some consider the two as noncomparable at this time. Other countries considered to be attractive as off-shore outsourcing sites include Malaysia, the Czech Republic, Singapore, the Philippines, Brazil, Canada, Chile, Poland, Hungary (Kearney, 2004), Russia, and Vietnam (*Computerworld,* 2004).

In the age of the Internet and World Wide Web, a company's location hardly matters. In the past, the educated and skilled labor from low-cost countries immigrated to the U.S. During the last decade, faster communications and improved information allow companies to easily send information oriented work to any location on the globe. Ultimately, countries with low-paid but well-educated workers will benefit greatly. However, the country of origin of the outsourcing also benefits. McKinsey Global Institute estimates that every dollar in spending that is diverted off-shore creates $1.45-$1.47 of value, of which the U.S. captures $1.12-$1.14 or 78% of the value (Arora & Arora, 2004, p. 23).

Why Do Firms Outsource?

Companies outsource functions for reasons that are organizationally driven, improvement driven, financially driven, revenue driven, or cost driven (Outsourcing Index, 2003). Moreover, outsourcing can be viewed as a component of corporate and industry international expansion and restructuring. A recent McKinsey Global Institute Report (Farrell; 2003) identifies five horizons of the global industry value chain:

*   **Market entry:** Entering a country for purposes of market expansion.
*   **Product specialization:** Specialization takes place in different locations. Each location may engage in final goods trade with each other.
*   **Value chain disaggregation:** Product components are manufactured in a certain location and assembled elsewhere.
*   **Value chain reengineering:** Reengineering processes to capture additional advantages from production cost differentials.
*   **New market creation:** New market segments are penetrated as a matter of capturing the full value of the company's global activities.

According to another McKinsey study:

effective outsourcing implies identifying and managing the 'natural owner' of every activity in he value chain. Off-shore outsourcing arises from the basic reality of the global environment: any company, in any country, may be the natural owner! It can then lead to a drastic restructuring, including 'unbundling,' of the companies affected. Indeed, as total interaction costs among companies and industries are changing, companies around the world are reorganizing themselves by providing the answer to their question: what business are we in? (Hagel & Singer, 2004, p.1)

A firm can use an outsourcing to supplement its core competencies, by contracting with outside providers for activities in which the firm has no unique capabilities. This "strategic outsourcing" (Quinn & Hilmer, 1995, p.1) can generate several benefits:

- Extracting the maximum benefits from internal activities, since they represent what the firm does best

- Maximizing their competitiveness and protecting or even expanding their market share

- Effectively utilizing suppliers capabilities

- Decreasing risks, shortening cycle times and fulfilling customer needs

A survey of 500 human resources executives (Arora & Arora, 2004, pp. 19-20) found that:

- 92% of the firms that had moved jobs overseas did so to cut costs.

- An average of 13% of jobs at each company are already located off-shore and an additional 12% could be relocated within the next three years.

- 45% of the 500 firms have overseas operations.

- 71% of the remaining companies planned to move some jobs abroad by 2005.

- Of the firms who are currently using off-shore labor, 29% began doing so in the years 1995-1999, while 43% began in 2000-2003.

When to Outsource: Factors that Support Outsourcing

Characteristics of today's outsourcing environment are many and varied. The strategic change to outsourcing is highly evident in the software industry. Frequent changes to software especially often result in an organization turning to outsourcing as a solution. Reasons studied for this (Agrawal, Haleem & Sushil, 2001; Agrawal, 2005a) can be generalized to all outsourcing, and include:

- The turbulent market will need corporations to be customer focused.

- There are pressures on corporations to continuously develop new product at reduced cost.

- Extensive customization is enabled by IT through mass customization.

- The market need can be fulfilled by flexible and adaptable organizational structure which is possible with IT-enabled processes.

Previously identified factors include time-compression, short product life cycles, strategic discontinuity, increase in knowledge intensity, and customer-focused approach (El Sawy, Malhotra, & Young, 1999). These changes and others will be discussed in subsequent paragraphs.

Customer Focus

In a traditional sellers' market, products and services provided by producers and suppliers are consumed. Today, most products and services exist in a buyers market, in which there is extreme competition with customers as a focal point. Moreover, customers have become much more sophisticated and knowledge-able, especially with the huge amount of product and service information available to them on the World Wide Web (Turban et al., 2006, p. 14). In many instances, customers can customize products or services and even name their own price. This provides customers with a huge amount of power (Pitt et. al., 2002). Companies need to be able to respond to that power. A company with no experience in doing so might be wise to turn to outsourcing as a solution to create and operate their customer relationship management (CRM) functions and related information systems (Greenberg, 2002).

Shrinkage in Product/Systems Life Cycle

Intense competition tends to decreases in the length of product or service life cycles. As new products or services are brought to market, the power of the modern consumer comes into play with demands for customization. Such continual customization is labor-intensive. Outsourcing, especially off-shoring provides a solution to contain those costs.

This impact is particularly evident in the software industry. In a survey of 118 senior financial executives, 73% of the respondents expected to have shorter replacement cycles for software over the next five years (Hoffman, 2005a). Shrinkage in systems life cycle is unfavorable for development of proprietary software and leads to extensive usage of off-the-shelf enterprise-wide software solutions (Agrawal et al., 2001; Agrawal, 2005a).

Global Economy

Many factors have led to the development of a global economy in which the boundaries of national and regional economic systems have become blurred. A reasonably more stabile world political environment has fostered trade between former Cold War opponents, especially those, like Russia and China that have moved into market oriented economic systems (Naisbitt, 1994). Regional agreements such as the North American Free Trade Agreement (United States, Canada, and Mexico) and the creation of a unified European market with a single currency, the euro, have contributed to increased world trade. Further reduction of trade barriers has allowed production and services to flow more freely around the globe (Turban et al., 2006, pp. 13-14).

The existence of a global economy makes it much easier for companies to shift resources from firm to firm internationally. It especially allows them to take advantage of the difference in labor costs. Labor that costs, say, $25 per hour in the U.S. might only cost $1 per hour in many developing countries.

Immense advances in telecommunication networks, the Internet and World Wide Web have made the global economy possible (Clinton & Gore, 1997; Kanter, 1995; Negroponte, 1995). The transition to an off-shore economy represents a new form of Internet-enabled globalization, the impact of which will dwarf prior globalization efforts (Robinson & Kalakota, 2005, p. 10).

Competition and Real-Time Operations

Strong competition is one of the hallmarks of today's business environment. The advent of the global economy logically has led to global competition. Rapid communications systems and improved transportation systems foster such international competition. When governments become involved to modify the competitive arena, challenges to businesses increase. Such government involvement might take the form of subsidies, tax policies, import/export regulations, and other incentives (Turban et al., 2006, p. 14). For companies not accustomed to dealing in such an intensely competitive environment, outsourcing of business functions that deal directly with competition or government regulations can provide the solution.

As the world economy moves ever faster, decisions must be made and actions must be taken more quickly in order for firms to remain competitive (Gates, 1999; Davis, 2001; Huber, 2004). Some companies, for example, Cisco Systems, have chosen to respond by closing their accounting books in one day, rather than the ten days previously required (McCleanahen, 2002). Developing systems to handle that might be beyond the capacity of a firm and that firm might turn to outsourcing to fill that need.

Changing Workforce and Job Loss

The workforce in both developed and developing countries is changing rapidly and becoming more diversified with more women, single parents, minorities, persons with disabilities, and employees who have deferred retirement in the workforce than ever before work in all types of positions (Turban, et al., 2006, p. 4). Additionally more workers are becoming knowledge workers (Drucker, 2002) and telecommuters. As much as half the U.S. workforce will spend two or more days per week working away from the office by the year 2010 (Cole et al., 2003). Those factors, plus the aging population and declining birth rates in developed countries will foster off-shoring (Robinson & Kalakota, 2006, pp. 12-13).

World demographics are changing. Developed countries have older average populations than developing countries. According to *Business Week*, 53% of India's population is considered to be the MTV generation (under the age of 25), vs. 45% in China. By 2020, 47% of Indians are going to be between 15 and 59 years old, compared with 35% now (Kriplani & Engardio, 2003).

A recent survey predicts that an aging U.S. population and slower population growth will lead to a shortfall in the domestic labor supply of 5.6 million jobs by 2010. Of these, immigrant workers will fill nearly 3.2 million jobs and another 1.3 million jobs will be filled by off-shoring (Arora & Arora, 2004, p. 23). Another survey indicates that 3,322,138 U.S. jobs will move off-shore by 2015, with the following breakdown by job category: management, 288,281; business, 348,028; computer, 472,632; architecture, 184,347; life sciences, 36,770; legal, 76,642; art/design, 29,564; sales, 226,564; and office, 1,659,310 (Forrester, 2002). In the IT field, that could translate to as many as 35% to 45% of U.S. and Canadian IT workers being replaced by contractors, consultants, off-shore technicians and part-time workers (Hoffman, 2003).

While the most alarming predictions point to the potential negative impacts of off-shoring on the U.S. economy and workforce, as well as those of other developed nations, there is evidence to suggest that off-shoring can lead to domestic job growth rather than reduction (Nakatsu & Iacovou, 2004). The logic supposes that U.S. companies that use off-shoring will keep their product and service prices lower, thereby sustaining competitiveness and maintaining or even increasing market share. As a result, U.S. companies will be able to expand their labor pools. Furthermore, jobs lost by off-shoring in one industry are offset by growth in other industries (*Times of India,* 2004). The saving created by outsourcing to India alone, could create $30 billion per year in new investments for U.S. companies by fostering 12,000 new strategic projects at an average of $2.5 million per year per project (Press Trust of India, 2004).

Technological Innovations and Obsolescence

Technology has played a critical role in creating an environment for global economy that fosters trans-border outsourcing, especially in the area of Web-based information technology (Carr, 2001; Evans & Motiwalla & Hashimi, 2003; Wurster, 2000). Technology also provides for other key factors in the outsourcing arena, such as creating and supporting substitutes for products and alternative service options, as well as providing products and services of a high quality (Turban et al., 2006, p. 15).

Another contribution of technology stems from its tendency to become obsolete quite rapidly. Such obsolescence, whether planned or not, thereby spawns competition to develop replacements, whether it is in the IT field itself or in medicine, biotechnology or any other technology-dependent field.

Other impacts of technology on the outsourcing game exist. Technology allows businesses to be more competitive by allowing them to provide their products and services on a 24/7/365 basis. Higher degrees of automation reduce the dependency on specialists, possibly allowing for easier outsourcing. Conversely, the lack of need for specialists might eliminate the need for outsourcing (Agrawal et al., 2001; Agrawal & Haleem, 2003).

Societal, Political, and Ethical Factors

The increase in outsourcing and off-shoring, in particular, in turn gives rise to many societal, political and ethical issues. The interface between businesses and consumers becomes more transparent as consumers become more powerful and businesses focus on customer relationship management. That transparency results in a tendency for consumers to place demands on businesses.

A case in point is the New Jersey state social services department which hired a company named eFund to provide electronics processing of food stamp and welfare benefits. In 2002, eFund moved its customer call center to Mumbai, India. The resulting public outcry that the move was inconsistent with the agency's intent to get people off welfare and into jobs caused eFund to move the call center back to the U.S. at an additional cost of $900,000 per year. The irony was that eFund's U.S. call center was in Wisconsin, which did nothing to create jobs for New Jersey citizens (Hopkins, 2003). A similar situation existed in

Indiana, where the public demanded the state cancel a $15 million IT contract with India's Tata Consultancy Services (Robinson & Kalakota, 2005, p. 15).

Despite such consumer involvement in business affairs, off-shoring is an unstoppable mega-trend. That will not stop politicians, however, to shape off-shore outsourcing via regulations to appease their constituents. However, government regulations cost money and make it more difficult to compete with countries that lack such regulations (Turban et al., 2006, p. 16). In general, deregulation fosters competition and lower prices to consumers. That concept is sometimes lost on the general public and politicians in today's fierce political environment.

Several national elements that encourage or discourage outsourcing have been identified (Koveos & Tang, 2004). They are:

- **Countries' attitudes toward international business:** Openness breeds openness!
- **Economic conditions:** Certain forms of outsourcing generate a great deal of resistance at home, especially when the domestic economy is struggling. Wage rate and productivity differentials between the home country and the provider country can also be a significant factor in the decision.
- **Labor market:** Regulations that make it harder to shift operations obviously add to the cost of engaging in an outsourcing activity off-shore.
- **Labor inflexibility:** Companies operating in many European countries, including France, Germany, and Scandinavian region find it very costly to lay off workers and restructure effectively.
- **The tax environment:** Higher taxes for domestic companies and for providers may serve as an obstacle.
- **Government intervention:** The freer the country is from government interference, the greater the ability to engage in off-shore transactions. On the other hand, incentives designed to keep business at home may discourage off-shore activity.
- **Culture, including language:** Similarities in the cultural attributes of the two countries can facilitate transactions.
- **Quality of labor force:** The greater the level of education and training of a country's workforce, the lower the costs of adjustment.
- **Technological sophistication:** The higher technological sophistication of the home economy, the greater opportunity to benefit significantly from outsourcing activities.
- **Infrastructure:** Outsourcingt companies tend to materialize within the countries that have a supporting national infrastructure.

- **The information and communications technology environment:** Adequate technologies are critical to support outsourcing of services related to or supported by IT.

- **The legal system, including protection of property and intellectual rights:** Lack of a well formulated legal system causes outsourcers to look elsewhere, especially if their intellectual property is not protected.

- **Local market characteristics, such as competition and suppliers:** A competitive market promotes outsourcing for cost advantages.

- **Experience with international market:** A history of success encourages future outsourcing endeavors.

Unfortunately, mention must also be made about the impact of terrorist attacks. Since September 11, 2001, there is ever increasing attention paid by organizations to protect themselves against terrorism. Geographically diversifying is one solution and off-shore outsourcing plays a large role in that. Another countermeasure is intensified security systems, and even intelligent systems that identify possible behavioral patterns to prevent cyber-terrorist attacks. The host company might not have the in-house expertise to handle such systems, thereby creating more opportunity for outsourcing (Turban et al., 2006, p. 16).

Other outsourcing issues relate to culture and ethics. Just as each country has its own culture, so does each country have its own norms for ethics. The same can be said of corporations and individuals. What is culturally acceptable and ethical to one country, company, or individual might not be culturally acceptable or ethical to the next. That provides challenges on both sides of the outsourcing equation to insure culture and ethical norms of the other party are not compromised or violated.

Organization Structure and Corporate Culture

Some organizations will implement outsourcing sooner, more effectively, and more efficiently than others for a variety of internal reasons, not the least of which is a company's self perception. Managers of some companies have a "small business" mindset and intend their firm to remain small. If a proposed new task can't be handled in the normal scheme of the business, then there is no reason to implement that new task. Such companies will be content to remain with classical outsourcing of legal, accounting, janitorial, or similar functions. Other companies similarly limit themselves by a "not invented here" mentality. If we haven't done it previously, why do we need to do it at all?

On the other end of the scale are those firms that consider changes as a normal phenomenon for survival and growth. Such companies tend to promote outsourcing as a means to reduce costs (Agrawal et al., 2003). The companies who are most successful with outsourcing will have identified and understand their core competencies and critical success factors. This will be elaborated in a subsequent section of this chapter.

When to Outsource:
The Risks of Outsourcing

Despite the purported benefits of outsourcing and the wide range of success stories that have stimulated an unprecedented growth rate, there are potential risks as well. An outsourcing project might fail because of poor selection of the vendor, mismanagement of the outsourcing contract, inferior performance by the vendor, lack of acceptance by the end consumer, or other reasons (Quinn & Hilmer, 1995). It might also be that outsourcing may have higher costs than insourcing the same function (King, 2005; Mears & Bednarz, 2005; Thibodeau, 2005a).

A survey of 25 large firms with a combined $50 billion in outsourcing contracts found 70% have had negative experiences with outsourcing projects and are now taking a more cautious approach. A quarter of the companies brought outsourced functions back in-house and nearly half have failed to see the cost savings of outsourcing they had anticipated (Mears, 2005).

In a time of lower revenues, outsourcing provides a tool to manage costs. However, there are other factors to consider that might cause increased costs. Disgruntled employees, ones who did not lose their jobs due to outsourcing, can cause problems and increase costs. When some business functions are outsourced, employees might not have an opportunity to apply as much skill variety, which can lead to lower productivity. Public perception can cause for a more negative corporate image within the community and can result in lower sales.

What to Do and Not Do to Outsource

Core Competencies and Critical Success Factors

Decisions as to what and whether to outsource should be tied to an identification and understanding of an organization's core competencies and its critical success factors (Luftman, Bullen, Liao, Nash, & Neumann, 2004, p. 320). Such an identification and understanding can be a lengthy process. However, it is the one true way to determine whether a project should be or should not be outsourced. While that recommendation was first applied to IT projects, it can be generalized to all business functions.

If a task is a both a core competency and a critical success factor, it should not be considered for outsourcing. Such tasks are at the heart of the company. Success or failure of such functions is directly tied to success or failure of the company as a whole. In general, such functions are critical to an organization's day-to-day operations, ability to competitively differentiate itself, ability to deliver value to customers and partners, and ability to innovate (Luftman et al., 2004, p. 320).

Tasks that are core competencies but not critical success factors should be reassessed. Why engage in such tasks if they are not critical? Often the answer to that is "because we can." It is typically not a good business decision to continue to engage in such tasks.

Those tasks which are not core competencies are the most likely candidates for outsourcing. The question is how to go about it. If such as task is a critical success factor, it might be wise to establish a strategic alliance; otherwise, a transaction partnership might suffice. The former is a more tightly-coupled arrangement than the latter. Strategic partnerships might even establish some form of mutual ownership or revenue sharing, whereas transaction partnerships are more typical outsourcing arrangements where a company simply contracts with a vendor to provide the service or product.

There is another consideration that lies outside the core competency-critical success factor matrix. If an organization intends to bring an outsourced task back in-house at some future time, managers should be cautious. There is overwhelming evidence that certain outsourced activities cannot be reversed, particularly in the IT arena (Luftman et al., 2004, p. 323). Once the expertise has been released to the outsourcer, it is difficult — if not impossible — to regain such expertise in-house.

Outsourcing Trends and Future Projections

As explained above, the overall trends toward outsourcing and off-shoring in all sectors are expanding. In particular, the trend in the IT sector is growing at a phenomenal rate. However, those trends vary geographically.

United States: Successful outsourcing and off-shoring by U.S. organizations from the early 1970's to the present day is well-documented (Rishi & Saxena, 2004, p. 63). U.S. off-shoring began as a means of taking advantage of cheaper labor in a handful of Latin American and Asian countries, such as Mexico, Korea, Malaysia, and Singapore. In the late 1980s and early 1990s, those practices expanded to include many more countries, including mainland China. The success of the North American Free Trade Agreement (NAFTA) in the mid-1990s greatly expanded U.S. outsourcing efforts in Mexico due to its geographically proximity.

The Y2K problem in IT and need to change information systems to handle the new euro currency in the late 1990s spurred U.S. expansion into India to take advantage not only of cheaper labor but also of greater expertise. Lack of caps on temporary L-1 visas allowed for foreign workers to be trained in U.S. businesses, then return to their country of origin to establish consulting firms with their new-found expertise. By 1999, 41% of software services were provided in India rather than on-site at the client's location, compared to only 5% in 1990 (Bajpai, Sachs, Arora & Khurana, 2004). Current estimates indicate that spending for global sourcing of computer software and services is expected to grow at a compound annual rate of almost 26%, increasing from approximately $10 billion in 2003 to $31 billion in 2008 (ITAA, 2004).

Japan: In Japan, outsourcing was stimulated differently (Koveos & Tang, 2004, p. 43) and is tied more to cyclical and structural challenges in the macro and micro foundations of the Japanese economy (Vietor & Evans, 2001). That included a number of measures aimed at restructuring the Japanese economy as well as purposeful promotion of greater integration of Japanese economic and business systems with the rest of Asia and the World.

Outsourcing was introduced in Japan in the 1980s by a company initially dealing with one service provider as a means of acquiring temporary help. In the 1990s, outsourcing evolved to include third party logistics (3PL) providers. Today, companies engage in strategic outsourcing policies to allow them to focus on their core competencies (WIT, 2001). A 1997 survey conducted by Japan's Ministry of International Trade and Industry, 20.1% of outsourcing firms outsourced job training services, 19.7% outsourced information systems services, 17.4% production processes, 14% accounting services, and 13% engaged in R&D outsourcing. More than 70% of Japanese firms had achieved their strategic outsourcing objectives (Murphy, 2000).

In Japan, the market for IT system development alone has been estimated at 6.7 trillion Yen a year (approximately $104 billion U.S.) (Rowley, 2004) with expected annual growth of 15.6% up to 2008 (Kajino, Kinoshita & Kobayashi, 2004, p. 1). Japanese companies have established relationships with providers in many countries, especially in Asia but also expanding to Europe and North America. Primarily, Japanese companies increasingly look to China (Rowley, 2004) and Russia (Outsourcing-Russia, 2004). They envision North America as a market in which they can offer their own outsourcing services (Koveos & Tang, 2004).

Europe: In Europe in the 1990's, various countries' economies have faced challenges such as budgetary issues, slumping demand at home, lack of global competitiveness, labor market inflexibility, lower levels of innovation, and production inefficiencies. Outsourcing certainly provided means to cut costs and provide greater organization flexibility, with more than 100 major companies routinely participating, each dealing with numerous subcontractors. However, their approach is seemingly haphazard and even counterproductive rather than as focused as in Japan (Quinn & Hilmer, 1995, pp. 2-13).

There are indicators that outsourcing is becoming better planned. A recent survey reports that 40% of Europe's 500 largest companies have engaged on off-shoring (Farrell, 2003). While the continent has already achieved more in post European Union (EU) times, Europe's economic and business environment are still plagued by pre-EU elements that might not be compatible with global sourcing practices, such as labor inflexibility, language differences, cultural openness, and tax laws (Pradhan, 2004).

There are bright spots in Europe, such as the Spanish automobile industry, which has intensified outsourcing as it expanded substantially and became more export-oriented (Pallares-Barbera, 1998). Likewise, throughout the United Kingdom (UK) the general European reluctance to outsourcing is not as evident (Dash, 2001; Gray, 2003a).

The International Trade Agreement (ITO) and other trade arrangements might hold promise for expanded European outsourcing as tactical and strategic mechanisms. ITO's emphasis is on individual systems or applications rather than entire systems which fosters outsourcing (Gray, 2003b, p. 5; Outsourcing Center, 1999).

Of the 58 billion euros ($76 billion) worth of major (greater than $40 million) outsourcing contracts awarded last year, Europe represented 49% of the value, while the U.S. took 44% and Asia 7%. European contracts doubled from 2002 to 2004. Germany is leading the way, accounting for 12.5% of the value of the worldwide contracts awarded in 2004, coming in at the heels of only the UK, with 20%, and the U.S. as the largest country market. Germany's share has increased from less than 1% in just four years (Pruitt, 2005).

Other Asian countries: Korea, Hong Kong, Taiwan, and other Asian countries besides Japan have developed outsourcing arrangements. For instance, Taiwan's MiTAK-SYNNEX Group can globally deliver 98% of its orders in two days, generating about $20 million per year, due to outsourcing 70% of its back-end operations to China (Miau, 2004). Nonetheless, Asian businesses are known more as suppliers of outsourcing contracts rather than as those that place contracts with others.

Specific industries and applications: Outsourcing of manufacturing has been a most logical application historically, primarily due to the labor cost savings and that such jobs only require the untrained labor pools available in developing countries. Consequently, outsourcing of production jobs perhaps is the most visible form as well. Rather than discuss manufacturing applications, the remainder of this chapter will present other less well known outsourcing applications.

Outsourcing of information technology functions is a huge marketplace (Hirschheim, Beena, & Wong, 2004). IT outsourcing began as a cost-reduction tool, but has evolved into a component of businesses' overall corporate strategies (Linder, 2004). It has grown from simple applications to a much wider set of business functions: logistics, payroll, human resources, legal, and so forth. It has become pervasive and strategic. Outsourcing has evolved from the one vendor-one client contracts to complex multiple vendor-multiple client partnerships and alliances, with parties sharing risks, rewards, and equity positions (Gallivan & Oh, 1999).

There are four growth areas in IT outsourcing. Web-based and e-business outsourcing partnerships are common and high growth areas (Dibbern, Goles, Hirschheim, & Jayatilaka, 2004). Another is the application service provider (ASP) industry, which buys, installs, and manages enterprise applications at remote data centers and hosts them for customers via a broadband connections (Kern, Lacity & Willcocks, 2002; Susarla, Barua & Whinston, 2003). A third is "back-sourcing," where companies try to bring back in-house previously outsourced functions when contracts end (Hirschheim, 1998; Overby, 2003). The fourth is IT off-shoring (Morstead & Blount, 2003; Robinson & Kalakota, 2005) which dominates overall off-shoring, rising 890% to $1.66 billion from 2002 to 2003 (E-Business Strategies, 2004).

Typical IT functions that are outsourced include:

- Applications development, maintenance and support, where 80% of code development is expected to go off-shore (Jepsen, Laplante, Williams, Christensen, Farrante, Chang, & Miller, 2004)

- Software quality assurance, where $16 billion is spent annually to save the $60 billion per year that software glitches cost U.S. industry alone (*Computerworld,* 2005)

- Security functions such as firewall management and network vulnerability assessment (Vijayan, 2005)
- Technical support via telephone and Web (Thibodeau, 2005c)
- Transaction processing for purchases, sales orders, deposits, withdrawals, time cards, and paychecks, insurance claims processing and policy administration, medical record administration and medical diagnostics, medical and legal transcription, digitizing of physical documents, e-mail response centers, and other lower level business processing services (Robinson & Kalakota, 2005, p. 185)
- Knowledge work such as reading CAT scans, MRIs, and ultrasounds at as little as half the cost of on-shore radiologists (Brice, 2003)

Outsourcing of pharmaceutical functions traditionally has taken the form of outsourcing drug development and manufacturing to contract research organizations (CROs) and contract manufacturing organizations (CMOs). Research and development and marketing were kept in-house as those were core competencies and critical success factors. Today, some of the research and development is also being outsourced globally in the light of proliferation of new technologies and new knowledge (Doshi, 2004, pp. 125-127). The cost of developing one new product increased from $131 million in 1987 to $802 million in 2001 and the average successful launch of a new drug is $250 million. Meanwhile, in 2000-2002, only one of thirteen discovered and clinically trialed drug makes it to market, compared to one out of eight in 1995-2000 (Gilbert, Preston, & Singh, 2003, p. 4). This huge and costly decline in R&D productivity has increased global pharmaceutical outsourcing opportunities to $40 billion per year.

Outsourcing of customer care functions by moving entire contact centers off-shore has become very popular. The functions performed by customer service centers are more important than their location. The discrepancy between labor, real estate and infrastructure costs on-shore vs. off-shore, makes this a logical function to outsource. Customer contact centers are a $650 billion industry (Cleveland, 2003). "The number of companies outsourcing and off-shoring their contact centers is rising steadily. For example, General Electric Information Services, which offers customer credit cards for retailers such as J.C. Penney, has 3,000 call center employees in the United States and 11,000 in India" (Goldstein, 2003). However the cost and complexity of increasing customer satisfaction has escalated over the past three decades. Robinson and Kalakota (2005, p. 107) estimate that live voice costs between $4 and $8 per contact, interactive voice response (IVR) costs about $1-$2 per contact, Web self-service between $0.05 and $0.3 per contact, and e-mail averages $3-$10 per contact.

Outsourcing finance and accounting (F&A) functions have been prevalent since the beginning of business. Now, there is a growing trend for F&A functions to be outsourced off-shore, primarily to save labor costs (Robinson & Kalakota, 2005, p. 131). For instance, Ford Motor Company has more than 400 people in its business services center in Chennai, India, conducting accounting operations for Ford worldwide. U.S. firms spent about $590 million on off-shore F&A services in 2004, while their European counterparts spent about $480 million. That is expected to increase by 2008 to more than $2 billion (Thibodeau, 2005b).

Outsourcing of human resource (HR) functions, such as payroll, recruitment, hiring, training, benefits management, employee assistance programs, executive compensation, as well as health, safety, and regulatory compliance, is gaining momentum (Robinson & Kalakota, 2005, p. 159). While providing and servicing qualified personnel might be critical success factors, they are not viewed as core competencies. There are also multiple points of potential failure in complex HR systems. It appears to be a logical application for outsourcing. For instance, British Telecom (BT) (BT, 2003) used outsourcing to handle its HR functions with Accenture HR Services in 2000, transferring 1000 HR employees to Accenture HR, which Accenture was able to reduce to just 600 staff members (Accenture, 2003). It is projected that HR outsourcing will increase at an annual rate of 16.1% to $16 billion in 2009 (Gonsalves, 2005).

Outsourcing in the entertainment industry has grown with many U.S. film companies contracting with Indian film companies to handle part of their production work (Abraham, 2005). For example, Global One Entertainment Inc outsourced the production of its film "The Woman from Georgia" to Fast Track Entertainment, an Indian company. They will save 80% of their production costs vs. shooting in the U.S.

Outsourcing of research and development (R&D) functions takes various forms. Above, the outsourcing of R&D in the pharmaceutical industry was discussed. In that instance, drug companies contract with outside firms to explore new compounds for possible testing and launching. A different form of R&D outsourcing is used by companies such as Dell, Motorola, and Philips which buy complete design of digital devices from Asian developers, tweak them to their own specifications, and attach their own brand names (Engardio & Einhorn, 2005). Another approach is that used by Boeing Co. which contracts with India's HCL Technologies to co-develop software for everything from the navigation systems and landing gear to the cockpit controls for its upcoming 7E7 Dreamliner jet (Engardio & Einhorn, 2005). Boeing is also in negotiations with India's Larsen & Toubro (L&T) to outsource engineering as well as aircraft-related IT services and aircraft parts manufacturing (Hardsamalani, 2005). Such trends will help control R&D budgets and reflect the shift in thinking about where R&D fits in a particular company in terms of critical success factors and core competencies (Engardio & Einhorn, 2005).

Summary

This chapter has explored the questions of what, when, and why to outsource. Definitions of outsourcing with off-shoring were examined and compared. An historical perspective on outsourcing was presented.

On the surface, the question of why to outsource is relatively simple. While there are many secondary reasons, there are two primary thrusts. In the case of on-shore outsourcing, the emphasis is on expertise that a company might not possess and finds the need to contract with an outside vendor. In the case of off-shore outsourcing, a primary motivator is cost savings, mainly due to lower labor costs in developing countries. In actual practice, the decision is usually more complex.

The question of when to outsource is equally complex. There are many factors that can support and promote outsourcing effectively. Many of those are internal to an organization. For instance, a company might set an intention to provide customer service, a company might see the life cycle of its products or services shrink, or a company might feel the impact of the global economy or increased competition. There are also many factors that are external to a company. These include changes in the labor pool and other economic factors, as well as political, ethical and societal considerations.

The question of what to outsource is answered by examining a company's core competencies and critical success factors. The chapter presents rules of thumb for each of the four possible combinations of those two factors. It also discusses outsourcing trends in specific companies and industries.

References

Abraham, T. P. (2005, May 24). Now, the mother of all outsourcing. *The Economic Times*. Retrieved June 15, 2005 from http://economictimes.com

Accenture. (2003, Dec. 11). *BT-human resources outsourcing*. Retrieved March 13, 2005, from http://www.accenture.com

Agrawal, V. K., Haleem, A., & Sushil. (2001). Trends in the demand for different categories of software and human resources. In *Proceedings of the Annual Conference of Midwest Decision Sciences Institute* (pp. 4-7).

Agrawal, V. K., & Haleem, A. (2003). Culture, environmental pressures, and the factors for successful implementation of business process engineering and computer-based information systems. *Global Journal of Flexible Systems Management, 4*(1-2), 27-46.

Agrawal, V. K. (2005). From proprietary software to off-the-shelf/ERP solutions: Identifications of critical factors. *National Social Science Journal, 23*(2), 9-32.

Agrawal, V. K. (2005a). Critical factors influencing the requirements of human resources engaged in IT applications. *National Social Science Journal, 24*(1), 1-32.

Agrawal, V. K. (2005b). Implications of environmental and cultural factors on the growth in end-user computing. *National Social Science Journal, 24*(2), 1-14.

Agrawal, V. K., Haleem, A., & Sushil. (2005c, June). Implications of environmental and cultural factors on the growth in the requirements of in-house software professionals. *Indian Journal of Economics and Business, 4*(1), 115-137.

Agrawal, V. K. (2005d). Implications of environmental and cultural factors on the trends in usage of various categories of software. *National Social Science Journal, 25*(1), 1-15.

Arora, H. K., & Arora, S. (2004). A primer on offshore outsourcing. *Indian Journal of Business and Economics, Special Issue, 3*(3), 1-10.

Bajpai, N., Sachs, J., Arora, R., & Khurana, H. (2004). Global services sourcing: *Issues of cost and quality* (CGSD Working Paper No. 16) New York: The Earth Institute at Columbia.

Brice, J. (2003, Nov 1). Globalization comes to radiology. *Diagnostic Imaging.* Retrieved March 13, 2005, from http://www.diagnosticimaging.com/db_area/archives/2003/0311.coverstory.di.shtml

BT. (2003, Dec 11). Outsourcing gives BT focus and adds value to bottom line. Retrieved March 13, 2005, from http://www.btglobalservices.com

Carr, N. G. (Ed.). (2001) *The digital enterprise.* Boston: Harvard Business School Press.

Cleveland, B. (2003, May 5). Author is the president of the Incoming Call Management Institute (ICMI). Retrieved April 15, 2005, from http://www.outsourceworld.org.

Clinton, W. J., & Gore, A. Jr. (1997, July). *A framework for global electronic commerce.* Retrieved March 13, 2005, from http://www.iitf.nist.gov/elec comm/ecomm.

Cole, C. L., Gale, S. F., Greengard, S., Kiger, P. J., Lachnif, C., Raphael, T., et al. (2003, June). Fast forward: 25 trends that will change the way you do business. *Workforce, 82*(6), 43.

Computerworld. (2004). Special report: Outsourcing offshore buyer's guide. Retrieved March 13, 2005, from http://www.computerworld.com/managem enttopics/outsourcing/report/

Computerworld. (2005, April 1). Indian software testing moves from boredom to boom. *Hindustan Times.* Retrieved June 15, 2005, from http://www.hindus tantimes.com

Dash, J. (2001). U.K. financial firms hand routine IT to CSC. *Computerworld.* Retrieved March 13, 2005, from http://www.computerworld.com/printthis/ 2001/0,4814,62661,00.html

Davis, B. (2001). *Speed is life.* New York: Doubleday.

Dibbern J., Goles, T., Hirschheim R., & Jayatilaka, B. (2004). Information systems outsourcing: A survey and analysis of the literature. *Database, 35*(4), 6-102.

Doshi, K. (2004). Pharmaceutical outsourcing: The next wave. *Indian Journal of Business and Economics, Special Issue, 3*(3), 125-136.

Drucker, P. F. (2002). *Managing in the next society.* New York: Truman Talley Books.

E-Business Strategies. (2004, August 10). Offshoring statistics: Dollar size, job loss, and market potential. Retrieved August 10, 2004 from http://www.eb strategy.com/outsourcing/trends

El Sawy, O. A., Malhotra, G. S., & Young, K. M. (1999). IT-intensive value innovation in the electronic economy: Marshall Industries. *MIS Quarterly, 23*(3), 305-335.

Engardio, P., & Einhorn, B. (2005, Mar 21). Outsourcing innovation: Special report. *Business Week*, 84-94.

Evans, P. B., &. Wurster, T. S. (2000). *Blown to bits: How the new economics of information transforms strategy.* Boston: Harvard Business School Press.

Farrell, D. (2003). *Can Germany win from offshoring?* San Francisco: McKinsey Global Institute, McKinsey & Co. Retrieved March 13, 2005, from http://www.mckinsey.com.

Farrell, D. (2004). *Multinational company investment: Impact on developing countries.* San Francisco: McKinsey Global Institute, McKinsey & Co. Retrieved March 13, 2005, from http://www.mckinsey.com

Forrester Research, Inc. (2002, November 11). *3.3 million US services jobs to go offshore.* Research report. Retrieved March 13, 2005, from http:// www.forrester.com/ER/ Research/Brief/Excerpt/0,1317,15900,FF.html

Gallivan, M. J., & Oh, W. (1999). Analyzing IT outsourcing relationships as alliances among multiple clients and vendors. In *Proceedings of the 32nd Annual Hawaii International Conference on System Sciences* (p. 15).

Gartner Group. (1997). *Gartner Group glossary of information technology acronyms and terms.* Lake Dallas, TX: InfoEdge

Gates, H. B. (1999). *Business @ the speed of thought.* New York: Penguin Books.

Gilbert, G., Preston H., & Singh, A. (2003). Rebuilding Big Pharma's business model. *The Business and Medicine Report, 21*(10).

Goldstein, M. (2003, January 20). Customer call center jobs exported from U.S. to India. *New York Daily News.* Retrieved March 13, 2005, from http://www. nydailynews.com/

Gonsalves, A. (2005, April 19). North America to have fewer developers than Asia/Pacific. *TechWeb,* Retrieved March 13, 2005, from http://www.tech web.com.

Gray, N. (2003a). Bike's manufacturer's redesign gets in high gear with product lifecycle management. *OutsorcingAsia.com, Outsourcing Center.* Retrieved March 13, 2005, from http://www.outsourcing-asia.com/bike.html

Gray, N. (2003b). European outsourcing catching up with U.S.: BPO becomes the big party in town. *OutsourcingInformationTechnology.com, Outsourcing Center.* Retrieved March 13, 2005, from http://www.out sourcing-information-technology.com/Europe.html

Greenberg, P. (2002). *CRM at the speed of light: Capturing and keeping customers in Internet real time* (2nd ed.). New York: McGraw-Hill.

Gupta, S. D. (2002, December 11). Outsourcing blues for Indian IT. *Business Standard.* Retrieved March 13, 2005 from http:// www.neoit.com/gen/ newsevents/news_contents/ Outsourcing_blues_for_Indian_IT.pdf

Hagel, J. III, & Singer, M. (2004, September). Unbundling the corporation. *McKinsey Quarterly.* Retrieved March 13, 2005, from http:// www.mckinsey quarterly.com.

Hardsamalani, R. D. (2005, May 28). Boeing in talks with L&T on outsourcing. *Times of India.* Retrieved June 15, 2005, from http://timesofindia. indiatimes.com

Havenstein, H. (2005, April 28). Pittsburg Medical Center taps IBM for IT consolidation. *Computerworld.* Retrieved June 15, 2005, from http://www. computerworld.com/ printthis/2005/0,4814,101375,00.html

Hirschheim, R. A. (1988, September). Backsourcing: An emerging trend? *Infoserver*. Retrieved March 13, 2005, from http://www.infoserver.com/ sep1998/html/academic.html.

Hirschheim, R., Beena, G., & Wong, S. F. (2004). Information technology outsourcing: The move towards offshoring. *Indian Journal of Economics and Business, Special Issue, 3*(3), 103-124.

Hoffman, T. (2003, January 24). Big shift in IT jobs to outsourcing predicted. *Computerworld*. Retrieved March 13, 2005, from http://www.computer world.com/action/ article.do?command=viewArticleBasic&articleId=77860

Hoffman, T. (2005a, April 1). IT users prepare to buy as budget thaw. *Computerworld*. Retrieved March 13, 2005, from http://www.computer world.com/action/article.do?command=viewArticleBasic&article Id=100806

Hopkins, S. M. (2003, August 10). State's contracts ship work to India. *Charlotte* (NC) *Observer*. Retrieved March 13, 2005, from http:// www.charlotte.com/mld/charlotte/

Huber, G. (2004). *The necessary nature of future firms: Attributes of survivors in a changing world.* San Francisco: Sage Publications.

Information Technology Association of America. (2004). 2004 IT workforce study. Retrieved March 13, 2005, from http://www.itaa.org

Jepsen, T., Laplante, P., Williams, J., Christensen, K., Farrante, D., Chang, J. M., et al. (2004, July-August). Software in the new millennium: Virtual roundtable. *IT Professionals, 6*(4), 10-17.

Kajino, M., Kinoshita, T., & Kobayashi, T. (2004, February 1). *Japan's IT market: Racing towards the second phase of growth* (NRI Papers, 43). Tokyo: Nomura Research Institute. Retrieved March 13, 2005, from http:/ /www.nri. co.jp/english/opinion/papers/2004/pdf/ np200473.pdf

Kanter, R. M. (1995). *World class: Thriving locally in the global economy.* New York: Simon and Schuster.

Kearney Business Consulting. (2004). Poland outsourcing services center attracts foreign companies to invest. Retrieved March 13, 2005, from http:/ /esmeap3.moeasmea.gov.tw/ smesr/info/ E11information3.htm.

Kern, T., Lacity, M. C., & Willcocks, L. (2002). *Net sourcing: Renting business applications and services over a network.* Upper Saddle River, NJ: Prentice Hall.

King, J. (2005, March 28). Homegrown. *Computerworld*. Retrieved April 15, 2005, from http://www.ruralsource.com/press/Homegrown.pdf

Koveos, P., & Tang, L. (2004). Offshore outsourcing: Japan, Europe and the rest of the world. *Indian Journal of Economics and Business, Special Issue, 3*(3), 43-62.

Kriplani, M., & Engardio, P. (2003, Dec 8). The rise of India. *Business Week.* Retrieved March 13, 2005, from http://www.businessweek.com/

Lewin, S. G., Lewin, S., & Mesisel J. (1987). Dynamic analysis of the adoption of a new technology: Case of optical scanners. *Review Economics and Statistics, 69*(1), 12-17.

Linder, J. (2004). *Outsourcing for radical change.* New York: AMACOM.

Luftman, J. N., Bullen, C. V., Liao, D., Nash, E., & Neumann, C. (2004). *Managing the information technology resources: Leadership in the information age.* Upper Saddle River, NJ: Pearson Education.

McCleanahen, J. (2002, April). The book on the one-day close. *Industryweek,* 31-33.

Mears, J. (2005, April 25). Study: Outsourcing loosing luster. *Computerworld.* Retrieved June 15, 2005, from http://www.computerworld.com/printthis/2005/0,4814,101380.00.html

Mears, J., & Bednarz, A. (2005, May 30). Take it all: Outsourcing on wane. *Computerworld.* Retrieved June 15, 2005, from http://www.computerworld.com/printthis/2005/0,4814,102168,00.html

Miau, M. (2004, Aug 31). The outsourcing model of MITAC-SYNNEX (lecture). Retrieved March 13, 2005, from http://www.gvm.com.tw/theme/in page_cover.asp?ser=9833.

Morstead, S., & Blount, G. (2003). *Offshore ready: Strategies to plan and profit from offshore IT-enabled services.* Houston, TX: ISANI Press.

Motiwalla, L., & Hashimi, A. (2003). Web-enabling for competitive advantage: A case study of Himalayan Adventures. *Annals of Cases on Information Technology, 5,* 274-289. Hershey, PA: Idea Group Publishing.

Murphy, M. (2000, February). Outsourcing Japan. *OECD Observer, 219.* Retrieved March 13, 2005, from http://www.oecdobserver.org/news/full story.php/aid=162

Naisbitt, J. (1994). *Global paradox.* London: N Breadly.

Nakatsu, R., & Iacovou, C. (2004, Dec 13). Debunking 10 myths of IT offshore outsourcing. *Computerworld.* Retrieved March 13, 2005, from http://www.computerworld.com/ managementtopics/outsourcing/story/0,10801,98252,00.html

Negroponte, N. (1995). *Being digital.* New York: Knopf.

Outsourcing Center. (1999, January). Changing nature of outsourcing fuels growth. *Outsourcing Journal*. Retrieved March 16, 2006, from http://www.outsourcing-journal.com/jan1999-suppliera.html

Outsourcing Index. (2003). *Outsourcing rationale*. Retrieved March 13, 2005, from http://www.outsourcingindex.com.

Outsourcing-Russia.com. (2004, Jul 4). *Delegation of Japanese IT companies visited Russia for first time*. Retrieved March 13, 2005, from http://www.outsourcing-russia.com/news/2004/07/09/01/

Overby, S. (2003. March). Bringing IT back home. *CIO*. Retrieved March 13, 2005, from http://www.findarticles.com/p/articles/mi_kmcio/is_200303/ai_kepm295310

Pallares-Barbera, M. (1998). Changing production systems: The automobile industry in Spain. *Economic Geography, 74*(4). 344-359.

Pitt, L. F., Berthon, P. R., Watson, R.T., and Zinkhan, G.M. (2002, July-August). The Internet and the birth of real consumer power. *Business Horizons, 45*(4), 7-14.

Pradhan, B. (2004). Why Europe is indifferent to outsourcing. *Rediff.com*. Retrieved March 13, 2005, from http://www.rediff.com/cms/print.jsp?doc path=?money/2004/mar/02basab.htm

Press Trust of India. (2004, December 16). Outsourcing to India benefits U.S. economy. *Press Trust,* from http://www.ptinews.com/pti/ptisite.nsf

Pruitt, S. (2005, January 14). Europe overtakes U.S. in big outsourcing deals. *Computerworld.* Retrieved March 13, 2005, from http://www.computer world.com/printthis/2005/0,4814,99086,00.html

Quinn, J. B., & Hilmer, F. G. (1995). Strategic outsourcing. *The McKinsey Quarterly,* 1. Retrieved March 13, 2005, from http://www.mckinsey quarterly.com.

Rishi, M., & Saxena, S.W. (2004). Is outsourcing really as bad as it is made to sound? Reassess- ment and some perspective. *Indian Journal of Economics and Business, 3*(3), 63-80.

Robinson. M., & Kalakota, R. (2005). *Offshore outsourcing: Business models, ROI and best practices*. Alpharetta, GA: Mivar Press.

Rowley, A. (2004, April 27). Japan's IT outsourcing has 6.7t yen potential. *Business Times*. Retrieved March 13, 2005 from http://www.asiaone. com.sg/cgi-bin/utils/it/printf.pl? newsprt

Susarla, A., Barua, A., & Whinston, A. B. (2003). Understanding the service component of application service provision: An empirical analysis of satisfaction with ASP services. *MIS Quarterly, 27*(1), 91-123.

Thibodeau, P. (2005a, March 7). Premier 100 Q & A: McKesson's Cheryl Smith on outsourcing. *Computerworld*. Retrieved March 13, 2005, from http://www.computerworld.com/printthis/2005/0,4814,100247,00.html

Thibodeau, P. (2005b, May 5). Datamonitor: Financial services sector outsourcing to grow. *Computerworld*. Retrieved June 15, 2005, from http://www.computerworld.com/printthis/2005/0,4814,101544,00.html

Thibodeau, P. (2005c, May 2). Offshore tech support still stirs controversy. *Computerworld*. Retrieved June 15, 2005, from http://www.computerworld.com/printthis/2005/0,4814,101456,00.html

Times of India, The. (2004, Dec 5). Developed nations need not fear outsourcing. Retrieved March 13, 2005, from http://timesofindia.indiatimes.com/articleshow/947001.cms.

Turban, E., Leidner, D., McLean, E., & Wetherbe, J. (2006). *Information Technology for Management: Transforming Organizations in Digital Economy*. New York: John Wiley.

Vietor, R. H. K., & Evans, R. (2001). Japan: Beyond the bubble. *Harvard Business Online*. Product #702004. Retrieved March 13, 2005, from http://www.hbsp.harvard.edu.

Vijayan, J. (2005, Mar 8). Premier 100: Outsourcing security offers benefits, risks. *Computerworld*. Retrieved March 13, 2005, from http://www.computerworld.com/printthis/2005/0,4814,100266,00.html

WIT. (2001). Win by borrowing other's abilities. *Wit Solution Journal Online*. Retrieved March 13, 2005, from http://www.ntt-west.co,jp/solution/eng/journal/tokushu_09/001spe_01.html

Chapter III

Planning for Information Systems Outsourcing

Vijay K. Agrawal, University of Nebraska - Kearney, USA

Donald A. Carpenter, Mesa State College, USA

Abstract

This chapter presents an overview of the pertinent aspects of planning for the outsourcing of information systems projects. The first major section of the chapter presents a historical perspective on the evolution of information systems outsourcing practices so the reader can understand subsequent sections of the chapter in context. The next major portion of the chapter deals with the need to examine goals, strategies, core competencies, and critical success factors as well as presenting all the functional areas of information systems that are candidates to be outsourced. Also included are discussions of the need to perform cost/benefits analysis and to consider cultural and other factors. The concluding section deals with all the factors that should be examined in preparing and administering outsourcing contracts.

Introduction

No industry has been affected more by outsourcing than the information sector! That has been both a boon and a challenge to information technology firms. For decades, as businesses in all industries have realized their lack of internal expertise to develop or manage their own information systems, they have outsourced portions or all of their IT departments to firms that specialize in that expertise. Yet, as salaries escalated for those with that needed IT expertise, general businesses as well as the IT firms themselves have turned to developing countries to provide the expertise at a lower cost. Thus, off shore outsourcing, or off-shoring, is exploding.

During the time of the amazing growth of the information sector of developed countries, there was an arrogant claim that is was natural to lose manufacturing jobs to foreign countries because that job loss would be exceeded by information technology companies which were said to have some form of exclusive hold on IT expertise. Reality is expressed more appropriately as:

Our labor force is not better trained, harder working or more innovative than our foreign competitors. The argument that we will create jobs in highly paying fields is simply not true. We have no comparative advantage or superiority in innovation. To assume that we are inherently more creative than our foreign competitors is both arrogant and naive. We are currently empowering our competition with the resources to innovate equally as well as we. (Warren, 2005, www.computerworld.com)

Rather, leaders in the IT field now see outsourcing as a natural evolutionary step in IT (McNurlin & Sprague, 2006, p. 304). Global competition affected only 10% of the U.S. economy in the 1960s, but rose to 70% in the 1970s and is arguably 100% today, as no businesses escape the impact of the global economy. In order to compete in that global economy — especially when the gap in the costs of local vs. off-shore labor looms so large — a majority of businesses must turn over some business functions outsourcing and off-shoring to be competitive. Due to their technical nature, IT functions are logical candidates for such outsourcing for a significant percentage of businesses. Consequently, outsourcing and off-shoring of IT functions is not just an IT issue, it is a primary business issue.

The purpose of this chapter is to provide a planning framework for the outsourcing of IT functions. First a brief historical perspective is presented in order for the reader to appreciate what has worked in the past as a predictor of what might work in the future. That is followed by a description of factors to consider prior to outsourcing information systems projects. Next the chapter presents an extensive examination of IS functions that are logical choices to outsource. Last is a discussion of how to contract for outsourcing and how to manage such contracts.

Evolution of Information Systems Outsourcing Patterns

Outsourcing has been an important information systems practice since the beginning of the computer industry in 1951. When a firm purchases prewritten software, it in effect has outsourced the processes of design and construction of programs. When a company retains a consultant to help identify information requirements, it has outsourced. When an enterprise hires a company to maintain its computer systems, it has outsourced. When a user organization acquires services from a value added network provider, it has outsourced (Singhal, & Singhal, 2002, p. 290).

The specific reasons for such outsourcing vary from one organization to the next. However, in general, the reasons boil down to one factor. It is less costly for the purchasing company to turn outside rather than do the work in-house (Niccolai, 2005). Perhaps it does not have the expertise and it is less costly to buy the expertise than build it. Perhaps it does not have the time to pull off a project. Perhaps it can take advantage of the economy of scale that the supplier has and which the purchasing company does not. Regardless of specific reasons, the host firm turns to outsourcing to save money.

Gradually, that gave rise to the growth of huge outsourcing firms such as Electronic Data Systems (EDS), to software giants such as Microsoft, and to consulting divisions within other companies such as in all the major accounting firms. It spawned the growth of the computer communications portion of the telecommunication industry. Furthermore, it provided myriads of opportunities for smaller firms such as one can find in the business listings of telephone books in any small, medium or large city.

The mid-1970s saw the beginning of outsourcing:

... megadeals, which consisted of outsourcing all of a company's data center operations for up to 10 years. These deals involved selling existing equipment to the outsourcer, transferring all software licenses, moving significant numbers of in-house IS personnel to the outsourcer's payroll, negotiating how the outsourcer would help in the transition and which party would carry which costs, establishing desired service levels and ways

to measure performance, and specifying every single service to be provided — because if it was not in the contract, it would be an added cost. (McNurlin & Sprague, 2006, p. 306)

Again the motivation of the host companies was to save costs — which usually occurred right away — and to guard against unpredictable expenses, by shifting the expertise and expenses to the supplier. For the suppliers, the deals were often money losers in the first year or more, but yielded large profits as start-up costs ended, operations stabilized, and the price of technology dropped. The sweetness of such deals could be soured by disagreements in the ambiguous wording of contracts, which often could lead to additional charges, or by culture clashes between the companies. The latter often occurred when former employees of the host company were transferred to the payroll of the supplier, yet former coworkers and supervisors maintained conflicting expectations.

Changes in information technology itself and changes in user organizations' needs led to corresponding changes in the nature of IT outsourcing. The impact of such changes was most noticeable as companies began to adopt client-server computing in the 1980s, then in the 1990s as industry began its efforts to solve their Y2K problems, to preadjust their information systems to accommodate the new euro currency, and to get on the dotcom bandwagon. In the latter three cases, the workload of IT departments in user enterprises increased beyond the level that could be handled in-house. Outsourcing was a logical solution as the Y2K and euro-conversion problems were both seen as temporary and the creation of corporate Web presences was seen as a new task that would require new investments whether it was outsourced or kept in-house. This gave rise to the concept of project-based outsourcing for specific, often short-term tasks.

The client-server phenomenon was another story, however, as companies chose to move to that environment in order to save costs associated with their mainframe computer systems. Some companies felt the switch to client-server computing had the potential to end their use of outsourcing. However, the reality for other companies was the need to engage in outsourcing due to their lack of internal expertise with the new paradigm. In many instances, the host firm used project-based outsourcing to install and launch their new systems. But another variation on outsourcing was also created, that of the help-desk functions both for end users within the host company but also for the IT staff as they dealt with multiple vendors and ever-changing protocol and systems software.

Such major shifts resulted in the availability of a smorgasbord of outsourcing services from which a host organization can choose. Termed "best-of-breed outsourcing" (McNurlin & Sprague, 2006, p. 307), it allows a user organization to pick and choose which specific IT functions they would like to outsource. It also allows them to choose how they go about outsourcing. One company might choose to outsource all its data center operations to a single vendor, while another might chose to contract with multiple vendors each for a specific function such as software development or Web site hosting. Still another company might choose to outsource specific IT processes or IT-based business processes such as order fulfillment or customer care, while another might choose to outsource functions that transcend functional areas, "such as e-mail, security, or redundancy" (Thickins, 2003).

Other growing trends relate to the nature of the outsourcing arrangement. Today, there is a spectrum of possibilities when a company chooses not to insource business functions in general or information systems functions specifically. Whereas traditional outsourcing contracts are alive and well, there are growing fields of opportunities for joint-venture partnerships and strategic alliances (McNurlin & Sprague, 2006, p. 308). Traditional contracts specify a structured relationship with the vendor supplying services to the host company. Conversely, joint ventures and alliances are trust-based with each party sharing risks and responsibilities. The rapidly growing e-commerce sector provides incredible and previously unachievable opportunities for such arrangements. Hence the business-to-business (B2B) e-commerce sector is growing at an incredible rate.

Another byproduct of project-based outsourcing that gained in popularity with the Y2K and euro-conversion projects is off-shore outsourcing, or off-shoring. White-collar off-shoring was most-likely inevitable as the service sector follows the footsteps of the U.S. manufacturing sector in which productivity grew by 330% in 50 years from the early 1950s largely due to taking advantage of lower labor costs in developing countries. In the same time, U.S. service sector productivity has only grown 47% (Altman, 2004, p. 39).

Project-based outsourcing gave the service sector, which is largely centered on IT, the boost it needed to explode to the point it is today. The sheer cost of the Y2K and euro-conversion problems and the lack of sufficient manpower in the U.S., forced many outsourcing contracts off-shore, especially to India. Today, that has expanded to other countries, many in Asia, including China (McNurlin & Sprague, 2006, p. 307).

Off-shore outsourcing has become a favorite political discussion point. Loss of U.S. jobs is seen as a negative issue. Some argue that off-shoring might actually be good because the living standards in developed countries increase as products and services produced in developing countries can be purchased at lower prices. Regardless, the reality is that off-shoring of services is inevitable. Rather than focusing on loss of jobs, the bigger concern is the loss of competitiveness of service firms, which need to "industrialization" themselves by applying strategies such as off-shoring, automation, and self-service (Karmarkar, 2004).

Identifying Information Systems Processes to Be Outsourced

Consider Goals and Strategies

As stated previously, the primary reason to outsource is to minimize costs (Niccolai, 2005). That is a worthy goal. There may be other reasons or goals. All goals should be formally stated and articulated with business strategies. Other criteria that might be included in goal statements for outsourcing projects are:

- If the process has a large cost base
- If the process is labor intensive
- If it has interlinkages that would be violated by relocation
- If the skills to complete the process are available off-shore
- If a significant wage level differential can be created by off-shoring
- If the process is not a source of competitive advantage (Robinson & Kalakota, 2005, p. 214)

Beyond that, a company needs to determine and formally state the scope of its outsourcing intentions Of course, it order to do that, the company must identify what functions it intends to outsource. Prior to that, the company must understand what is possible to outsource. The remainder of this section intends to provide a method to follow in that process.

Consider Core Competencies and Critical Success Factors

Decisions as to what and whether to outsource should be tied to an identification and understanding of an organization's core competencies and its critical success factors (Luftman, Bullen, Liao, Nash & Neumann, 2004, p. 320). Such an identification and understanding can be a lengthy process. However, it is the one true way to determine whether a project should be or should not be outsourced. While that recommendation was first applied to IT projects, it can be generalized to all business functions.

If a task is a both a core competency and a critical success factor, it should not be considered for outsourcing. Such tasks are at the heart of the company. Success or failure of such functions is directly tied to success or failure of the company as a whole. In general, such functions are critical to an organization's day-to-day operations, ability to competitively differentiate itself, ability to deliver value to customers and partners, and ability to innovate (Luftman et al., 2004, p. 322).

Tasks that are core competencies but not a critical success should be reassessed. Why engage in such tasks if they are not critical? Often the answer to that is "because we can." It is typically not a good business decision to continue to engage in such tasks.

Those tasks which are not core competencies are the most likely candidates for outsourcing. The question is how to go about it. If such as task is a critical success factor, it might be wise to establish a strategic alliance; otherwise, a transaction partnership might suffice. The former is a more tightly-coupled arrangement than the latter. Strategic partnerships might even establish some form of mutual ownership or revenue sharing, whereas transaction partnerships are more typical outsourcing arrangements where a company simply contracts with a vendor to provide the service or product.

There is another consideration that lies outside the core competency–critical success factor matrix. If an organization intends to bring an outsourced task back in-house at some future time, managers should be cautious. There is overwhelming evidence that certain outsourced activities cannot be reversed, particularly in the IT arena (Luftman et al., 2004, p. 323). Once expertise has been released to the outsourcer, it is difficult — if not impossible — to regain such expertise in-house.

Consider Functional Aspects of IS and the Future of the IS Department

As an organization considers outsourcing for its information systems functions, it should recognize that the IS department really performs four interrelated major functions (Cox, 1994):

1. Running computer and communications operations

2. Developing and maintaining systems

3. Developing the strategies and overall architecture for both IT and information

4. Identifying business requirements in conjunction with users

Each of those four areas requires a different knowledge set, varying skills, and distinctly different tools. Each should be managed from its own appropriate strategy. As the company looks to outsource IS, it should consider that each of those four areas should be considered differently in terms of core competencies and critical success factors. As a result, it might make sense to outsource some of those four functions but not others.

The roles of running computer-communications systems and developing/maintaining systems tend to be those that are more logically outsourced than the more strategic roles of developing architecture plans and defining business requirements. To outsource the first two and not the latter two might lead to what is becoming known as "IS lite" (Woolfe, 2000) and reduce budgets for in-house IS functions by 90% (McNurlin & Sprague, 2006, p. 300).

As a firm decides to make a major shift in the IS department that will result from extensive outsourcing, it should consider the long-term impact. Trends indicate two elements that cry out for consideration: (1) how IS will be coordinated in the future and (2) how corporate data and content will be controlled (Markus, 1996). The argument is strong that there still needs to be corporate coordination of IS functions. The argument is also strong that the organization should continue to control its own data and content rather than contract externally for another firm to control them (Hickey, 2005). For these, there is a continued need for an IS staff.

Consider Specific Information Systems Processes

The discussion immediately above identified four general information systems functional areas that might be subject to being outsourced. This section takes a different tack as it presents a listing of 38 information technology management processes (Luftman et al., 2004, p. 119), each of which is subject to being outsourced. The 38 processes are grouped according to a familiar scheme: the three levels of management decision making, long-term strategic, shorter-term tactical, and day-to-day operational. The descriptions of the 38 items are summarized below. For each of the functions, there is an indication as to whether the function should be kept in-house, be considered further for outsourcing, or be considered as a joint responsibility shared between in-house and outsourcing staff.

Consider Costs vs. Benefits

Successful managers recognize that a cost/benefit analysis should be included as part of any major financial decision. Both tangible and intangible benefits, plus both direct and indirect costs should be included. The challenges for most information systems projects traditionally have been quantifying benefits and

Table 1. Categorized IS functions to consider for outsourcing (Modified from Luftman, 2004, p. 119)

• Long Term, Strategic Planning and Control		
1. Business strategic planning	In-house
2. IT architecture — data, apps, computer, network — planning/definition	Outsource
3. IT strategic planning and control	Joint
• Short Term, Tactical Planning and Control		
○ Developmental planning functions		
4. Application portfolio planning and scheduling	Outsource
5. Data needs planning	Outsource
6. Network planning	Outsource
7. System planning	Joint
8. Project planning	Joint
○ Service planning functions		
9. Service level planning and management	In-house
10. Recovery planning and management	Outsource
11. Security planning and management	Outsource
12. Audit planning and management	Outsource
○ Resource planning functions		
13. Capacity planning and management	Joint
14. Skills planning and management	Outsource
15. Budget planning and management	In-house
16. Vendor planning and management	In-house
○ Management planning functions		
17. Management systems planning & management	Joint
• Day-to-Day, Operational Planning and Control		
○ Project management functions		
18. Project assignment	Joint
19. Project scheduling	Joint

Table 1. continued

20. Project controlling	In-house
21. Project requirement control	Joint
22. Project evaluating	In-house
○ Resource control functions	
23. Change control	Joint
24. Asset management	Outsource
○ Service control functions	
25. Production and distribution scheduling	Outsource
26. Problem control	Joint
27. Service evaluating (keep in-house)	In-house
○ Development and maintenance functions	
28. Software development and upgrade	Outsource
29. Software procurement and upgrade contracts	In-house
30. Hardware procurement and upgrade contracts	In-house
31. Systems maintenance	Outsource
32. Tuning and system balancing	Outsource
○ Administration services functions	
33. Financial performance	In-house
34. Staff performance	In-house
35. Education and training	Outsource
36. Recruiting, hiring, and retention	Outsource
○ Information services functions	
37. Production	Outsource
38. Service marketing	Outsource

identifying all of the costs. For many outsourcing projects, especially off-shore outsourcing, the complexity of determining costs and benefits "will increase further because of off-shore arrangements where many variables may be unknown till the project is completed" (Robinson & Kalakota, 2005, p. 215).

The temptation is to jump into an off-shoring project simply on the basis of cost savings as such projects can offer great reductions in capital requirements and long-term operating expenses. Initial cost differentials can be as much as 40% (Hickey, 2005). For example, a software application maintenance worker in India earns about $25 per hour, compared with $87 per hour in the U.S., according to Gartner (Wolfe, 2000).

However, the potential cost saving can erode rapidly. There are costs associated with establishing and administering the outsourcing contract. There might be costs associated with receiving a lower-quality product or service than had been anticipated. This differential can be significantly eroded, however, as companies incur additional costs to manage and administer these outsourced functions. As wages in developing countries catch up with those in the country of origin of the host company, there might be less cost savings over the long run. Most businesses push work overseas in the hope of cutting labor costs. Furthermore, there might be hidden expenses for communications, travel, and cultural training. Off-shore deals that last a relatively short time might not pay off in as big a manner as anticipated (Niccolai, 2005).

Such challenges emphasize the need to perform a thorough cost/benefits analysis. The details as to how to perform such a task go beyond the scope of this chapter, but can be found elsewhere.

Consider Cultural and Other Factors

The cultural differences inherent in off-shore outsourcing can be overcome with cultural training. Such training has become more prevalent in recent years to familiarize employees of both client and provider with information about both country and company cultures. Including an arbitrator who is familiar with both cultures is advisable.

Languages differences might or might not exist. For example, a U.S. company dealing with an Indian outsourcer will benefit in that English is the official language of each. However, regional dialects and accents still can present a challenge, as can colloquialisms. Parties in such an outsourcing arrangement would be wise to avoid such nuances and potential conflicts. As rules of thumb, parties should use short, concise terms and phraseology and should place all agreements in writing.

Differences in legal, regulatory and ethical issues can also provide stumbling blocks in off-shore arrangements. Particularly troublesome are laws pertaining to privacy and intellectual property rights. Retaining legal representation that is familiar with laws and requirements of both countries is costly but invaluable.

One additional consideration bears noting. An outsourcing arrangement can result in atrophy of knowledge and skills in the client organization. To avoid that, the parties might enter into a "co-sourcing" arrangement in which "the vendor and client collaborate so closely that the vendor can replace or augment the client's IT competencies" (Kaiser, & Hawk, 2004). Usually that results in employees from each party working together on the same project team. Similar a mechanism can prove essential in communicating initial requirements as well.

Managing Outsourcing

Outsourcing adds complexity to already complex information systems projects and functions. As was discussed in the Evolution of Information Systems Outsourcing Practices section above, the issue of how to outsource can require managers to decide between creating software or buying a prewritten package, hiring a consultant for a short term or executing a long term contract for ongoing advice, farming out projects or forging a "megadeal," entering into a joint venture partnership or a strategic alliance, outsourcing locally, or going off-shore. Furthermore, as was discussed in the previous section on Identifying Information Systems Processes to be outsourced, before an enterprise engages in outsourcing, managers should consider the firm's goals and strategies, its core competencies and critical success factors, the present nature and future of its information systems functions, the wide range of specific information systems functions that can be outsourced, costs vs. benefits of candidate outsourcing ventures, as well as cultural, language, political, and ethical factors.

Once all that consideration has taken place and the decisions have been made as to what and how to outsource, there is still more work to do to insure the outsourcing adventure is managed properly. Managers have more decisions to make related to the management structure and control, the selection of the vendor, the nature of the outsourcing contract, the launching and implementation of the project, and the monitoring, evaluation and renegotiation of the contract. This section of the chapter discussed those additional topics in greater detail.

Management Structure and Control

Regardless of the management structure, management style and span of control within the companies that are party to an outsourcing contract, the contracted activities must be managed jointly. "Jointly" usually translates to "differently than the firm is accustomed to managing noncontracted activities."

For example, a manager, who might be used to making internal decisions individually and quickly, will encounter the need to make decisions relating to the outsourcing contract cooperatively and probably more slowly. Another manager might be challenged as he adjusts to managing expectations rather than staff.

High quality communications between parties to an outsourcing project is the key to success of the outsourcing endeavor (Niccolai, 2005). However, the customary communications structure and procedures change from what managers usually experience within their respective organizations. Both formal and informal communications channels change when dealing with outside workers.

Interestingly, adjusting to new communications channels can yield unexpected positive results. As managers and employees adjust to the new communication processes, they encounter more formality than what typically exists within their own company. Increased formality demands more rigorous planning and more thoroughness in execution. Those, in turn, can result in improved quality.

To handle such decision-making, parties typically establish layers of joint teams (Robinson & Kalakota, 2005, p. 225). There should be a team of strategic managers from each contract party, a team of tactical managers, and a team of operational managers. The members of each team are responsible to their team but also responsible to the manager within their own company at the higher team level.

Robinson and Kalakota (2005, p. 223) also advocate the use of service level agreements (SLA) as a means to govern outsourcing projects and to monitor performance. "For every contracted service, its SLA spells out responsibilities, performance requirements, penalties, bonuses, and so on. Completeness is an important attribute of good SLAs; generally everything should be detailed, perhaps even with times of deliveries, who will deliver what to whom, and so on." An SLA should also include rules that parties follow when making decisions as well as metrics to be able to measure compliance and rules.

Vendor Selection Criteria

When selecting a vendor for outsourcing projects, managers in the client company should follow the same tried and true methods that are prescribed for all similarly complex purchases. After determining how and what to outsource, as discussed in the previous sections of this chapter, the firm needs to spell out in great detail all its expectations regarding the project. Those detailed explanations should be provided to vendors who have expressed an interest in the project. That should take the form of a formal request for proposal (RFP) to which the potential vendors should be required to respond with detailed formal proposals.

In addition to detailed explanations about the project, the RFP should include extensive discussions as to the vendor's required qualifications and how the project will be managed, monitored and evaluated. The information asked about the vendor should include topics of size, longevity, financial stability, management style and infrastructure, retention experience with its employees, training and educational levels of its employees, experience and procedures with security and privacy, experience and procedures with protecting data and intellectual property, quality management such as IS9000 and Six Sigma compliance, experience with reporting and meeting deadlines, and references from other clients (Robinson & Kalakota, 2005, pp. 230-242).

Once vendors' proposals have been received, the evaluation process begins. Of course, the client company should examine the proposals in depth to be certain that all its requirements can and will be met. Moreover, each vendor should be evaluated as to how well it fits with the client company in light of the future need for communications between the parties as they cooperatively manage the outsourced project.

After narrowing the set of potential vendors to a short list, the client company should schedule reciprocal site visitations to verity capabilities. It should also require demonstrations of capabilities by means of visits to other clients of each vendor or even prototype projects. Performance guarantees should also be worked out prior to deciding on the final vendor.

It might turn out that more than one vendor is required to fulfill all the requirements of the outsourcing project. The RFP should require prospective vendors to explain their plans for and experience with interfacing among multiple vendors. In a related vein, the client company might choose to divide the project among multiple vendors and even among multiple countries in order to minimize risks. In that light, the RFP should include questions that relate to the prospective vendor's location. Those include assessment of the current political climate and cultural differences, as well as disaster recovery and business continuity plans and experiences (Hickey, 2005).

The complexity of the RPF process might seem overwhelming to managers in a client firm and especially if the managers have not been through such a process previously. However, failure to consider thoroughly all the details will predict problems later. Consequently, the client firm might choose to retain the services of an experienced consulting firm. Engaging such a neutral "informed buyer" (Feeny, 1998) might be costly but it most certainly will be worthwhile.

Whether or not an external consultant is used, the final selection of outsourcing vendor(s) should be handled by a vendor selection committee. The magnitude of potential risk of an outsourcing project decision should dictate the managerial level of the members of such a committee. The decision should be reviewed prior to implementation by the client company's top management team, legal advisors, and pertinent stakeholders (Luftman et al., 2004, p. 317). Additional approval should occur prior to, during, and following contract negotiations.

Outsourcing Contracts

Outsourcing contracts can be complex due to the level of detail that needs to be included to insure that all parties understand each others' expectations. Robinson and Kalakota (2005, pp. 219-236) present a general framework for what should be included in outsourcing contracts. That framework is summarized in the following list:

- Price structure
- Billing and payment arrangements
- Price stability
- Payment terms
- Treatment of hidden costs
- Flexibility and tolerances
- Change management
- Conflict resolution
- Term expiration and renewal
- Work to be accomplished
- Vendor's responsibilities
- Define scope and objectives
- Time line and deadlines
- Deliverables
- Performance measurement criteria
- Service level agreements (SLA)
- Communications mechanisms
- Warranties, liabilities, confidentiality
- Protecting of intellectual property

- Security and privacy of data
- Ownership of data or source code
- Compliance with local regulations
- Failure to perform duties
- Terminating the relationship
- Enforcement of contract rights
- Recovery of damages

Many of the items in the above list have been discussed previously in this chapter. Most of the remaining items in the list are fairly straightforward and do not require elaboration. However, the concept of performance measurement does bear expansion.

Measuring performance of information systems is always a challenge. Putting expectations for performance measurement in contractual terms for an outsourcing project can be a greater challenge. The following paragraphs are intended to shed some light on that.

According to Bruton (2004, p. 179) the four main measurements for outsourcing projects are: quantity, performance, quality, and value. Measuring quantity is the easiest of the four — determine how much work was accomplished: how many invoices were processed, how many lines of program code were written, how many workstations were installed. Once quantity is known, performance can be determined by comparing quantity against preset targets or standards. Value of information systems is a little trickier to measure unless it is defined tightly as to whether the project made business sense, whether it advanced the company, or whether it saved the company from higher costs or other losses. The goals of quantity, performance, and value can be relatively easily be put into words in an outsourcing contract.

Quality of information systems is the difficult one to measure and to put in contractual terms. Robinson and Kalakota (2005, p. 81) note that quality of information systems can be tied to customer satisfaction. Turney (1992) writes that "quality is doing it right the first time." Both of those help the reader to understand the nature of quality, but there would be obvious challenges in writing either of those approaches into outsourcing terms.

Parasuraman, Zeithaml, and Berry (1985) provide a little more help with their list of "determinants" of service quality, which are in essence:

- Reliability (consistency/dependability)
- Responsiveness (timeliness/promptness)
- Competence

- Access (approachability/convenience)
- Courtesy
- Communications ease
- Credibility (trustworthiness/honesty)
- Security
- Understanding customers and their needs
- Tangible evidence of service (including facilities, personnel appearance, tools, and equipment)

While those are more definitive, and can be used as critical success factors (Luftman et al., 2004, p. 361), they do not necessarily lend themselves easily to contractual terminology. Myers, Kappelman, and Prybutok (1997) list eight IS success dimensions that can be more easily worded into an outsourcing contract: (1) service quality, (2) system quality, (3) information quality, (4) use, (5) user satisfaction, (6) individual impact, (7) work group impact, and (8) organizational impact. The contractual wording would depend on the specific nature of the outsourcing project.

Implementing, Monitoring, Evaluating, and Renewing Outsourced Projects

Robinson and Kalakota (2005, pp. 224-229) strongly emphasize the need to develop plans to implement outsourced processes and encourages the early formation of teams to oversee (1) knowledge transfer between client and supplier organizations, (2) facilitation of initial and ongoing communications at all levels of the participating firms, (3) management of employees, especially those transferred from one firm to the other, and (4) management of the quality of the fulfillment of the project. Hayes (2003) agrees that setting up the management of outsourcing implementation needs to happen as quickly as possible. Luftman et al. (2004, pp. 319-320) reinforces the need to develop vendor relationships and partnerships and advocates use of steering committees to build those through frequent meetings with vendor councils. For long-term, complex engagements, Robinson and Kalakota (2005, p. 230) even go to the point of prescribing relationship managers for each of the parties to the outsourcing contract to serve as the folks that resolve conflicts at a high level.

Regarding monitoring of outsourcing contracts, evaluating performance and conducting periodic reviews, Feeny (1998) writes that those should be considered critical success factors and should become core competencies of the IS staff. In other words, the success of the outsourcing project resides in the monitoring, evaluation, and reviewing of the parties' performances. Service level agreements (SLA), coupled with incentives and penalties, can be excellent tools to measure quality of the project against predetermined metrics (Luftman et al., 2004, p. 319) such as the vendor's performance against the service level agreement and accepted industry benchmarks of quality. There might be an infinite number of questions that could be asked regarding whether SLAs are being adhered to, for example: Are SLA deadlines being met and adhered to? Is reporting timely and accurate? Is the quality of work consistent with the defined SLAs? Is the number of people on the projects accurate? Does the vendor have valid software licenses in place? (Robinson & Kalakota, 2005, p. 235).

Other critical factors in contract management are assessment of risks and appropriate adjustments. Robinson and Kalakota (2005, p. 234) note that things change during the course of a contract and risks change as a result. Both parties in an outsourcing arrangement need to keep their fingers on the pulse of those factors that can produce risks. This is especially true in a global economy where factors change very rapidly and in a world of unstable political environments. "To insure business continuity, companies must engineer availability, security, and reliability into every offshore process" (Robinson & Kalakota, 2005, p. 234).

Monitoring the activities of an outsourcing project helps to identify problem areas and opportunities to improve performance. There are times when contract monitoring can identify changes that result in a need to renegotiate the contract. Examples of such changes are:

- Expiration of the contract at its logical and predetermined end
- Material contract breach by vendor, for example, poor performance, security lapses, criminal activity
- A major change in the organization's management or industry, for example, bankruptcy, merger
- Significant change in price for the same service by the same or other vendor
- Advent of new technology that could improve the project (Luftman et al., 2004, p. 319)

Robinson and Kalakota (2005, pp. 232-233) point out a rule of thumb is that process designs become obsolete every five years. This can be due to any number of causes, but points to the potential need to renegotiate contracts.

Summary

This chapter has provided an overview of the processes and considerations for planning for outsourcing of information systems functions. It began by framing the present state of IS outsourcing processed in a historical context. The nature of IS outsourcing has evolved through the years for several reasons. Each of the evolutionary processes is available for use today.

There are many factors that should be considered prior to outsourcing information systems functions. Managers should consider the firm's goals and strategies, its core competencies and critical success factors, the present nature and future of its information systems functions, the wide range of specific information systems functions that can be outsourced, costs vs. benefits of candidate outsourcing ventures, as well as cultural, language, political, and ethical factors. Similarly there are many IS functions which might be candidates to be outsourced

After deciding how and what to outsource, managers begin the process of restructuring the organization to accommodate outsourcing. Then there are the elaborate processes of selecting the right vendor and negotiating the outsourcing contract. The work does not end with the signing of the contract. Indeed some of the most critical tasks lie ahead with the monitoring, evaluation, and possible renegotiation of the contract.

References

Altman, D. (2004, May 1). A more productive outsourcing debate. *Business*. Retrieved March 13, 2005, from http://money.cnn.com/magazines/business2/business2_archive/2004/ 05/01/368257/index.htm

Bruton, N. (2004). *Managing the IT ServicesPprocesses*. Burlington, MA: Butterworth-Heinemann.

Cox, G. (1994, June). Time to reshape the IS department? *Wentworth Research Program (*part of *Gartner Executive Program)*. Retrieved March 13, 2005, from http://www.gartner.com

Feeny, D. (1998, Spring). Core IS capabilities for exploiting information technology. *Sloan Management Review, 39*(3), 9-21.

Hayes, M. (2003, August 4). Doing offshore right. *InformationWeek,* 77-78.

Hickey, T. (2005, January 31). Outsourcing decisions: They're strategic. *Computerworld.* Retrieved March 13, 2005, from http://www.computer world.com/printthis/2005/0,4814,99316,00. html

Kaiser, K., & Hawk, S. (2004). Evolution of offshore software development: From outsourcing to cosourcing. *MIS Quarterly Executive, 3*(2), 69-81.

Karmakar, U. (2004, June). Will you survive the services revolution? *Harvard Business Review,* 101-107.

Luftman, J. N., Bullen, C. V., Liao, D., Nash, E., & Neumann, C. (2004). *Managing the information technology resources: Leadership in the information age.* Upper Saddle River, NJ: Pearson Education, Inc.

Markus, M. L. (1996). The future of IT management. *Database for Advances in Information Systems, 27*(4), 68-84.

McNurlin, B. C., & Sprague, R. H. Jr. (2006). *Information systems management in practice.* Upper Saddle River, NJ: Pearson Prentice Hall.

Mearian, L. (2005, April 8). Feds force tighter oversight of outsourcers. *Computerworld.* Retrieved June 15, 2005, from http://www.computerwor ld.com/printthis/2005/ 0,4814,100962,00.html

Myers, B. L., Kappelman, L. A., & Prybutok, V. R. (1997). Comprehensive model for assessing quality & productivity of information systems function: Toward theory for information systems assessment. *Information Resource Management Journal, 10*(1), 6-25.

Niccolai, J. (2005, June 22). Gartner: Five reasons why offshore deals go bust. *Computerworld.* Retrieved July 13, 2005, from http://www.computerworld. com/printthis/2005/ 0,4814,102677,00.html

Parasuraman, A., Zeithaml, V. A., & Berry, L. L. (1985). A conceptual model of service quality and its implications for future research. *Journal for Marketing, 49*(4), 41-50.

Robinson, M., & Kalakota, R. (2005). *Offshore outsourcing: Business models, ROI and best practices.* Alpharetta, GA: Mivar Press.

Singhal, J., & Singhal, K. (2002). Supply chains and compatibility among components in product design. *Journal of Operations Management, 20,* 289-302.

Thickins, G. (2003, April). Utility computing: The next new IT model. *Darwin Magazine.* Retrieved April 15, 2005, from www.darwinmag.com/read/ 040103/utility.html.

Turney, P. B. B. (1992, January). Activity-based management. *Management Accounting,* 20-25.

Warren, S. (2005, May 23). Eye on offshoring: Aligning IT strategy with the business strategy. *Computerworld.* Retrieved March 13, 2005, from http:/ /www.computerworld.com/managementtopics/outsourcing/story/ 0,10801,101896,00.html

Woolfe, R. (2000, July). IS lite. *Gartner EXP.* Retrieved March 14, 2006, from http://www.gartner.com.

Chapter IV

Strategic and Tactical Planning of Outsourcing in MIS

Jeanette Nasem Morgan, Duquesne University, USA

Abstract

This chapter lays out a set of steps for organizations to traverse in considering and crafting an outsourcing strategy for the firm. Outsourcing in management information systems (MIS) is defined. The chapter proceeds through the steps of strategic and tactical planning, addressing particular issues at each level, and concludes with operational level planning for outsourcing projects. These disciplines prepare an organization to manage and execute a MIS project or ongoing service that will be provided by an outsourcing partner. Lessons learned from good techniques for integrating planning across the firm are included. Planning serves as the introduction to outsourcing selected functions, services, or products. Best practice methods and decision models for outsourcing are crafted from both outsourcing success stories as well as numerous failures, and are covered in subsequent chapters. The chapter includes suggestions for how to address and consider the option of outsourcing MIS projects as part of an overall strategic plan. Project management considerations in this decision are included. Ethical considerations such as humanitarian consequences and theological considerations are addressed.

Strategic Planning in the Organization

This section addresses how organizations approach strategic planning. It concerns the steps and decisions that an organization progresses through while contemplating outsourcing of MIS functions or services which are appropriate and beneficial to the organization's overall strategy. First, as depicted in Figure 1, defining an organizational strategy that recognizes outsourcing to international or even national or regional external service providers makes sense for overall competitiveness when the firm has a disciplined approach to strategic planning. Strategic or "institutional level" management defines the vision, mission, and goals of the organization. Through the defining characteristics of the firm's vision identified by executive level planning, lower levels of management are empowered to seek out innovative techniques and projects that can implement the mission of the organization. This vision is concerned with "Where do we want to be?" Second, midlevel and division or department management is involved in crafting the mission and appropriate goals that will carry out that vision of the organization. This tactical or "organizational level" planning activity involves the coordination and exercise of control over core business functions that differentiate the firm from its competitors. Mission planning answers the question "How will we get there?" This level may analyze and approve certain projects because they carry out the mission of the organization.

Finally, for the strategic vision and mission to permeate the very culture of the organization, management involves the operational or "technical level" management and staff in identifying and selecting appropriate projects that will implement the goals of the organization. The operational level is generally concerned with the day-to-day transactions that produce goods, manage business processes, and execute transactions to achieve project objectives. This places them in the unique position of being able to give senior management a "reality check" as to the reasonableness and attainability of the goals. Operational, ground level planning addresses the question, "What must we do?" as well as reports on "How are we doing?"

Figure 1. Three steps to planning in organizations

Step 1. Define Corporate Strategy by the *Vision:* The Public Image of the Organization

Organizations need to periodically reevaluate the progress and perception of where they stand in relation to their vision. A vision is said to be the way the organization views itself. *The Vision Statement describes a picture of how the organization wants to be seen by the outside world.* In evaluating what it wants to be known for and what is its image, an organization is often identified with the kinds of projects that are approved. An organization that dispenses with unprofitable business lines is seen as agile and self-correcting. Shareholders view these type of actions clinically and approve of an adroit Board of Directors who divests the organization of businesses that drain profitability from other units, or hinder the organization from remaining competitive. In this way, the organization improves efficiency.

However, in some cases, Board actions to remove a forward thinking CEO has made the organization turn in on itself and shareholders may flee from stock ownership of a volatile organization. Frequent changes at the top of an organization may make shareholders unsure of the intentions of the Board of Directors and the owners are left feeling the ship has become too rocky to stay the course. This can be a danger of outsourcing core functions to overseas providers. When shareholders see key business functions such as new research and development

Figure 2. Roles and scope (intent of/planning in organizations)

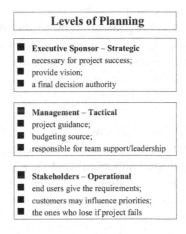

Levels of Planning

- **Executive Sponsor – Strategic**
- necessary for project success;
- provide vision;
- a final decision authority

- **Management – Tactical**
- project guidance;
- budgeting source;
- responsible for team support/leadership

- **Stakeholders – Operational**
- end users give the requirements;
- customers may influence priorities;
- the ones who lose if project fails

of new product innovations, or management of projects moved to external organizations, there may be a real fear of breakup of the firm and loss of control over organizational autonomy and competitiveness. This may be an appropriate fear, as all of us have seen less of competitive advantage when innovation is outsourced.

Vision statements are used by effective organizations as a management instrument to provide strategic focus on specific long-term mission objectives (Step 2) throughout an organization. When effective, vision statements influence day-to-day decisions in a way that the cumulative effect moves the organization on a path to meet its long-term goals (Step 3). The vision statement is also a statement of the inspirational purpose that appeals to the higher values in both employees and the organization's customers. Figure 2 illustrates the roles and scope of what is included in each level of organized planning

The public persona of a firm can be damaged by actions that appear to the investing public (generally not to the "clear-eyed" and shrewd institutional investors) as unsavory and unpatriotic. So decisions to outsource MIS functions may be viewed as counterproductive from the standpoint of the public understanding of the organization's vision.

Step 2. The Threefold *Mission* of the Organization: What is the Service Line of Our Business? Where Do We Do Business? Who Are Our Customers?

The next step of organizational strategic planning involves defining the mission of the organization. Strategic planning is best done once a year in organizations. The mission is said to help the organization more specifically define the three operational aspects of its vision when it embarks to implement that vision. To do so, the organization must articulate a *Mission Statement that explains what the organization wants to achieve, what role will it play in its marketplace, and who the community is in which it operates.* The mission statement is usually a few sentences that describe in more detail how the organization distinguishes itself to achieve its vision as can be seen in Figure 3. Some organizations dispense with a vision statement and encapsulate the essence of the organization in a one-sentence, clear, concise mission statement that says who the company is (the name), what it does, for whom, and where it operates. The mission themes should be easy to understand, noncontroversial, and translate into behavior that can gain support.

Consider the mission statement for Disney, mentioned in the text box, for example. They aim for people to have fun — not just their customers, but anyone

Figure 3. Sample organization mission statements

Sample Mission Statements (found on company Web sites in 2003)

- **Entertainment - Disney**: "To make people happy"
- **Defense - Boeing Phantom Works**: "To be the catalyst of innovation for the Boeing Enterprise"
- **Non-profit - United Community Center**: "A 501(c)(3) human service agency providing emergency assistance, daycare, social services and recreational activities for low-income children and families at risk in inner city Atlanta, Georgia".
- **Technology - IBM**: We strive to lead in the creation, development and manufacture of the industry's most advanced information technologies, including computer systems, software, networking systems, storage devices and microelectronics. We translate these advanced technologies into value for our customers through our professional solutions and services businesses worldwide.

---

associated with Disney enterprises. They want their employees to have fun. They arrange corporate gatherings and celebrations for employees to engender team spirit. This can be difficult in an organization that is heavily using outsource providers located a continent or more away. Disney wants people to escape the grind and stresses of their regular lives with enjoyment and fantasy. The mission statement should also express the themes of the core businesses of the organization.

What is the organizational theme? Does it deal with a product, service, or both? Can it be easily understood and interpreted by both employees and customers? In some cases, it may have to be mildly controversial to provoke thought and discussion.

Mission statements should be clear enough for tactical management to formulate goals that can be quantifiably defined and that can then be measured and carried out within a one to five year planning horizon. The mission should stay relatively stable and only require alterations every three to five years. Evidence that a firm does not clearly know what business it ought to be in is often found when organizations change their vision or mission statement annually.

Step 3. Identify Organizational Goals: What to Accomplish in the Next One to Two Years

The final step in strategic planning in the organization is to carefully define the five or so Organizational Goals that will drive what the organization does for the

Figure 4. Engender support for corporate goal-setting

Engender Support for Corporate Goal-Setting

1. Communicate with Action Plans that help Visualize the Goals. Demonstrate your corporate commitment and follow through with concrete plans that can be linked to specific initiatives and projects in the organization. Consider creating committees and work groups that help build the excitement and determination to succeed.

2. Focus on the Key Attributes of the Service or Products. Take the example of Boeing, mentioned in the textbox sidebar earlier. Does your organization want to push the leading edge of technology to achieve one or more of its goals? This may be necessary when outsourcing a project or a service overseas. Do you accept the risks and challenges and are you postured to undertake the steps that others in your industry won't or can't? Are the potential problems in executing these goals too difficult and challenging to solve? Do these goals bring value to your customers and shareholders?

3. Don't Rush the Goal Identification Process. Brainstorming and creativity take time. Be sensitive to the process of vertical communications that are required across the organization as well as the end result of identifying goals. Participants want to see that their experience and hopes for the firm are incorporated. Some organizations just wanted a rubber stamp on the executive mission and goal setting process, never considering it will be the rank and file (as well as the outsource partners they work from week to week to carry out those goals. This is a critical opportunity to build commitment, trust and morale in the organization.

---

coming year. Figure 4 summarizes guidelines for organizations to disseminate and engender multi-level support for the organizations' goals. Questions that should be asked to help prepare each Goal Statement include what broad areas does the firm want to focus on to achieve the mission. What measurable improvements do we want to implement in the near term? What changes or actions must this organization undertake and complete in order to be competitive or to improve bottom line financial results? These organizational goals will be used to evaluate and select specific projects that help execute the goals. Goals also help the firm to communicate exactly where the firm is going in the following year. By providing solid, measurable goals, the tactical levels of management as well as the operational, in-the-trenches managers and team leaders know what the firm's annual performance targets are. Having measurable goals, managers know what they are expected to aim for to help the firm achieve its vision and mission. Goals are revised annually to keep staff and teams *accountable* as well as provide incentives for performance.

Organizations that tie personnel performance plans (which are usually done on an annual basis) to corporate goals help further solidify employee commitment to organizational performance. In this way, goals become part of the operating culture of the organization, enhance cross communication between management and staff, and get everyone involved in the mission.

Lastly, when validating these as the correct goals, the organization must map each goal back to the mission statement. If there is only a one-sentence or otherwise vague mission statement, this validation task will require more creative rationalizing of projects. A bulleted mission statement is easier (and examples can be found on most any corporate or government Web site home page). Consider evaluating whether your mission statement adequately and sufficiently expresses what the organization wishes to accomplish in the near term planning horizon.

The following suggestions can be used to validate that the goals and the mission statement are aligned and clear:

- **Statement of vision:** What is your vision of the organization, and how does it appeal to the employees and customers? Do the goals carry out the vision intent?

- **Statement of value:** What corporate values link the organization's vision to the more specific mission? Are these values that employees can be proud of? Can the stated goals be achieved within the reasonable time frames expressed in the mission?

- **Statement of expected behaviors:** How do employee and supplier behaviors relate to customer perceptions of value? Can the goals be realistically achieved with external outsourcing partners?

- **Statement of corporate culture:** Is the organizational culture casual and informative in terms of communications lines or is it structured and formal with clear lines of hierarchy? What changes are implied in the goals?

Clearly, cross-checking goal statements against how adaptable the organization is, is vital to actually achieving the goals. A final note: goals should be stated in a way that includes or clearly implies the measurable results that are to be attained by successful completion of each of the goals. Statements that express growth targets, product or service line profitability rates, reduction in errors or loss rates, and market share figures are examples of measurable goods. These can be aligned to the subsequent projects that will be selected to execute goals. The same goal metrics can then be used to hold outsourcing partners and vendors to similar quantitative performance targets. The remaining steps of planning MIS outsourcing are addressed in subsequent sections. We now address some specifics relevant to outsourcing in strategic and tactical planning.

The Role and Tactics of Outsourcing: How Outsourcing Differs from Insourcing Strategic and Tactical O/S MIS

A lot of press has addressed the pros and cons of outsourcing, particularly that of off-shore outsourcing. One hardly needs to write a book about it. However, too many horror stories exist as to the unseen costs and lackluster benefits to not address it in a consolidated guide that can help management make appropriate decisions as to when and how to outsource certain or all MIS functions. Because MIS is so broadly characterized, we know it includes any technological support for core functions, the systems that manage the production of goods, as well as the internal support functions that foster improved worker productivity or help introduce new channels for selling products. MIS also adds value by integrating access to critical corporate data, and streamlines work processes to support more agile organizations and more profitable ways of doing business. Outsourcing of MIS occurs because the organization determines that the cost of doing certain business functions can be better done, or more quickly done, or more cheaply by an outside party. However, the provision of services is not only limited in strategic planning to external providers. The entire spectrum of sourcing includes outsourcing, insourcing, off-shoring, near-shoring, and rural sourcing within national boundaries. The scope of this book is focused on outsourcing and off-shoring; however, the principles, tools, techniques, and considerations can be applied to any organization with tailoring to address any types of sourcing of MIS projects or activities.

Outsourcing, therefore, is loosely defined as work done for an organization by people other than the organization's full-time employees. (See Figure 5 for some

Figure 5. Technical vs. business process outsourcing

Outsourcing – the Way it is...

■ Best Technology Outsourcing Options:
- ■ Ongoing software maintenance
- ■ Software Conversion Projects (e.g. modernizing, reengineering)
- ■ Original application development

■ Best Business Process Outsourcing Areas:
- ■ Consumer rebate processing
- ■ Medical records, dictation transcription
- ■ Claims handling and payment authorization
- ■ Credit card transaction processing

Figure 6. Trends facilitating outsourcing

Outsourcing *Business Processes –*
Why it Now Works…

- Cheaper labor resources abroad for "body shop" work.
- Overseas education levels are also high, but at a fraction of the cost of U.S. graduates and employees.
- Cultural attitudes toward quality and "work ethic" may mean higher worker productivity levels.
- Maturation of infrastructure for telecommunications, energy, etc. in many under-developed countries.
- Internationalization of "English" and ability to "telecommute" removes traditional barriers to "move to higher paying countries for job opportunity"

examples of typical outsourcing sources.) The terms and specific conditions for the outsourcing relationship between an organization and its partner or vendor is specified in some sort of agreement. The agreement or contract for services or products is concluded between a client organization and a service provider for the ongoing activities related to a part or to the whole of MIS. The types of services or products that are typically outsourced include:

- Business functions (e.g., human resources, marketing, payroll, billing/ collections)
- Infrastructure (e.g., information systems, security systems, telecommunications)
- Software development (e.g., software applications, databases, software customization, transaction processing, networks)
- Support services (e.g., help desk, customer support, facilities)
- Operating processes (e.g., procurement of raw materials, production, operation of a telecommunications network)

The actual differences between insourcing vs. outsourcing are often viewed as significant. With an internal service provider you have the same organizational culture, share the same vision and mission. Employees march to the same set of organizational goals. Staff is held accountable to the same performance measurement techniques and their compensation systems are tied to the same corporate standards and practices. Penalties as well as rewards for compliance to MIS objectives are direct. With an external service provider, it becomes necessary to converse about the expected cultural norms, agree upon operating principles and practices. In many cases, this involves lengthy negotiation. Contracts address penalty and reward systems and there is often little latitude for backing out of an outsourcing arrangement. This is covered subsequently in Chapter V in greater detail under "Negotiating Outsourcing Contracts and Terms."

However, all the types of sourcing require the organization define the performance characteristics and the objectives of the MIS project. In this way, if we do not actually differentiate the metrics and decision models applied to sourcing MIS projects, we may have a greater likelihood of success. These issues are supported in Chapter VII. It will become readily evident that all forms of sourcing are appropriate as "bona fide tools in the CIO's tool belt" as Mary Brandel offers in the article, "The 'O' Word Reconsidered" (Brandel, 2005).

As an outgrowth of strategic planning, the organization has to also weigh the costs and benefits as well as determine if outsourcing fits the image expressed in the vision and the scope expressed in the original mission. Questions such as when to insource and when to outsource become thorny management issues. Figure 6 outlines some trends, both cultural as well as technical, responsible for making outsourcing feasible for the new millenium. Using analytical models such as activity based costing (ABC) can help the firm to measure the current cost of providing MLS services in house. When the business case demonstrates a vendor or partner can perform that function for a significantly lesser cost, the case for outsourcing becomes compelling. However there are many hidden or unforeseen costs that are often overlooked. Other techniques such as project management earned value analysis (EVA) techniques provide a means to monitor and gauge if the external party is performing as anticipated. These are covered in greater detail later in this chapter.

Some of the reasons Morgan (2004) found that make off-shore outsourcing a compelling business arrangement include cheaper labor, higher education levels, cultural attitudes toward quality and work ethic, worker productivity, maturing infrastructure, telecommunications availability and lower costs for these, as well as an availability of local labor educated to converse well in English:

- Cheaper labor resources exist abroad due to lower standards of living, lower education levels, and fewer social welfare programs. This results in an opportunity for local, private companies to establish training programs to develop a specifically trained labor force for specific "body shop" work. In this scenario, specialized labor may be then made available for "niche" outsourcing contracts with larger companies abroad who do not wish to diversify and dilute their core business focus.

- Overseas education levels in certain underdeveloped countries are high due to government focus on educating their population in areas like technology. Because of government investment in this retraining of their labor force, higher education comes at a fraction of the cost of U.S. graduates and employees.

- Cultural attitudes toward quality and "work ethic" in many Asian and Eurasian nations often translate to a population that believes in personal sacrifice for the good of the homeland. Dedication to state-fostered education programs as well as to state-run entities may mean higher worker productivity levels.

- Maturation of infrastructure for telecommunications, energy, and so forth in many underdeveloped countries have made long-distance outsourcing obstacles a thing of the past. International aid agencies like the International Monetary Fund, the World Bank Group, and governments themselves have invested to stabilize infrastructure and develop higher bandwidth telecommunications capabilities. These technological advances, such as fiber optic cabling, come at a lower cost today than many of the U.S. companies that invested in technology early, when the costs were still relatively high. Nowadays, countries invest in shared satellite communications and other mechanisms for global communications capability.

Figure 7. Five different types of outsourcing MIS

Many Forms of "Sourcing"

Insourcing – Defined service levels and memoranda of understanding concerning response times, application support services. Performance may be tied to annual personnel evaluations to encourage good performance. Less cultural strife or differences as it's al the same employer. May include one subsidiary serving another within the same conglomerate corporation.

Local outsourcing – Hiring local companies to provide services or support. Reduced labor investment on short-term projects; used to acquire expertise not readily available in-house. Used for staffing for "peaks" in seasonal business.

Rural outsourcing – Establishing contractual agreements for a workforce in a non-metropolitan area. Dedicated labor pool; usually domestic labor, not foreign, but infrastructure or education levels may not be satisfactory. Eliminating a contract in the future may have political backlash against the client organization.

Near-shoring – Hiring foreign companies to provide specific services, but within same time zone as the client organization. Easier to manage than providers located across the globe. Good for 24 x 7 services in non-peak hours, and for routine, non-sensitive work.

Offshore outsourcing – Establish contracts for specific work or support services in another geographical region. Helps provide global support to business that is also global in nature, such as securities trading or back-office support for which oversight is not very important.

- The internationalization of "English" and the ability of many countries to "telecommute" remove traditional barriers to job opportunity. Local labor can now provide services, as quasi-employees or representatives to larger firms for higher paying salaries, without having to deal with immigration laws, or having to move families and uproot themselves to better their means (Morgan, 2004).

Outsourcing MIS to local, rural regions with educated, available local citizenry within national borders can have advantages from the cost standpoint that far outweigh the risks of going overseas for MIS service providers. Dell, a computer manufacturing company that also sells direct to companies and consumers learned the hard way that off-shore outsourcing is not as attractive and can backfire in many ways. Other organizations have found rather than going far off-shore to another time zone, sending MIS work nearby to a neighboring country makes the work easier to manage and oversee. This has led to an increase in establishing outsourcing centers in Mexico and Canada proximate to U.S. client organizations (see Figure 7). Later sections describe these different outsourcing options in greater detail. Chapters V and VII address some of the techniques and technologies available for managing geographically disparate teams.

Moving to Development of Tactics: Organizational Global Warfare in the Financial and Performance-Based Trenches

Up to this point we have presented the background of planning that must occur before an organization can realistically determine if MIS functions that support business processes can be outsourced. An outgrowth of strategic planning activities is the identification and initiation of eligible projects in the organization. While, in some instances, ongoing core business functions such as human resource management, payroll, help desk, and other continuous MIS activities are considered for outsourcing, in many cases outsourcing is treated as a defined project. A project is commonly identified as a temporary endeavor undertaken to accomplish a unique purpose and that is aligned to the company's strategic goals. As such, each project has specific objectives it must accomplish as part of its purpose. Project management performs against the targets in hopes that the projected objectives will each be met. Strategic management, accordingly, views project objectives in light of their contribution to meeting overall organizational goals, such as decreasing costs of raw materials, or increasing sales revenues in Web-based business lines. Projects that are outsourced may include a vendor developing an Internet software application that creates a new customer portal to accept customer-entered orders, while automating the inventory decrementing activities and the pick-and-pull order shipment functions. Such a project's objectives would likely include lowering costs of telephone sales staff, reducing lost sales due to out of stock situations, lowering shipping costs, and increasing customer positive feedback.

Other project objectives may be more social in nature — providing easier access to information by the public, personalizing the customer experience by instituting an outsourcer that responds to incoming customer calls to replace a voice response telephone system. In such cases, the metrics of project objectives may be intangible, and involve goodwill. In the case of governmental or nonprofit organizations, the reasons for outsourcing may not be financial. Once the financial or other intangible benefits case has been made, the organization needs to consider corporate citizenship. This may mean local, national, or global citizenship. What are the implications of choosing partners outside the organization to help implement strategy? What are the impacts to the local community; what happens in the outsourcer's country?

The organization that is looking seriously at off-shore outsourcing needs to consider the viability of any particular host country as to its political stability, the state of its infrastructure and local services, such as water, transportation, and availability of trained, skilled labor. Political stability can affect supplies and the availability of human resources if local or national conflicts ensue.

In addition, there may be further aspects of domestic goodwill and public outcry when the organization considering the outsourcing option is a large, publicly traded firm or a national governmental agency. Firms must consider the ethics as well as the financial wisdom of such a venture. The outsourcing commitment means there will be a loss of high technology jobs domestically. Public awareness spurred by either a federally mandated or locally published "reporting requirement" can have negative consequences. Host countries that tax excessively or permit excessive work hours, or undemocratic, inhumane working conditions can impact both the client firm as well as the local populace of the outsourcer. Overall, however, the globalization of labor as a commodity has been coming, just as technology has sought to reduce the amount of manual, noncreative labor that mankind has to contend with. The internationalization of telecommunications has largely renewed the closed borders limitations against global commerce.

Overseas Outsourcing: A Political Football or a "Hot Potato"?

Other issues from overseas outsourcing have arisen that are more political and emotional. In France, legislation was enacted to require reporting of outsourcing activities in all public companies. In the U.S., congress requires that government contracts report where the work will be performed. Companies involved in public activities where goodwill and public opinion are vital to their continued success, may consider seriously the benefits of near-shoring in U.S. states or territories such as Guam on west coast time zones, or Puerto Rico in the eastern time zones.

Another point often ignored is that moving jobs out of the organization's country has additional problems when sales are dependent on the prosperity of a large portion of the local population. If the outsourcer's host country cannot make up for lost sales, then the organization may need to consider that unemployed citizens can ill afford their products.

National ethical considerations include questions that ask how the unemployed in a nation share in the savings that an organization gains from outsourcing. Are the countries receiving these job opportunities using their increased spending power in humanitarian and egalitarian ways? A large organization involved in outsourcing to a village in a foreign land that is generally underdeveloped can divert part of the profits from the lowered cost of labor or infrastructure to establish housing, schools, churches, hospitals, and other public services that benefit and educate the local host country citizens. Organizations have a companion moral obligation to also assist local officials to carefully direct and monitor the impact to the local host country economy from the sudden inflow of dollars as a result of increased local incomes of their citizens. One example broadly reported in the press in the last decade was television host Kathy Lee Crosby's clothing manufacturer who unwittingly used child labor to produce products that were sold in Kmart and otherstores to U.S. consumers. Once this situation was brought to light, both the public opinion forum as well as the courts put an immediate stop to the human rights abuses. Bad press, as well as shareholder backlash can have very negative consequences to the public persona of an organization that elects to do off-shore outsourcing in a country that does not conform to the generally acceptable practices for worker treatment and welfare. As such, the decision to outsource must be considered a strategic decision.

In fact, there is more realistic evidence that outsourced projects are, in fact, not decimating U.S. offices or white collar jobs; the actual numbers of displaced American workers in 2004 numbered in the 250,000 range (Myers, 2004). This is not an epidemic in a nation with a 250 million populace. In a nation experiencing increasing productivity levels, the economy will not run out of jobs. Rather, there will continue to be a shift in how some service activities are performed in the U.S., as well as in how they will be done abroad by non-U.S. workers.

Since the 1940s, advances in industrial equipment and factories caused shifts from manual labor to skilled and automated labor. Technology has largely eliminated back-office administrative jobs since the 1970s. Unemployment is not a staggering number when compared to other nations across the globe. Industrialized nations are experiencing a shift in labor concentration. There has been some backlash to companies overseas that are subjects of the outsourcing trend. Public outcries over loss of jobs in various rural areas of the United States have had a backlash against the outsourcers themselves. The "ugly" side of this sort of negative publicity for outsourcing done well has been that "some Indian software companies that once publicized their new U.S. customers no longer do so, for fear of adverse publicity" (Johnson, 2004, p. 56). However, the flip side of the coin is that rural companies can also set up shop with English-speaking, stable infrastructure and even educated work forces within the national borders far less expensively than in Silicon Valley east or west. In this way, even U.S. companies have benefited from the trend towards cost management through outsourcing near shore or rurally.

Aligning MIS Projects for Outsourcing in the Organization

This section considers project management disciplines and feasibility analysis as drivers of MIS projects in an organization. Feasibility analysis is a technique for aligning projects to organizational goals, and is a necessary process when considering outsourcing as a tactic for MIS. The section discusses the specifi-

Figure 8. Main questions inserted at different levels of planning

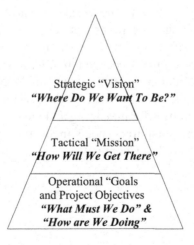

Figure 9. What's different about project vs. "normal" management

Line Management	Project Management
☐ Finite timeline and resources ☐ Specific technical constraints ☐ Crosses functional boundaries ☐ Relies heavily on influence and persuasion ☐ Draws together different skills, resources and outlooks ☐ Creates change in the organization	☐ Continues indefinitely ☐ Tends to be hierarchical ☐ Based on formal authority ☐ People tend to have common skills and attitudes ☐ Maintains the organization ☐ Budgets and operations are continuous over time

cation of requirements for a project that may be outsourced, as well as how to go about determining appropriate partners to outsource with. Figure 8 illustrates the planning perspectives of each management level in strategies, tacical and organizational planning.

Step 4. Aligning Projects that Implement and Carry Out Organizational Goals

The previous section addressed some sample project objectives that could be indicative that outsourcing is a viable option for particular projects. The next question then becomes how do we define project objectives and then select the right candidate projects to outsource? The first step is in identifying those things that the project must achieve in order to be successful. In some cases, it is having the exact, right set of technical skills to utilize a particular software development toolset. In other cases, it may be necessary to have stakeholders actively involved in order to get the specifications right. In still other projects, the organization may need sufficient, knowledgeable staff to respond to incoming call queries by end users within a specified number of telephone call rings (see Figure 9). For each candidate project, it is vital to develop the correct critical success factors (CSFs) and convey those to the service provider. From those CSFs, we will develop metrics for managing and measuring adherence to those metrics and how well the outsourcer meets them. Development of metrics for project evaluation is covered in Chapter V.

Figure 10. The project charter

THE PROJECT CHARTER

- o   Project Description and Concept of Expected Operations
- o   Project Objectives and Metrics of Performance
- o   Deliverables and Products or Services to be Outsourced
- o   Schedule for Delivery, Reporting, Reviews
- o   Key Personnel, Experience and Specific Skills
- o   Environment and Infrastructure to be Provided

Step 5. Managing Projects vs. Managing Line Functions

Understanding how to manage outsourcing also requires strong, skilled managers with experience to navigate the special nuances of communication and oversight roles with external partners or service providers. In the case of a partner, contracts and mutual understanding of the customized relationship characterize the transaction. In the case of a vendor or service provider, the services are usually not customized to the customer organization. Services, like Web site hosting or an Internet service provider, or telephone answering service may be generic and is routinely provided to numerous clients in a similar fashion to your organization. Nonetheless, the client organization's manager must be cognizant that the functions of managing a distinct project are different that what is expected in managing line activities.

One of the tools that the project manager may use is the Project Charter (Figure 10). The project charter is used to develop and confirm a common understanding of the project scope and purpose. This charter lays out the overall concept and framework for the project, as well as defines the architecture of how the project will be executed. Just as a set of blueprints define different aspects of a home or office building construction job, the project charter lays out an understanding from both the business and financial, as well as the technical viewpoints. The project charter should include:

- A project justification — aligned to the organization's mission statement(s)
- A brief description of the project's products or services
- The project objectives that determine project success
- How the project will be executed and time frame

Figure 11. Documentation and tools for project management

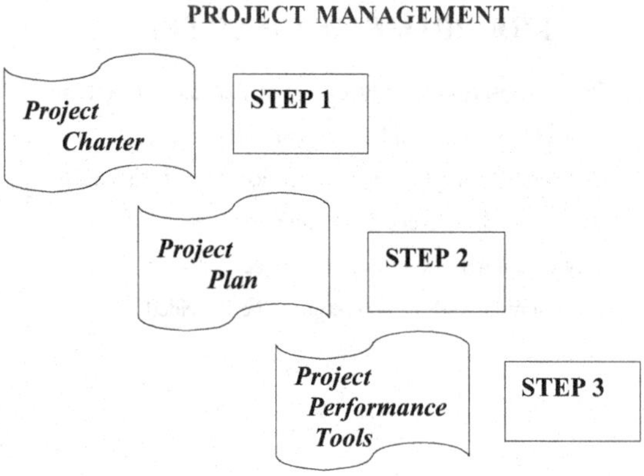

PROJECT MANAGEMENT

- A description of the climate or environment that the project is operating within: political, competitive, regulatory, or other aspects of importance

This charter later becomes the basis for applying decision models that either affirm outsourcing as a viable option or not. Another aspect of the charter may include validation that the objectives meet the "SMART" test: Specific, Measurable, Attainable, Realistic, Time-bound. From the charter, the next step in defining the project is development of a Project Plan. A project plan is a document used to coordinate all project elements. It describes the project's objectives and management approaches, as well includes the schedule and resources expected to carry out the project. Its main purpose is to guide the project execution. In outsourcing, the plan will also assist the project manager in leading the project team and assessing project status and performance of the outsourcing provider or partner (see Figure 11).

Project performance should be measured against a baseline project plan. This can be created in commercial off the shelf (COTS) software packages such as Microsoft's Project, Primavera, or Artemis Project Manager tools. Selection of the best tool depends largely on the size and complexity of the outsourcing project, as well as on the number of deliverable products that will be produced and the number and location of resources. A challenge in managing MIS projects that are being executed either partly or entirely by outsourcers is coordinating and monitoring progress on the various tasks of a project. Managing projects with e-mails, spreadsheets, and desktop applications is neither conducive to productivity, nor reliable for keeping outsourcers on track and synchronized with the rest of the organization. Dysfunctional outsourcing arrangements can actually cost more than having kept the work in-house. When a project manager is calling the outsourcing partner for status updates, copying and pasting information from emails to create separate reports, and sifting through correspondence to find the latest project documents — there is very little relationship being cultivated. Centralized project tools can alleviate a lot of the communication disconnects.

Chapters V and VII address some specific areas and techniques for using and applying automated tools to manage tasks, issues, budgets, resources and documents in one place. Through the use of a Web-based project management toolset, information is shared instantly with anyone on the team. Through the use of identity management, access to discreet information can also be controlled. Tools exist for this aspect of outsource management as well, and are discussed under security in Chapters V and VII. Permission for access to certain areas, documents, or versions of data can be granted to internal team members, clients, and outsource partners or vendors. Regular updates and viewing of appropriate information through direct Internet access into these tools leverages up-to-the-minute project management.

Some tools, such as Primavera and Artemis, lend themselves adequately to dispersed teams, with summary level management reporting while others like Microsoft Project are more easily used on a desktop for centralized reporting and tracking.

Step 6. Selecting the Right Projects: Project Objectives That Indicate Outsourcing

The next step in strategic planning for an organization is to select the projects that will help implement and support achievement of organization goals through outsourcing. Many techniques may be used to continuously improve operations and therefore achieve operational savings. One technique utilizes financial management and process measurement to quantify the cost of work flow processes. Activity based costing (ABC) helps to determine where the best bang for the buck can be garnered by using an outsourcing partner. At its basic level, tools permit the systems analyst to capture hourly human resource, facilities and machine cost data on all process activities that will be subsumed or somehow changed with the outsourcing agreement. Data is collected on how often that activity is performed each day and in what volumes. The ABC tool then sums the total dollar cost of performing the activities. Through subsequent analysis, the organization may determine there are some activities that are likely candidates for MIS to lower the overall costs in sufficient magnitude to justify outsourcing. Morgan (2005) describes the applicability to MIS projects:

Figure 12. Most popular areas of outsourcing

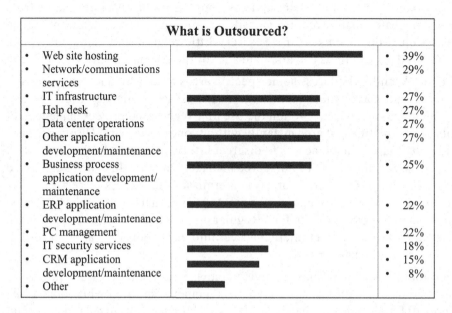

What is Outsourced?		
• Web site hosting		• 39%
• Network/communications services		• 29%
• IT infrastructure		• 27%
• Help desk		• 27%
• Data center operations		• 27%
• Other application development/maintenance		• 27%
• Business process application development/ maintenance		• 25%
• ERP application development/maintenance		• 22%
• PC management		• 22%
• IT security services		• 18%
• CRM application development/maintenance		• 15%
• Other		• 8%

ABC may be used to model the scope of an IT project. Requirements gathering for an MIS project may include recording ABC data. Most process analysts or users themselves are readily able to complete a data entry form describing activities and the time they take to perform. In some organizations, hourly tasks are tracked on employee time cards which allocate costs to a job unit or specific project code, so cost data may already be available. Activities to be automated in an MIS are one way of forecasting tangible future Return On Investment for the arrangement. Comparison of before and after activity costs give net savings data for activities the IT project will subsume or alter. (p. 54)

CIO Magazine (2003) reported that the majority of outsourcing technology projects was in the area of hosting Web sites, as illustrated in Figure 12. This will continue to evolve over the next decade as tools for global management become more widely used and companies gain expertise in managing distributed projects.

Once activity costs for a candidate outsourcing project have been quantified, ABC models can be leveraged to determine the performance of an outsourcer in terms of cost savings for a selected workflow process. In addition, the metrics used to capture the cost of labor or machine time, as well as the cost of handling selected volumes of transactions, like Web site portal sales for a catalog business, can help point to circumstances where an application service provider will provide satisfactory levels of service at a much lower cost than hosting the portal in-house. In other cases, the outsourced MIS project may be indicated because the customers are located elsewhere. Everyone thought the dot-com craze was an economic disaster. But, in fact, the rapid rise of profit seekers and venture capitalists hoping to tap into international marketplaces without buying an airline ticket and wearing out the leather soles on their feet, found they could establish a store on the Internet highway. Proposals were constructed on an assumption that everyone who passed in cyberspace might stop for a browse, an inquiry, and a buy. However, the costs of establishing a business line in-house and then competing heavily on price soon caused the "dot-com" bubble to burst for many entrepreneurs. Costs like communications, maintaining inventory, and shipping as well as costs of billing, collections, and infrastructure eroded profitability.

Many people lost their Web designer and developer jobs when it was discovered that online stores are still burdened with shipping costs, all the headaches of logistics and customer service, poor supplier throughout and stiff, rapid competition. They could not, in general, sustain the costs of inventories and staffing when shoppers abandoned their online store and went elsewhere for the buy. Larger institutions such as eBay and Amazon had to find ways to charge for listing and selling items, for belonging to their Web site or through partner relationships, for a "fee".

Figure 13. Three types of outsourcing relationships

Three Different Types of Outsourcing Relationships

Partner – paid against percentage of sales, or in equity sharing of total profitability, e.g. sharing 50% of profits from the supported line of business, while responsible for 100% of support costs.

Service Provider – Administer and operate MIS applications; may develop special custom software applications for the line of business; contracts are flexible to respond to changing needs of the organization.

Vendor – Provides hardware, telecommunications, backup and recovery services of client-developed and managed applications. Fees are for specific services and billed, based on tiered levels of usage, size of database records, etc. Contracts usually escalate fees based on levels of usage of line item services.

Step 7. Conducting Research into Types and Locations of Service Providers

It has become evident up to this point that outsourcing MIS is not necessarily a panacea to conducting those operations in house. However, the option of looking at different outsourcing models is worthy of examination, as it affords a degree of flexibility that is not gained when simply keeping the functions inside the organization's walls.

Costs for staffing, training, and providing personnel benefits can far outweigh the direct cost of "sharing" resources from an outsource provider or partner. However, depending on the nature and extent of strategic value or criticality of the work to be outsourced, there are a number of criteria to be used to select the correct "type" of service provider for the specific service we have decided to outsource. Considerations of legal arrangements, fees, and price escalation as well as where the outsourcer's staff may be located are all factors to be considered.

Development of a decision model that best serves strategic needs is described in Chapter VII. Once the project objectives have been decided upon, the nature of the outsource relationship becomes important (see Figure 13). An outsource arrangement may require a partnership arrangement, or it may be that the MIS project can be managed in house, yet still use outsource service providers for aspects of the work, such as software development only. A third arrangement is to turn over complete operation to an outsource vendor, such as developing, maintaining, and managing the operations of a Web site for providing information on the company, or for order-taking and fulfillment.

In the first type of relationship, a partner is motivated and incentivized through equity partnership. In this type of arrangement the **outsource partner** shares in the potential rewards or savings from an outsource contract arrangement. The partner, who exceeds expectations or specifications such as net profit on sales, will also earn a percentage share of profits from the successfully executed arrangement. In the second type of arrangement, the **outsource service provider** may offer simple hosting of applications or Web services, or another business service. The outsource service provider may even provide complex hosting where parts of the MIS are managed by the service provider, and other business functions, such as order fulfillment and billing are handled by the client organization, in a distributed fashion. Custom dedicated hosting provides very specific services and functionality to the organization. The service provider will not only host and manage the services, but is also contracted to perform the software development of the MIS, load balancing and management to ensure that performance levels are maintained. The custom service provider may be contracted from time to time to develop additional capabilities or features as the need arises on an ad hoc, custom basis for the client (Applegate, 2003).

The third type of outsource arrangement is with an **outsource vendor**. This arrangement is simply providing a standard service that is the same or distinctly similar to that provided to numerous other clients. This is the lowest risk and often the simplest outsourcing contract. Typically, little knowledge is given up by the organization and the service levels reporting are fairly standardized in contract boilerplate language.

The next decision, once the scope and type of services or products have been decided upon, is to address the decision of where the outsourcers should be found. Different considerations are involved whether we elect to go overseas or stay local. Globalization in laws governing international transactions, Web sales, authentication and digital commerce means sovereign to issues and legal enforcment of international contracts have become less of a risky business. Nations like Ireland saw the jobs potential for a nation of technologically savvy citizens that could compete for jobs across national borders. Ireland invested in post secondary technology education for their citizenry. The outsourcers are in virtually every corner of the globe now. India also anticipated the software development boom, and invested millions to advance the presence of telecommunications networks that would support global commerce and communications between outsource providers and client organizations.

The strategic importance of telecommunication is even greater in the software and other information processing industries, where the product itself is information. Low cost telecommunication has been a major contributor to the software export success of nations such as India and Ireland. (Press, 1993, p. 66)

Figure 13. Where is outsourcing going? (Source: Computerworld, September 15, 2003)

Where is Outsourcing Going?
▫   India –> 38%
▫   China –> 6%
▫   Mexico –> 5%
▫   Ireland –> 5%
▫   Canada –> 5%
▫   Malaysia –> 4%
▫   Philippines –> 4%
▫   Russia –> 4%
▫   Singapore –> 4%

Legal and contractual aspects of overseas outsourcing are covered in Chapter V on managing metrics. However, global outsourcing is only one model for an organization to evaluate when addressing tactical decisions to lower costs or seek outside expertise for provisioning services.

Portfolio Management of Outsource Projects

This section addresses project management considerations in the context of a portfolio of many projects an organization will be involved in at any given time. Issues related to selection of the right outsourcing partner and where they will be, as well as how to package the arrangements, are discussed. Finally, techniques used for managing multiple vendors, as well as third party subcontractors, for effective management of the organizational portfolio are discussed.

Selecting the "Best" in Class Partner

The last two sections in tactical outsourcing involve considerations for selecting the outsource partner, provider, or vendor. If we, as previously mentioned, elect to go overseas for cost or convenience sakes, it is important to also have done an in-depth study of the local infrastructure and local legal environment of the host country as well as the reputation of the outsourcing company.

When considering off-shore or even near-shore outsourcing the organization must assess the maturity of services that will be needed for the organization to monitor the performance of the outsourcer. The firm, as well, needs to consider the viability of any particular host country as to its political stability, the state of its infrastructure and local services, such as water, transportation, and finally consider the availability of trained, skilled labor amenable to the type of work being outsourced. Political stability can affect supplies and the availability of human resources if conflicts ensue. Several aspects and actions factor into the long term viability of an outsourcing portfolio:

• Carefully define the project — what skills may be outsourced

• Document processes and the project oversight schedule

• Compare quality and cost (workers' availability) of different outsource suppliers

• Plan every step of the project through deployment and post-deployment

- Maturity of existing infrastructure — communications, electricity, water, heating, crime, housing, and so forth

- Evaluate obstacles (availability and location of technology, airports, shipping ports)

- Evaluate local politics, safety and hazards of local conditions

- Education, language, and local culture may limit skilled expertise

- Legal and human rights considerations

- Determine applicable local policies, laws, and regulatory environment

- Define, procure, install coordination infrastructure (databases, connectivity, networks, equipment)

- Outsourcing requires close management, clear requirements, communication across cultural and language barriers (Morgan, 2004)

As noted in the above list, the presence of skilled or English-language speaking labor does not necessarily translate to availability. It is important to do the background checking of the outsourcer to be sure they have a history of performing to specifications. Strictness of contract terms also varies from culture to culture. The client organization must be aware of local laws concerning nonperformance by local outsource. Some countries permit the service provider an unlimited amount of time to perform, not compensating for delays, while others are more western in nature, recognizing that time delays in performance constitute the breach of contract term, in most cases, and allow for contract cancellation or even the pursuit of penalties by the client organization.

Next, the client organization should also undertake an independent evaluation of the state of the local infrastructure in the host country of the outsourcer. Press (1993, p. 67) notes that some lesser developed nations recognized the need for lower cost software development and made preliminary investments in infrastructure that today are helping their local industries reap the benefits. Additionally, countries to which many of the outsourcing jobs are going have taken additional steps to attract international contracts:

Tax and financial incentives can entice software companies to open subsidiary offices and invest in a country. For example, Ireland offers a variety of incentives, such as a 10% corporate tax rate for computer services companies, employment grants for jobs created, and capital grants toward the cost of computers, equipment, office furniture and buildings. It also offers training grants, rent subsidy grants, and research and development grants.

A reduction in trade barriers (tariffs, quotas, currency conversion restrictions, and bureaucracy) on computers, software, communication equipment, and related information processing products ... make it easier for software companies ... A larger domestic information technology industry provides demand for software products, employment buffers, and support for university growth.

Software development in Japan, Taiwan, South Korea, and Singapore ... is likely to be made through a national, government-directed, and publicly funded initiative ... Chile has also high-level coordination between universities, the government and software companies.

Encouraging students to study information technology by investing the body of professionals needed to establish a healthy local software industry and user community, build the local infrastructure, and staff foreign offices ... The investment in universities should include the establishment of contacts and relationships with major universities in other nations.

Pre-university education will, in the long run, lay a fundamental foundation for the software industry. Widespread computer literacy programs lead to a demanding local market and provide future developers. Nations including Chile, Costa Rica, Cuba, and Malaysia have programs underway for universal deployment of computers and networks in schools and community centers.

The "brain drain" has been a major problem for less-developed nations. Some of their best students remain abroad after obtaining an advanced degree ... Declining hardware and communication costs make it increasingly feasible to establish major computer science research centers in any nation. Such centers offer powerful incentives for gifted students to remain at home and can be a continuing source of innovation for exportable products.

Ireland has established Industrial Development Agency offices in 17 cities in North America, Europe and the Far East, and many other nations have similar offices. In Chile, the Economics Ministry subsidizes technical assistance and consultation, market research, preparation of promotional material, marketing design, and quality certification.

Figure 15. Oft-overloaded risk aspects of outsourcing (Source: Perkins, 2003)

Outsourcing with Sub-Contractors

▢   **Changing Leadership** – Outsourcers frequently bring in a
    sales team different from the performing team (new team needs
    to build "ownership" of the contract)
▢   **The Contract is not a Relationship** – Contracts don't
    guarantee success; original intent needs to be clear ; do put into
    writing; reasonable flexibility and compromise necessary for
    dynamic global business; strong counterpart relationships.
▢   **Sales Puffery** – Proposals by sales people are often puffed up
    to "win" the work: "show me!"
▢   **Appetite for Risk** – Adventurers yield rewards or suffer career
    consequences. Outsourcers are paid to play it safe, to meet
    SLAs and consistency. Make visionary changes *first*.
▢   **Insufficient Performance Monitoring** – Regular, fact-based
    reviews foster continuous improvement. May use third-party to
    provide IV&V of performance.
    Outsourcing does not mean divestiture of your responsibility

---

*The biggest "opportunity" in software export is the stopping of piracy ...
Software piracy is a dilemma for a developing nation. Piracy may be the
only means of obtaining software to sustain development in a capital-
starved nation, yet to develop a domestic software industry, copyright laws
must be passed and enforced (legally and by persuasion).* (Press, 1993)

Conduct the Background Investigation

Finally, the organization must have a set of criteria that are used to select the
"right" service provider (see Figure 15). Part of this also includes conducting a
background investigation of the vendors. Several considerations are of note
here. First, ensure that sufficient, documented evidence is presented and verified
that the supplier is financially sound — *verify* with regulatory or audit organizations, as well as leading financial institutions. Letters of credit for the full value
of the contract may be secured through correspondent banking relationships and
may be well worth the insurance cost. Speak with past clients as to the reputation
and performance of the outsource vendor.

Understanding local legal climates and including contract provisions concerning
notification of developments that may prevent fulfillment of contracted services

are ways that the organization can legally require the outsourcer to provide updates whenever accepted norms goes awry. Service level agreements (SLAs are discussed in more detail in a subsequent chapter) also provide specifications for selected levels of performance by the outsourcer. The same policies and provisions are applicable whether the outsourcer is local or across the globe.

The monitoring function becomes significantly more complex when the provider is farther away. SLAs may include provisions for periodic reviews and remedies, as well as how and when the possibility of amendments may be entertained. Consider that if key personnel are part of the outsourcing decision, the organization may want to include a right of termination for change of ownership of the outsource provider or loss of key personnel. As with all projects, monitoring, reporting, and management are key components of project success.

Defining Work Packages for Multiple Outsource Partners

As an organization begins to realize the savings and agility that can be attained by using outsourcers, the organization may find that it has accumulated a variety of outsourcing relationships. Some of these may be insourcing where a sister company or parent organization is providing certain services for a fee, such as infrastructure support or help desk services for employees. Still others may include outsource vendors such as those providing Internet access, but no custom or complex hosting of MIS applications. Yet others may actually involve detailed outsourcing contracts that specify levels of performance for response time, levels of MIS availability, or even software development services.

In some cases, the outsource arrangement is given to a single provider or vendor but that provider relies upon a third party to provide some of the services for the

Figure 16. "Portfolio" project management

Outsourcers "Portfolio" Project Management

- Decide on common requirements like monthly reporting, billing, communication
- Tailor performance requirements to the task
- Select the best providers for each task
- Establish governance structure
- Use web-based program management tools
- Track compliance with a Balanced Scorecard Dashboard

client. In this case, the client really does have a multiple vendor arrangement, although the contract relationship is with a single provider. The organization must be diligent to ensure that the third party service provider is also of good repute and has the necessary skills. Financial arrangements such as secured and unsecured bank letters of credit can secure against possible losses or failure to perform the client's domestic bank can usually handle these insurance arrangements through agreement banking relationships. It is vital to ensure that the same critical success factors are incumbent on both the outsource provider and the subcontractors, contractually and in practice.

Outsource providers are selected based on reputation and skill in certain MIS areas. In this case, the organization may have to develop expertise in managing multiple vendors. There are unique problems associated with multiple contracts and multiple relationships. Each of these must be considered a strategic partnership, whether or not there is equity sharing in the outcome of the arrangement. The solution approaches for manage multiple vendors must also be flexible and robust to handle the different MIS services and products.

One way of connecting the interrelationships and reporting requirements among multiple outsourcers that are connected by a common MIS program is to create individual work packages (see Figure 16). Work packages segregate specific requirements for performance to the individual outsourcers. However, the common underlying contract creates common performance requirements for things like use of a virtual online program management information system, common configuration management policies, and use of program tools for same, and so forth. In MIS, it is not unusual to have multiple service providers and vendors supporting different aspects. But the use of a central contract for many boilerplate activities that leverage common practices across the projects can increase overall quality. This is also referred to as "portfolio" project management. Portfolio project management presupposes that standard procedures for governance of performance will be more effective for the organization. The limitation is only that it requires substantial buy-in and adherence to an outside organization's procedures by each outsourcer. It is recommended that balanced scorecards or other common dashboard reporting techniques are used across all outsource contracts to maintain visibility into the nuances that can go wrong in any of the MIS projects. These techniques are covered in Chapters V and VII.

References

Applegate, L. M., Austin, R. D., & McFarlan, F. W. (2003). *Corporate information strategy and management: Text and cases*. New York: McGraw-Hill.

Brandel, M. (2005, May 16). The "O" word reconsidered. *Computerworld, 39*(20), 9-14.

Johnson, M. (2004, January 26). Unspeakable candor. *Computerworld, 18*(4), 56.

Morgan, J. N. (2004, July 16). *The rise of international project management as a national and corporate strategic advantage: The impact of outsourcing technology and business process projects in the new millennium.* Paper presented at Academy of Business and Administrative Sciences (ABAS), Tallinn, Estonia.

Morgan, J. N. (2005, January-February). A roadmap of financial measures for IT project ROI. *IT Professional, IEEE Computer Society, 7*(1), 52-57.

Myers, L. (2004, October 21). *U.S. underestimates jobs lost to outsourcing, labor experts assert.* Retrieved June 6, 2006, from http://www.news.Cornell.edu/chronicle/0/10.21.04/outsourcing-jobs.html

Perkins, B. (2003, November 10). Outsourcing's dirty little secret. *Computerworld, 37*(37), 12.

Press, L. (1993, December). Software export from developing nations. *IEEE Computer, 26*(12), 62-67.

Section II

Decision-Making Issues in Management Information Systems Outsourcing

Chapter V

Establishing Performance Metrics for Managing the Outsourced MIS Project

Jeanette Nasem Morgan, Duquesne University, USA

Abstract

This chapter presents the tactics and metrics an organization applies after having made a decision to use outsource providers. Tactics are used to define the nature and specifics of the outsourcing arrangement, as well as to select the contractual basis of the agreement. Organizations that elect to use providers geographically distant from the client site are cautioned to carefully evaluate capabilities, as well as legal and security issues related to external outsourcers. For these purposes, it is critical to align measures of performance compliance in the form of metrics on each MIS outsourcing relationship. When negotiating and establishing the terms of the outsourcing arrangement, management should ensure that appropriate performance metrics are identified and included, as well as flexibility for change is built in to the contract. This chapter addresses some of the methods, as well as some of the metrics that might be used in such contract agreements. The use of contracts and service level agreements are discussed, as well as in depth techniques for conducting validation and background checks on outsource suppliers. Sample outlines for service level agreement preparation and performance specifications are included for the practitioner.

Executing the Tactics
of Outsourcing MIS

This section presents the tactics that an organization should draw upon after having made certain decisions related to the use of outsource partners. Topics include establishing agreements for service or support, managing geographically dispersed teams of providers, and appropriate metrics to be used to manage these types of global projects — across international datelines and multiple time zones. Issues related to quality, contract investigation and issuance, as well as preparing to monitor the outsourced project are identified. The importance of service level agreements to monitor and manage performance under outsourcing contracts is addressed. Problems that arise out of poor or inferior communications and reporting are illustrated by example.

Role of the Service Level Agreement

Even before the vendor has been selected, an exploratory process must take place within the organization that is considering outsourcing work. A process for defining the scope of the work was described in Chapter IV, "Strategic and Tactical Planning of Outsourcing in MIS." Figure 1 shows the steps for refining the scope of work, which is then used to craft the agreement as to service levels defined for the outsourcing relationship in the agreement. The purpose for a service level agreement (SLA) is to describe the scope and terms of the outsourcing arrangement. The scope constitutes a high level understanding of the nature of the agreement. By defining the type of services or products to be delivered, there is a general understanding of agreement as to the concept of the deal. The terms of the outsourcing arrangement should cover the scope of specific performance expectations, such as volumes of transactions, turnaround times for the work, response times for infrastructure support, security, backup and recovery services for MIS outsourcing, or may include scenario based behaviors or scripts for business process outsourcing arrangements. For each specific service being contracted, there will be levels of performance criteria and metrics associated with the services or products.

Figure 1. Preparing the request for outsource work

□ Research your needs
□ Benchmark processes and areas of automation to
  develop target metrics
□ Develop Requirements (RFP)
  □ Statement of Work – contains the specifics of
    what the outsourcer is to accomplish or provide.
  □ List specific "Schedule C" numbered
    requirements
  □ Provide models of current infrastructure
    (*Zachman, 1987*) – networks, nodes,
    configurations
□ Evaluate respondents
□ Perform site visits, background checks – ask for
  demonstrations
□ Best and finals (BAFO)
□ Finalize contract terms

A pricing model is negotiated for the contracted services, and that model will allow for escalation of price as more services are requested, or as the work expands or increases in volume, and so forth. The SLA should also include provisions for oversight by the customer organization as well as reporting expectations to help in monitoring the contract.

Steps in Creating the Outsourcing Arrangement and SLA

First, we learned in the previous chapter that the client organization must preliminarily take steps to ensure the outsourcer is financially sound and experienced by reputation. This is often accomplished by working with local, independent auditors and consultants who verify the outsourcer's financial and human resource assets, as well as those subjects of the contract obligations for equipment, infrastructure, and facilities. A local consultant will be familiar with the reputation and quality history of the outsourcer. The local contact may also later negotiate on the organization's behalf when flexibility is required, or minor changes need to be dealt with. If local regulations or local governmental authorities need to be involved, the local contact can be an invaluable asset to have in the pocket. Companies who plan to expand globally need to think strategically about partnering with local distributors as well as suppliers in order to take advantage of local expertise and access to materials. Partnering locally gives the advantage of minimizing initial investment risk, and is a means for gaining early penetration, as well as cost savings.

Figure 2. SLA table of contents

☐   Scope/specific services to be performed
☐   Technical specifications for performance
☐   Where the work will be performed
☐   Node and components architecture diagrams
☐   Performance tracking and reporting mechanisms
☐   Capacity forecasts (see textbox on *"Benchmarking"*)
☐   Transaction specifications and volumes
☐   Problem management
☐   Fees and rates (facilities, equipment, labor, levels of service)
☐   Customer duties & responsibilities

Figure 3. SLA reporting

1. Services or products to be provided.
2. Timely notification of changes needed by either party.
3. Established process for modifying contract requirements.
4. Formal reviews conducted monthly, quarterly, annually.
    a. Requirements baseline
    b. Critical design reviews
    c. Prototype reviews
    d. Implementation readiness reviews
    e. User acceptance reviews
    f. Operation readiness reviews
5. Informal reviews conducted as scheduled:
    a. Preliminary requirements reviews
    b. Preliminary design reviews
    c. Structured walkthroughs
    d. Test readiness reviews
    e. Unit test, and systems integration test reviews
    f. Pre-implementation reviews
6. Ad hoc reviews as needed for spot check of
    documentation, in-process progress checks, etc.
7. Financial arrangement, fees and service levels
8. Service level metrics (e.g. response time, frequency of
    backups, call handling, etc.)

Second, SLA contract provisions should be considered to ensure the outsourcer's timely notification of any developments, whether internal or externally caused, that could conceivably impact the ability of the outsourcer to perform or complete the contract provisions. Because most outsourcing arrangements are for ongoing support services, it is likely over time that service terms must change to accommodate changing conditions or levels of service required.

Contract agreements may be described in terms of the size of the system being managed, the number of incoming customer calls that must be dealt with, or even the nature of the support services. Organizations that keep track of the metrics of call hang-ups, unresolved customer problems, and the nature of customer problem calls go a long way in establishing a knowledge base that can be used for continuous improvement in call handling. These requests need to be handled as part of the SLA negotiations.

Use of tools such as Peregrine or Remedy for customer call tracking, problem classification and reporting are helpful for the firm who wishes to track any drop in customer service or even who wishes to leverage product or service knowledge across the outsourcer's staff for improved customer service handling. Metrics drawn from customer calls abandoned by callers, number of minutes to resolve problems, number of problem reoccurrences are good metrics associated with customer service business process outsourcing. The objective is to include reporting of appropriate metrics — tied to the type of service the outsourcer is providing. A sample table of contents outline for what should go into a typical SLA is included in Figure 2.

Third, operating agreements should be addressed between the parties to ensure verbal communications will be open and regular, in addition to formalized reporting mechanisms established. SLA arrangements should include a means for conducting regular formal reviews, in addition to periodic informal reviews, and an allowance for "spot checks". Figure 3 lists several types of formal and informal reviews for MIS that should be considered important to keeping a constant finger on the pulse and condition of the outsourcer level of service. Comprehensive reporting should include contract, deliverables, and cost/budget reviews as well.

Fourth, the ability of both parties of the contract to discuss and agree upon ad hoc modifications for changed circumstances or revised requirements should exist in the relationship. SLA terms should be flexible enough to allow for changes in processes, as well as in what is being managed as the client organization continues to evolve and new products or services are introduced. Many of us know of instances where we purchased the latest computer or cellular phone, yet when calling customer support to inquire for assistance, the nonnative English speaking representative seems to know less about the equipment than we do, having just bought and having read the instructions ourselves. New technologies or outsourcer capabilities will evolve and the client organization should have enough contrast flexibility to take advantage of these advances without penalty or infringement.

What Happens without Formal SLA Management

In one case, an outsourcer learned not having agreements as to the nature and formality of communications can backfire on the client, and wind up burning the outsourcer as well. Halper and Hudson (1993) report a case where inland revenue (IR), the UK government tax authority, outsourced its IT services to electronic data systems (EDS) for 10 years starting in April 1994. EDS purchased the existing IT equipment from Inland Revenue and hired 2,000 of the 2,500 IR IT employees thus taking over, in place, the entire IT operations of the tax authority. Inland Revenue planned to retain 300 employees but reduce costs and gain improved technology by this arrangement. The arrangements appeared to operate effectively for several years into the 10-year contract. In 1999, Collins (2003) describes, the UK government announced new tax credits to be introduced in April 2003. EDS, as the main IT supplier, was to develop and implement the software to handle the new tax credits. The plan was to create two releases, a Release One version to commence development in October 2000 for deployment January 2003, the Release Two version to start 6 months later in April 2001, with development in parallel and deployment by April 2003.

Shortly after this new outsourcing arrangement, it became clear that IR failed to provide firm requirements as scheduled. By April 2001, 6 months behind schedule, EDS began work on Release One even though uncertainty about the design and business processes remained. EDS resorted to heroics to put over 500 labor-years of work into Release One so it could go live on schedule, though EDS apparently did not formally communicate with the release risks. The consequence was Release Two work started April 2002, 12 months late. During the delayed start for Release Two, the scope for requirements increased by about half for new complexity introduced by the client IR. Even as November 2002 testing was due to start, IR had 60 new MIS change requests open. In spite of these issues and the failure of the last MIS test safety mechanism which was in review by the Office of Government Commerce, IR gave approval to go live with Release One on schedule. The accumulated project management failures began the final rush to critical mass implosion.

In January 2003, IR discovered 100,000 tax returns entered in Release One MIS had incorrect national insurance numbers entered. IR stopped sending award notices. This soon resulted in so many phone inquiries, the IR phone system jammed. To resolve the critical national insurance number errors, IR and EDS compounded Release Two's schedule problem by freezing testing at Release One so it could be corrected before proceeding with Release Two.

The corrections were completed and Release One resumed operation the following month. IR shortened the Release Two test schedule to four weeks instead of the planned twelve weeks. The outsource partner, EDS, warned the reduced testing increased the risk of problems in Release Two. EDS did not officially request a delay of deployment and IR did not delay the deadline. EDS heroics again completed Release Two on schedule, but this time over one million claims were incomplete or had errors, an order of magnitude greater problem than in the Release One in January. The resulting extra workload also exposed system capacity limitations that had not been found in the severely shortened testing phase. Both MIS systems crashed several times per day until stability was restored in June 2003.

The major fault is directly traceable to lack of clear contract terms for communication, a change control process, and means for granting extensions or altering critical schedules when necessary changes were needed. These are all components of a service level agreement between a client and an outsource partner. Collins (2003) suggests IR failed to establish its own requirements on schedule and failed to comprehend the impact of milestones and schedules missed. EDS, as a partner, failed to establish a functional change control process that would have rejected the continued stream of late changes or demanded schedule extensions to accommodate delayed testing.

Both IR and EDS shared in the final fatal flaw of slashing the Release Two test cycle to correct errors in Release One data and then proceeding with both systems even though EDS knew, and made IR aware, of the increased risk of in-service failures. Although IR faced political and bureaucratic ramifications if they publicly announced a delay and although EDS was well aware they were approaching contract negotiations at the end of the ten-year contract, both parties ignored the basic outsourcing rule to have in place project management and control procedures to address each problem as it was identified along with clear requirements, deliverables, and baseline schedules.

Metrics for Managing the Outsourced Project

This section discusses various metrics programs for quality and for organizational process maturity. Metrics are used both in selection of outsource partners, as well as for managing their performance. The section presents suggestions for how to measure and track productivity of the outsourcer and how to manage difficulties, as well as ongoing communications. Suggestions for appropriate metrics and the underlying management processes to support continued awareness of these are given. Use of a Balanced Scorecard is presented as well as actions appropriate to managing critical success factors.

Figure 4. What constitutes quality in MIS projects

Quality in MIS
- Complying with requirements
- Zero defects
- Project on-budget delivery
- On-time delivery
- Meeting user's expectations
- Achieving performance objectives
- Getting it right the *first* time
- Degree to which project is integrated and supported by the organization and its culture
- Quick resolution of issues which arise during the project

Using Internationally Recognized Quality Metrics Programs: TQM, ISO 9000x, SEI CMM

Many firms and government agencies have learned that selecting a provider with internationally recognized credentials can prove to be one safe harbor for assuring that the outsourcing work will be done according to customer requirements. As depicted in Figure 4, quality is defined in many different ways by different organizations. Some definitions of what constitutes quality in the arena of MIS are illustrated in the textbox. However, questions arise as to how to maintain the quality benchmark of outsourced projects, while still making them cost-effective. Several quality models and certifications exist that provide guidance.

The U.S. Congress signed the Malcolm Baldrige National Quality Award into law on August 20, 1987; it is an established standard of the National Institute of Standards in Technology (NIST). The Award is named for Malcolm Baldrige, whose managerial excellence contributed to improvement in government efficiency and effectiveness reports Morgan (2005). The award may contain self serving aspects that make certain its use in arbitrarily selecting an outsourcer on this basis alone. To apply for the award, an organization completes self assessment questions, which is then followed by a study of the candidate organization. The candidate organization selects which key factors will be evaluated, irrespective of whether these are the "right" set of practices for that industry in which they claim to demonstrate recognition-worthy quality.

The Malcolm Baldrige Award is not charged to validate the efficacy of specific practices such as software engineering in the candidate organization. It rather looks for artifacts to evaluate competency. Leadership, planning, customer awareness, culture, and other characteristics which may not be relevant to the client's outsourcing requirements are evaluated. So, while shedding light on an outsourcer's quality culture, it may not truly demonstrate their ability to fulfill an outsourcing agreement's terms and requirements. On the other hand, where a strong customer-focused culture is important to service levels, such characteristics may be very relevant and appropriate.

The International Organization for Standardization publishes updates to the ISO 9000 quality models originally developed for manufacturing production processes in 1987. Many believe the ISO 9000 models can be applied to measure quality processes for MIS. However, clients must regard ISO 9000 certification as an incoming qualification but should actually consider the specific high-mark processes that are part of the outsourcing arrangement before determining the applicability of the quality processes that earned the outsourcer an ISO 9000 certification qualification.

Finally, the Software Engineering Institute (SEI) Capability Maturity Model (CMM) for software and more specifically, the newer Integration Capability Maturity Model (CMMi) may be more applicable to outsourcing. These models enumerate key process areas containing qualifying practices to measure an organization's competency level. The model is not a standard, but has been adopted by the U.S. Government and is broadly used in international business related to MIS transactions. Several agencies require offerors to demonstrate their organizational competency in software engineering with qualification at CMM level three or higher. Specifically, the newer CMMi contains four integrated models to select among depending on the type of MIS service or product: systems engineering, software engineering, integrated product and process development, and supplier sourcing. The last model can actually be used by the client organization as a model for selecting outsourcers.

The supplier sourcing model can be used when outsourcing complex work efforts, such as when projects use suppliers to perform different functions or to add modifications to products. The CMMi is used when the outsourcing supplier activities are critical, where enhanced supplier source selection processes are used, or when acquiring products from suppliers. It also includes critical processes for monitoring outsource supplier activities before product delivery. The SEI uses a rigorous assessment methodology with independent appraisers that identify strengths and weaknesses in all key process areas.

Metrics in the Service Level Agreement

As a company considers outsourcing, there are the legal and contractual aspects that must be considered as well. As previously described in this chapter, the client firm should ensure that the outsourcer is financially sound, by independent audit and verification of financial assets, as well as contract obligations of the outsourcer for equipment, infrastructure, and space location. Include contract provisions to ensure timely notification of any developments, whether internal or externally generated, that could conceivably impact the ability of the outsource supplier to perform or complete the contract provisions. Ensure expectations for written and verbal communications are fully described. The ability of both parties to the contract to make easy modifications for changed circumstances or revised requirements should be addressed in the contract. Statistics of what services will be provided and benchmark estimates of size of the MIS and the volume and description of transactions expected are relevant. The ability to modify service statistics from time to time, based on actual events, should be included in the SLA.

For standard services covered by a vendor's normal outsource service offerings, usually the boilerplate outsourcer offered metrics associated there under would be sufficient. If there are any special circumstances concerning the nature of the outsource services requested, appropriate metrics for monitoring performance and controlling outcomes should be described in detail, with examples in the SLA.

The elements of a network SLA, for example, should cover the characteristics of the network itself, connection characteristics, and network security. The network SLA should identify the IP performance levels that a service provider guarantees in the course of delivering services to the customer. It should also define the type of network infrastructure that the service provider will deliver. Understanding the nature of a network's physical components helps providers set customer expectations on the performance levels they will receive. The network SLA also spells out network availability, measured in percent of uptime, and throughput, measured in bits per second. A key element of a network SLA is specifying penalties for downtime during critical business hours vs. overall downtime: For instance, downtime at 2:00 a.m. may not disrupt business, but it could be unsatisfactory in an e-commerce environment. "Most service providers probably will guarantee 99.5 percent uptime; few promise 100 percent" (Lee, 2000). Another key part of guaranteeing network service is the connection, which spells out acceptable data losses and delays, plus bandwidth provisioning. A security section should address the level of encryption, where data is encrypted, and the penalties for security breaches.

An application SLA should require the institution of application specific metrics that define performance levels that relate to application utilization. For example, Menasce (2002) states an application SLA should define the percent of user interactions, such as downloads or data requests, to be executed without failure. It should also define the acceptable time lapse between a user's request for data and the moment the updated data screen appears, as well as an acceptable rate for data transfer in a transaction session. A time-lapse guideline should work in conjunction with the execution guideline, ensuring that while a download is deemed successful even if it takes several hours, it would still violate the SLA for taking so long.

Hosting SLAs ensure the availability of server-based resources, rather than guarantee server performance levels. Hosting SLAs should cover server availability, administration of servers, and data backup and the handling of storage media. A server availability SLA, measured in percentage of uptime, usually guarantees a minimum of 99% uptime. The server-administration part of a hosting SLA should detail the management responsibilities of a hosting service, specifically, the acceptable response times for restoring failed servers, as well as performing data backups. For example, a hosting SLA should mandate that a host provider respond to a restoration request for a failed server within a set period of time (such as 1 or 2 hours); it should also guarantee that the server would be returned to service within another specified period (such as 12 to 24 hours). The percentage of scheduled data backups that will actually be conducted should also be defined. A data backup might also require the hosting service to create a disaster-recovery plan. This could include contingencies that would give a customer access to temporary computing facilities when the customer's own site is unavailable (Ferengul, 2002). Service level agreement provisions should include periodic formal reviews, in addition to informal reviews, and an allowance for "spot checks" against the appropriate metrics.

Controlling, Pricing, and Managing Changes in the Outsourced Project

There is a saying in the information technology fields that the only thing inevitable is change. Because change is often unpredictable, it is vital to plan for it in crafting the outsourcing agreement. Addressing the procedures for making and pricing amendments is a vital part of the negotiation. The process for documenting significant changes and for accepting minor changes should be discussed and agreed upon early on. Some changes should be acceptable, such as when product offerings on an onsite store change — this is part of the business of an online retail operation, and is an expected part of the application service provider (ASP) hosting services. Understanding what recourse there may be when changes are undesirable, such as a change in ownership of the outsourcer or loss of key personnel should be considered. Legal aspects of contract change and undesirable events are covered later in this chapter.

The possibility of amendments should be provided for in the outsourcing contract language, so that the terms can be flexible enough for changes, but not flexible as to how they may be interpreted. Wherever possible, benchmark expectations

Figure 5. Benchmarking MIS systems

☐ Capture specifications on workload
☐ Average size of each transaction (consider both inputs and outputs)
☐ Largest historical size of a transaction, and largest forecast future size of a transaction
☐ Largest historical number of transactions at peak times, and largest forecast number of transactions at peak times
☐ Total current storage capacity requirements for data
☐ Total forecast storage capacity requirements for future data
☐ Peak utilization of the central processing unit at particular times during the 24-hour day

of performance to metrics should be required to ensure statistical collection on processes or contract performance items to avoid misunderstandings. Use of selected benchmarks to clarify expectations on size and capacity are a key ingredient to ensuring agreement as to the level of support expected. Figure 5 illustrates a benchmarking process for determining the size and performance expectations for MIS service.

Finding the Right Outsourcers where They Live

Some of the concern regarding outsourcing is loss of competitiveness. As we consider outsourcing MIS functions the terms "software factory" and "assembly line" come to mind. Experience with outsourcing software development has yielded many success stories, while others that are "service" related have not. Other concerns have centered around the potential for security breach of customer or other key corporate data, and associated loss of competitiveness. However, where firms have retained the creative, or innovation-driven design functions, it seems that success in cost reduction or increased efficiencies can be compartmentalized.

For 20-odd years we have witnessed industry/manufacturers "horizontally stratify" work: outsourcing parts manufacturing and general-assembly tasks to low-wage countries, while keeping the high-wage, high-level design work close to home. The danger occurred for some firms when they allowed the design jobs to follow the manufacturing jobs overseas too. In many cases, it just made more sense to have the design proximate to the manufacturing floor. Technology advances in third world countries, fueled by globalization and domestic support for advanced telecommunications capabilities, satellite communications supporting videoconferencing, e-mail, and fiber optics have made them all viable contenders for outsourcing work. Chapter IV reported on the top nine countries where the bulk of the outsourcing has gone. The list of countries will continue to expand as opportunity for globalization in MIS as well as business process support becomes increasingly lucrative to poorer nations, as a way to build gross domestic product and revenues for trade.

Careful consideration of the scope of the outsourcing arrangement needs to be given. There are proprietary risks to horizontally stratify high-value-added activities (whether manufacturing or building software), parcel out the work, and attempt to retain control over intellectual design property, research and development, and the organization's long-term competitive advantage. In a lesson gone "bad," Logitech took an initiative to outsource 80% of the production of its "mouse" hardware and design. However, in the first year, Logitech found that market design changes were evolving so rapidly that the outsourcer was unable, either contractually or knowledge-wise, to help Logitech maintain its innovative edge. Competitors were able to test and implement changes to design, function, or price more rapidly because they controlled production lines (Johnson, 2004).

Yes, the organization can horizontally stratify, and they can farm out product design and get a temporary, short-term cost advantage, but very possibly at the cost of losing control of critical new product development (Applegate, 2003). Likewise for MIS, it may be a risk to outsource all the work from requirements specification through software/system design to coding. It may be more prudent to farm out the coding, but retain the competitive edge in design. Eventually design gets farmed out too, and all that is left are the marketing and distribution. When the local outsourcer becomes the competition and figures out that since they now control the entire life cycle of the product, they do not need the client organization's name for marketing either, the game is up for the client.

The Request for Proposal Process

In evaluating an outsourcer, we have addressed the need for local consultants or experts in arranging outsourcing deals. Even before the SLA is negotiated and signed, preparation must begin. Figure 6 illustrates some of the steps in preparing for the bidding process.

Finally, once all candidate responses have been collected, it is vital to evaluate each vendor's adequacy to the tasks to be outsourced. Much of this was covered in Chapter IV on *Strategic and Tactical Planning of Outsourcing in MIS*. Yet it is also worth repeating that due diligence means looking beyond stated capabilities, to reputation and stability of the firm. A good vendor evaluation

Figure 6. Steps to prepare for evaluating outsourcers

☐ Review Outsourcer's descriptive information to evaluate if technical approach is reasonable
☐ They have previous experience
☐ Approach and management style fits our strategy & culture
☐ Review financial information (stability, banking relationships)
☐ Analyse schedule & plan (compare deliverables; milestones; reviews; communications)
☐ Look for realistic risk mitigation plans
☐ Evaluate service level guarantees (past history, pricing; SLA components, metrics used)
☐ Compare pricing schemes (labor rates, capacity or utility computing pricing, flexibility to upsize or downsize, etc.)

Figure 7.

Hard Metrics	Soft Metrics
☐ Net worth of the business	☐ Technical capability
☐ Accounts Receivable/Payable Status	☐ Management experience
☐ Production capability	☐ Cash Flow and Banking Relationships
☐ Accounting Systems	☐ Quality assurance program
☐ Depth of Past Performance experience in similar contracts	☐ Inventory control measures
	☐ Packing, marking and shipping capabilities

includes looking at both hard facts about the firm, as well as their potential ability to perform the required activities. Figure 7 gives additional distinction between the various aspects.

In the final analysis, there will be considerable work that can largely be reduced by advance research and planning. Aspects of due diligence also include the contractual side of the outsource relationship. Some of the actions that have proven useful are to actually travel to the outsourcer location and meet with technical staff as well as management. In some cases, it may be that the vendor will also use subcontractors. It is advisable to take the time and effort to also meet the staff and management of the subcontractors as well as verify past experiences and project results of all service providers who will be involved in the MIS arrangement. Whenever feasible, it is advisable to personally talk to past clients, or to verify with the local experts. Ask questions about the operating principles of the outsourcer with regard to end-to-end quality.

A key component of the contract will be time and materials' costs. It is important to confirm labor rates for different types of work under the outsourcing contract. Lastly, part of the SLA itself should include an agreement concerning the oversight role of the outsourcer for their subcontractors, as well as the role of the client organization in direct oversight of the arrangement (Strassman, 2004).

The Balanced Scorecard for Monitoring Progress

One of the successful ways that has evolved in upper management circles is the use of the Balanced Scorecard. Like an automobile dashboard, a quick review of the key indicators on a project can quickly highlight a potential problem or series of related problems that are developing, before they become large and unmanageable. A scorecard can be established with methods for reviewing the health of the myriad components of an SLA. One of the first aspects to developing an outsourcing scorecard is to identify the critical success factors (CSF) for each MIS project. The scorecard translates corporate strategy into operational terms.

Critical success factors are those pertinent components of project management that must be done right, consistently, for the overall project to be a "Success." These CSFs are applicable to the metrics included in the SLA, as previously discussed. CSFs become the variables by which we measure compliance, progress and ultimately, the achievement and closeout of the project. To be successfully implemented in an outsourcing arrangement, the scorecard must be adopted by all levels of the organization, as well as throughout the operations of the outsourcer.

The Balanced Scorecard Institute reports that the *balanced scorecard*:

... approach to strategic management was developed in the early 1990's by Drs. Robert Kaplan and David Norton. Recognizing some of the weaknesses and vagueness of previous management approaches, the balanced scorecard approach provides a clear prescription as to what companies should measure in order to "balance" the financial perspective. The balanced scorecard is a management system (not only a measurement system) that enables organizations to clarify their vision and strategy and translate them into action. It provides feedback around both the internal business processes and external outcomes in order to continuously improve strategic performance and results. (Arveson, 1998)

For outsourcing projects and other MIS projects that are distinctly defined and managed out of the mainstream of core business processes, certain key factors

Figure 8. Selecting and defining appropriate critical success factors for the outsourced MIS project

Stakeholders	**Financial or Business Benefits**
• Are project "owners" committed and involved? • Are decision-makers and funding authorities supportive? • Do users or subject matter experts (SMEs) make time for this project? • Do we have management support for project needs and goals?	• Is the project achieving planned benefits to the corporation/constituency? • Are requirements aligned to achieve good return on investment (ROI)? • Doe this project help the company achieve a Corporate Goal? • Are the Goals reasonable and achievable by this project?
Team & Resources	**Cost Management**
• Is project staffing appropriate, do we have the right skills that are needed? • Do we have the correct equipment and facilities to do the job? • Is the infrastructure sufficient and stable to support the work?	• Do we have sufficient finances to complete the project; are we expending costs as planned? • Are reporting processes in place for cost control? • Are costs in line with competitor organizations with similar levels of quality and experience?
Work & Schedule	**Scope**
• Is the project schedule and work realistic? • Is the project schedule complete and up-to-date with progress reported? • Will we be able to deliver the requirements as planned? • Are forecasting and productivity targets being realized; are schedule adjustments accommodated? • Are staff able to perform the work within planned timelines?	• Have new requirements been presented that stretch the available resources? • Are we adding additional "features" while not finishing those already agreed to? • Are additional requests "priced" to ensure adequate scope coverage? • Are we expending resources doing activities that don't add value?
Risk Management	**Delivery of Products or Services**
• Are we managing all our risks and addressing issues as they arise? • Are we tracking issues management on a regularly reporting basis? • Do risks occur without being resolved or without contingency plans?	• Is the project acknowledged as "successful" at Enterprise levels? • Is the project delivering upon stated expectations? • Are interim deliverables delivered on time with good quality? • Are we given ample time to review products before acceptance?

should be considered in development of an understanding of the project's CSFs. These factors are Stakeholders, Team and Resources, Work and Schedule, Risk Management, Financial and Business Benefits, Cost Management, Scope, and Delivery of Products or Services. Defining the CSFs for an insourced vs. an outsourced project simply requires that management look more carefully at the

Figure 9. "Dashboard" type of balanced sources

Stakeholders	Team	Schedule	Risks	Benefits	Costs	Scope	Deliverables

communications mechanisms that will be used to convey and receive progress reports on the relevant CSFs for an externally managed MIS project. Figure 8 provides relevant questions to be asked in data mining the rigth CSFs for the candidate project.

Invoking the aforementioned regular reporting along the lines of these eight key CSFs, the organization can quickly assess where there may be impending problems arising. Individually asking sample questions for each CSF area like those included in the Using Critical Success Factors (CSFs) to Monitor Projects text box, management is assured that CSFs are addressed in specific elements of the outsourcing scorecard. A logical connection exists between use of the Balanced Scorecard which illustrates the *Green-Yellow-Red* status of each CSF and the early detection of problems with the individual projects making up the MIS (see Figure 9).

Furthermore, a rather simple approach of requiring the outsourcing organization to report weekly as to the condition of each CSF and how it is progressing according to plan can be implemented. Using a Web-based virtual project management reporting system, comments can be provided weekly by the teams performing the outsourcing work. Items that may become problematic can be explained and any variances drilled down into by the simple click of a radio button. Buttons would indicate by color the condition in that week, of that specific CSF reporting area.

Buttons are highlighted as one of three colors: *Green,* indicating there is no known problem or aberration from plan, *Yellow,* indicating that deviations from expected plan or results are anticipated or have been encountered, or *Red,* which means management action must be taken immediately to avoid or minimize further loss or exacerbation of the severity. This dashboard management technique is equally applicable to our outsource partners when they are included in the same reporting structure, as described under subsection on SLA reporting in this chapter.

Figure 10. Characteristics and special requirements for virtual teams

Virtual Teams
- Managing people at a distance using technology to provide access to office tools and resources.
- Reduce travel costs for meetings and coordination activities by up to 50% with huge gains in team productivity and morale.
- Can be high risk unless all levels of the organizations involved are committed in process discipline.
- Requires an investment in technology as well as in team training and ancillary support to the supporting systems.
- Means maintaining close working relationships with colleagues in many locations, without the need for as many meetings as traditionally needed.

How to Construct a Virtual Teaming Organization

Tactics for constructing and managing virtual teams are presented in a step by step manner to guide the manager in establishing such teams. A discussion of considerations and information related to technology for managing information security are provided. Finally, technological issues such as trends towards open architectures, global "time-independent" services and Web service-enabled MIS applications are discussed in the context of their applicability for executing and supporting the outsourced project.

This subsection deals with the mechanics of how to facilitate good, regular, and formalized reporting between the outsource provider and the client organization. The challenges include technology, time and distance, as well as cultural practices and norms that may be different between the outsourcer and the client. One way of addressing the disparity that can occur to damage the outsourcing of MIS is to adopt the concept of Virtual Teams.

Figure 10 lists some of the defining characteristics and requirements for successful implementation of virtual teams. Virtual teams are distinct groups of human resources that cooperate for the purpose of completing a service or aspect of a project, but are geographically separate. This definition works quite well for the outsourcing arena, as the outsourcing arrangement frequently means that the provider or vendor is not in a proximate location to the client, although this is certainly possible. When physical distance is not an issue, such as with rural outsourcing or even simple outsourcing to a local provider, the need for communications and reporting structures as well as for managing the terms of the arrangement is still necessary. Effective virtual team relationships help improve both productivity and increase the likelihood of outsourcing success.

In the virtual team arrangement, productivity is measured by adherence to schedule and fulfillment of requirements, within a prescribed cost structure. Part of the cost of facilitating the virtual team relationship is, of course, the establishment of and support of the technology to make this work. A firm cannot simply put up a LotusNotes database and expect teams to populate it correctly and frequently. Training needs to be provided, as well as operating procedures for frequency of reporting and to help define the type of documentation that will be included in the virtual database. There are several technologies in the marketplace that provide global accessibility to information resources, such as LotusNotes, Microsoft Project Central, and various others using .NET or J2EE technologies for converting internal employee intranet Web sites into globally accessible Web-based extranet Web sites. Once a tool has been selected, systems administrator support for managing the virtual team room environment will also be needed.

Managing Resources and Ongoing Productivity: The Globe-Trotting Project Managers

This subsection deals with some examples of the unique challenges of outsourced projects in different time zones. In most cases, organizations have discovered that there is a right balance of organic resources for oversight and project management and outsourced resources to get the job done in MIS projects. The following examples describe some of the techniques used to manage the outsourcer half a globe away.

In studying lessons learned from companies that have outsourced projects, certain universal considerations emerge. Some of these relate to the importance of good communication channels, others relate to the mix of outsourced labor to project management personnel and where they should be located, and finally to legal considerations when executing an outsourcing contract. The following points address some of these lessons.

- Consideration for outsourcing should be to reduce operating costs, but do not outsource the control functions for the project.

- Capitalize on the outsourcing provider's newer hardware and software technologies.

- Provide mechanisms for geographically disbursed teams to maintain the focus on corporate objectives and goals, clear direction, and frequent checkpoints.

- Use a centralized project management information system (PMIS) to centrally control configuration of the MIS and all reporting documentation; helps provide a visual "big picture" view of the context of the outsourced project within the overall client organization.

- A Web-based PMIS supports online status reporting and project by project accountability. Balanced Scorecards tied to measures of success support the project manager's "finger on the pulse" of all vital signs.

- It is critical to establish a "culture" and set of "norms" that are synchronized across the client organization and their outsourcing partner.

- Use Project Management techniques and documentation to monitor control, and execute appropriate corrections as needed.

In one "good" case, Patni, Inc. uses a three-tiered project approach to execute outsourced projects for net cost savings. Johnson (2004) cites their outsourcing projects as being characterized by 7,000 employees in India, another 1,500 project managers who shuttle between India and U.S., and the 150 U.S. industry experts based in U.S. This approach ensures that the outsourced projects are managed with domestic, business knowledgeable staff, and continually supported by subject experts who maintain the open lines of communications by being housed where the core business functions are initiated. Patni recognized that the in-depth business knowledge of the U.S. staff was vital to continued good service. While travel is frequent for the 150 U.S.-based project managers, this model works and is highly cost-effective.

In another case, State Street Financial recognized that investment clients across the globe required 24 hour service, seven days a week (24/7). This could not be accomplished with a domestic work-force without incurring huge overtime expense and shift work. State Street found by placing outsourced teams, supported by IT staff in various time zones, they could comfortably provide 24/7 service to their customers through the use of selected outsourcing partnerships.

In a third but unsuccessful case, Nielsen Media Research which collects, collates, and analyzes television viewer data found the coordination efforts of data collection and analysis using off-shore assets too cumbersome and ineffective. In order to effectively manage the critical path activities of their projects, Nielsen needed to bring the work back to domestic shores to be able to adequately control analysis and reporting for clients. Clearly the cost of collaboration and the role of monitoring and coordination are key functions in outsourcing projects.

Outsourcing teams and client organizations require an added infrastructure to facilitate reporting and coordination among virtual teams. Today's technology provides Web-based tools that include ready made templates for virtual teams to coordinate project(s) across time zones and sovereign borders. In some cases, the online virtual team tool can also be used as an electronic meeting venue, complete with video conferencing, as well as electronic white-board capabilities. Centralizing documentation and providing a balanced scorecard for weekly status reporting and monitoring goes a long way to alleviate the necessity of a full-time project manager on-site at the outsourcer.

Companies considering the use of such online collaboration tools need to study the costs and benefits of a particular suite of tools. Ease of setup and low technology maintenance is vital. It is important for the outsourcing team to be an active player, and training to ensure broad entrenchment and understanding of the virtual team collaboration site is critical to success.

The key to success in these cases was that establishing cultural "operating norms" across the company and including their outsourcers in those norms was vital to the virtual teams' cross-border coordination.

Off-Shore Projects Require Leveraged Technology and Higher Education

The success of off-shore projects require enhanced understanding of the technologies that enable projects to come in on budget, on time, while meeting the organization's performance and business requirements. An adroit project manager has the skills of American corporate politics and communication in their bag of qualifications. Statistics involving IT projects in the 1990s gave many IT projects a bad report. A 1995 Standish group study found that only 16% of IT projects were successful. Nearly a third were cancelled before completion. Yet, in 1998, corporate America initiated 200,000 new IT projects; in 2000, 300,000 new IT projects were initiated; and by 2001, over 500,000 new IT projects were started. This growth in the demand for IT projects and the corresponding expansion of available, cheaper technology makes outsourcing reasonable today. International developments in infrastructure and technology posture developing nations for involvement and competitive position in the global services marketplace:

•   Telecommunications costs from the late 1980s to 1990s dropped by a factor of 30 and continue to drop at even greater rates.

•   Lesser developed countries invested in technology education for labor forces while U.S. graduates in the engineering sciences have significantly dropped.

•   Computing power doubles every 18 months, affording even more opportunity to leverage lower cost technology in lesser developed nations.

Through the use of collaborative and virtual team software, and through secured use of the Internet for cross-border communications, the U.S. project manager brings a set of skills unmatched in parts of the world where outsourcers are proliferating. Jeanette Morgan reported in March 2004 at the IEEE and Pittsburgh Technology Council Summit on Outsourcing that this is the skill area where public focus and politicians need to look for retraining MIS-educated citizens. Retraining unemployed, educated professional workers with special project management skills and tools is one way to keep MIS outsourcing managed from home base. Skills required to manage off-shore projects and to integrate the use of technologies for virtual teaming relationships is vital to globalization of these relationships. Institutions with industry and public sector experience in Web-based collaborative work environments share their experiences and lessons for how to effectively manage geographically dispersed development efforts across the world. Incoming college students must understand the new roles professional careers will require in both the skills and knowledge of intercultural teamwork. Education and exposure in the academic environment to global "gaming," team play and communications, and the use and application of Web-based project management tools for sharing team based products is critical (Morgan, 2003).

Current and Evolving Enabling Technologies for Globalizing Project Management

We have discussed how virtual teams can leverage available technology for managing performance under outsourcing contracts, as well as for coordinating activities and documentation. Another area for outsourcing organizations to consider is the use of enabling technologies such as collaborative software. With collaborative software technologies, in addition to the PMIS for reporting and documentation, as well as project schedule management, additional features may be deployed to further enhance the teamwork to make the outsourcing relationship seamless to organic projects:

- Conduct teleconferences directly from personal workstation PCS or even mobile personal digital assistants (PDAs).
- Hold online (video) meetings with numerous participants across several global connections.
- Share software applications and data access.
- Present prototypes of outsourced MIS under development for instantaneous feedback.
- Team members can ask questions and see responses in real-time for group decision support. Tally responses for immediate quantitative results.

- Conduct MIS testing and create problem reports for developers to access on the PMIS.

However, collaboration on outsourcing MIS does not always involve Internet technologies. Another innovative approach to near-sourcing work involves artificially creating local proximity of outsourced staff. Romero (2005) reports one new company, Sea-Code, Inc. will deploy a cruise ship with living quarters and offices, three miles off the coast of Silicon Valley, Los Angeles, CA staffed with 600 software engineers. Workers will initially be onboard ship for 4 month assignments. The company anticipates that the lower cost salaries for staff who originate in India, will make the venture attractive. (Romero, 2005) The operational feasibility of being in the same time zone as many software development client organizations will likely offer a new alternative to off-shore outsourcing with companies across the other side of the globe. This will bring jobs closer to the United States while still maintaining the imprimatur of near-shore outsourcing.

A Final Word on Negotiating Outsourcing Contracts and Terms

Before leaving this section, it is worth noting that outsourcing arrangements that cross national borders do so with some degree of risk that is not experienced when outsourcing rurally or locally. International law governs these transactions. In some cases, domestic political unrest or sovereign actions such as nationalizing foreign assets, have thrown outsourcing arrangements into disarray. With the proliferation of the Internet and electronic commerce, the courts have had to address many of these concerns. The preponderance of evidence suggests that arrangements that go awry where there is a difference of opinion on the outcome of the arrangement, courts may tie up final legal verdicts for years, rendering the outsourced MIS hostage to the arrangement. In such cases, it is advisable to retain legal advice and handling by experienced firms which have strong local representation. Services for negotiating resolution may include arbitration, litigation, mediation, negotiation, or other alternative dispute resolutions such as resumption of work by the outsourcer through an extension of time or transference of the contract to a third party for completion and satisfaction.

The aim in using legal resources to resolve disputes is to attempt to not have to force litigation action in courts. Since successful dispute resolution is about achieving attainable results in the most cost effective and timely manner, and international courts can be capricious, it is best to avert the necessity of legal action by close monitoring throughout the outsourcing process.

CIOs negotiating the outsourcing contract should be aware of the Unfair Contract Terms Act 1977 (UCTA) and the Court's interpretations of the law as pertain to outsourcing agreements. With respect to MIS contracts, it has long been standard practice for the supplier to include provisions to limit their potential liability for losses or damages due to MIS functions or bugs that become evident after the contract is executed. Outsourcers typically include self-protection against liability or litigation through Limitation and Exclusion clauses. The traditional obstacle to the outsourcer's attempt to limit and exclude liability has been recently litigated with interesting results under the Unfair Contract Terms Act 1977 (UCTA) and the Court's interpretation of reasonableness (Shoosmiths, n.d.). Recent international judgments under this law have presumed the parties negotiating a contract were fully cognizant of the ramifications of all aspects of the outsourcing agreement. The client organization can no longer simply state "failure to perform" allegations under the UCTA. It is incumbent on the client organization to adequately address the risk factors involved in an outsourcing contract and at least attempt to negotiate on the outsourcer's Standard Terms and Conditions before accepting these clauses.

The most obvious advice is to read and understand the terms and conditions related to limitations and exclusions. Should subsequent litigation be required, the client organization will have at least illustrated to the Court the imbalance in negotiating power, if limitations have been artificially imposed by the outsourcer. Failure to object to limitation clauses in an outsourcer's standard service contract are interpreted as silence and considered tacit acceptance.

Another aspect of governance in negotiating an outsourcing agreement is the concern for protection of the organization's intellectual property rights. This was commonly referred to in international agreements as the technology transfer block exemption (TTBE). Shoosmiths (n.d.) describes the European Union and United Kingdom competition law which addresses issues of technology transfer with an aim to promote innovation, but still protect patents and copyright laws across national borders. In some cases, TTBE may require the client organization to conduct an economic analysis of the impact of an agreement on the market. The former 1996 block exemption for technology transfer was widely criticized as being:

- Too narrow in that it addressed patent and know-how licensing, but not most other forms of intellectual property, such as software design and new product functions

- Too prescriptive, for example, prohibiting noncompete clauses which are often benign and difficult, if not impossible, to enforce and prove violation under

- Too formulaic and restrictive leaving many circumstances out of step with modern competition law, particularly in the area of information technology developments

Shoosmiths (n.d.) feels the new TTBE is an improvement in some areas, but may be difficult to apply without detailed analysis, which could lead to an unsatisfactory interpretation of the law in some cases. Organizations that are involved in software or MIS licensing need to be careful to structure agreements to fall within the protection of the new TTBE. They also need to review existing agreements – those which fall within the current TTBE will be protected for a transitional period of 18 months, but after that date, they must comply with the new arrangements or risk being unenforceable. (Shoosmiths, n.d.). Bear in mind that international litigation is extremely slow and painstaking. The Internet is prolific, as are technology vulnerabilities, and attackers are hard to track down. Even when there is a clear dispute and violation, both enforcement and proof are hard to come by. Governments are often slow or reluctant to take action. Let the buyer beware!

Securing the Strategic Nature of the Relationship

This section addresses some of the procedural as well as technical issues that are considered as part of the outsourcing relationship. Examples of security vulnerabilities as well as threat identification techniques are presented. Finally, considerations that can be included in contract terms, as well as due diligence of oversight before entering into the contractual relationship are discussed. Suggestions for appropriate steps that the organization can take to address security of data as well as assets entrusted to the outsourcer are discussed.

Issues Related to Information and Process Security

The proliferation of hacker attacks resulting in denial of service to company customers, or logjams in processing transactions via Web-based servers has caused organizations to reevaluate the dangers as well as the advantages of outsourcing. One danger of outsourcing is that control over corporate assets is no longer under the ownership and purview of the organization. Instead, this control is turned over to the outsourcer to whom it has been entrusted. On the other hand, when the outsourcer has more robust hardware and software assets and that is its main business concern, then greater security measures with deeper experience in managing information assets can be brought to bear on behalf of the client organization.

Recently, it was reported that in the U.S. Department of Defense, there were over 38,000 attacks identified, of which over 27,000 resulted in unauthorized access to data. Of these, only 988 were actually detected by users, and only 267 were reported to authorities. These statistics are relevant in that they highlight the glaring reality that the vast majority of security breaches are, in fact, never even detected. Therefore the organization that outsources MIS work must be proactive in ensuring that the outsourcer has a tactical plan for addressing information security. Technology can actually help in assuring secure management of MIS and data. However, it can also be a danger as the trend towards more open architecture may actually provide an easier opportunity for violations of secure systems and transfer of sensitive data. Mechanisms such as firewalls as well as complex security monitoring procedures and an architecture of tools can help minimize the threat of technological vulnerabilities in outsourced MIS.

Best Practices Related to Off-Shore Outsourcing Security Risk

Risk management in any project is a matter of process enforcement and oversight functions. It is also a matter of responsibility. Leishman and Van Buren (2003) define risk as "A possible future event that, if it occurs, will lead to an undesirable outcome." Risks can come from either internal sources, such as infrastructure weaknesses or incompetent or disgruntled staff, or external events, such as supplier material outages, weather or cyber-security violations. Organizations need to ensure that their outsourcer practices safe security and data protection. Koch (2005) highlights five best practices, in Figure 11, that should be considered part of an outsourcing relationship.

First, organizations that turn over services to an outsourcer may elect to still specify and even retain responsibility for implementing the infrastructure. In this manner, the hardware and networks will be dedicated to that organization's workload and there is no risk of sharing databases on common platforms. The

Figure 11. Five best security practices for outsourcing

1. Control the assets: consider providing your own MIS equipment to the outsourcer.
2. Use security consultants to background check outsourcers and their employees.
3. Manage outsourcer's access to data.
4. Verify security processes and facilities.
5. Control where the work is done.

Figure 12. International standards for information security

```
□   Security policies and management
    procedures in place
□   Maintain accurate inventory of IT assets
□   Workers and business partners are qualified
    to fulfill duties and responsibilities
□   Data centers are physically protected against
    access by unauthorized parties
□   Comprehensive business continuity plans
    have been developed and tested
```

drawback of this approach is that it is more costly, but companies that insist on ownership or at least on specifying the configuration of their hardware assets retain more control over the operating environment of the outsourcer, inasmuch as that is critical. In addition, some organizations also monitor network traffic to ensure that they can detect security lapses at the outsourcer site before it gets out of control.

Second, due diligence to investigate the vendor is necessary to ensure that the reputation and capabilities of the outsourcer are as stated. Some firms even hire security consultants on the ground, in the host countries to report on the outsourcers. Local consultants can also assist the organization in structuring the contract to best leverage regulations and local laws, as part of the outsourcing agreement.

Third, organizations that also take responsibility for the hardening of the assets at the outsourcer may have better control over security infrastructure. Some companies use software tools that permit remote control and virtual management of the local assets including outsourcer login and validation. Access control management by the outsourcer that is retained by the client organization is another way security can be managed at the data access level.

Fourth, Koch suggests regular verification activities by the client organization. Standards such as the International Standards Organization (ISO) 17799 (see Figure 12) as well as other standards for auditing procedures should be considered for use in verifying the practices and in-situ processes at the facilities of the outsourcer.

Considerations of facility security should also be addressed to ensure proximity does not permit accidental, unauthorized access to client data or MISs. Lastly, taking careful stock of the political environment and regulatory environment of the outsourcer is another avenue that should be addressed by the client organization. Local civil strife or conflicts, as well as sweeping government actions such as Mexico's nationalization in the 1970s can have disastrous affects on the client organization's business, and are often not reversible. However, international tribunals and international commerce law is are strengthening protections for global commerce, partly just so that lesser developed nations can in fact participate in the global labor marketplace for services.

Vendor Hardening and Other Security Measures with Technology

Due diligence on the part of the organization who will outsource some aspect of an MIS includes consideration of several security approaches. The fundamental components of an outsourcing relationship require an investigation of the vendor infrastructure. Core technologies include:

*   **Networks:** Fiber, hardware (routers, switches, etc.), network operating systems, identity management, network monitors, and so forth
*   **Processing:** Enterprise applications, servers, clients (PCs), peripherals (printers, etc.)
*   **Facilities:** Data centers, managed services, buildings, power supply

The mathematical probability of a catastrophic failure or loss of systems decreases with added redundancy of those systems, but increases with the number of interconnected components existing in the infrastructure (Applegate, 2003). Therefore, it is prudent to evaluate what protective measures are taken at each juncture point of multiple components. Security measures can be Systemic or Procedural, or some combination of both, as applicable to the nature of the outsourcing scope and services.

Systemic measures are built-in, and designed to operate automatically. They include software for firewalls, monitoring software with business rules defining normal transaction patterns, as well as digital certificates. "Normal" transaction patterns are defined based on benchmarking that captures typical transaction contents and patterns.

Procedural measures must be created and customized to the actual business processes. These include development of security policies such as user profiles and valid data access definitions, the use and maintenance of passwords, host and network authentication, and even encryption which can include key encryption or digital-signatures. Some encryption mechanisms can be automated to be systemic.

Figure 13. Continuity of operations planning

COOP Objectives

1.   Ensure continuous performance of essential
      functions/operations;

2.   Protect essential facilities, equipment, records, and other
      assets;

3.   Reduce or mitigate disruptions to business;

4.   Reduce loss of life, minimize damage and losses;

5.   Achieve a timely and orderly recovery from an emergency and
      resumption of full service to customers.

A security framework should be deliberate: it may be acquired through the use of commercial tools such as virus protection software, as well as development of policies and procedures that are policed and proactively enforced. Security procedures should also be reviewed with constant vigilance to changes in cyber-criminal activity. The outsourcer's security framework must be evidently disciplined with change management practices and deployment of available patches as soon as they are available. The framework should be evidently pervasive across the company — staff and users are educated; enforcement of things like password changes and data access are automated, and so forth. The outsourcer should be cognizant of and be able to demonstrate a multilevel security architecture, depending on the sensitivity of the client data.

Lastly, in the event of the unforeseen or unavoidable occurrence, the outsourcing agreement should stipulate a common understanding of how the outsourcer will provide for continuity of operations (COOP). COOP planning is done to ensure operations can continue despite a wide range of potential events or risks. The objectives of a COOP plan are illustrated in Figure 13. The COOP assists the organization to continue some or all operations under varying ability levels until return to full normal operations.

Degrees of partial operation may include cessation of all ability to function, a limited set of capabilities, or simply degraded performance with all capabilities working in some fashion. Finally, the COOP must address the procedures for returning to normal operating mode, as well as procedures for recovering lost or damaged data.

References

Applegate, L. M., Austin, R. D., & McFarlan, F. W. (2003). *Corporate information strategy and management: Text and cases.* New York: McGraw-Hill.

Arveson, P. (1998). *What is the balanced scorecard?* Retrieved March 15, 2006, from http://www.balancedscorecard.org/basics/bsc1.html

Collins, T. (2003, December 16). Inland revenue should not put all blame for tax credit failure on sacked supplier. *Computer Weekly,* 14.

Ferengul, C. (2002, January 31). *Best practices in Web hosting service-level agreements.* Retrieved March 15, 2006, from http://techupdate.zdnet.com/techupdate/stories/main/0,14179,2843179,00.html

Halper, M. (1993, November 29). UK tax agency will outsource to EDS. *Computerworld, 27*(48), 47.

Hudson, R. L. (1993, November 24). EDS wins $1.48 billion contract to run computers for Britain's tax agency. *Wall Street Journal* (Eastern Edition).

Johnson, M. (2004, January 26). Unspeakable candor. *Computerworld, 18*(4), 56.

Koch, C. (2005, May 15). Don't maroon security. *CIO Magazine, 18*, 46-51.

Lee, M.-Y. (2000, November 10). Check that network service level agreement. Savvy Business Shoppe. Retrieved March 15, 2006, from http://www.bizjournals.com/austin/stories/2000/11/13/smallb4.html

Leishman, T., & Van Buren, J. (2003). *The risk of not being risk conscious: Software management basics* (STSC Seminar Series). Hill AFB, UT.

Menasce, D. (2002, September-October). Mapping service-level agreements in distributed applications. *IEEE Internet Computing, 8*(5), 23-31.

Morgan, J. N. (2004, March). *2004 Outsourcing Summit.* Retrieved June 5, 2005 from http://www.pghtech.org/Events/speakers.org

Morgan, J. N. (2004, July 16). *The rise of international project management as a national and corporate strategic advantage: The impact of outsourcing technology and business process projects in the new millennium.* Paper presented at Academy of Business and Administrative Sciences (ABAS), Tallinn, Estonia.

Morgan, J. N. (2005, January-February). A roadmap of financial measures for IT project ROI. *IT Professional, IEEE Computer Society, 7*(1), 34-47.

Romero, P. (2005, May 3). Un Barco-Factoria de "Software" en Alta Mar, el Colmo de la "Deslocalizacion"[A ship's factory of software in the Atlantic Ocean, the culmination of offshore outsourcing]. *El Mundo, 15*.

Shoosmiths. (2005, May 25). *Preparing the way to outsource — What should I consider?* Retrieved March 15, 2006, from http://www.shoosmiths solicitors.co.uk

Strassman, P. A. (2004, April 5). Pick your perspective on IT outsourcing. *Computerworld, 30*(21), 31.

Zachman, J. A. (1987). A framework for information systems architecture. *IBM Systems Journal, 26*(3).

Chapter VI

The Case for Centralized IT Contract Management:
A Four Force Model

Anthony Briggs, Best Buy, USA

Eric Walden, Texas Tech University, USA

James J. Hoffman, Texas Tech University, USA

Abstract

In this chapter a model is developed that describes four forces that move organizations toward centralized IT contract management. Specifically, the model illustrates how centralizing IT contract management enhances organizational performance in four areas. First, centralizing IT contract management allows for a corporate level view of technology, which supports not only interoperability, but also optimizes software license inventory. Second, it combats vendor opportunism by creating a set of contract negotiators who have as much knowledge as the vendor's contract negotiators. Third, it enhances information retrieval, but locates the physical contracts in a central location, which allows the legal department, project managers, and senior managers to quickly and reliably locate contract details. Fourth, it provides the proper motivation to project managers and contract negotiators by rewarding each job separately rather than by lumping the rewards for timely project completion together with the rewards for efficient contract negotiation.

Introduction

Senior executives used to be concerned with whether or not to outsource information technology (IT) resources. Now they are more concerned with figuring out how to efficiently manage the portfolio of IT resources that they have outsourced. From hardware to software, and from help desk to temporary help, organizations today have dozens, or even hundreds, of active IT outsourcing contracts.

Outsourcing of IT is an important area of study since over 90% of U.S. companies outsource some activity and the total outsourcing market in 2004 was over $350 billion (Study, 2004). This explosive growth in the volume of contracts offers an excellent opportunity for cost savings. However, in order to maximize cost savings, contracts must be negotiated, enforced, and renewed or canceled at the appropriate time.

There are two basic ways an organization can manage contracts. The organization can use a decentralized approach where project managers negotiate and manage contracts. Alternatively, an organization may form a central contracting authority that receives requests from project managers then negotiates and manages the contracts centrally.

In this chapter we briefly review the organizational structure literature and then develop a model that describes four forces that move organizations toward centralized IT contract management.

Organizational Structure

Jackson and Morgan (1978) define organization structure "as the relatively enduring allocation of work roles and administrative mechanisms that creates a pattern of interrelated work activities and allows the organization to conduct, coordinate, and control its work activities." The major theoretical dimensions of organizational structure that are of interest in technology-structure research are complexity (including vertical and horizontal differentiation), centralization (including hierarchy of authority and participation) and formalization (Child, 1977; Ford & Slocum, 1977; Gerwin, 1979; Hage & Aiken, 1967; Hall, 1977). The primary dimension of organizational structure that we are examining in this chapter is decision making structure. Decision making structure involves the centralization and decentralization of decision making. Organizational decision making has been formally defined as being the process of identifying and solving problems within organizations. Given that organizational performance is determined at least in part by how well problems are identified and solved, it can be inferred that an organization's decision making structure is one of the most crucial areas in terms of its influence on organizational performance. Thus, it can also be inferred that whether IT contract management is centralized or decentralized will impact organizational performance.

The Four Force Information Technology Procurement Model

As mentioned above, from hardware to software, and from help desk to temporary help, organizations today have dozens, or even hundreds, of active IT outsourcing contracts. This multitude of negotiations and relationships is leading

Figure 1. Four underlying forces driving organizations toward centralized IT contract management

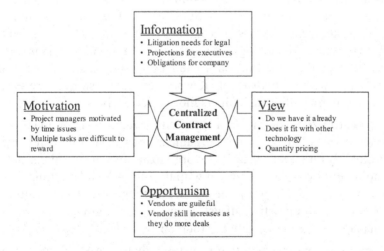

organizations as diverse as Best Buy, Clackamas County, Oregon, and National City Corp to centralize their IT contract management. It can be theorized that there are four primary forces that come into play as an organization's outsourcing portfolio grows. The forces are *accountability*, *technology*, *opportunism*, and *motivation,* and are displayed in the ATOM model in Figure 1. Each of these forces favors centralized, independent management of IT contracts. Taken together, these four forces create a very strong argument for the creation of a centralized IT contract management office.

View

View, in this case, refers to the contract negotiator's point of view of an organization's technology needs. A project manager has a very detailed view of the exact technology needed to facilitate his project, and none can better evaluate a tool's ability to solve a specific problem than the project manager. However, actions are not taken in a vacuum, and the choice of technology has impacts, not only on the project manager's specific project, but on other areas of the organization as well. Only with a centrally located contract management office can contract managers view the overall infrastructure of the business. The contract manager sees the technology needs and abilities of the entire organization, and is much better able to determine the *total* impact of a new technology. This high-level view confers three advantages.

First, it is not uncommon for a large organization to have extra licenses for a particular technology available internally. Clearly, if an organization needs a resource, it makes sense to first check to see if that resource is available internally. In the case of technology, internal availability usually means software, which has been paid for, sitting on a shelf collecting dust. The centralized contract manager with his high-level view can see what resources are available internally, and thereby allocate budgets more effectively.

Second, a centralized contract manager can evaluate the impacts that a particular technology will have on the organization as a whole and thus optimize resources globally rather than locally. No organization today is a blank slate, and new technologies have to be integrated with the old. A locally optimal solution may cause massive integrations issues, while a second-best local solution may integrate easily with the existing infrastructure. Only the global view allows the contract manager to fully evaluate the total cost of a technology.

Third, a centralized contract negotiator can take advantage of volume discounts. Many different projects will require the same technologies. If the same technology is acquired in small lots by different people within an organization, the negotiation costs are multiplicative, and the per unit costs will be higher. If many units of a technology are acquired by a single entity and distributed within the organization, then a contract needs only be negotiated once, and the per unit costs will be lower.

Opportunism

Opportunism is the knee-jerk response for why a Centralized IT procurement is necessary, and rightly so. Opportunism has been defined by Williamson (1975) as "self-interest seeking with guile." The important part is *guile*. It means that vendors will wheedle, cajole, and dazzle in pursuit of better contract terms for themselves. Vendors, and vendor salespeople in particular, operate in direct opposition to the client organization. The primary task of the sales person is to charge the client more money. Salespersons are well compensated for this task, usually working on commission, so that every extra dollar they convince the client to pay is money in their own pocket — money that they can use to pay their mortgage, buy presents for their children, or take their spouses out for a night on the town. It is not that they are bad people, just that the incentive scheme forces them to play an us-or-them game.

Opportunism occurs in a decentralized setting because of the differences in skill levels between vendor sales people and project managers. A project manager devotes his time to learning about information technology and may only negotiate one or two contracts a year. The salesperson negotiates contracts full time. Every day they are in the trenches, learning, practicing, and getting better at what they do. The project managers are in trenches too, but different trenches.

A contract manager in a centralized setting is a specialist who dedicates his full time to negotiating and managing contracts. Just like the vendor salespeople, the centralized contract manager spends every day honing his negotiating skills. In fact, many centralized contract managers are former vendor salespeople. Thus, a centralized contracting office can negotiate better terms because the centralized contract managers are more skilled negotiators.

Information Needs

Various entities within an organization need to have access to the information contained in the contracts. The legal department needs to know the terms and conditions of the contract in the case of litigation or potential litigation. Without access to the contracts the legal department cannot effectively address vendor disputes. Contracts also contain the prices and quantities of goods and services to be purchased. Organizational accountants need access to this information to make projections for future budgets. Senior executives may also need to consider indemnification clauses and contract durations to understand the organization's long-term obligations or obligations in different situations.

Decentralized contract management makes this information difficult to access. If each project manager independently maintains these records, then it requires multiple points of contact to retrieve the information. Moreover, each project manager may have a different method of recording and accessing the contracts so that there is no standard way to retrieve desired information, and no guarantee that the information will be in the same format. It is not uncommon for a project manager, who has only one or two contracts to manage, to have no system whatsoever for recording and accessing contracts. In other words, the contract may be lying in someone's drawer. Further, because project managers are mobile, it is unlikely that a new project manager will even be able to locate a contract.

A centralized IT contract management office solves these problems by relegating the storage and retrieval of contract information to a persistent entity rather than an individual. Centralized contract management provides a single point of contact for the legal department, accounting department, and senior managers to access all information about all contracts.

Motivation

Motivational issues arise when one person is given multiple tasks, each with their own reward structure. The person must then choose how much effort to dedicate to each task. If the tasks are rewarded equally, then effort will be distributed equally. However, if tasks are rewarded differently, then differential effort will be exerted. This is referred to as the multitask problem (Holmstrom & Milgrom, 1991). Project managers are rewarded for being on time and on budget. These two outcomes are easy to verify and because of this, a project manager should, and does, work very hard to bring the project in on time and on budget.

Unfortunately, contract negotiation does not have such a clear-cut outcome. It is certainly easy to judge the final price paid, but it is nearly impossible to judge whether the price is reasonable. Software vendors have something called *list price*, which is the price they will quote, if pushed. However, list price for software is something like sticker price for an automobile — no one should pay it. In fact, list price is far more variable. The actual price paid may be anywhere from 5% to more than 100% of the list price. It is clear that the people who pay more than list price are doing a poor job of negotiating contracts, but what about the people who pay 50% of list? Is 30% of list with vendor A better or worse than 40% of list with vendor B? It is not obvious when a negotiation is done well.

On top of this, contracts contain terms that are much harder to evaluate than prices. How much is it worth to have an international enterprise license rather than a nationwide enterprise license? It can be very valuable if the company expands internationally. However, at the time the contract is negotiated it is not clear which terms will be invoked. Each term has some option value, but it is difficult to gage that value at the time the contacts are written; hence it is difficult to reward an individual for negotiating a contract.

In the absence of centralized IT procurement, the project manager is faced with three tasks — bringing the project in on time, bringing the project in on budget, and negotiating contracts. The time to complete the project is easy to observe, and thus, the project manager is sure of his reward for speed. The project expenditures are easy to observe, and thus, the project manager is sure of his reward for budget. The quality of the contract is difficult to observe, and thus, the project manager is uncertain of his reward for good contract negotiation. It is only reasonable that the project manager focuses his or her efforts on the first two tasks and largely ignores the last.

This discussion, of course, begs the question of how to compensate contract managers for negotiating contracts. Clearly, project managers have other tasks that tend to take precedence over contracting because contracting is hard to observe. But what about those people who have only the task of contracting? They still need to be motivated and rewarded for a job well done, or they will not do a good job.

The contract negotiator must be judged on subjective criteria. This requires that a judge, with the tacit knowledge of contracting, offer good subjective evaluations. Luckily, by its very existence, centralized IT procurement generates a group of such people. Having centralized IT contract management in place, with dedicated contract managers who negotiate contracts on a full-time basis, results in a group of people who have the knowledge necessary to offer high-quality subjective evaluations of contract negotiators' performances. Thus, centralized IT contracting not only removes the conflicting motivations due to poor measures of contract negotiation performance, but it also improves the measurability of the contract negotiation process.

Conclusion

As organizations grow ever-larger portfolios of IT contracts, the potential gains (or losses) from managing that portfolio appropriately grow. Although IT personnel may be very gifted in certain areas, in general, they are not talented at negotiating, enforcing, and managing contracts. In fact, contract management is antithetical to IT personnel's training. Contract management is adversarial, while IT personnel are accustomed to working in cooperative environments. Contract management is about limiting options, while IT is about expanding options. Contract management is focused on legal aspects of *inter*organizational relationships, while IT is focused on *intra*organizational technical aspects. This results in an opportunity for cost savings when the burden of contract management is placed with a group of nontraditional IT personnel, rather than forced upon the project managers who are ill equipped by training and disposition to deal with it.

One particularly effective tool for managing a large portfolio of IT contracts is to create a centralized contracting office. Such an office creates a group of negotiation specialists, who can serve as a single point of contact for IT outsourcing needs of the entire organization. The centralized office has the high-level view, the appropriate skills, and the proper motivation to handle contract negotiation and management more efficiently than decentralized project managers.

Given that contracting for IT services is a large budget component in any modern corporation, it makes sense to look for efficiencies in the process. In a large organization, a centralized office that has the skills, the motivations, and the perspective to manage the process can most effectively do this. Centralized IT contract management offers that kind of centralized procurement and has the potential to generate drastic savings for an organization. This is because as the portfolio of outsourced resources grows, problems develop in the decentralized approach. At the same time gains from specialization and scale accrue to a centralized approach. Therefore, for large organizations, or small organizations with a large portfolio of IT outsourcing, it can be theorized that centralized procurement is superior.

 Overall, it is hoped that this chapter sheds additional light on the benefits associated with the centralization of IT contract management. It is also hoped that this chapter will serve as the basis for additional research regarding the benefits of centralized IT contract management.

References

Child, J. (1977). *Organizations: A guide to problems and practice.* London: Harper & Row.

Ford, J., & Slocum, J. (1977). Size, technology, environment, and the structure of organizations. *Academy of Management Review, 2,* 561-575.

Gerwin, D. (1979). The comparative analysis of structure and technology: A critical appraisal. *Academy of Management Review, 4,* 41-51.

Hage, J., & Aiken, M. (1967). Relationships of centralization to other structural properties. *Administrative Science Quarterly, 12,* 72-93.

Hall, R. (1977). *Organization structure and process.* Englewood Cliffs, NJ: Prentice Hall.

Holmstrom, B., & Milgrom, P. (1991). Multitask principal-agent analysis: Incentive contracts, asset ownership, and job design. *Journal of Law, Economics, and Organization, 73,* 24-52.

Jackson, J., & Morgon, C. (1978). *Organization theory: A macro perspective for management.* Englewood Cliffs, NJ: Prentice Hall.

Study: Outsourcing market exceeds $350 billion. (2004, January 24). *Charlotte Business Journal.*

Williamson, O. (1975). *Markets and hierarchies: Analysis and antitrust implications.* New York: Free Press.

Chapter VII

Decision-Making Methods in MIS Outsourcing:
Case Studies of Successes and Failures

Jeanette Nasem Morgan, Duquesne University, USA

Abstract

This chapter commences with a discussion of corporate and government decision-making processes and the management sciences that support development of decisions. Special decision-making considerations, trade-offs analyses, and cost-benefit studies all figure into decisions that result in outsourcing. Technologies that support different methods of decision-making include data warehouses and data mining, rules-based logic, heuristical processes, fuzzy logic, and expert-based reasoning are presented. The chapter presents case studies and current and evolving technologies. The following sections will address the decision-making methods that are used in considering, executing and monitoring outsourced MIS projects or in service lines related to provision of information services in the organization.

The Structure of Decision Making in the Organization

This section addresses the history and evolution of decision sciences in corporate planning and project management. The chapter includes sections on how decision making has evolved from traditional, line of business functional decisions to the need for negotiating services and even core processes to outsource partners. Examples are given from current industry and government experiences with outsourcing, highlighting key success factors and failure indicators that exemplify the best and worst of decision making as it relates to the outsourcing decision in the information technology arena.

Define Corporate Decision Making in MIS and Information Technology

Corporate decision-making is supposed to be done by committee of an executive board, representing all parts of the core business functions in an organization: finance, production, manufacturing, marketing, human resources, IT, sales. In many cases, the CEO will exercise authoritarian decision-making based on perceptions or a solitary sense of purposeful guidance. In some cases, CEOs look externally to secure endorsement for their ideas or initiatives. In other cases, a more systematic approach is used to generate sound decisions.

In the field of decision science, Marshall, Kneale, & Oliver (1995) state that there are six concepts that factor into the arrival of a decision (see Figure 1). Every decision has an entering objective, for example, to lower costs of MIS support, or, to provide speedier response to customer support calls. Every decision being considered has certain *characteristics*. For example, costs of MIS include equipment costs and staffing and lower consumption costs, as well as space costs. Costs of providing customer service include cost of the systems and staff hourly labor to answer calls.

Next, *attributes* of each characteristic are measurable ways that we can evaluate the costs of the characteristics: for example, dollars and cents, or time in minutes and hours. Quality of customer service support may be expressed in number of complaints or number of hang-ups before an operator answers the call. Next, *continuing* the aforementioned two examples, each attribute also has an associated *criterion* that is the level by which we measure improvement, or satisfactory performance or other levels of success.

For costs of an MIS, the criterion may be to lower the dollar costs by 20% per year, without a negative change in the level of service, as evidenced by a change

Figure 1. Decision model components

```
1.  Objectives
2.  Characteristics
3.  Attributes
4.  Criteria
5.  Trade-Offs
6.  Constraints
```

in the number of help desk calls. For customer service, the criterion may be an improvement in customer perception of our support as evidenced by the number of positive responses to a customer survey done every three months.

Next, we have *trade-offs* which are exchanges of attributes to achieve a benefit to the organization. For example, we may accept higher costs (in dollars) for a lower rate of customer complaints (in number of negative responses). Lastly, all decisions are framed with some *constraints* that we must understand in order evaluate the feasibility of a decision. Constraints to lowering costs for an MIS might include fixed costs already incurred for investments made, or for mainte-nance contracts entered into. Constraints to improving the quality of customer service support may be the comparative level of quality of the underlying products we have sold. In some cases, a company will bring in outside support to help negotiate a particular decision, in order to take the perception of close association with a decision away from senior management, or to help the decision appear more objective.

Fisher Scientific is an advanced instrumentation company. Consultants were used to endorse outsourcing IT with mixed results. In the late 1990s, senior management created an independent, but internal Operational Strategies Group (OSG) to explore untapped areas for increased profitability. The OSG project reported directly to the CIO. The group enlisted external consultants to give further weight and credence to their steering committee studies and recommen-dations. OSG worked on projects ranging from enhancement of data warehouse capabilities to determining the causes of profit margin erosion. The group even recommended restructure of the sales force to better fit market conditions. In this instance the CIO also used consultants to get an outside second opinion. The consultants recommended to OSG and the CIO that the firm outsource much of the existing IT department to cut costs and to bring a fresh view of the architecture.

The internal changes implemented by the OSG were successful. The IT outsourcing was pilot-tested but did not achieve the success of the internal projects. While using independent consultants is often useful for fresh perspectives and innovative insights, sometimes all the factors of a good decision are not taken into account. In this case, the complexities of Fisher Scientifics' legacy systems was too intricate for outside consultants to comprehend, and the outsourcer was unable to completely handle migration of the MIS services. Only internal IT staff with many years of experience with the MIS were able to handle them.

It is evident in terms of decision models, that when one decision works for a particular set of projects, the same decision model criteria applied to a slightly different operating or MIS model may not yield the same results. In this case, constraints were not accurately understood, and the attribute of lowered cost alone was not sufficient as a criterion for successful outsourcing MIS. Therefore, every decision should be evaluated for both infrastructure as well as a detailed understanding of what currently goes into maintaining an MIS. When the parameters for a current maintenance activity require historical perspective and specialized expertise, it may be dangerous to try and outsource that work. Alternatively, if the organization could have rather ported the MIS to an outsource provider's newer platform, this may have proved less risky than assuming all would continue as in the past.

Another area where consultants are often used to drive a decision model to outsourcing is in politically sensitive decisions. As firms increasingly find public outcries and furor over loss of thousands of jobs due to closure of MIS support offices, they find that using external parties to convey these recommendations makes them more palatable. Consider the point that many outsourcing firms are no longer publicizing their mega-outsourcing deals for fear of backlash.

As the boardrooms of large corporations have come to recognize both the large budgetary impact of IT decisions, as well as the strategic advantage that can be wrought by effective uses of IT for e-commerce and new market penetration, corporate executives are paying closer attention to how IT is leveraged for strategic and tactical advantage. In the past, senior executives have often turned to the chief financial officer to analyze trends and to provide quantitative guidance as to productivity, financial results, and for forecasting sales and profits. The chief information officer is now standing at a par with the financial executives. It is no surprise that the marriage of IT with finance represents such a strong decision model for business. By using financial analysis models to support IT proposals, the CIO has a better chance of convincing their peers in the board room of the wisdom of outsourcing arrangements. This is discussed further in the section on decision-making models.

One outsourcing deal occurred well before the advent of millennium scares and enterprise resource planning systems and Internet e-commerce MIS. *CIO Magazine* (1999) discusses how Kodak used multiple outsourcing vendor arrangements as part of its IT strategy as early as 1989. Kodak hired multiple vendors to handle data center operations, telecommunications, and desktop support. Kodak's decision to outsource to multiple best-of-breed vendors was considered risky due to the possibility of loss of control to its customer and production systems. However, by using vendors to provide basic IT resource management services, within a year, Kodak's IT capital costs dropped 95%, PC support costs dropped 10%, and mainframe operations' costs dropped by 15%. Kodak continues to outsource these support services, and continues to save IT support costs, through renewal of the original deals with many of the original vendors as well as with new vendors (CIO, 1999). The obvious decision model attributes for these multiple arrangements were cost related. Kodak, however, did not ignore quality as an attribute and customer perception as criteria for the quality attribute. In selecting its outsourcing partners, Kodak uses reputation as a means of gauging the ability of its outsourcers as equal criteria for selection, equal to lower cost and greater efficiency of operations. In another sad case, however, cost alone was the attribute of importance. Level of cost in comparison to price was the criteria — and the lower the better for Armstrong.

In 2003, Armstrong World Industries outsourced much of its computer systems applications support in a joint deal with Computer Sciences Corporation (CSC) and Satyam, an off-shore outsourcing firm based in India. The deal was valued at $2.6M annually for a term of three years. Forty-three long-time Armstrong employees were fired as a result of the deal although they were given incentives to stay for three months to transfer knowledge to the outsourcer (Applegate, 2003).

The structure of the deal was unusual in that Armstrong would only have contact with CSC as the intermediary. CSC was to gather work requirements and communicate these to the third party outsourcer, Satyam, for development. In essence, CSC outsourced the most important part of the outsourcing activity, the programming, to another outsourcer. This needlessly complex arrangement only served to add costs and create a communication chain where messages from Armstrong were often misinterpreted by the time they reached the Satyam programmers.

The arrangement began in February of 2003 and productivity dropped by 60%, as measured in work orders closed per employee. While productivity was dropping, the rate of programming requests increased. The resulting "bottle-neck" caused nearly all IT work to halt. So much administrative paperwork was involved in authorizing work that the programmers in India often spent entire days with nothing to do awaiting authorization, despite a growing work backlog at CSC and the client. Despite the fact that CSC increased staffing and hired back as many former Armstrong programmers as possible, the backlog contin-ued to grow. Less than nine months after the agreement was signed, Armstrong terminated the agreement, citing CSC's inability to meet its target performance metrics. The primary cause of the outsourcing failure was underestimating the amount of business and system knowledge that was lost when Armstrong immediately fired the 43 people that had been supporting the system. The criteria for successful productivity numbers, work orders closed, was artificial, an ineffective bellwether of success for Armstrong. Communication breakdowns between Armstrong, CSC, and Satyam also doomed the effort.

To further exacerbate the arrangement, security of data also became an attribute that was not well managed in the outsourcing arrangement. Many corporations will still not consider outsourcing their security. In fact, an analysis of the Armstrong case points to the need for even more knowledgeable in-house security and disaster recovery experts to deal with the complexities of a global, inter-networked, outsourced environment. The internal security staff actually increased from four to five people to handle the increased work from the new outsourcing arrangement.

It is clear that some outsourcing deals work well for all parties while others are destined for failure. Good communication, comprehensive metrics, excellent knowledge transfer, and common sense are all key ingredients in making a successful outsourcing deal. The place to begin is in defining the objectives and planning the structure of the outsourcing arrangement well before concluding the contract.

Decision-Making Science: What It is and Its Applicability to IT

Decision-making science requires that management understand the rudiments of how outsourcing decisions related to MIS are made. What are the expectations and how will they be achieved? The value of using managerial sciences to approach this decision is to understand the motivation drivers that justify MIS and IT outsourcing decisions.

Chapter V addressed financial models such as activity based costing (ABC). ABC models quantify the current cost of providing MIS services or business processes that can be outsourced. An advanced, ongoing project management technique, is also useful for monitoring outsourced projects. Earned value analysis (EVA) helps us to compare the costs budgeted for a project against the results of ongoing efforts and actual costs there under. Using EVA analysis models, we create forecasts of actual costs to complete an MIS project, based on the level of expenditures to date, and an assessment of how much has been accomplished to plan.

Figure 2. Process for framing discussion components

```
                    Rational Framing of Decisions

          1.  Define the Problem
          2.  Identify the Criteria
          3.  Weight the Criteria
          4.  Generate Alternatives
          5.  Rate the Alternatives on each Criteria
          6.  Compute the Optimal Decision
```

When applying a rational view to consideration of an outsourcing arrangement, there are six steps that are recommended for framing and considering the decision. Once alternative approaches to the MIS project have been formulated, the expected costs and benefits of each can be weighed and then rated, to arrive at the best approach. Computing mathematical outcomes based on selecting one alternative over another, helps to determine if outsourcing is a viable decision.

Processes and Tools of Decision Support

This section addresses quantitative and process-driven approaches to defining the type and selection of services to be outsourced. Techniques such as detailed project feasibility analysis also factor into decision models that consider outsourcing as an option. These project management disciplines are often the drivers of MIS projects in an organization. Biases can enter into quantitative models and are discussed in the context of cases where management heuristics resulted in outsourcing decisions. Decision support tools such as knowledge bases and data warehouses are also presented, along with the techniques and benefits of crafting the decision model with data mining and business intelligence tools.

The SLA As Part of the Decision Model

The previous chapter on metrics framed the need for the process for managing service level agreements (SLAs). In crafting the SLA for the MIS outsourcing project there are three levels of service that are defined as part of the SLA Model: basic, medium, and advanced. In the *basic* category a single level of service is established. Metrics are defined for the specific service and measured on an ongoing basis. In most cases, the metrics are even captured automatically, such as volumes of transactions, or number of calls, or consumption of resources like disk space. In the *medium* category of service, "services (are) done to support line-of-profit application systems. These are the application systems, hardware, software, and related support. Include these in the catalog if the business unit has the freedom to choose components, options or service windows" (Sacks, 2005). The automation of metrics data enables more comprehensive and less labor intensive reporting of service level achievement. The objective is to match service and cost levels with long-term goals to increase service levels while decreasing costs to the client organization.

Advanced category services are embedded in overall processes enabling dynamic allocation of resources either externally or internally to meet changing business conditions. "These are infrastructure devices, security and business continuity services, and other things deemed to be 'overhead' functions" (Sacks, 2005). The goal of advanced services is to provide a seamless mix of services, costs and appropriate, multiple outsource providers at better than competitive rates without sacrifice of control or continuity of operations.

CIO Magazine's Meyer (2005), recommends that individual SLAs be negotiated for different services. They can be negotiated at the same time, as a bundle, but making the agreements distinct allows for different service periods, different service organizations even within the same outsourcer, as well as different pricing strategies. In one project example, imagine that the organization is upgrading the PCs across the organization while at the same time deploying a new sales application for marketing. Departments can receive the PCs without the sales application, and the application will work without the newer PCs. This situation describes two distinct services, and thus, should be covered under separate SLAs. They might be bundled and negotiated at the same time for convenience, but the pricing strategies for acquisition and deployment of hardware may be at different labor rates, and with different levels of time responsiveness than for deployment of a software application. The decision to model the specific services to be provided and how to construct the SLA or even the bundle of SLAs as part of an outsourcing arrangement requires looking at the components and measures of success for the outsourcing decision.

Feasibility Analysis in Modeling Alternatives

Feasibility analysis is a technique used in project management and portfolio management for selecting viable projects. A natural outgrowth of the problem definition and planning phase, feasibility analysis is a set of processes that consider the required resources, skill sets, experience, and facilities against an organization's availability of these. When a project has high feasibility but the organization is lacking in one or more of these required elements, outsourcing becomes a reasonable avenue to pursue. Therefore, in any organization there are triple constraints on any project: Scope, Time, and Cost. Once the MIS project has been defined in terms of what the concept of operations is, who the stakeholders are, and where the funding comes from, there are steps in making the decision to do the project: is it feasible? Five specific criteria are used for project selection:

- Backed by management
- Timed appropriately for commitment of resources
- It moves the business toward attainment of its goals
- Practicable and reasonable in its technical approach
- Important enough to be considered over other projects

A feasibility study assesses the merits of the proposed project. There are three types of feasibility analysis that factor into the decision: Technical, Economic, and Operational feasibility. *Technical* feasibility assesses whether the current technical resources have the skills, tools and knowledge sufficient for the project. Outsourcing becomes a reasonable alternative in the decision model if the organization does not consider this a core process. If the resources are not available, can they be acquired, or training provided? Another technical question is to determine if the organization has the right tools to do the project; or can the MIS be upgraded to provide the level of technology necessary for the new system? When upgrading MIS or entering a new realm of experience, another concern is the maturity of the technology. It is important to note if the technology exists in the marketplace and whether it has already been proven. When crafting a new innovation, it helps to have an outsourcing partner that has done similar MIS projects before, or who has direct and deep experience in that business area. If it is to be "sourced" in house, it will be vital to address if the organization has the experience to do the job, as well as ensure that the right team members are, in fact, available so that resource contention does not become the wedge that makes the project fail.

In some cases, after performing the technical feasibility study we discover that the costs are prohibitive, or that to do the MIS project successfully from the technical standpoint, we have under-estimated the financial commitment. Perhaps the ABC analysis proved that existing processes can't really be improved without major investments of capital. In such cases, the project must also undergo an *economic* feasibility analysis to determine whether the time and money are available to develop the system. The project proposal must be carefully examined to be sure that management has the right understanding of all costs, both real and "implied costs," for example staff time away from other assignments, time to train staff in the new processes, consultants that may be needed to help transition the MIS project. These are all economic cost factors that cannot be forgotten in the cost model.

Other costs include the purchase of new equipment, hardware, software, and maintenance. The economic analysis also weighs the costs against the perceived benefits to ensure that the expected results are compelling. Lastly, economic feasibility must address the availability of sufficient funding and whether that funding is actually appropriated or only "earmarked." Many firms have embarked on risky outsourcing arrangements hoping to pay for the services or the infrastructure from the expected savings, only to find that the "undocumented costs" of knowledge transfer, or the outsourcer's lack of experience in legacy applications made the costs of supporting the outsourcer higher than expected, and resulted in the arrangement being less advantageous than envisioned.

The last aspect of feasibility analysis concerns the cultural or operational feasibility of a project. *Operational* feasibility determines if the human resources are available to operate the system once it has been installed. Another aspect is that the project must have executive sponsorship and management support for the time it will take from their other duties to implement or transition the project. In outsourcing it is generally the case made that the time savings of outsourcing will pay for the services wrought. User acceptance of a project that was done elsewhere can be an issue, such as in the case of a software development SLA. If users do not want a new system they may prevent it from becoming operationally feasible. When the MIS is to be paid for by departments having to forego some part of their budgets, due to fewer operations required because of the new MIS, the organization may suddenly find all support for the new project disappeared. Operational feasibility also requires evaluation of related issues for potential risks:

- Computer competency of user community
- Computing comfort level of potential clients and customers
- Perceived loss of decision control by employees
- Shift in power away from traditional business processes
- Fear of job changes
- Fear of employment loss
- Reversal of longstanding procedures

Finally, not all costs and benefits can always be measured. Some intangible benefits might include increased levels of service, improved customer satisfaction, the necessity of the MIS for competitive survival, or simply a need to source the project with organic resources to develop in-house expertise. On the flip side of the model, intangible costs might include reduced employee moral, lost productivity, or even poor customer perception resulting in lost customers or sales.

Decision Making Biases: Heuristic-Based and General Biases Decision Theory and Models

Having appropriately identified the components of the decision, and then framing the alternatives, we can remove most of the guesswork and assumptions from the decision process. In many cases of outsourcing, it is evident that the organization tries to outsource a business process or entire MIS system based on how it internally defines the operating procedures for that function. In cases where the decision was arrived at by a single individual in the organization, it may be the result of a general or heuristical bias that the organization should focus of core business rather than on supporting processes. While in many cases this makes good business sense, it does not always translate that it makes good economic sense. Bias occurs when a faulty model is applied to an unrelated decision, and the resulting decision does not follow the expected outcome of success. The reasoning for the decision based on a preexisting bias does not follow a rational pattern of arguments and key points, but rather a general sense of similarity.

There are certain assumptions made that the outsourcer will duplicate the same methodology and business rules to operation of that function, or provision of that service, which are consistent, or even identical to the client organization's. Operational biases arise when the operation proceeds in a manner that the client organization views as detrimental. In some cases, this can be alleviated and corrected with a flexible contract arrangement and good operating relationships and communications on both sides of the contract. An example of an outsourcing case where the client organization had to adapt its expectations to the outsource provider's model turned out to be a good approach.

First American Bank is an Illinois based bank located in the suburbs of Chicago (Ward, 2004). First American, like many other financial institutions, found their business needs changing due to advancements in electronic banking via the Internet. To make matters more complex, First American was also processing information for four other financial institutions. They outsourced systems recovery and continuity activities to Comdisco Inc. in Rosemont, Illinois. They now believe it is time to bring this operation back in-house. Two issues led the bank to question its current outsourcing situation. The first issue is the ability to adequately maintain "self-service-oriented" platforms such as the Web and voice response systems: "First American was encountering difficulties in making the systems available during periods of down time because of the bank's limited arrangements for back-up" (Ward, 2004). The second issue was the availability of test time the bank was allotted. Ward (2004) reports Noel Levasseur's comments on this topic:

Our annual allotment of test time always seemed to be thin. It was a challenge to test other than locally, because the communications infrastructure was connected to the main IT location. That did not lend itself to platform-or silo-specific recovery. (p. 4)

Ultimately, First American decided to bring the work back in-house and utilize a product called DataMirror for advanced infrastructure support capabilities. Following implementation, the new product provided automated handling for testing and would offload processing to a second machine. In this example, outsourcing was not a failure in terms of the provider's service. The failure was merely that First American found they could rethink their business model in light of changing technology availability in the environment. In some cases, as IT continues to evolve, the organization may discover that the outsourcing model no longer fits due to the criticality of the service and development of newer, cheaper IT support tools.

Another bias that is frequently introduced into making outsourcing decisions is that of heuristical bias. In heuristic bias, assumptions creep into the decision-making bias disguised as fact, rather than just potential attributes. Decisions are then made to weigh one alternative over another based on an otherwise unfounded set of assumptions about performance to criteria that constitute the basis for the rational decision. Decisions based on a heuristics framework are arrived at largely due to familiarity and a degree of confidence in our assumptions. When some of the constraints, such as sunk costs or congruency of operating capabilities are made as part of the decision-making algorithm, the resulting decision may no longer be entirely objective. Yet, in most cases, the decision-makers are not completely aware of the bias towards that which they are familiar and comfortable which may lead them to overlook drawbacks or limitations in the solution. Confidence is a great blind. The "goal is to help you 'unfreeze' your decision-making patterns by showing you how easily heuristics become biases when improperly applied" (Bazerman, 2002, p. 140).

Normative vs. Descriptive (Process-Oriented) Models

In other cases, decision-making follows an assumption that what services were performed well by one outsourcer means that the same firm can handle a variety of other tasks as well. As noted in the previous chapter, outsourcers often bring in a marketing team to sell services that are different than the performing team. One firm learned through a bittersweet experience just how such a normative decisions model may not always be reliable when crafting what work can be reasonably outsourced to the same vendor.

This firm wished to outsource part of its IT function. The company entered into a contract to outsource the help desk functions. The help desk outsourcing project worked so well that after only three months, the client company decided to expand the work and start outsourcing the local area network (LAN) department as well, for management of all network and support functions. This effort did not go as smoothly, but the outsourcer adapted well to the change in contract scope.

Initially, the outsourcing firm used the same staff who participated in the help desk project to start outsourcing the LAN project. This was done because the staff who had worked on the help desk had acquired a feel and familiarity with the client company and had also developed internal operating relationships with organic staff at the client. However, the selected staff did not have the proper skill sets to adequately perform LAN administrator and network technician roles necessary to this MIS project. The outsourcing firm responded immediately when this became apparent and moved to bring on more experienced and technologically skilled individuals to fill the LAN jobs.

Since this chapter deals with theories and applications of decision theory we have begun with giving some examples of outsourcing decisions based on past experiences the firm had with successful cases of outsourcing certain MIS or business processes. Since *normative* or *prescriptive* decision theory is concerned with identifying the best decision to take, sufficient analysis of alternatives and preparations of the best model for outsourcing is necessary. A decision to outsource a project assumes that we are fully informed as to requirements and conversely, as to the capabilities of the outsourcer. The decision-maker is able to predict the likely outcome or result of outsourcing the MIS with perfect accuracy and the truths regarding requirements vs. capabilities are fully rational. This requires the use of descriptive models that accurately mirror the constructs and services of the outsourcing arrangements.

Decision analysis also uses tools, methodologies and software to help managers make better decisions. The most systematic and comprehensive software tools developed in this way are called decision support systems (DSS). Many DSS have as basic underlying structure, data warehouses constructed with analytic tools for data mining and business intelligence. In some cases, these tools are used to monitor the performance of the outsourcer. Data warehouses are organized for fast queries and management reporting.

To further facilitate access to formatted data, data warehouses often contain precreated standard or recurring reports available online. Data warehouses are also optimized for answering complex queries as opposed to normal operational databases that are constructed for performance and speed of update. Warehouse reporting uses relationships and indexing that would bog down the performance of operational, transaction-focused databases, and uses online analytical processing (OLAP) for business analysis. OLAP tools are now available in many operational databases as well.

Data Warehouses, Data Mining, and Business Intelligence in Decision Support

One of the greatest decision aid aspects of data warehouses is that multiple databases are integrated and have been processed so that common data are uniformly defined or have been cross-mapped to standard data elements, for cross-organizational mining of knowledge. This can be particularly valuable to the outsourcer who needs access to many databases in order to provide a customer-facing service for their client.

Since organizations do not typically behave in optimal ways, data warehouses are ideal for supporting the related area of decision modeling study which is *descriptive*, attempting to describe what people will actually do. Since the prescriptive decision often creates hypotheses for testing against actual behavior, the two fields of decision science are closely linked. Using descriptive decision models, the outsourcer, in cooperation with the client, can use decision models and dialog questions to understand the client's dynamic nature of business. Assumptions of perfect information, rationality and "conned" unimagi-

Figure 3. Using case-based reasoning methods in decision support

Case-based Reasoning Methods

- retrieve most similar case (or cases) comparing the current problem case to the library of past cases;
- use parameters from the retrieved case to try solve the current problem;
- revise and adapt the proposed solution if necessary;
- save the new final solution as part of a new case in knowledgebase.

native telephone scripts can be eliminated to produce different prescriptions for MIS actions that are more appropriate in practice.

In the case of the firm that outsourced first help desk functions, and then tried to apply the same model to LAN administration, a bad normative model was corrected and the outsourcing parameters were adjusted to save the MIS project and convert the outsourcing episode to a successful one.

Lastly, rules and case-based reasoning (Figure 3) fit into the outsourcing decision by helping to develop models based on analogies to the services or MIS project we seek to outsource. By creating databases of past MIS projects and lessons learned from these the organization builds a descriptive model for making proper and appropriate outsourcing decisions.

Decision-Making Models for Intelligent Outsourcing

This section discusses the evolution from cognitive, human-based decision-making to the development of models that specify a project that may be outsourced.

Cognitive and Motivational Models for Outsourcing

In some cases, it may be appropriate to create databases of rules to provide better operational models to the outsourcer. Three approaches to generating such client business process knowledge bases are often used in the outsourcing field:

- **Knowledge acquisition from experts:** through query and conjecture as well as by extraction of rules used by experts, models can be generated that reflect the heuristical inputs experts typically use.

- **Knowledge-based models like expert systems:** tools such as trouble call knowledge bases can be developed and used as expert systems for issuing repair orders, or for tailoring customer support scripts for outsourcers involved in customer service.

- **Construction of knowledge-based models:** a decision is generated by a model engine based on the problem description. The decision model construction consists of studying, selecting, and collecting causative and associative relationships from an historical knowledge base of similar cases. The system continually evolves the decision model structure with analytical processing, so that decisions are directed to increasingly robust options applicable to the incoming context for the decision question (Wellman, 1994).

Modeling with Knowledge: Human Cognitive Architectures for Decisions

The availability of technology and reporting tools has helped make outsourcing to off-shore incumbent staff much more feasible than in the last century. Many of us recall the telemarketers who ring with "standard pitches" for products or for collecting bills. When we offer objections or seek to discuss a problem with an account they do not seem prepared, much less empowered by their organization to actually help us solve the problem. In most cases, they do not even know the features or even the function of the product they are selling or seeking to service through this phone interaction. It leaves us feeling frustrated and wondering why they bother with the service or the marketing effort.

Data warehouses and rules knowledge bases have now become so common place that minor training is needed before users can take advantage of and query powerful expert-based search engines. These tools include intelligent search agents for "sounds like," "is synonymous with," and other algorithms to provide the right information to questions or to offer telephonic services that have greatly enhanced the online, outsourcer experience. In many cases the customer is not even aware they are dealing with a third party.

In fact, data mining tools now afford a further level of business intelligence capability to the databases that house customer history data, buying patterns,

Figure 4. Data mining patterns in DSS

> ☐ Associations - patterns that occur together, i.e., Grocery store offers gasoline discounts for food purchases, customers patronize those gas stations and fill up when empty.
> ☐ Sequences - patterns of actions that take place over a period of time, i.e., Regulations concerning air fares change, price competition to fill last minute seats at the airport result in advance fare prices coming down as well; predictions of foul weather and increased purchases of canned food.
> ☐ Clustering - patterns that develop among groups, i.e., A new neighborhood is constructed near a major hospital – new home buyers are doctors.
> ☐ Trends - patterns that are noticed over a period of time, i.e., Pink clothing sells in London; magazines report this, youth start buying pink in response to ads.

market sequences, and clustering that further enhance the total experience of the outsourcer with the organization's customer. Data mining is the process of identifying patterns that a human would not naturally detect through statistical analysis, decision trees, and other modes of data visualization. With all of this information and data visualization tools at their fingertips, customer service personnel, or other business process outsourcer personnel now have the same powerful analytics that the client organization used to rely upon to "know the customer." Figure 4 illustrates some of the decision models used in data mining.

In some cases, however, organizations have discovered that crafting a knowl- edge model for designing the outsourced support may not be directly transferable to an outsource provider. In the case of Dell, one student of the author reported the following experience from working as a collection agent for Dell. "Dude, Buy a Dell???" is how this individual entitles his story.

"Good Morning. Dell Customer Collections, may I speak with the owner of the home please?" The irate customer, who bought a Dell computer some time back, replies. "Is this Dell? I told you to stop calling me. I paid off my computer and I have phone records. I called to close my account, but I spoke with some Indian guy who claimed to be named Charles. I opened the preferred customer account, paid my bill and closed it off. I refuse to pay for some Indian guy's mistakes. What type of customer service is this anyway? Why don't you try calling them, maybe you can talk to this 'Charles'! I'm never buying a Dell again and neither is anyone else that I know. I'll make sure of that!"

This true, yet short conversation actually happened to Corey who worked at Dun & Bradstreet Collections, whom Dell hired to collect debt for overdue preferred customer credit accounts. Through his brief stay there, he encountered numer- ous customers who refused to pay. They all had the same complaint, poor customer service call routing to Indian representatives who spoke from written scripts, using fake names and were just outright harsh to customers. In an article for E-Commerce News, Columnist Keith Regan writes, "Newspapers located near Dell's Austin, Texas headquarters reported that customers were complain- ing not only about having their calls answered by technical support staff who spoke with accents but also about receiving scripted responses to their questions rather than one-on-one support" (Regan, 2003). Though the company was attempting to save money, they were actually cannibalizing their own market share.

After taking a stroll through a Best Buy retail store one can see the large number of computer manufacturers with extremely low prices. Now that prices have drastically decreased, the remaining factor of differentiation is customer service.

Dell was originally praised for its personalized customer service, but is now being blackballed by a number of angry customers. Such customers have vowed to never return to Dell and have made every effort to spread the word.

However, in light of the extensive media coverage on this topic, Dell learned a lesson in the importance of customer service. The company pulled most of its business customer service support calls from India. However, they did not pull out of off-shore outsourcing for the personal computer (PC) customer service activities. As Regan points out, "In the case of computer sales especially, the customer is also looking for the overall value and if there's a sense that's being eroded by a lower level of service, that's a concern." Dell may soon find that their once heroic motto of custom-building every PC for each and every customer has been overtaken by the after the sale impression.

Outsourcing Core Business Processes, MIS Development Projects, or IT Support Service

In some cases, companies have had to learn the difficult way that the outsourcing model may not work for all IT services. In Dell Computer's case, they spent a considerable amount of money to divest themselves of customer support functions to focus on product development and production. Yet in their business, after the sale customer support is a key differentiator for future success. Future business depends upon customer goodwill, and product reputation, as well as customer support. These could not be outsourced and left to others. It is clear quantitative models and financial cost-benefit analyses that point toward potentially significant cost savings from outsourcing a business processes or an MIS function do not stand alone. The previously discussed technique of ABC helps to quantify and even identify key operating metrics for inclusion in outsourcing SLAs. In this manner, the parameters of the cost savings become the metrics in decision making as they relate to IT or MIS projects.

References

Applegate, J., Austin, J., & McFarlan, J. (2003). *Corporate information strategy and management: Text and cases* (6th ed.). New York: McGraw-Hill Higher Education.

Bazerman, M. H. (2002). *Judgment in managerial decision-making* (5th ed.). Hoboken, NJ: John Wiley & Sons.

Marshall, K. T., & Oliver, R. M. (1995). *Decision making and forecasting,* New York: McGraw-Hill.

Meyer, N. D. (2005). *Beneath the buzz — SLAs — service level agreements are fundamental to the integrity of IT.* Retrieved March 15, 2006, from http://www.cio.com/go/index.html?ID=4944&PMID=22093223&s=3&f=1

Regan, K. (2003). *Dell recalls tech support from India after complaints.* Retrieved March 15, 2006, from http://www.ecommercetimes.com/story/32248.html

Sacks, S. (2005). *Taking the first step toward reducing IT costs with demand management.* Retrieved March 15, 2006, from http://www.computerworld.com/managementtopics/management/story/0,10801,98555,00.html

Ward, J. (2004). First American gains multi-channel stability. *Bank Systems & Technology, 41*(3), 4-12.

Wellman, M. (1994). *Knowledge-based decision model construction.* Retrieved March 15, 2006, from http://ai.eecs.umich.edu/people/wellman/KBMC.html

Chapter VIII

Lessons Learned from Successes and Failures in Information Systems Outsourcing

Kathryn M. Zuckweiler, University of Nebraska - Kearney, USA

Abstract

This chapter presents a process map of information systems outsourcing decisions and factors which influence the outcome of the outsourcing project at each decision point. The author takes a broad view of outsourcing projects and examines IS outsourcing successes and failures in context of project phase. Brief examples are provided to illustrate various outcomes of the decisions faced by both outsourcing vendor and client. The chapter also presents a summary of lessons learned about information systems outsourcing and recommendations for future research.

Introduction

The rapid advances in information technology over the past twenty years have fueled what some are calling the "knowledge economy" (Due, 1995). A knowledge economy is partly characterized by the strategic role of information systems in creating and disseminating knowledge and information. Specifically, information systems (hereafter referred to as IS) enable more timely spread of information that is rich and deep. IS have also reduced the asymmetry of information between buyers and suppliers. While this is most commonly thought of between consumers and businesses, these benefits also accrue in business to business relationships. These benefits can lead to more efficient and effective communication between businesses and their customers, which at least in theory could favorably impact the performance of the company. With so much potential gain from the strategic use of IS, many companies look for ways to realize these benefits. However, the rapidity of IS change, evolving technological standards (hardware, networking, etc.), and dizzying array of software choices make it challenging to develop and maintain the resources and competencies necessary to manage IS. So, companies have increasingly turned to IS outsourcing as a means of retaining focus on core product or service competencies and keeping IS strategic by buying IS competency from vendors (Allnoch, 1997).

This has not proved to be as simple or straightforward as it might seem. While IS outsourcing successes garner much publicity, there are an unknown number of IS outsourcing failures, some of them staggering in the cost and scope of the failure (Anderson, Davison, & Lepeak, 2004). Researchers are beginning to study IS outsourcing failures as well as successes to attempt to learn more about the determinants of IS outsourcing outcomes. To date, most research examines IS outsourcing outcomes from either a success or a failure standpoint. This chapter aims to synthesize the academic research related to IS outsourcing successes and failures, combined with examples from business, to take stock of what has been learned about IS outsourcing. As outsourcing itself is a multistage process, successes and failures will be presented and analyzed at each stage of the process. The chapter concludes with a discussion of lessons learned and suggestions for future research.

The Outsourcing Process

A review of the existing literature on IS outsourcing indicates that there are several stages through which most, if not all, outsourcing projects progress. These stages are graphically represented in a process map shown in Figure 1.

Figure 1. Information systems outsourcing process map

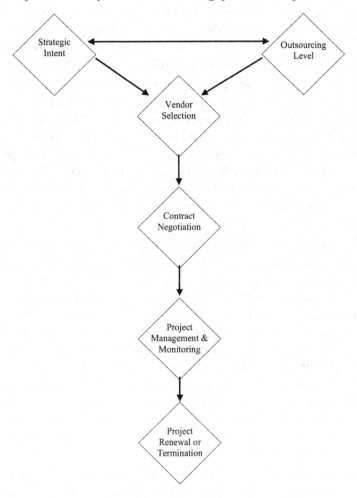

Each stage will be briefly introduced in this section. A detailed discussion with examples will follow in subsequent sections. Two decisions regarding IS outsourcing must be made in the early stages of the project: strategic intent and outsourcing level.

Strategic intent refers to the outsourcing company's goals for the project. DiRomualdo and Gurbaxani (1998) discuss strategic intent in three categories: IS improvement; business impact; and commercial exploitation. IS improvement is aptly named — companies pursuing outsourcing for IS improvement seek to reduce costs and enhance efficiency of IS resources (DiRomualdo & Gurbaxani, 1998). Business impact is concerned with improving the IS contribution to company performance within existing lines of business (DiRomualdo & Gurbaxani, 1998). Companies using IS outsourcing for commercial exploitation focus on leveraging technology-related assets, including applications, infrastructure, and knowledge, in the marketplace through the development and marketing of new technology-based products and services (DiRomualdo & Gurbaxani, 1998).

Decisions relating to outsourcing level can be dichotomized as either total IS outsourcing or partial IS outsourcing. Lacity, Willcocks, and Feeny (1996) coined the term "selective outsourcing" to describe the practice of outsourcing only part of a company's IS activity. Selective outsourcing is defined as the decision to source selected IT functions from external providers while still providing between 20% and 80% of the IT budget internally (Lacity & Willcocks, 1998). Total outsourcing, by contrast, is the decision to transfer more than 80% of the IS budget for assets and accompanying management responsibility to an external vendor (Lacity & Willcocks, 1998).

Once decisions are made regarding strategic intent and level of IS outsourcing, companies must then select a vendor (or vendors). Issues presented in the literature as relevant to vendor selection decisions include benchmarking vendor costs against internal costs (Hall, 2003), evaluating vendors' capabilities and resources to complete the project (Ferguson, 2004; Kim & Chung, 2003; Willcocks & Lacity, 1999a); and completing due diligence of prospective vendors (Lankford & Parsa, 1999). Additionally, Kern, Willcocks, and van Heck (2002) discuss the implications of a "winner's curse" for selecting IS outsourcing vendors. While vendor selection is obviously a critical component of the outsourcing process, contract negotiations with the chosen vendor codify many important elements of the relationship between vendor and outsourcing company (for clarity, the company that purchases outsourcing services will hereafter be referred to as the client).

Contract negotiations between client and vendor are discussed to some extent in much of the IS outsourcing literature. Oft-mentioned contract considerations include flexibility and dealing with uncertainty (Kern et al., 2002; Lee, Huynh, Kwok, & Pi, 2003), performance measures (DiRomualdo & Gurbaxani, 1998), service level (Ferguson, 2004), length of contract (Willcocks & Lacity, 1999a), and structure of rewards and penalties (DiRomualdo & Gurbaxani, 1998). Some authors (Quittner, 2004; Willcocks & Lacity, 1999a) indicate that clients should assume that the original contract will need to be renegotiated as the project progresses and prepare for the process of renegotiation in the early stages of the relationship with the vendor.

At the completion of contract negotiations and commencement of the project, clients enter the project management and monitoring phase of the outsourcing process. During this phase, the nature of the relationship between client and vendor takes center stage. Several researchers have studied the determinants and results of this relationship (including Allen, Juillet, Paquet & Roy, 2001; Ferguson, 2004; Lee, Huynh, Kwok, & Pi, 2003; Natovich, 2003; Quittner, 2004), but all agree the manner in which the relationship between client and vendor is managed plays a central role in the outcome of the outsourcing project. Additional IS outsourcing project management issues include conflict resolution (Natovich, 2003), retained skills and capabilities (Willcocks & Lacity, 1999a), and level of commitment to the project for both client and vendor (Natovich, 2003). These additional issues are, to varying degrees, related to the nature of

Table 1. Information systems outsourcing stages, issues and relevant citations

Outsourcing Stage	Issues	Relevant Citations
Strategic Intent	• IS improvement • Business impact • Commercial exploitation	Anderson et al. (2004), DiRomualdo & Gurbaxani (1998), Quittner (2004)
Outsourcing Level	• Total outsourcing • Selective outsourcing	Barthelemy & Geyer (2004), Chain Store Age (2004), Gupta & Gupta (1992), Natovich (2003), Quittner (2004), Willcocks & Lacity (1999a, 1999b)
Vendor Selection	• Due diligence • Vendor capabilities & resources • Benchmark v. internal costs • Winner's curse	Chain Store Age (2004), Ferguson (2004), Hall (2003), Kern et al. (2002), Kim & Chung (2003), Lankford & Parsa (1999), Strassman (2004), Willcocks & Lacity (1999a)
Contract Negotiation	• Flexibility & dealing with uncertainty • Performance measures • Service level • Length of contract • Structure of rewards & penalties	Allen et al. (2001), DiRomualdo & Gurbaxani (1998), Lee et al. (2003), Quittner (2004), Willcocks & Lacity (1999a)
Project Management & Monitoring	• Nature of relationship between vendor & client • Conflict resolution • Retained skills & capabilities • Level of commitment – vendor & client	Lee et al. (2003), Natovich (2003), Nonprofit Business Advisor (2004), Willcocks & Lacity (1999a)
Project Renewal or Termination	• Choice between renewal and termination • Tone of project termination	Anderson et al. (2004), Natovich (2003)

the client-vendor relationship, which is a further indication of its centrality to the entire project.

The final stage of the IS outsourcing process is project renewal or termination. This stage is largely a function of the contract terms and client-vendor relationship. Natovich (2003) and Quittner (2004) discuss project termination when the original contract term is abbreviated. Willcocks and Lacity (1999a) describe ways to mitigate the risks associated with project termination. As with other types of projects, renewal or termination of IS outsourcing projects can be a delicate issue for both client and vendor, particularly when the project is not going well. However, it offers insight into the entire IS outsourcing process that may be informative for future projects.

A summary of the stages of the IS outsourcing process, related issues, and relevant citations is presented in Table 1. Each of these topics is discussed in greater detail in the next section and illustrated with examples of successes and failures of IS outsourcing in business. From these vignettes, a collection of lessons learned is presented in the final section of the chapter and summarized in Table 2.

Successes and Failures in IS Outsourcing

Stories of outsourcing successes are well-publicized and generally easy to find in both the academic and business press. It requires a little more digging to turn up information on failed outsourcing projects. This may be partially attributable to a lack of clear, unequivocal criteria for success or failure. Rather, these are anchor points on a continuum with most IS outsourcing projects falling somewhere other than on an end point. Further complicating assessment of IS outsourcing projects is the tendency of companies to "spin" the story to emphasize successes and mitigate the impact of failures. For example, when JPMorgan Chase announced that it would restructure its $5 billion IS outsourcing deal with IBM and bring much of the previously-outsourced systems back in-house, IBM publicly stated that despite its sunk costs in the project the cancellation would have a positive impact on earnings (Anderson et al., 2004). Both companies also emphasized that they would continue to have an outsourcing relationship, but with a reduced scope.

Given the inequities in availability of information on IS outsourcing successes and failures, the number of examples presented at each phase of the outsourcing process is limited to one or two that succinctly illustrate the relevant issues. In addition to the examples, insights specific to each phase are discussed.

Strategic Intent

As DiRomualdo and Gurbaxani (1998) describe the three types of strategic intent (IS improvement, business impact, and commercial exploitation) for IS outsourcing, they highlight the need to align strategic intent with actions taken during the entire outsourcing project duration. Companies need to articulate their strategic intent for IS outsourcing in terms of desired outcomes. In other words, what does a company hope to gain by outsourcing its information systems? Clearly expressing strategic intent sets the tone for the entire outsourcing project and provides a general framework from which to make decisions.

IS improvement outsourcing projects are perhaps most well-known, as this type of strategic intent includes outsourcing to reduce costs and enhance efficiency of IS resources. In general, companies that undertake IS improvement projects "want better performance from their core IS resources — the hardware, software, networks, people, and processes involved in managing and operating the technology and supporting users" (DiRomualdo & Gurbaxani, 1998, p. 70). In addition to cost reduction and enhanced efficiency, companies may seek service quality improvement and acquisition of new technical skills and management competencies from IS improvement projects (DiRomualdo & Gurbaxani, 1998). To achieve these objectives, companies turn to outside specialists, who they believe are better able to keep pace with new technologies and skills, to manage their IS resources.

According to DiRomualdo and Gurbaxani (1998), success for IS improvement projects comes through "exploiting economies of scale and expertise, deploying proven processes for cost reduction and service improvement, and bringing distinctive technical expertise to bear for the client" (p. 71). Causes of failure include "the vendor's lack of appropriate technical and management skills, cost shifts and postponements instead of real reductions, and added coordination costs that exceed the savings from outsourcing" (p. 71). Thus, achieving the goals of IS improvement projects depends on technical and operational processes and skills.

Outsourcing for business impact involves working with vendors to deploy IS to significantly improve critical aspects of business performance (DiRomualdo & Gurbaxani, 1998). "Realizing this goal requires an understanding of the business and the link between IT and business processes, and the ability to implement new systems and business change simultaneously. This form of outsourcing brings new skills and capabilities that link IT to business results rather than those related purely to technology" (p. 72). Examples of outsourcing for business impact include developing the capabilities to deliver innovative IS, such as automating order fulfillment, inventory management, or customer management processes, and the competencies related to business process analysis and management, such as using technology to reengineer business processes. Frequently companies find that the most effective approach to outsourcing for business impact is to focus on jointly developing complementary skills and capabilities, rather than relying solely on those of the vendor (DiRomualdo & Gurbaxani, 1998).

Success for business impact projects is evaluated from a business, rather than technical, perspective. Factors such as fitting IS to business needs, managing change projects, and balancing management expertise and technical knowledge are important to the success of a business outsourcing initiative. Because technology has significant potential to create business value in this type of outsourcing arrangement, companies must retain ownership of the user management and IS innovation processes focusing on the discovery of new ways to exploit technology in the business, and make explicit provisions to ensure the continuous transfer of knowledge about the impact of emerging technologies from vendor to client (DiRomualdo & Gurbaxani, 1998). Failure in business impact outsourcing projects can result from the vendor's incomplete understanding of the client's business, and the lack of a direct link between business results and vendor payments and incentives. Thus, achieving the goals of a business impact outsourcing project depends on business and strategic knowledge.

Outsourcing for commercial exploitation involves partnering with vendors to offset IS costs or generate new revenue and profit from IS resources. This can be accomplished by licensing systems and technologies originally developed for internal use, selling IS products and services to other companies, or launching new IS-based businesses (DiRomualdo & Gurbaxani, 1998). DiRomualdo and Gurbaxani (1998) found that companies pursuing commercial exploitation of IS resources often had developed innovative information systems, but could not justify further investment in new technologies based on internal returns. Only when the commercial revenue potential of proposed innovations is considered does the investment become viable.

However, commercial exploitation is currently the least-often used type of outsourcing. This is due in part to the rarity of IS organizations that:

... have the capabilities required to exploit IT in the marketplace: the know-how to commercialize and sell IT products and services originally developed for use by a single company, the ability to establish new distribution channels for IT-based products and services, the skill to port systems to various technology platforms, and the wherewithal to support and enhance products and services after they are sold. (DiRomualdo & Gurbaxani, 1998, p. 76)

One way to gain these commercial exploitation capabilities is through relationships with outsourcing vendors.

Success factors in commercial exploitation outsourcing projects include product development, technical innovation, and sales and marketing skill (DiRomualdo & Gurbaxani, 1998). Failures can result from misjudging or failing to realize synergies of assets and capabilities, failing to fulfill commitments to internal customers, and failing to ensure that the rewards received by the partners are commensurate with the risk that each assumes (DiRomualdo & Gurbaxani, 1998). Thus, achieving the goals of commercial exploitation projects relies on both vendor and client making significant investments of management and staff, technology resources, and funding (DiRomualdo & Gurbaxani, 1998).

The three types of strategic intent may be viewed as falling along a continuum, with projects potentially shifting intent as they progress. For example, an outsourcing project may begin as an IS improvement initiative and progress to one that has business impact as in the case of Pacific Bell Telephone. Pacific Bell Telephone needed to replace its aged and inflexible customer billing system and its IS staff lacked the skills and competencies to upgrade the old system and manage the new one, so the project was outsourced to a vendor (DiRomualdo & Gurbaxani, 1998). Over time, the project evolved into a joint venture to facilitate knowledge transfer and continued development of the system after implementation (DiRomualdo & Gurbaxani, 1998).

Xerox Corporation clearly identified its strategic intent for an IS outsourcing project as business impact, which helped guide its efforts and ensure the success of the project. Xerox:

decided to outsource as part of its move to completely transform the IT resource — technology, processes, and people. Outsourcing was integral to the company's broader effort to reengineer and retool its business capabilities. The company outsourced most of the existing infrastructure and 70% of its IS staff people to EDS — thereby giving them an opportunity to develop new career paths. This freed financial and management resources to concentrate on creating future business-critical IT infrastructure and applications and acquiring new IT-related skills for remaining staff.

According to Jagdish Dalal, a Xerox executive then involved in the outsourcing and reengineering initiatives, "I would not have even thought of reengineering if we hadn't outsourced, because we would have been busy reorganizing, letting people go, consolidating data centers, whatever. Xerox had to reduce its IT spending and redirect it, and the best way to do that was outsourcing.

To help realize the project's objectives, Xerox designed the outsourcing contract to ensure continuing high-quality and cost-effective service levels from the existing IS processes and resources while making it possible to eventually replace them by funding new IT infrastructure and systems. The contract addressed the company's cost and service objectives, but more importantly, it made liquid a significant portion of the IT asset base to provide seed money for the new IT infrastructure and for process and systems reengineering. (DiRomualdo & Gurbaxani, 1998, p. 73)

If the strategic intent of an IS outsourcing project changes during the project or if there are material changes within the organization, the success of the project (and sometimes even the outsourcing project itself) may be in jeopardy. This was the case with banking giant JPMorgan Chase & Co., which in September 2004 announced it would cancel a $5 billion outsourcing deal with IBM Corporation that was to have lasted until 2010 and involved 4,000 employees (Quittner, 2004). The cancellation came in the wake of JPMorgan Chase's merger with Bank One Corporation and the decision by the newly-merged company to bring many technology assets back under internal control. JPMorgan Chase indicated that it saw an opportunity to gain competitive advantage via its IT infrastructure and wanted to exploit that opportunity and more tightly control its IS resources (Anderson et al., 2004). While IBM had some sunk costs for work performed to date, it indicated that the cancellation would have a positive impact on earnings which suggested that the deal was not profitable for IBM.

Both companies put a positive public spin on the cancellation and pointed out that they will continue to work together on other outsourcing projects. However, cancelling an outsourcing deal with such a large financial and personnel scope suggests that there were significant problems. JPMorgan Chase decided that the strategic management of their technology assets could be better handled by in-house staff than by the vendor. While details about the factors that led to cancellation of the deal may never be publicly known, it is feasible that differing views regarding the strategic intent of the project contributed to the cancellation.

What are the lessons for IS outsourcing regarding strategic intent? First, there is no "one size fits all" approach to IS outsourcing — each type of strategic intent for IS outsourcing requires different approaches and tactics to be successful (DiRomualdo & Gurbaxani, 1998). Also, the strategic intent for an IS outsourcing project "must drive the operating philosophy of the relationship [between client and vendor] and be reflected in the critical features of the outsourcing contract: contract type, pricing provisions, reward and penalty mechanisms, performance measures, and nonpricing provisions" (DiRomualdo & Gurbaxani, 1998, p. 79). Finally, because strategic intent may change during the course of the project, the relationship between vendor and client and associated contract must be designed to accommodate change.

Decisions about the strategic intent of IS outsourcing projects often are made concurrently with decisions about outsourcing level. These two decisions define the goals and scope of an outsourcing project and thereby establish the foundation for actions and decisions by both client and vendor throughout the project.

Outsourcing Level

Outsourcing level, as previously mentioned, refers to the scope of the outsourcing initiative undertaken by the client usually measured as the percentage of IS budget under third-party management. In general, projects that involve 80% or more of a company's IS budget being outsourced to a vendor are considered "total outsourcing," while projects that transfer 15% to 25% of the IS budget to a vendor are considered "selective outsourcing" (Willcocks & Lacity, 1999a).

Decisions about outsourcing level are important because the scope of the project is frequently correlated with the risks and rewards for both vendor and client. Total outsourcing projects typically incur more risks than smaller, selective outsourcing projects but also typically have greater expected rewards. This can have a major impact on the success or failure of the project. Willcocks and Lacity (1999b) analyzed 116 sourcing decisions over a period of 8 years and assessed objectives against outcomes, cost savings expected against those achieved, and satisfaction levels in client companies. They found 38% of total outsourcing projects were considered successful, 35% deemed a failure, and 27% had mixed results (Willcocks & Lacity, 1999b). By contrast, 77% of selective outsourcing projects were successful, 20% ended in failure, and only 3% had mixed results (Willcocks & Lacity, 1999b).

The superiority of selective outsourcing over total outsourcing can be attributed to the fact that IS is a heterogeneous function, encompassing such diverse elements as data centers, telecommunications networks, applications development, and systems integration (Barthelemy & Geyer, 2004). Selective outsourcing is a way to meet client needs while minimizing the risks associated with total outsourcing approaches. Barthelemy and Geyer (2004) found that companies tend to favor selective outsourcing when performance improvement motivation is strong, IS departments are large, and the company is in an IS-intensive industry. However, companies tend to choose total outsourcing when they need to quickly cut IS costs (Barthelemy & Geyer, 2004).

Copperweld Corporation is an example of a successful total outsourcing project that arose from the need to quickly cut costs. Copperweld, a steel fabricator based in Pittsburgh, PA, was strapped for cash when the U.S. steel industry was in financial trouble during the early 1980s (Gupta & Gupta, 1992). In an effort to rapidly cut costs, Copperweld outsourced its entire IS department to Genix Enterprises, Inc., another Pittsburgh-based company. The project was a success — estimates showed that Copperweld saved approximately $4 million a year, or about half of what it cost to run its IS operations (Gupta & Gupta, 1992).

KeyCorp, a bank based in Cleveland, Ohio, is engaged in a successful selective outsourcing project with ABN Amro for trade finance processing (Quittner, 2004). ABN Amro is one of the largest banks for trade finance and has developed significant expertise and capabilities in facilitating import and export letters of credit and collections, open account processing, and purchase order management (Quittner, 2004). The agreement between KeyCorp and ABN Amro allows KeyCorp to tap into the prowess of ABN Amro and offer private labeled state-of-the-art trade finance products and services, while minimizing customer attrition (Quittner, 2004). This project is described as a "carefully focused and managed outsourcing strategy" (Quittner, 2004, p. 32) that leverages ABN Amro's IS skills to improve the competitiveness of KeyCorp, thereby satisfying the needs of both companies.

One of the prime reasons for failure of outsourcing projects is the inability (or failure) to specify the scope, or level, of the project (Willcocks & Lacity, 1999a). This was the case with the outsourcing arrangement between Bezeq, a telecommunications company and the client, and AMS, a software company and the vendor. The original project called for AMS to work with two other software vendors and Bezeq's IS department to deliver a new billing system. However, the scope of the project continually broadened and eventually reached a point where AMS could no longer fulfill Bezeq's requirements (Natovich, 2003). After two years, Bezeq cancelled the project, claiming breach of contract by AMS, and one year later, Bezeq recovered all payments made to AMS in an out-of-court settlement (Natovich, 2003).

There are a few key lessons to be learned regarding outsourcing level. First, the level of the proposed project, either selective or total, should be clearly specified as this decision influences all other stages of the outsourcing project. Also, outsourcing level should be matched to strategic intent to ensure consistency between project objectives and scope. Finally, it bears mentioning that at this stage of the process the question "Should we outsource?" is still valid and "No" is an option. Even though IS outsourcing has become all the rage, it may not be a good option for every firm. Companies, including giants like Wal-Mart, may evaluate their options and conclude that regardless of the level or strategic intent of IS outsourcing, it is not currently in the company's best interest to pursue outsourcing. According to Linda Dillman, Wal-Mart Stores CIO and executive vice president:

We don't do any outsourcing. That's kind of a controversial stance to take, but it's worked for us. We've had CIOs tell us we're doomed to failure if we don't outsource, and that it isn't cost-effective to do everything ourselves. But we've found that with outsourcing, although the cost per labor hour is cheaper, the overall project cost is higher. (Chain Store Age, 2004, p. 20A)

Vendor Selection

There are several important considerations related to selecting a vendor (or vendors) for IS service provision. One, as pointed out by Ms. Dillman (Chain Store Age, 2004), is to benchmark vendor costs against the cost of providing IS services internally to assess whether cost savings can be realized through outsourcing. Another critical aspect is for both client and vendor to be sensitive to the potential of a so-called winner's curse, where the vendor's bid is lower than its projected expenses for the project (thus guaranteeing a loss on the contract), and take steps to avoid the resulting problems. Finally, the client must perform due diligence to evaluate prospective vendors' resource availability and capability to complete the project.

For companies to assess the economic impact of outsourcing, they must first be able to quantify their internal costs on the IS products or services being considered for outsourcing. For example, Strassman (2004) offers the case of a computer mouse that retails for $40, with $20.50 in total costs. If an IS outsourcing contract were signed for this product that generated 10% IS cost savings, approximately 6.6 cents of total costs would be saved on each mouse (Strassman, 2004). This is important information for companies to have because "more than 50% of IT outsourcing agreements fail for lack of comparative information" (Hall, 2003, p. 10). Additionally, companies:

... often discover that much of the money saved by sending work outside is eaten up by the costs of managing the outsourcer relationship. Also common is for the outsider to bungle the service quality. Arming yourself with apple-to-apple comparisons and measurable service level agreements can boost outsourcing success rates to higher than 75% ... That's because you might discover that the best and most cost-effective work can be done inside the organization, so you outsource fewer tasks. (Hall, 2004, p. 10)

Understanding internal costs provides an objective benchmark against which vendor proposals can be compared.

If prospective vendors want to win an outsourcing contract badly enough (for prestige, long-term business opportunities, etc.), they will sometimes engage in bidding at or below their projected costs, virtually guaranteeing a loss on the project while assuming that additional business will arise upon which they can make a profit. This is called a "winner's curse" by Kern, Willcocks, and van Heck (2002) because the vendor who wins the contract is cursed with a financial loss on the project. The problem sometimes occurs unintentionally when vendors bid on contracts with incomplete information and the scope of the project grows beyond what the vendor can deliver for the originally agreed-upon price, as in the case of Bezeq and AMS. A winner's curse can cause severe strain on the relationship between client and vendor and have a negative impact on the entire project (Kern et al., 2002). If companies have an internal cost benchmark, they can use this information to evaluate vendors' bids and try to avoid a winner's curse by ensuring that the outsourcing arrangement is viable for both parties.

In addition to understanding the cost aspects of vendor selection, companies should be prepared to undertake rigorous due-diligence processes to ensure that the selected vendors possess the resources and capabilities necessary to fulfill the outsourcing project's objectives (Lankford & Parsa, 1999). Kim and Chung (2003) state that vendor capability is the most critical factor for successful implementation of IS outsourcing because companies usually turn to outsourcing when they lack the needed capabilities internally. Therefore, the vendor must have the experience, technical competence, and financial resources to meet the client's strategic and technical goals for the duration of the project (Kim & Chung, 2003).

Due-diligence processes frequently involve both client and vendor asking questions and exchanging information beyond that included in the request for proposal and bid. This is important because the IS environment of an organization is often too highly integrated to objectively evaluate the actual service costs and technical requirements (Kern et al., 2002). Companies find that:

... selecting a supplier is a costly undertaking in terms of time, effort, and resources. However, the investment in identifying the right supplier and contract bid is paramount to the success of the overall outsourcing venture. (Kern et al., 2002, p. 48)

A successful vendor selection effort can lead to a successful outsourcing project, as in the case of Polaris outsourcing their software development to Logica (Willcocks & Lacity, 1999a). Before soliciting bids, Polaris outlined detailed selection criteria and quantified its internal service levels and costs (Kern et al., 2002). Once Logica was identified as the preferred vendor, a 3-month due-diligence period was undertaken to assess Logica's ability to fulfill the objectives of the project (Kern et al., 2002). These steps laid the foundation for a successful partnership between Polaris and Logica that eventually led to new business opportunities for both companies (Kern et al., 2002).

Vendor selection efforts are not all as successful as Polaris. Enetfinity Technologies LLC chose an outsourcing partner based in India without fully evaluating the vendor's capabilities (Ferguson, 2004).

Kelvin Johnson, vice president of sales and marketing and a technical consultant at Enetfinity, [says] "Our experience [has been] that a lot of people there are good at programming, but they aren't good at the business-logic part of application development. ... You can give them a project to work on, and they'll do maybe a good 75 percent of what you want. But there's that 20 percent you'll end up pulling your hair out about that you'll have to redo or bring other people in from over here to finish or redo." (Ferguson, 2004, p. 10)

When the contract expires, Johnson says:

I'm not sure what we'll do, to be quite honest. They have done some good things, but you contract for more — we expected more than we've got. Most people are just looking for results. When there's money involved and you end up losing, that doesn't put a good taste in your mouth. (Ferguson, 2004, p. 10)

The lessons associated with vendor selection are: first, benchmark the internal costs and service levels for the IS products and services to be outsourced prior to soliciting bids; second, carefully analyze the reasons for a low vendor bid and whether the bid can result in a profit for the vendor; and third, undertake a rigorous due-diligence process before a contract is finalized (Kern et al., 2002). As previously noted, vendor selection is a critical stage in the outsourcing process for IS projects. Kim and Chung (2003) studied 207 outsourcing relationships and found that vendor capability is a significant predictor of IS outsourcing success. Once a vendor (or vendors) is selected and due-diligence is completed, the focus shifts to contract negotiation.

Contract Negotiation

During contract negotiations, project details such as scope of work, service level, length of contract, performance measures, and structure of rewards and penalties are spelled out. The contract should reflect both the strategic intent and level of the outsourcing project.

Senior managers must understand that for each kind of strategic intent, the nature of both the risks and rewards are different, and therefore the control mechanisms must be different. The challenge is to design the contract and relationship so that the selected options contribute to the client company's objectives. (DiRomualdo & Gurbaxani, 1998, p. 69)

Several authors (DiRomualdo & Gurbaxani, 1998; Lee et al., 2003; Quittner, 2004) indicate that outsourcing contracts must be flexible enough to accommodate changes in the project. Additionally, provisions for dealing with uncertainty should be specified to the extent possible (Lee et al., 2003). Performance measures should be clearly defined and easy to calculate (Quittner, 2004). Service levels should also be specified and included in the assessment of vendor rewards and penalties.

Successful contract negotiations can help mitigate risk and transition into the project management phase. In the case of Polaris' outsourcing deal with vendor Logica, flexibility and risk management were addressed through staged contracting (Willcocks & Lacity, 1999a).

This can be seen in the Polaris deal with the possibility of termination after 3.5 years, and a right to terminate with 6 months notice thereafter, though the declared intention is a 7-year contract period. Risk is also mitigated by a continuity clause requiring the vendor to smooth transition to any preferred arrangement in the event of termination. The contract also has highly detailed price-service level resource requirement stipulations, with mechanisms in place for regular review to ensure all prices are competitive. Regular review builds in contractual flexibility needed to deal with changes in volume and/or type of business and technical requirements. There are also a battery of 20 sets of performance measures against which the supplier is monitored regularly and can be penalized on. (Willcocks & Lacity, 1999a, p. 176)

However, if the contract for an IS outsourcing project does not match the strategic intent and level of the project it can contribute to the failure of the entire project.

Recently, the state of Connecticut in The United States spent millions of dollars and over three years negotiating one the of the most ambitious outsourcing deals of a government ever, only to see the deal collapse before completion. Both parties, the government and the primary vendor, provide amicable, though contrasting explanations for the deal's demise. While no single factor is evident, it is fair to conclude that the requisite mix of political acceptability and profitability could not be achieved in an adequate fashion due, in part, to a tremendous emphasis on contracting specifications, objectives, terms and conditions — a process fundamentally at odds with the trust and collaboration required to partner on such a massive scale. (Allen et al., 2001, p. 99)

There are a few lessons to be learned about contract negotiation. As with all other stages of an IS outsourcing project, the contract must be aligned with the strategic intent and level of the project. Also, contracts must be intentionally designed to be flexible to accommodate changes in the project or available technology. Performance measures must be clearly defined and linked to service level agreements. However, contracts should not be "Byzantine documents thick with legalese" (Quittner, 2004, p. 32) that prohibit formation of trust, commitment, and mutual interest between client and vendor. Striking a balance between contracts that are sufficiently specific and those that are too rigid and inflexible is as much an art as a science. It relies on collaboration between client and vendor and sets a tone for the remainder of the project.

Project Management and Monitoring

Upon completion of the outsourcing contract, the project enters the management and monitoring stage, when the work really begins. "Robust contracts mean little if the client then sees outsourcing as 'spending, not managing' and turns away from active management of the supplier" (Willcocks & Lacity, 1999a, p. 176). If the client fails to take an active role in the outsourcing project, it risks its ability to leverage the vendor's performance and may even compromise the project outcome. Key issues in project management and monitoring of IS outsourcing projects include the nature of the relationship between client and vendor, conflict resolution mechanisms, retained skills and capabilities for the client, and the level of commitment to the project of both client and vendor.

The nature of the relationship between client and vendor should be a reflection of the strategic intent of the IS outsourcing project. As projects move toward business impact and especially commercial exploitation intents, an effective partnership between client and vendor becomes a key predictor of outsourcing success (Lee et al., 2003). If the partnership sours, conflict resolution mechanisms such as arbitration, mediation, and sometimes renegotiation must be employed in an effort to repair the relationship and save the project (Natovich, 2003).

As the project progresses, the client must work to retain the skills and capabilities necessary for future IS operations beyond the duration of the outsourcing project (Willcocks & Lacity, 1999a). Retained skills and capabilities for the client are often included in contract negotiations as the vendor must facilitate the transfer of skills and capabilities to the client's in-house staff. Retained skills and capabilities important to the client may include business systems thinking capability, applications maintenance and support, and technical skills related to technical architecture and technology "fixing" (Willcocks & Lacity, 1999a).

As the project wears on toward conclusion (or if the relationship between client and vendor is in conflict), both client and vendor must sustain their level of commitment to the project. Natovich (2003) indicates that in addition to full commitment to the IS outsourcing project by the client's management, the vendor management's commitment is critical to project success. Usually contractual obligations are sufficient to ensure the vendor's sustained commitment, but in cases where the vendor incurs financial losses on the project, vendor management may choose to de-escalate its commitment to reduce or prevent additional losses (Natovich, 2003). However, financial loss may be offset and de-escalation of commitment avoided if the project has strategic value for the vendor beyond the current project (Natovich, 2003).

An example of successful project management and monitoring and client-vendor partnership is Saint Vincent Catholic Medical Centers (SVCMC) in New York. In 2000, SVCMC signed a 7-year IS outsourcing contract with Computer Sciences Corporation (CSC) (One nonprofit's award-winning, 2004). The project was intended to generate significant business impact and was a nearly total outsourcing arrangement (One nonprofit's award-winning, 2004).

The key factor that made the outsourcing deal a success was that the arrangement was viewed as a "strategic partnership" — not merely the contracting out of an organizational function ... "CSC locked in on our strategic direction and mission, enabling us to maximize our operations and provide better service to our patients," said David J. Campbell, CEO and president for SVCMC. On the same token, SVCMC regarded CSC as more of an 'insourcer,' treating it just like a member of the organization, indistinguishable from other departments or employees. (One nonprofit's award-winning, 2004, p. 5)

In addition to the partnership quality, SVCMC actively worked with CSC to ensure the project's success by monitoring progress against pre-established benchmarks and maintaining a high level of commitment to the project (One nonprofit's award-winning, 2004).

Not all projects are as collaborative as the SVCMC-CSC deal. The IS outsourcing project between Bezeq and AMS discussed previously suffered from frequent conflicts between client and vendor over critical issues, including scope of work and cost. "It is interesting to note that, during the long history of the disputes ... the possibility of arbitration was not exploited, although this dispute resolution mechanism was clearly prescribed by the contract" (Natovich, 2003, p. 413). Due to the inability to resolve the problems related to project scope and costs, AMS notified Bezeq that it "intended to withdraw from its commitment to the project owing to expected heavy losses" (Natovich, 2003, p. 414). This led to termination of the project and eventual litigation.

Because IS outsourcing arrangements are projects, they rely on active project management and monitoring of the vendor by the client for success. The relationship between client and vendor should be aligned with strategic intent. Specific conflict resolution mechanisms should be included in the outsourcing contract and employed if conflicts arise. The client must sustain its commitment to the project through continuous involvement with the vendor, which also facilitates retention of skills and capabilities needed after project completion. Finally, vendor commitment to the project should be supported by structuring the contract to ensure the project's profitability for the vendor and reinforced through communication with the client.

Project Renewal or Termination

The stages of an IS outsourcing project are cumulative, and at some point the aggregated actions lead to a decision about renewing or terminating the project. This can be a delicate point in the relationship between client and vendor as each party tries to look after its own interests, while keeping open the option for future collaboration. Anderson et al. (2004) estimate that approximately 70% of existing outsourcing agreements are renewed, "yet many of these renewals often encompass reduced scope, modified service levels, price changes, and alteration to duration of the original agreement." When projects are terminated, either at or before the end of the contract, both companies try to put a positive spin on the termination to preserve dignity and reputation. As Anderson et al. (2004) remind companies facing the termination of an outsourcing project, "discretion is the better part of valor."

JPMorgan Chase and IBM heeded this advice as their massive outsourcing project was cancelled three years into an eight-year contract. Both companies downplayed the early termination, instead choosing to highlight their ongoing outsourcing relationships in other areas of business (Anderson et al., 2004). However, the end of a project is not always so civilized. Bezeq and AMS spent approximately four months, after it became apparent that the conflicts between them could not be resolved, "continu[ing] with the project, tread[ing] carefully so as not to breach the contract, and wait[ing] for the other party to do so" (Natovich, 2003, p. 415). Eventually, Bezeq accused AMS of breach of contract and cancelled the project, which led to a series of lawsuits and counter lawsuits that culminated in an out-of-court settlement (Natovich, 2003). In the end, neither company achieved their objectives for the project and both lost time and money (Natovich, 2003).

It is interesting to note that successful project renewals receive little press compared to project terminations. It is possible that this is a case of "no news is good news," but it may also provide tacit support for the 70% renewal rate for outsourcing projects cited by Anderson et al. (2004). Further, the outcome of an IS outsourcing project is a symptom of the foregoing stages, such that projects with clearly articulated and integrated strategic intent and level, carefully selected vendor(s), thoughtful contract negotiations, and diligent project management and monitoring are set up for renewal or amicable termination. In this way, the lessons associated with project renewal or termination are essentially a summation of the preceding lessons. Some authors point to a key element as critical to the outcome — success or failure — of an outsourcing project. This chapter contends that there is not one key element that makes or breaks a deal, but a series of interconnected decisions that cumulatively create the project outcome. Put another way, the whole is greater than the sum of the parts in IS outsourcing projects.

Conclusion

Information systems outsourcing is expected to continue to grow as more companies seek to leverage the IS-specific competencies of vendors. As evident from the preceding discussion, IS outsourcing projects are complex undertakings that require a considerable investment of time, effort, and money from both client and vendor. The examples of IS outsourcing successes and failures presented in this chapter offer some lessons for companies considering IS outsourcing. Perhaps the first lesson is to clearly articulate and integrate the strategic intent and level of the outsourcing project. These two decisions establish the basis for the entire project and deserve thorough consideration. Sometime during these initial stages, the client must quantify its internal costs for providing the products and/or services being considered for outsourcing. This creates a benchmark against which to evaluate bids from potential vendors. When selecting a vendor, the client must verify that the vendor possesses the resources and capabilities to meet the stated strategic intent and level objectives. Further, the client has a responsibility to ensure that the proposed deal is viable for the vendor to avoid the complications of a winner's curse. The contract between client and vendor must balance the competing demands of specific enumeration of scope of work, service levels, and performance measures and the flexibility to accommodate changes in the project. The contract negotiations stage should also anticipate conflict between the parties and detail appropriate conflict resolution mechanisms. During the project management and monitoring stage, both client and vendor must sustain their commitments to the project and proactively work to resolve any conflicts that may arise. De-escalation of commitment by either party jeopardizes the project outcome. Finally, when it is time to renew or terminate the project, this decision in shaped by all the preceding stages. Conscientious management of the project's earlier stages should make renewal or termination a smooth and natural outcome. These lessons are summarized in Table 2.

This chapter takes a macrolevel view of the IS outsourcing process and considers the interconnectedness of all stages of the project. Examples of success and failure are presented at each stage. One of the challenges of research into IS outsourcing is the difficulty in generalizing across companies and industries because information systems are so heterogeneous. Focusing on the process of IS outsourcing, rather than specific techniques, may help overcome these difficulties. Avenues for future research into the process of IS outsourcing include refinement of the process map presented herein, possible empirical tests of the strength of relationships between stages, and exploration of methods to "fail-safe" the process.

Table 2. Lessons learned about information systems outsourcing

Lesson
• Articulate and integrate the strategic intent and level of the outsourcing project.
• Quantify client's internal costs for providing the products and/or services being considered for outsourcing.
• Verify that the vendor possesses the resources and capabilities to meet the stated strategic intent and level objectives.
• Ensure that the proposed deal is viable for the vendor.
• Balance the competing contractual demands of specific enumeration of scope of work, service levels, and performance measures and the flexibility to accommodate changes in the project.
• Anticipate conflict between client and vendor and detail appropriate conflict resolution mechanisms in the contract.
• Sustain client's and vendor's commitment to the project and proactively work to resolve any conflicts that may arise.
• Manage the earlier stages of the project to make renewal or termination a smooth and natural outcome.

References

Allen, B. A., Juillet, L., Paquet, G., & Roy, J. (2001). E-governance & government on-line in Canada: Partnerships, people and prospects. *Government Information Quarterly, 18,* 93-104.

Allnoch, A. (1997). Outsourcing can boost profitability. *IIE Solutions, 29*(8), 9.

Anderson, D., Davison, D., & Lepeak, S. (2004). *JPMorgan and IBM: Breaking up (outsourcing deals) is hard to do, but sometimes you should.* Retrieved March 15, 2005 from http://www.itproportal.com/8C2 970FE82D1DD4487FC227ED38DC571/article.asp

An eye toward outsourcing. (2004, November). *Chain Store Age, 80,* 18A-20A.

Barthelemy, J., & Geyer, D. (2004). The determinants of total IT outsourcing: An empirical investigation of French and German firms. *Journal of Computer Information Systems, 44,* 91-97.

DiRomualdo, A., & Gurbaxani, V. (1998). Strategic intent for IT outsourcing. *Sloan Management Review, 39*(4), 67-80.

Due, R. T. (1995). The knowledge economy. *Information Systems Management, 12*(3), 76-78.

Ferguson, R. B. (2004). Bringing IT home again. *eWeek, 21*(36), 9-10.

Gupta, U. G., & Gupta, A. (1992). Outsourcing the IS function. *Information Systems Management, 9*(3), 44-50.

Hall, M. (2003). Outsourcing deals fail half the time. *Computerworld, 37*(44), 10.

Kern, T., Willcocks, L. P., & van Heck, E. (2002). The winner's curse in IT outsourcing: Strategies for avoiding relational trauma. *California Management Review, 44*(2), 47-69.

Kim, S., & Chung, Y.-S. (2003). Critical success factors for IS outsourcing implementation from an interorganizational relationship perspective. *Journal of Computer Information Systems, 43,* 81-90.

Lacity, M. C., & Willcocks, L. P. (1998). An empirical investigation of information technology sourcing practices: Lessons from experience. *MIS Quarterly, 22,* 363-408.

Lacity, M. C., Willcocks, L. P., & Feeny, D. F. (1996). The value of selective IT sourcing. *Sloan Management Review, 37*(3), 13-25.

Lankford, W. M., & Parsa, F. (1999). Outsourcing: A primer. *Management Decision, 37,* 310-316.

Lee, J.-N., Huynh, M. Q., Kwok, R. C.-W., & Pi, S.-M. (2003). IT outsourcing evolution: Past, present and future. *Communications of the ACM, 46*(5), 84-89.

Natovich, J. (2003). Vendor related risks in IT development: A chronology of an outsourced project failure. *Technology Analysis & Strategic Management, 15*, 409-419.

One nonprofit's award-winning IT outsourcing setup. (2004, April). *Nonprofit Business Advisor, 7*(175), 5-7.

Quittner, J. (2004). A reversal of fortune? *Bank Technology News, 17*(12), 31-33.

Strassman, P. A. (2004). Pick your perspective on IT outsourcing. *Computerworld, 38*(14), 30.

Willcocks, L. P., & Lacity, M. C. (1999a). IT outsourcing in insurance services: Risk, creative contracting and business advantage. *Information Systems Journal, 9*, 163-180.

Willcocks, L. P., & Lacity, M. C. (1999b, April). Information technology outsourcing — practices, lessons and prospects. *ASX Perspective,* 44-49.

Chapter IX

Information System Outsourcing Decision:
Case Study on the Automotive Industry

Rafael Lapiedra, University Jaume I, Spain

Joaquin Alegre, University Valencia, Spain

Ricardo Chiva, University Jaume I, Spain

Steve Smithson, London School of Economics and Political Science, UK

Abstract

Outsourcing decisions in information technology (IT) research has yielded contradictory findings and recommendations. However, companies are increasingly outsourcing all or some of their information systems (IS) activities. This chapter examines the potential problems a company may face under this strategy. For this purpose, we conducted an empirical study in a European car manufacturing company that has followed the outsourcing alternative. The case analyzed offers insights about the outsourcing decision process and the difficulties the company faced when trying to adapt the software developed to the new business requirements. The problems that came out pushed the company to move back to the internalisation of the IS functions. The case shows a greater involvement of users on in-house developed projects. Our findings indicate that outsourcing is a good alternative when the IS activity is a technical one which does not require specific knowledge of the company.

Introduction

Information systems (IS) development is a complex activity that requires close communication among users, information systems personnel, and senior managers. From the 1980s on, among business organisations there has been a trend towards the outsourcing of information systems functions. IS outsourcing may be defined as the act of subcontracting a part, or all, of an organisation's IS work to external vendors to manage on its behalf (Altinkemer, Chaturvedi, & Gulati, 1994).

Some authors have analysed the reasons why companies outsource (Ang & Cummings, 1997; Ang & Straub, 1998; Lacity & Willcocks, 2000; Slaughter & Ang, 1996). The experience of outsourcing has brought the desired results to some companies, but others have suffered many difficulties (Ang & Toh, 1998). Outsourcing always entail some dangers. The companies should evaluate the problems related with the transfer of its IS to an outsider.

This chapter addresses three research questions. First, following prior research in IS outsourcing, we outline reasons why many companies have moved towards outsourcing. Second, we will try to identify the risks and problems associated with outsourcing. Finally, the chapter attempts to provide an answer to the questions regarding which IS projects could be outsourced. We have followed a qualitative approach analysing a detailed case where, after having suffered the problems associated with the previous decision of outsourcing software development, the company makes the decision to start from the beginning with an in-house development.

Theoretical Background

It is necessary to remark that, as far as organisational strategy is concerned, there is no generalizable universally valid solution. The current conditions in which enterprises must develop their activities demand, more than ever, a deep analysis of their competitive position, their strengths and weaknesses, and an awareness of the threats and opportunities existing in the new context. Every enterprise has to study carefully the different options, and choose a strategy that furnishes better prospects for survival and success.

The enterprise must select from a series of alternatives to obtain the necessary resources and reach sufficient flexibility to successfully face up to the new conditions:

1.   Resorting to new investments that facilitate the acquisition of the elements the company lacks.

2.   Getting the necessary resources by means of mergers or acquisitions of other companies.

3.   Going to the market to purchase the required resources.

In economics terms, the set of variables affecting the choice comprises reaching scale economies, technological supplying, profitability level, the endowment of experience and knowledge levels, the availability of financial resources, and transaction costs.

Traditionally, transactions within a particular economy can be regulated by two basic types of institutions: companies and markets (Jarillo, 1989). The market model assumes a framework where the relationship between the economic agents becomes just a set of buying and selling operations, by means of which an agent pays a price, perfectly known by him and, in turn, he receives a service. The relationship between the agents is completed once the exchange has been performed. The market displays some restrictions for managing specific trans-actions and these give rise to what are known as transaction costs (Jarillo, 1989).

Many companies have recently decided to focus on their core competencies, concentrating on what the organisation does better than anyone else while outsourcing the remaining activities. Within this general context, some compa-nies consider the IS function as a noncore activity, whose cost can be reduced through outsourcing.

From the late 1980s there has been a trend towards the outsourcing of information systems. Hoffman (1997) states that 40% of the biggest companies in the United States decided to outsource parts of their information systems. Even the U.S. Department of Defense outsourced some portions of their information systems (Brower, 1997). Some authors give reasons why companies outsource their information systems (Ang & Cummings, 1997, Ang & Straub, 1998, Lacity & Willcocks, 2000, Slaughter & Ang, 1996). In the next section we will summarise those reasons.

Reasons for Outsourcing

The IS literature offers many reasons that justify the decision to outsource the information system function. We have grouped those reasons into five blocks: strategic, economic, market efficiency, managers' expectations, and technical reasons.

Strategic

- Companies focus on their core competencies and consider that the IS function is a noncore activity or a utility (Lacity & Hirschheim, 1993).
- Employees may focus on their own core competencies (Polo, Piattini & Ruiz, 2002).
- In the case of a merger or acquisition of a company, outsourcing helps to solve the technical incompatibilities and absorb the excess IS assets (Lacity & Hirschheim, 1993).

Reduction of Costs

- Savings in personnel, training, and management.
- Transfer from fixed to variable costs.
- Development of cost process control; with outsourcing it is easier to gain an accurate estimation of costs before the service is provided. The company receives a service whose price is perfectly known (Kirsch, Sambamurthi, Ko, & Purbis, 2002). In IT outsourcing, the contract between the client organization and the vendor organization states explicitly the specific terms and conditions of the relationship between them.
- When the IS function is offered internally users usually demand and consume resources excessively. When a business unit hires an outsourcing service it has a better control of the cost, and it helps to reduce excessive demands for information systems services.

Market Efficiency

- IS activities are developed by external skilled people whose essential competence is focused on those activities; this means a specialist who, in order to maintain himself in the market, must invest in research and development for profit.

Managers Expectations

- Most business unit managers consider the IS function as a utility, or commodity (Carr, 2003), whose cost should be minimised. Business managers perceive that outsourcing is likely to save them money because external companies gain economies of scale and can pass them on through lower costs, an option that is normally not open to internal IS departments.

- In many organisations there is a dissatisfaction with the services provided by their in-house IS departments (Ho, Ang, & Straub, 2003). This is one reason for initiating outsourcing evaluations where there is a tendency to evaluate the function solely on cost efficiency (Quinn, Doorley, & Paquette, 1990).

Technical Reasons

- Access to technical talent. Senior managers may believe that through outsourcing the company can profit from the technical expertise and talent of external experts (Lacity & Hirschheim, 1999).

- Outsourcing is one way to gain access to new emerging technologies.

Problems with Outsourcing

Companies are increasingly outsourcing some or all of their IS activities (Cross, 1995; Huber, 1993; Lacity & Hirschheim, 1993). The information systems literature has mostly seen outsourcing positively but we believe that a company should take the decision to outsource its information systems very carefully as outsourcing carries with it many disadvantages. A company that decides to outsource parts of its information system suffers a loss of control and loses an important source of learning that should contribute positively to the know-how of an organisation. When outsourcing, the company loses knowledge of the software and has a greater dependency on the supplier.

Information systems development is a complex, intensive and dynamic activity that requires close cooperation and contribution among diverse stakeholders: users, information systems personnel, and senior managers (Beath, 1987). When a project is developed internally and users and developers belong to the same organisation it is easier to acquire this interconnection but when the developer is remotely located there is a loss of communication richness (Carmel, 1999), and coordination problems may arise.

Socialization, shared experiences, and rituals promoting shared beliefs and common goals are more difficult to achieve between members of two different companies (Lacity & Willcocks, 2001) and there is a high probability of suffering a lack of "teamness" (Carmel, 1999).

In an outsourced project, direct observation of the actions of the developer is harder than in internal development projects (Nicholson & Sahay, 2001). The design and use of effective, cross-organizational information systems that reliably inform the company about the development progress are likely to require a greater investment of a manager's time in an outsourced context than in internal development projects (Choudhury & Sabherwal, 2003). Kirsch (1997) states that in the case of an outsourced development project, it requires the establishment of formal controls, but these never give the continuous feedback that can be achieved with the internalisation of the development process.

Ring and Van de Ven (1994) proposed that an interorganisational relationship evolves through sequences of negotiation, commitment, and execution. Doz (1996) identified different cycles of learning, reevaluation, and readjustment of long term interorganisational relationships. As the two sides learn from their interactions, they reassess the alliance and make adjustments. Lapiedra, Smithson, Alegre, and Chiva (2004) describe the adaptation process between companies that create a network.

In the following section we analyse the case of a European car manufacturer that, after a period when the outsourcing alternative seemed ideal, is now moving back to internalise most of the IS function.

Research Methodology

The purpose of our study was to obtain a richer description and understanding not only about the nature of the phenomenon, but also about the factors affecting it, and effects arising from expectations within an organisational context. According to our objective we considered it appropriate to follow a qualitative approach for our research. In order to select a company as a case study, three attributes were sought: (1) an outsourced IS development, (2) recent completion, and (3) top management's willingness to allow a detailed case study. These conditions were satisfied by a big European car manufacturing group, whose top management gave us access but preferred to remain anonymous.

The senior manager who allowed the case study was interviewed first and asked to describe the IS development process and identify the participants. The participants interviewed were the leader of one IS project and the head of organisation and systems of the related business unit. We also interviewed some of the system users.

We followed semi-structured interviews with managers and system users of the company. The project was related to the development of a software package to manage their relationship with large customers. The software developed was being implemented to substitute software developed by an external company.

The interview sessions were conducted over a 2-week period. The interviews lasted an average of two hours and we had two interviews with each of the managers and with some users of the system. Previously, we developed an interview protocol to guide the interviews in describing the decision process to outsource, its repercussions, and especially the reasons for undertaking the software development internally. The questions followed three main themes:

1.   Reasons to outsource the IS function

2.   Evaluation of the system and relationship with the vendor

3.   Decision process to internalise IS function

In each interview one of the authors led the discussion and another author took notes, which were compiled and transcribed for analysis.

The following section presents the case study with some samples of responses that illustrate the views of our interviewees and which provide insight concerning the decision process of outsourcing, and the reasons which influence any decision to internalise the information system function of the company.

Case: Software Development for Managing Large Customers

In the case analysis, we study the development of software specially designed to manage large customers. We study the process followed from the need for the development to the subsequent decisions taken to outsource and finally develop in-house the computerised tool.

The idea to develop the system came from the users, as the Head of Organisation and Systems recognized:

The users requested a specific application for the management of large customers, but the head office rejected the proposal because it hadn't been budgeted for at the beginning of the financial year. For this reason, one business unit, bearing in mind the usefulness of the tool, decided to develop this application for themselves.

After making the decision, the pioneering business unit had to choose between either the in-house development of the software or hiring an external company. After a financial comparison between the alternatives and taking into account that the external company was able to meet the demand faster and cheaper, the business unit decided to outsource the request:

An estimate was made of the cost of developing the application internally which was far higher than that established by the consulting firm.

The choice to outsource was based on a combination of a very reduced time frame and a reasonable price offered by the vendor, who signed a fixed-price contract for the development. The contract included a formal specification of the required system functionality, although some aspects were specified at a broader level.

In many organisations there is dissatisfaction with the services provided by their in-house IS departments. During the interviews we heard sentences like:

The IS department delivered systems late and 40% more expensive than initially budgeted.

The developed software never matches our expectations. It is always necessary to include adjustments and this requires time.

Senior managers think that through outsourcing the company may profit from the technical expertise and talent of external consultants.

The business management agreed to contract the services of an external consulting firm charged with developing the application. The necessary administrative procedures were followed and the services of a consulting firm with a very competitive price were contracted to develop the application.

They observed that early on in the project, efficiency benefits from outsourcing were considerable, but later, as the project moved to use and maintenance, the costs of managing the external vendor might become too high. As the interviewee responsible for the project stated:

A company is not a static thing, but rather, its processes change and require its systems to change at the same time. Thus, after a few years of working with the tool, an update was requested, and the estimate for this work from the consulting firm far exceeded cost expectations.

This view was underlined by the Head of Organisation and Systems:

The improvement of the tool had a very high cost.

The company did not have access to modify the software developed externally, and the vendor was clearly in a strong bargaining position; "they tried to make use of this better position" as the Head of Organisation and Systems said.

In the same way that the group applications are closed to the outside, we do not have access to the source code of the program designed by the consulting firm. We buy the application, not the source. (IT Project Manager)

Then, the company began to think about the possibility of starting again from the beginning with the in-house development of the software, so they would not have such a dependency on the vendor and would have better control of the process. The business unit also took into account in the decision process that there were skilled people within the company to develop the system. As the Head of Organisation and Systems recognised:

We have a very competent IT Department, possibly small sized companies might require more help from external assessors.

Successful development requires a mixture of capabilities but also motivation and involvement of the people working on the project.

The staff in our IT department is much more involved with the company than the consultant who has a mere contractual relationship in which a service is provided in exchange for economic remuneration.

Members of the IT department staff are much more receptive to suggestions from the users for changes in the tool being developed if they can appreciate that the application with the changes included is more to the users' liking, although at times this may mean spending more time on the project than was at first envisaged.

In the in-house development period there was close communication among the participants, including programmers, analysts and users. The outcome of these frequent interactions was a strong sense of shared values and goals and shared responsibility for the project success.

We were part of the project. We all wanted it to be successful. (System user)

Everyone was working very hard for the system to work properly. We were like a team in the competition game. (Project leader)

A project may be qualified as a success when it has an adequate implementation. The analysed case may be considered as successful, according to the opinions of the different participants:

I haven't noticed any change in the IT tool. It works just the same, the only difference being that it now looks more like the other applications we use. (System user)

Internally, the connections with the group systems enable data introduced by the user to be integrated, thus making the process more automatic and avoiding the need to type the data in for a second time. This is only done once, which reduces the risk of errors being introduced. (Project leader)

We have used other technologies better adapted to our internal system that allow the system to absorb and integrate the data introduced in a terminal by the user. We could not do this with the old system designed by the consulting firm, which had one of their employees working in our company to introduce the data. (Project leader)

By dealing with the development of an application internally, the cost of introducing data is shared amongst various applications that integrate these data. (Head of Organisation and Systems)

Probably the best way to measure the success of the project is to review the words that the senior business unit manager said to his subordinates during an informal meeting:

The Large International Accounts department is studying the possibility of using the tool developed by this business unit for the whole group.

Nevertheless, the entire IS functions cannot be considered as one homogeneous utility. There are parts of the IS activities which can be easily outsourced at a lower cost than its internal realisation. As the Head of Organisation and Systems recognised:

However, this does not mean that we do not have to outsource part of our work and take advantage of low labor costs in countries such India, China, or Argentina, which in certain cases enable us to take advantage of time differences in order to reduce the application implementation time needed. For instance you can send something off at the end of your working day to be done in India and have it in your computer first thing in the morning the next day.

We still outsource mainly the parts of the computer system that can be developed without specific knowledge of the company, such as the migration of data in the updating of the version of a program. To give an example, we are now moving from Oracle.8 to the version Oracle.9, and this migration, which is a purely technical job, is being done for us by a company in Argentina with lower labor costs, and moreover ,they are experts in Oracle while our company has no expert in Oracle.

Conclusion

This chapter sought to examine and extend findings from research on the outsourcing of IS activities. There are an increasing number of vendors and services available in the market for IS outsourcing. As the outsourcing contracts evolve our learning about their implications also evolve. Our research found that practitioners must analyse the long term implications of choosing market offerings. This analysis must include a right understanding of the IS project contribution to the current and future company strategy. In our case, the interviewed managers highlighted only costs, but we think that the right alignment of the IS with company strategy may contribute significantly to competitive advantage also on differentiation. This desired alignment is more likely to be attained through the in-house alternative.

Information systems development is a complex activity that requires close communication among users, information systems personnel, and senior managers. Through a rich and continuous communication among those participants, it is easier to exchange information and ideas that can be transferred for the improvement of the IS project.

An important issue that should be included on the decision to outsource is the user acceptance of the new system. The early involvement of users in the information system development may increase their predisposition to work hard on the development of the new information system. The user's involvement should have a continuity and provide quick feedback to the IS personnel. In our case study, users felt much more motivated to work when the software was developed internally by the IS department.

References

Altinkemer, K., Chaturvedi, A., & Gulati, R. (1994). Information systems outsourcing: Issues and evidence. *International Journal of Information Management, 14*(4), 252-278.

Ang, S., & Cummings, L. L. (1997). Strategic responses to institutional influence on information systems outsourcing. *Organization Science, 8*(3), 235-256.

Ang, S., & Straub, W. (1998). Production and transaction economics in information systems outsourcing: A study of the U.S. banking industry. *MIS Quarterly, 22*(4), 535-552.

Ang, S., & Toh, S. (1998). Failure in software outsourcing: A case analysis. In L. Willcocks & M. Lacity (Eds.), *Strategic sourcing of information systems* (pp. 351-368). New York: John Wiley.

Beath, C. M. (1987). Managing the user relationship in information systems development projects: A transaction governance approach. In *Proceedings of the 8th International Conference on Information Systems* (pp. 415-427).

Brower, J. M. (1997, September). Outsourcing and privatising information technology. *The Journal of Defense Software Engineering,* 28-30.

Carmel, E. (1999). *Global software teams.* Englewood Cliffs, NJ: Prentice Hall.

Carr, N. G. (2003, May). IT doesn't matter. *Harvard Business Review*, 41-49.

Choudhury, V., & Sabherwal, R. (2003). Portfolios of control in outsourced software development projects. *Information Systems Research, 14*(3), 291-314.

Cross, J. (1995, May-June). IT outsourcing: British Petroleum's competitive approach. *Harvard Business Review,* 94-102.

Doz, Y. L. (1996). The evolution of cooperation in strategic alliances: Initial conditions or learning process. *Strategic Management Journal, 17,* 55-83.

Ho, V. T., Ang, S., & Straub, D. (2003). When subordinates become IT contractors: Persistent managerial expectations in IT outsourcing. *Information Systems Research, 14*(1), 66-86.

Hoffman, T. (1997, March). Users say move quickly when outsourcing your personnel. *Computer World, 77.*

Huber, R. L. (1993, January-February). How Continental Bank outsourced its crown jewels. *Harvard Business Review,* 121-129.

Jarillo, J. C. (1988). On strategic networks. *Strategic Management Journal, 9,* 31-41.

Kirsch, L. J. (1997). Portfolios of control modes and IS project management. *Information Systems Research, 8*(3), 215-239.

Kirsch, L. J., Sambamurthy, V., Ko, D., & Purvis, L. (2002). Controlling information systems development projects: The view from the client. *Management Science, 48*(4), 484-498.

Lacity, M. C., & Hirschheim, R. (1993). The information systems outsourcing bandwagon: Look before you leap. *Sloan Management Review, 35*(1), 72-86.

Lacity, M., & Willcocks, L. P. (2000). Survey of IT outsourcing experiences in U.S. and U.K. organizations. *Journal of Global Information Management, 8*(2), 5-23.

Lacity, M., & Willcocks, L. P. (2001). *Global information technology outsourcing.* Chichester, UK: Wiley.

Lapiedra, R., Smithson, S., Alegre, J., & Chiva, R. (2004). Role of information systems on the business network formation process: An empirical analysis of the automotive sector. *Journal of Enterprise Information Management, 17*(3), 219-228.

Nicholson, B., & Sahay, S. (2001). Some political and cultural issues in the globalisation of software development: Case experience from Britain and India. *Informatics Organization, 11,* 25-43.

Polo, M., Piattini, M., & Ruiz, F. (2002). Integrating outsourcing in the maintenance process. *Information and Management, 3*, 247-269.

Quinn, J., Doorley, T., & Paquette, P. (1990). Technology in services: Rethinking strategic focus. *Sloan Management Review, 31*(2), 79-87.

Ring, P. A., & Van de Ven, A. (1994). Developmental process of cooperative interorganizational relationships. *Academy of Management Review, 19*(1), 90-118.

Slaughter, S., & Ang, S. (1996). *Communications of the ACM, 39*(7), 47-54.

Chapter X

Outsourcing Information Technology:
The Role of Social Capital

James J. Hoffman, Texas Tech University, USA

Eric A. Walden, Texas Tech University, USA

Mark L. Hoelscher, Illinois State University, USA

Abstract

The current chapter explores the role that one factor, social capital, may have on the success of IT outsourcing. It extends current understanding of outsourcing success and failure by examining the effect of social capital on outsourcing success. The chapter proposes that social capital has potential impact on information technology (IT) outsourcing success. Specifically, it is theorized that social capital has an inverted "U" shape relationship with outsourcing success.

Introduction

Factors that affect the success of the outsourcing of information technology (IT) resources is an important issue since over 90% of U.S. companies outsource some activity and the total outsourcing market in 2004 was over $350 billion (Study, 2004). Firms have now started considering IT outsourcing as a strategic activity. Firms that earlier outsourced only minor information system (IS) services are now outsourcing entire IS departments (Mazzawi, 2002). Because of this senior executives who use to be concerned with whether or not to outsource information technology (IT) resources, are now more concerned with figuring out what factors can lead to the success or failure of outsourcing relationships.

Social Capital Theory

The term social capital first arrived on the scene in the sociology literature. It initially appeared in community studies, highlighting the central importance of networks of strong, crosscutting personal relationships developed over time that provide the basis for trust (Nahapiet & Ghoshal, 1998). The literature suggests that social capital can be separated into five distinct dimensions. They are information channels, social norms, identity, obligations and expectations, and moral infrastructure. Listed below are the separate dimensions and a more complete description of their makeup.

Information Channels

Information channels are social networks within the organization and also are the mechanisms that connect them to the outside world. Information channels are the most obvious example of social capital. They are the directly observable inventory of social capital. Information channels also contain the formal structure of an organization. This dimension of social capital consists of personal relationships that people develop with each other through a history of interaction.

The major benefits that a well-developed information channel provides are abundant and strong ties within the network. These ties, in turn, provide closure (Coleman, 1988). Closure can be described as the existence of sufficient ties within a social network to guarantee the observance of social norms. Within businesses, closure provides for more intense adherence to norms, a stronger feeling of obligations and expectations and a heightened sense of identity.

Social Norms

Social norms provide for social control in an organization. They are general, internalized sets of accepted behavior for members of the social network. Social norms are a common belief system that allow participants to communicate their ideas and make sense of common experiences (Adler & Kwon, 2000). They are shared strategic visions, systems of meanings, and normative value orientations (Nahapiet & Ghoshal, 1998). Social norms increase efficiency of action and reduce external unknowns. They also contain shared knowledge and history for an organization. They are the accumulated history of the organization in the form of social structure appropriable for productive use by any member of the social network in the pursuit of his or her interests (Sanderfur & Laumann, 1988).

Obligations and Expectations

Lesser (2000) viewed this dimension of social capital as the positive interactions that occur between individuals in a network. These interactions have been viewed as positive largely because of the levels of trust and reciprocity that they engendered (Putnam, 1993). The existence of these obligations and expectations of future benefit are nurtured in an organizational environment containing strong social ties and are hampered by the absence of these ties.

Within a network, obligations and expectations lead to collective trust, which becomes a potent form of expectational asset (Knez & Camerer, 1994; Nahapiet & Ghoshall, 1998). Collective trust allows group members to rely on each other more generally to help solve the everyday problems of cooperation and coordination (Kramer, Brewer, & Hanna 1996). With collective trust present, group members can rely on one another to follow through with things expected of them and obligations owed by them. Group members are then more willing to work for the group with the knowledge and expectation that the group will work for them when the time comes. Collective trust strengthens obligations and expectations.

Identity

Identity occurs when individuals see themselves as one with another person or group of people (Nahapiet & Ghoshal, 1998). The individual takes the values or standards of other individuals or groups as a comparative frame of reference (Merton, 1968; Tajfel, 1982). Identity with a group or collective enhances concern for collective processes and outcomes, thus increasing and strengthening group norms and collective goals. This group identity increases perceived opportunities for information exchange and enhances frequency of cooperation (Lewicki & Bunker, 1996). In contrast, where identity is not present there are significant barriers to information sharing, learning, and knowledge creation (Child & Rodriques, 1996; Pettigrew, 1973; Simon & Davies, 1996).

Moral Infrastructure

The fifth dimension of social capital is moral infrastructure. While support for the dimension of moral infrastructure as a part of social capital is somewhat limited in the management literature, there is support for it in the sociology literature. A moral infrastructure is identified as the structure or network, which allows an organization to encourage norms of conduct within the organization's scope of influence. Putnam (1993) refers to this dimension at the community level as networks of civic engagement. Civic engagement refers to people's connections with the life of their community and includes such things as membership in neighborhood associations, choral societies, or sports clubs (Blanchard & Horan, 1998; Putnam, 1995). These networks, whether existent within an organization, or within a community, provide an additional pathway for network actors to learn of the trustworthiness of individual actors within the network. This provides additional closure for social norms and gives individuals, acting in their own rational self interest, solid reasons to act in ways that adhere to formal and informal codes of conduct in their organization (Blanchard & Horan, 1998).

Portes (1998) notes that members of communities with a substantial stock of social capital find it much easier to work. This is largely a result of the trust engendered through social capital effects such as the existence of closure and social norms (Coleman, 1988). These items, then, provide the structure from which organizations can pin their belief systems and from which formal and informal codes of ethics can flow. This is the moral infrastructure of an organization.

A Multidimensional View of Social Capital

Without strong information channels which create strong ties between individuals within the organizational network, there is no opportunity for the organization to experience closure (Coleman, 1988). Without closure, there is no opportunity for the organization to develop strong social norms and for identity to begin to take hold. And, finally, without strong social norms, there is no opportunity to develop a system of obligations and expectations and to provide for the adherence to a set of ethics, both formal and informal (the moral infrastructure).

While each of these dimensions is separate and each provides distinct benefits to the organization, they are mutually dependent on each other for their development. Lesser (2000) summed it up nicely when he said, social capital, at its core, is about the value created by fostering connections between individuals.

Social Capital, Knowledge Management, and Increasing Outsourcing Success

Social Capital and Knowledge Management

Most organizations possess valuable knowledge relating to their products, processes, management, and technologies. However, often these organizations do not communicate as well as they might or apply this knowledge for maximum advantage (King, Marks, & McCoy, 2002). Organizations that are able to manage this knowledge and communicate it to their information technology vendors often have a competitive advantage over those organizations that are not as adept at knowledge management.

Knowledge management has been defined as the process of accumulating and creating knowledge, and facilitating the sharing of knowledge so that it can be applied effectively throughout the organization (Turban, Rainer, & Potter, 2003). Knowledge management involves four main processes. The first process is the generation of knowledge which includes all activities that discover "new" knowledge. The second process is knowledge capture which involves continuous scanning, organizing, and packaging of knowledge after it has been generated. Knowledge codification is the third process and it is the representation of knowledge in a manner that can easily be accessed and transferred. The fourth process, knowledge transfer, involves transmitting knowledge from one person or group to another person or group, and the absorption of that knowledge (Pearlson & Saunders, 2004).

It can be theorized that social capital can enhance an organization's ability to manage knowledge because it has the capacity to do a variety of things. In terms of knowledge creation, social capital helps to facilitate the development of collective intellectual capital by affecting the conditions necessary for exchange and combination to occur. In this vein collective intellectual capital is defined as the knowledge and knowing capability of a social collectivity, such as an organization, intellectual community, or professional practice (Nahapiet & Ghoshal, 1998). Social capital can also facilitate the development of intellectual capital. Since intellectual capital depends on the combination of knowledge and experience of different parties, intellectual capital's creation is greatly facilitated by the existence of social capital. Social capital has also been theorized to play a role in the development of core competencies (Kogut & Zander, 1996) which are vital to knowledge creation.

The presence of social capital can also enhance knowledge capture, knowledge codification, and knowledge transfer. Social capital enhances these knowledge management processes because it contributes to a firm's ability to create value in the form of innovation through the facilitation of combination and exchange of resources in a firm (Kanter, 1988; Kogut & Zander, 1993; Schumpeter, 1937). Social capital also increases the efficiency of action (Lesser, 2000) and encourages cooperative behavior (Coleman 1988; Nahapiet & Ghoshall, 1998). Additionally, social capital has been theorized to serve as an important element in the development of human capital (Coleman, 1988) and to provide access to resources through network ties (Burt, 1992).

From an overall perspective social capital can enhance the entire knowledge management process because it makes collective action more efficient, because it becomes a substitute for the formal contracts, incentives, and monitoring mechanisms that are necessary in systems with little or no social capital among organizational members (Fukuyama, 1995; Leana & Van Buren, 1999). In the language of economics, social capital can reduce transaction costs, thus making the knowledge management process more efficient.

However, social capital also introduces rigidities into the interactions among knowledge workers. When individuals share the same norms, identity, and communication channels their ability to come up with novel solutions to problems is limited (DiMaggio & Powell, 1983). Thus, social capital provides strong, but specific support for knowledge sharing. If a new type of knowledge is required, social capital will limit the ability of organizations to develop new knowledge.

Effectively using IT requires two types of knowledge: business knowledge and technical knowledge (Walden, 2005). Business knowledge is concerned with *what* the IT needs to do in order to support the business goals of the organization. Technical knowledge is concerned with *how* the IT needs to be configured to do what the business needs. These two types of knowledge are different. Business knowledge is stable, but is often focused on people, and thus, is soft knowledge. Technical knowledge changes rapidly, but focuses on scientific artifacts, and hence, is more concrete.

Few organizations are good at developing and managing both types of knowledge. Usually, an organization outsources its IT specifically because its social capital is geared toward the development and management of business knowledge. Conversely, IT vendors' social capital is geared toward the development and management of technical knowledge.

Social capital has the capacity to enhance the management and communication of knowledge between firms and their IT vendors, and thus allows for better communication of both what should be done and what can be done. However, the creation of social capital requires that clients and vendors establish similar identities, norms and communication channels, which undermine each organization's specific strengths. We believe that moderate levels of social capital will facilitate the sharing of vital knowledge between organizations, but high levels of social capital will compromise each organization's ability to offer a unique contribution of knowledge to the relationship. Thus, we propose:

Proposition 1: Social capital has an inverted "U" shape relationship with outsourcing success.

The Creation of Social Capital

Before firms and their IT vendors can benefit from social capital, the firms and their vendors must first create social capital. Time is important for the development of social capital since social capital depends largely on stability and continuity of the social structure. Long standing outsourcing relationships may be deriving a large part of their success from this underlying prerequisite for social capital. New outsourcing relationships, on the other hand, must expend large amounts of resources and time in order to achieve the same level of social capital.

Because, at its core, social capital is about relationships, it is eroded by those factors that make people less able to be interdependent (Lesser, 2000). Factors that enhance interdependent relationships are trust (Adler & Kwon, 2000; Lesser, 2000), reputation (Coleman, 1988), reciprocity (Lesser, 2000), and closure (Coleman, 1988). Interaction, which promotes things like trust and reciprocity, is a precondition for the development and maintenance of dense social capital (Bourdieu, 1986; Nahapiet & Ghoshall, 1998). It is quite likely that many variables that are described in the literature as outcomes of social capital, in fact, operate reciprocally with it, that is, trust (Leana & Van Buren, 1999). Adler and Kwon (2000) went so far as to suggest that trust might actually precede social capital. It is also quite likely that organizations can also develop social capital by selecting only those vendors who share its values and goals.

Once social capital is created between a firm and its IT vendors, use of social capital is also an important factor in its growth since, unlike many forms of capital, social capital increases, rather than decreases, with use. This is a result of the close connection between social capital and relational and network ties (Burt, 1992). These ties, necessary in the creation and maintenance of social capital (Adler & Kwon, 2000) are maintained, extended, and strengthened through use (Sanderfur & Laumann, 1988).

Discussion

This chapter examines the relationship between social capital and IT outsourcing success. Theoretical work in the field of social capital was used as the foundation on which to examine this relationship (Adler & Kwon, 2000; Burt 1992; Coleman, 1988; Nahapiet & Ghoshal, 1998; Putnam 1993). Because there is no existing literature that has examined the relationship between social capital and outsourcing success, this chapter extends prior research on outsourcing by providing a new theory of how social capital can impact the probability of outsourcing success.

The theories developed in this article have practical implications for managers of firms engaged in outsourcing relationships. This article argues social capital has an inverted "U" shape relationship with outsourcing success. Since resources within all businesses are relatively limited, and particularly so when the business is small relative to its competitors, the revelation that certain levels of social capital between firms and their vendors can lead to a sustained competitive advantage makes the decision to support and nurture it much more credible. Outsourcing firms can then make a more informed decision on whether to commit a portion of their limited resources toward its creation and maintenance.

Overall, it is hoped that this chapter will serve as a point of reference for future research on the relationship between social capital and outsourcing success. Additionally, it is hoped that it will serve as a foundation for future studies looking at possible competitive advantages that some firms engaged in outsourcing have over other firms engaged in outsourcing.

References

Adler, P., & Kwon, S. (2000). *Knowledge and social capital.* In E. L. Lesser (Ed.). (Reprinted from *Social capital: The good, the bad, and the ugly.* Paper presented to the OMT division of the Academy of Management, 1999, p. 2). Butterworth-Heinemann.

Blanchard, A., & Horan, T. (1998). Virtual communities and social capital. *Social Science Computer Review, 16,* 298.

Bourdieu, P. (1986) *The forms of social capital.* In J. G. Richardson (Ed.), *Handbook of theory and research for the sociology of education* (pp. 241-258). New York: Greenwood.

Burt, R. S. (1992). *Structural holes, the social structure of competition.* Cambridge, MA: Harvard University Press.

Child, J., & Rodriques, S. (1996) The role of social identity in the international transfer of knowledge through joint ventures. In S. R. Clegg & G. Palmer (Eds.), *The politics of management knowledge* (pp. 46-68). London: Sage.

Coleman, J. S. (1988). Social capital in the creation of human capital. *American Journal of Sociology, 94*, 95-120.

DiMaggio, P. J., & Powell, W. W. (1983). The Iron Cage revisited: Institutional isomorphism and collective rationality in organizational fields. *American Sociological Review, 48*, 147-160.

Fukuyama, F. (1995). *Trust: The social virtues and the creation of prosperity.* New York: Penguin Books.

Kanter, R. M. (1988). When a thousand flowers bloom: Structural, collective, and social conditions for innovation in organizations. In B. M. Staw & L. L. Cummings (Eds.), *Research in organizational behavior* (Vol. 10, pp. 169-211). Greenwich, CT: JAI Press.

King, W., Marks, P., & McCoy, S. (2002). The most important issues in knowledge management. *Communications of the ACM, 45*, 93-97.

Knez, M., & Camerer, C. (1994). Creating expectation assets in the laboratory: Coordination in "weakest link" games. *Strategic Management Journal, 15*, 101-119.

Kogut, B., & Zander, U. (1993). Knowledge of the firm and the evolutionary theory of the multinational corporation. *Journal of International Business Studies, 24*, 625-645.

Kogut, B., & Zander, U. (1996). What firms do? Coordination, identity, and learning. *Organization Science, 7*, 502-518.

Kramer, R. M., Brewer, M. B., & Hanna, B. A. (1996). Collective trust and collective action: The decision to trust as a social decision. In R. M. Kramer & T. R. Tyler (Eds.), *Trust in organizations. Frontiers of theory and research* (pp. 357-389). Thousand Oaks, CA: Sage.

Leana, C. R., & Van Buren, H. J. III (1999). Organizational social capital and employment practices. *Academy of Management Review, 24*, 538-555.

Lesser, E. L. (2000). Leveraging social capital in organizations. In E. L. Lesser (Ed.), *Knowledge and social capital* (pp. 3-17). Woburn, MA: Butterworth-Heinemann.

Lewicki, R. J., & Bunker, B. B. (1996). Developing and maintaining trust in work relationships. In R. M. Kramer & T. M. Tyler (Eds.), *Trust in organiza-*

tions: Frontiers of theory and research (pp. 114-139). Thousand Oaks, CA: Sage.

Mazzawi, E. (2002). Transformational outsourcing. *Business Strategy Review, 13*, 39-43.

Merton, R. K. (1968). *Social theory and social structure.* New York: Free Press.

Nahapiet, J., & Ghoshal, S. (1998). Social capital, intellectual capital, and the organizational advantage. *Academy of Management Review, 23*(2), 242-266.

Pearlson, K., & Saunders, C. (2004) *Managing and using information systems.* Hoboken, NJ: John Wiley & Sons.

Pettigrew, A. M. (1973). *The politics of organizational decision-making.* London: Tavistock.

Portes, A. (1998). Social capital: Its origins and applications in modern sociology. *Annual Review of Sociology, 24*, 1-24.

Putnam, R. D. (1993). The prosperous community: social capital and public life. *American Prospect, 13*, 35-42.

Putnam, R. D. (1995). Bowling alone: America's declining social capital. *Journal of Democracy, 6*, 65-78.

Sanderfur, R., & Laumann, E. O. (1988). A paradigm for social capital. *Rationality and Society, 10*, 481-501.

Schumpeter, J. A. (1934). *The theory of economic development.* Cambridge, MA: Harvard University Press.

Simon, L., & Davies, G. (1996). A contextual approach to management learning. *Organization Studies, 17*, 269-289.

Study: Outsourcing market exceeds $350 billion. (2004, January 24). *Charlotte Business Journal.* Retrieved March 15, 2006, from http://charlotte.bizjour nals.com/charlotte/stories/2004/01/26/daily4.html

Tajfel, H. (Ed.). (1982). *Social relations and intergroup relations.* Cambridge, MA: Cambridge University Press.

Turban, E., Rainer, R., & Potter, R. (2003). *Introduction to information technology.* Hoboken, NJ: John Wiley & Sons.

Walden, E. A. (2005). Intellectual property rights and cannibalization in information technology outsourcing contracts. *MIS Quarterly, 29*, 699-720.

Chapter XI

Outsourcing of Services by Service Firms:
An Empirical Investigation

Masaaki Kotabe, Temple University, USA

Janet Y. Murray, University of Missouri - St. Louis, USA

Maneesh Chandra, ZS Associates, USA

Abstract

The traditional "make-or-buy" decision has been widely studied in the context of the theory of the firm and vertical integration. One of the most popular frameworks for examining this strategic decision has been the transaction cost analysis (TCA) framework. However, much of past research has focused on the make-or-buy decisions of product manufacturing activities, to the neglect of services. The make-or-buy decisions of services and service activities, due to their inherent characteristics (i.e., intangibility, inseparability, heterogeneity, and perishability) and the unique nature of their "production" and "delivery," necessitate modifying and revamping the existing framework. The authors develop and empirically test a conceptual framework that examines factors influencing a firm's decision to use outsourcing or in-house sourcing for a service (service activity).

Introduction

Due to intense pressure to improve the efficiency and effectiveness of procure-ment efforts, firms are seeking new ways to perform these critical functions and to reduce costs in the value-added process (Cannon & Perreault, 1999). Increasingly, both large and small firms are outsourcing various service activities that were traditionally performed within the firm by shifting them to external suppliers. Outsourcing of routine operational service activities alone amounted to more than $1 trillion worldwide in 2000 (Auguste, Hao, Singer, & Wiegand, 2002). While firms have obviously embraced outsourcing of service activities to an overwhelming extent, their experience has been mixed (Hsieh, Lazzarini, & Nickerson, 2002; Lacity, Willcocks, & Feeny, 1995). The reasons are the lack of documentation of good business practice for the buying firm to evaluate its service suppliers, the lack of a practical management framework to guide managers to critically evaluate how to enhance value by deliberately managing outsourcing of services, and the variability in performance when outsourcing of services is used. One of the most critical decisions in outsourcing is how firms decide which service activity should be outsourced or retained in-house (i.e., in-house sourcing). As Venkatraman (1997, p. 60) points out, "the issue that senior managers face is not whether to outsource, but what to outsource."

Although scholars in operation research have made valuable contributions in purchasing or sourcing related issues, for example, inventory management, reorder points, order lot sizing, discount pricing, and order proportioning among multiple suppliers (Das & Handfield, 1997), research in services sourcing is lacking. Likewise, Fisk, Brown, and Bitner (1993) have explicitly identified outsourcing of services as one of the research gaps in services research, and extant literature reflects little work in this area. Furthermore, researchers should critically rethink previously embraced theories, empirical findings, and normative prescriptions in the area of outsourcing of goods before they should be applied to outsourcing of service activities, since some of which are becoming outdated in today's highly competitive global markets (Cannon & Perreault, 1999, pp. 8-9). Our study aims at filling these research gaps. Thus, the purpose of our study is to contribute to both the operations research and service literature by developing and empirically testing a framework to help describe the factors that influence a firm's decision to use outsourcing or in-house sourcing for a service activity. Furthermore, we develop our framework from the perspective of the firm using outsourcing for a service activity (i.e., potential/actual buyer of the service activity). The buyer of the service activity is the firm outsourcing the activity, and is termed the "outsourcer." The firm to which the service activity is outsourced (i.e., potential/actual supplier of the service activity) is the "outsourcee."

Theory and Hypothesis

We define outsourcing of services as the purchase of any service activity from an external source, irrespective of whether it was previously performed within the firm. This "make-or-buy" activity is a critical decision that has been tightly linked to the literature on vertical integration. Past research on "make-or-buy" decisions has mostly focused on transaction-cost analysis (TCA) in that under certain conditions, it is more efficient for a firm to create and use an internal market, rather than incurring the prohibitive transactions costs of an outside market (Williamson, 1975, 1985). Although the TCA framework has received much empirical support to substantiate its explanatory power in make-or-buy decisions (Balakrishnam & Wernerfelt, 1986; Joskow, 1987; Monteverde & Teece, 1982), most empirical work has been conducted in manufacturing industries. Furthermore, while TCA focuses on transactional economies as a basis for make-or-buy decisions, it fails to incorporate various market imperfections and other motives to integrate, such as: extension of market power (Caves & Porter, 1977) drive for unambiguous control, and avoidance of conflicts with partners (Contractor & Lorange, 1988). In the global context, a stream of research has evolved pertaining to outsourcing of manufacturing activities (Kotabe, 1990, 1992; Kotabe & Swan, 1994; Murray, Kotabe, & Wildt, 1995). Much of the underlying basis for this research is the internalization theory (Buckley & Casson, 1974) and the core competency argument (Prahalad & Hamel, 1990), both of which relate to the market imperfection motivation for outsourcing decisions. A limitation of this research stream is that it focuses on outsourcing of manufacturing activities, to the neglect of service activities. Moreover, it fails to specifically incorporate the transactional and technological motivations of outsourcing.

The above discussions highlight the need for a decision framework for outsourcing of service activities by incorporating TCA and non-TCA motivations. The TCA motivations (e.g., asset specificity, uncertainty, and complexity) have been well documented in the literature (Williamson, 1975, 1985). The non-TCA motivations, such as market power, (related to market imperfections) should also form an important part of any decision framework. Erramilli and Rao (1993) have asserted that non-TCA benefits flowing from integration is particularly relevant and important to service firms. In many service industries, the fixed costs associated with internalizing activities, or the switching costs, may be relatively small, with the true value-generating assets in the form of human resources being relatively mobile. Furthermore, the characteristics of services introduce new elements that have implications for two opposing forces — desire for greater control and the difficulty in monitoring what is received from an outsourcee (supplier). The desire for greater control arises most noticeably due to the intimate contact between the producer and the customer during the process of service delivery, and customer involvement in the coproduction of the service. The difficulty in monitoring arises due to the intangibility of the service.

Propensity to Use Outsourcing

The objective of our study is to develop a decision framework that examines the factors (i.e., antecedents) influencing a firm's decision to use outsourcing or in-house sourcing for a service activity. Thus, the propensity to use outsourcing is the likelihood that a firm would source a service activity from independent suppliers. We categorize the antecedent variables into three groups: the characteristics of service activities, market conditions, and the nature of interaction between the outsourcer and the end-customer. We provide discussions leading to the hypotheses in the following section.

Characteristics of Service Activities

Intangibility

Intangibility has been cited as the most critical differentiation between goods and services. It refers to the service characteristic of not being seen, felt, tasted, or touched in the same manner in which goods can be sensed (Zeithaml, Parasuraman, & Berry, 1985), and not reasonably be stored (Mills & Margulies, 1980). Unlike physical goods, services are usually performances or processes. The degree of intangibility varies across the spectrum of services, with no service being entirely intangible (Clark, Rajaratnam, & Smith, 1996; Zeithaml, 1981). Service intangibility is a continuum, with the extremes being pure services (e.g., consulting services) and those embedded in goods (e.g., car rental). As intangibility increases, monitoring the performance (and quality) of services delivered becomes increasingly difficult. For example, in the case of air travel, it is quite difficult to monitor the performance of in-flight attendants since the service they provide is a performance/experience. Thus, airlines generally do not outsource their in-flight attendant service. Conversely, monitoring the quality of food served in-flight is easier since food is more tangible in nature. Hence, service intangibility creates unique problems in exchanges of services. For physical goods, an exchange results in physical ownership/possession. However, for services, "the object of exchange is often an experience that can neither be touched nor possessed" (Bowen, 1990; Shostack, 1977). If the outsourcer experiences difficulty in evaluating the outsourcee's performance due to the level of service intangibility, it is less likely to outsource the service activity.

H₁: The higher the intangibility of the service activity, the lower the propensity to use outsourcing.

Customization

Customization refers to the extent to which a good or a service is modified to meet the individual customer's needs and wants. Since most services are produced and consumed simultaneously, and the customer is often involved in the production process, firms have more opportunities to tailor the service to meet their customers' needs (Lovelock, 1983). However, the extent to which services can be customized varies significantly. For example: in-flight food services are highly standardized while in-classroom teaching is highly customized. The more standardized a service is, the easier it is to monitor and evaluate the quality of the service received. Conversely, the more customized a service is, the more difficult it is to monitor and evaluate the service.

H₂: The higher the customization of the service activity, the lower the propensity to use outsourcing.

Inseparability

Inseparability refers to the closeness of the consumer to the producer (Fuchs, 1968; Mills & Margulies, 1980), attributed to the simultaneous production and consumption of most services (Regan, 1963). Inseparability forces the buyer into intimate contact with the production process (Carman & Langeard, 1980). While goods are generally first produced, then sold and consumed, services are generally first sold, then produced and consumed simultaneously (Zeithaml et al., 1985). In buyer-seller interactions, inseparability has two significant implications. First, it necessitates the tight coordination of the demand and supply of the service activity (Bowen & Jones, 1986). Second, it requires close interactions between (employees of) the outsourcee and (employees of) the outsourcer. This provides an opportunity for the service provider to adjust the service to better match the particular needs of each customer at the time of the service delivery (Bateson, 1989). Firms manage both of the above conditions most effectively when they retain the service activity in-house. Therefore, it is hypothesized:

H₃: The higher the inseparability of the service activity, the lower the propensity to use outsourcing.

Core vs. Noncore Service Activities

Extant literature has emphasized that an activity can be outsourced as long as it is not a core one (Bettis, Bradley, & Hamel, 1992; Huber, 1993; Kelley, 1995; Lacity et al., 1995; Mullin, 1996; Murray & Kotabe, 1996; Piesch, 1995; Rothery & Robertson, 1995), and outsourcing noncore activities is consistent with the core competency argument (Prahalad & Hamel, 1990). Core services are essential services that the firm must provide in order to participate in the market. In this study, the distinction of core vs. noncore service activities relates to the activity being a resource or a skill that represents a source of sustainable competitive advantage (Bharadwaj, Varadarajan, & Fahy, 1993). Consistent with the core competency argument, it is hypothesized:

H$_4$: There is a higher propensity to use outsourcing for noncore than core service activities.

Market Conditions

Uncertainty

The growing uncertainty and unpredictability facing businesses have significant implications for organizational decision-making (Lacity et al., 1995). Most extant research has treated uncertainty as unidimensional (Klein, Frazier, & Roth, 1990). However, Larsson and Bowen (1989) have highlighted the multidimensionality of uncertainty including tasks (e.g., the use of different technologies), the environment (e.g., customer demands), and inputs to production (e.g., raw material quality). The multidimensional nature of uncertainty has also been referred to in the context of outsourcing (Piesch, 1995). Moreover, researchers have cautioned that treating uncertainty as a unidimensional construct may lead to unreliable conclusions regarding the outcome of the strategy implemented to counteract environmental uncertainty. Two forms of uncertainty have received much attention with specific reference to outsourcing: demand and technological uncertainty.

Demand Uncertainty

Demand uncertainty refers to the fluctuations of demand for the service activity being outsourced. Based on TCA, demand uncertainty would lead to frequent mismatches between supply and demand for services outsourced, resulting in higher transaction costs (Walker & Weber, 1984). Consequently, Klein et al. (1990) argued that internalization allows the absorption of uncertainty through specialization of decision making and savings in communication expenses, facilitating an adaptive, sequential decision process. Walker and Weber (1984) have found support for demand uncertainty leading to internalization of a manufacturing activity. Therefore:

H$_5$:   The higher the demand uncertainty associated with the service activity, the lower the propensity to use outsourcing.

Technological Uncertainty

Technology uncertainty refers to the rate of technological changes. Information technology-related outsourcing, characterized by significant uncertainty due to the rapid pace of technological innovations and change, is the most prevalent form of outsourcing. However, technological uncertainty can be associated with any activity faced with rapid changes in the conversion processes involved, irrespective of whether the activity involves any "hardware" or "software." The traditional view denotes that as the number of contingencies associated with high technological uncertainty increase, it becomes more difficult and expensive to monitor contracts between the outsourcer and outsourcee; thus, the preferred mode would be to integrate vertically. However, Balakrishnan and Wernerfelt (1986) empirically found the opposite relationship. They assert that integrating under situations of high technological change results in reduced flexibility. Internalizing activities that have short life cycles, due to high rates of technological change, diminishes the incentive to internalize activities in-house since the firm has to keep replacing its technology, thus incurring huge costs. More importantly, the reduced life expectancy of the technology affects the profitability of the industry, thus reducing the incentive to integrate. To take an extreme case, Balakrishnan and Wernerfelt (1986) state that "at the limit, where the industry profitability goes to the competitive rate of return, there is no incentive to integrate since there are no profits to bargain over and thus *no* transaction costs to save." Empirically, Balakrishnan and Wernerfelt (1986) found support for an inverse relationship between technological uncertainty and vertical integration. Hence:

H$_6$:   The higher a service activity is characterized by technological uncertainty, the higher the propensity to use outsourcing.

Complexity of the Service Activity as a Moderator

Although research grounded in both strategic management theory and TCA considers uncertainty as an important factor affecting the decision to vertically integrate (Porter, 1980; Walker & Weber 1984; Williamson, 1975), empirical findings regarding the effects of uncertainty on vertical integration contradict one another (Sutcliffe & Zaheer, 1998). Studies utilizing TCA provide empirical support that vertical integration is an efficient response to environmental uncertainty (Anderson, 1985; John & Weitz, 1988; Walker & Weber, 1984). Contrarily, empirical studies in strategic management suggest that firms facing uncertainty require greater flexibility; consequently, uncertainty results in a *lowered* rather than an increased degree of vertical integration (Balakrishnan & Wernerfelt, 1986; Grant & Baden-Fuller, 1995). Central to the inconsistency of empirical findings based on the above two schools of thought may be due to the lack of consideration of the nature of the activity to be outsourced or retained in-house. The popular press has mentioned outsourcing as a mechanism to tackle uncertainty. A closer look reflects that most service activities outsourced under high uncertainty have been simple noncore service activities. To examine whether a service activity should be outsourced or retained in-house, it is important to investigate the potential moderating effect of the level of complexity involved in the service activity on outsourcing decisions. We conceptualize complexity as the number of steps and sequences that constitute a particular service activity.

The role of complexity as applied to make-or-buy decisions is not a new one. It has been cited in the TCA literature as being associated with the construct of uncertainty and bounded rationality (Williamson, 1975). Williamson (1975) posits complexity to increase the impact of bounded rationality, thus increasing the positive relationship between uncertainty and vertical integration. More specifically, he argued that if the task is simple (not complex), then the problems associated with bounded rationality would be limited. Under conditions of low task complexity, there would be limited incentive for the firm to internalize an activity even under conditions of high demand uncertainty. For example, for a firm to transport its executives, it may be more efficient for the firm to depend on outsourcees (i.e., airlines). This is because although the task may involve considerable demand uncertainty, it is a simple one (low complexity). However, when the complexity of task increases, the problems of bounded rationality magnify. Taking the example of product designing activities, design engineers are involved in complex activities including development tasks and communication of tacit and uncodifiable knowledge among themselves. One may arguably compare the demand uncertainty to be similar in both cases for transporting and product designing activities. However, the latter is a far more complex task, and a firm would be less likely to outsource its product development activities. The bounded rationality argument would hold true for both demand and technological uncertainty; for the same level of uncertainty, the higher complexity of the service activity would lead to the lower propensity to use outsourcing. Therefore:

H$_{7a}$: The higher the complexity of the service activity, the stronger the inverse relationship between demand uncertainty and propensity to use outsourcing.

H$_{7b}$: The higher the complexity of the service activity, the weaker the positive relationship between technological uncertainty and propensity to use outsourcing.

Number of Alternative Suppliers

The number of alternative suppliers is akin to the idea of "small numbers" proposed in TCA (Williamson, 1975). For a firm to outsource a service activity, there have to be potential suppliers who can deliver it. The extent of competition among potential outsourcees also affects their propensity to behave opportunistically. If there were only one outsourcee, the outsourcer would be less inclined to use outsourcing for a service activity as there would be the risk of becoming completely dependent on the supplier. Based on this small numbers argument, we hypothesize:

H$_8$: The smaller the number of potential outsourcees of the service activity, the lower the propensity to use outsourcing.

Nature of Interaction Between Outsourcer and End-Customer

"End" Customer Contact

Earlier, we discussed that inseparability brings the outsourcer's employee in direct contact with the outsourcee's employee. For a specific service activity to be potentially outsourced, the outsourcer is the customer while the outsourcee is the service provider. However, as we stated earlier, the outsourcing decision in this study is being viewed from the outsourcer's perspective. The outsourcer may have various service activities that take place within its premises. Some of the activities may involve interaction with the end-customers of the outsourcer, while others may involve no interaction with the end-customer. Hence, end-customer contact refers to the contact between the outsourcer and its customers, while inseparability refers to the interaction between the outsourcer and the outsourcee.

Zeithaml et al. (1985), Shostack (1977), Lovelock (1983), Berry (1980), and Levitt (1981) have highlighted various differences between the delivery of services and goods. One of the differences is the need for firms to focus on additional elements as part of the service delivery: participants, physical evidence, and process of service assembly. These additional elements recognize the importance of the social and physical context of services and highlight the criticality of the service encounter (Bitner, 1990; Kohnke, 1990). Since these additional elements in the service encounter form part of the service that the consumer receives, they have a significant impact on the customer's view of the service provided. In many service encounters, the very success of a particular service vendor rests on the quality of the subjective experience between the customer and the contact employee of the service firm (Solomon, Surprenant, Czepiel, & Gutman, 1985).

Besides being part of the service experience of the customer, the service organizations involved with the actual delivery of the service also serve the important role of acting as the listening posts, and as a link between the firm and the customer. This is a critical activity for obtaining customer feedback on a regular basis (Heskett, 1986). For the reasons stated above, interactions with the customer are considered critical for service firms. Service activities that involve interaction with the customer go to the very heart of why a service firm exists. The point of customer interaction is the place where the service is assembled and delivered by the contact employee to the customer. Therefore, we hypothesize:

H_9: The higher the contact that the service activity involves with the end-customer, the lower the propensity to use outsourcing.

Moderating Role of the Type of Customer Contact

The two types of customer contact refers to the nature of interaction between the outsourcer and its end-customer; they are direct or indirect contact. The impact of the three additional elements (i.e., participants, process, and physical evidence) on the service outcome is likely to be higher in direct contact as the customer is being directly exposed to these elements. Conversely, their impact is likely to be less in indirect transactions since the customer is exposed to extremely limited forms of these elements. To demonstrate the difference between transactions that involve direct or indirect contact, we consider the process of purchasing an airline ticket. An airline ticket could be bought at the check-in counter at the airport. This is an example of direct contact between the service provider and the end-customer. Since the customer interacts directly with the service provider, the three additional elements of participant, process, and physical evidence would most likely have a significant role in providing service to the end-customer. The airline ticket could also be purchased through a centralized 1-800 telephone line. The latter is an example of an indirect contact transaction where the participant, process, and physical evidence are relatively less important in providing service to the consumer. In this example, we would expect the latter case to be more amenable to outsourcing than the former case. Indeed, many firms are now using outsourcing of customer service from call centers of independent suppliers. Hence,

H_{10}: The propensity to use outsourcing for those service activities involving indirect interaction between the outsourcer and the end-customer will be higher than those involving direct interaction between them.

Empirical Investigation

Sampling

Outsourcing of services occurs both in product manufacturing and service firms. For the purpose of this study, we have chosen to focus on service firms. Extant literature has stressed the need to examine various phenomena across a range of service industries rather than focusing on a few specific ones (Bowen, 1990). Based on SIC codes at the four-digit level contained in the 1997 *Directory of Corporate Affiliations*, there are over 400 service industries. Most of the studies that have examined effects across multiple industries have done so on a few select industries. Furthermore, they have not explicitly provided a basis for their choice of industries. One of the notable exceptions to this includes Parasuraman, Zeithaml, and Berry's (1985) study. Similar to studies conducted by Parasuraman et al. (1985) and Schmenner (1986), we used a service classification framework identified in the literature to identify the service industries across which the activity of outsourcing is examined.

To fulfill our research objective discussed earlier, we conducted a survey in two stages to empirically examine the hypotheses. The sampling frame included fourteen service industries that were identified from the *Directory of Corporate Affiliations*. These were chosen to be representative of the categories in the classification scheme by Schmenner (1986). The population of U.S. public and private firms for the industries identified formed the initial sampling frame. Firms with sales fewer than $10 million were not included as they were expected to be too small to be considering outsourcing. We identified 1,793 U.S. service firms.

In the first stage of the survey, we sent letters to the CEOs/Presidents of 1,793 firms seeking their participation in the study. After one reminder letter, 131 prospective respondents expressed interest in participating in the survey. In the second stage, we mailed a survey questionnaire to the 131 prospective respondents and also reminders a month later. As a result, we received a total of 102 usable responses, with 55 and 47 service activities involving outsourcing and in-house sourcing, respectively. Responding firms had sales revenues that ranged from $15.4 million to $24.9 billion, and represented the industry categories identified by Schmenner (1986). The number of employees ranged from 82 to 120,000 employees.

Measures

We developed the survey questionnaire based primarily on existing scales. For the few constructs with no existing scales, conceptualizations in the literature formed the basis for their measurement. We conducted in-depth interviews to help assess the validity of questions and identify possible sources of measurement error. The Appendix contains the measurement (adapted from previous studies) and its reliability for the variables.

We measured *intangibility* with two items regarding the degree of intangibility and the proportion of cost of the service attributable to tangible objects (Cronbach's $\alpha = 0.56$). *Customization* was measured by two items reflecting the extent of adaptation/standardization that was required to meet the firm's specific needs (Cronbach's $\alpha = 0.87$). We measured *inseparability* by a single item on the extent of the production and consumption of the service occurring simultaneously. The distinction between *core vs. noncore service activities* was measured by three items on whether the service was imitable, other competitors had access to the same service, and whether it significantly influenced the firm's effectiveness or efficiency (Cronbach's $\alpha = 0.54$).

We measured *demand uncertainty* by two items reflecting fluctuations in the requirement of the service, and inaccuracy of volume estimates (Cronbach's $\alpha = 0.67$). *Technological uncertainty* was measured using three items on the frequency of change of the processes, likelihood of improvement in the future, and difficulty in forecasting future changes (Cronbach's $\alpha = 0.60$). We measured *complexity* using two items reflecting the number of steps/sequences to perform the service, and the simplicity of the tasks (Cronbach's $\alpha = 0.55$). The *number of alternative* suppliers, *end-customer contact*, and the *type of customer contact* (i.e., direct or indirect) were each measured by a single item.

Model Estimation

We used logistic regression to estimate the effects hypothesized in the conceptual framework. The use of logistic regression is appropriate when: (1) the dependent variable is binary, and (2) the underlying assumptions of multivariate normality may not be met (Afifi & Clark, 1984; Erramilli & Rao, 1993; Kachigan, 1986). We modeled the propensity (i.e., probability) of using outsourcing or in-house sourcing for a service activity as a function of the main effects (independent variables and moderator variables), and interaction effects (interactions between the independent and moderator variables):

Propensity to use outsourcing for a service activity = $1/[1 + \exp^{(-Y)}]$, where

$$Y = \beta_0 + \beta_1 X_1 + \beta_2 X_2 + \ldots + \beta_n X_n$$

Table 1. Results of logistic regression

Effect (hypothesized sign)	Standardized Beta Estimate	Standard Error	Significance
Intangibility (-)	-.210	.252	.20
Customization (-)	-.239	.288	.39
Inseparability (-)	-.453	.247	.03 [b]
Core vs. Non-Core (-)	-.099	.288	.37
Demand Uncertainty (-)	-1.454	.735	.02 [b]
Technological Uncertainty (+)	.556	.654	.20
Dem. Uncertain. X Complexity (+)	2.202	.983	.01 [a]
Techn.Uncertain.X Complexity (-)	-2.083	.977	.04 [b]
No. of Alternate Suppliers (+)	.916	.533	.04 [b]
End-Customer Contact (-)	-.350	.838	.33
End-Cust. X Type of Customer Contact (-)	.099	.288	.37
Model Chi-Square = 26.58, df = 11, p-value = .005			
-2 Likelihood = 112.05			
Nagelkerke R^2 = 31.1%			
Correct Classification Ratio = 72.5%			

[a] = $p < .01$
[b] = $p < .05$

Dependent variable= propensity to use outsourcing; 0=in-house sourcing; 1=oursourcing

In the previous equation, X_1, X_2, ... X_n represent the explanatory variables (independent variables, moderator variables, and interactions between the independent and moderator variables). We estimated the model parameters using the maximum likelihood estimation procedure. Table 1 presents the parameter estimates and a summary of effects.

Hypothesis Testing

The negative parameter estimates of -.210 and -.239 for intangibility and customization, respectively, would seem to support the hypotheses that the higher the intangibility (or customization), the lower the propensity to use outsourcing. However, the parameter estimates are not significant, thus not supporting H_1 and H_2. One possible reason for the weak effect could be that firms may choose to structure the relationships between the outsourcer and the outsourcee in a way to counteract the difficulty of monitoring performance of the outsourced service activity. For example, they may choose to adopt more relational norms, as opposed to transactional norms (Heidi, 1994) to manage uncertainty, which in this case is the result of difficulty in monitoring performance. Hypothesis H_3 is strongly supported ($\beta = -0.453$), that is, the higher the inseparability associated with the service activity, the lower the propensity to use outsourcing for that activity.

The parameter estimate of -0.099 for core vs. noncore service is in the hypothesized direction, but it is not statistically significant. Hence, H_4 is not supported. The result seems to suggest that the use of core vs. noncore is at best a weak factor for firms in deciding whether to use outsourcing or in-house sourcing for a service activity, thereby substantiating the main issue, that is, the need for a more comprehensive decision framework that more effectively captures the factors that influence the make-or-buy decision for service activities. The parameter estimate of -1.454 is in the hypothesized direction for demand uncertainty. This parameter is statistically significant; therefore, H_5 is supported. Technological uncertainty has a parameter estimate of 0.556 that provides directional support; however, this result is not statistically significant; hence, H_6 is not supported.

We hypothesized that for the same level of uncertainty, there would be a lower propensity to use outsourcing for service activities that are more complex. More specifically, the greater the complexity of the service activity, the stronger the inverse relationship between demand uncertainty and the propensity to use outsourcing. Similarly, the higher the complexity of the service activity, the weaker the direct relationship between technological uncertainty and propensity to use outsourcing. Both of these effects were found to be statistically significant and in the hypothesized direction. Hence, H_{7a} and H_{7b} are both supported.

As hypothesized, the greater the number of alternate suppliers for the service activity, the higher the propensity to use outsourcing ($\beta = 0.916$). Hence, in line with the predictions, H_8 is supported. The parameter estimate of -.350 for end-customer contact is in the hypothesized direction; however, the effect is not significant; therefore, H_9 is not supported. The parameter estimate for the type of customer contact was not statistically significant. Hence, H_{10} is not supported.

Discussion

Conceptually, the framework for outsourcing of service activities developed in this study complements the TCA-based literature on the make-or-buy issue. It does this by explicitly incorporating the characteristics of service activities, role of customer interaction, and market imperfections (core competency argument). The empirical results from testing the framework are encouraging. This high-lights the need to refine the conceptual frameworks for examining the make-or-buy decisions in the context of services. The framework presented in this study is an important first step in this direction.

Our findings show that the higher the inseparability associated with the service activity, the lower the propensity to use outsourcing for that activity. Indeed, the inseparability characteristic of many services poses many challenges when delivering services to their customers. From an operational point of view, because many service activities are produced and consumed at the same time, it is crucial for firms to be able to respond to "service recoveries." Service recoveries involve attempts by firms to rectify consumer-perceived service failure. Although it is unlikely that service firms can eliminate all service failures, they can effectively respond to failures once they do occur (Maxham, 2001). However, the quality of the recovery can either reinforce customer relationships or further exacerbate the failure (Hoffman, Kelley, & Rotalsky, 1995; Smith, Bolton, & Wagner, 1999). In this respect, the way in which a firm recovers from service failure could become a sustainable competitive advantage in the market-place (Maxham, 2001). If the service is being outsourced, then the service recovery would be in the hands of the outsourcee. The outsourcee may choose not to make any recovery effort or the recovery may not be adequate. If this is the case, generally two scenarios would take place. Some customers may take the initiative to complain to the outsourcer, which provides an opportunity for the outsourcer to eventually take corrective action. If no complaint is filed with the outsourcer, the outsourcer may not even be aware of the problems that arose, and the outsourcer may lose the customer forever, in addition to further damage through negative word-of-mouth. In general, it costs much less to keep a current customer than it does to attract a new one, so inadequate service recovery efforts may eventually hurt the outsourcer's bottom line (Hart, Heskett, & Sasser, 1990). In addition, if the service activity that is being outsourced represents a subset of an overall inseparable service package, the outsourcee would become a noticeable third party instead of a seamless part of the overall service package (Greer, Youngblood, & Gray, 1999).

We found that the higher the demand uncertainty, the lower the propensity to use outsourcing for a service activity. In addition, complexity exerts a positive moderating effect on the negative relationship between demand uncertainty and the propensity to use outsourcing for a service activity. Because of the perishability characteristics of many service activities, it is quite costly if the supply and demand of the service activities involved is not managed well, which is worsened in situations when the service activity is highly complex. If the service activity is outsourced, the outsourcee may not take the responsibility of correcting the problem when it occurs. In addition, how well the outsourcee is able to satisfy the customers in the case of service failure/recovery encounters are affected by both the service failure context (i.e., type and magnitude of failure) and service recovery attributes (i.e., compensation, response speed, apology, and recovery initiation) (Smith et al., 1999). In order to ensure that customers are satisfied with service recoveries, it is important for firms to tailor their service recovery efforts that have the greatest positive impact on customer response (Smith et al., 1999). However, it is doubtful that a contract can be written in such a way as to spell out all the contingencies listed above, especially when highly complex service activities are involved.

Companies are increasingly assessing each customer individually and make decisions on how best to serve the customer (Sheth, Sisodia, & Sharma, 2000). With technological advances, companies are able to utilize technology to effectively customize service offerings (Bitner, Brown & Meuter, 2000). However, technological advances often induce high levels of uncertainty in "acceptable" technological standards. Therefore, technological uncertainty leads to "competence destroying" for firms due to the shorter life cycle of certain technologies (Tushman & Nelson, 1990); the situation is made more pronounced when high levels of complexity are involved in the service activity. Indeed, new technology implementations often disrupt the relationship between service production experience and productivity improvements when they are obsolete, inappropriate, or difficult to utilize (Adler & Clark, 1991; Boone & Ganeshan, 2001). This results in the difficulty of developing outsourcing contracts that include all the contingencies that may arise, thus complexity exerts a negative moderating effect on the relationship between technological uncertainty and the propensity to use outsourcing for a service activity. Indeed, if technological uncertainty mandates extensive coordinated adaptation, then outsourcing would be discouraged (Poppo & Zenger, 1998). Our findings also supported the hypothesis that the greater the number of alternate suppliers, the higher the propensity to use outsourcing for the service activity. The reason is that the outsourcer does not have to be overly dependent on the current supplier if there are many another outsourcees available.

On the substantive domain, we contribute to the literature in operations research in sourcing-related issues by investigating the factors influencing outsourcing of service activities. Most past studies have examined the make-or-buy decision in the manufacturing context. This study is one of the first to explicitly examine this issue in the context of services. The conceptual implications of the differences between the traditional TCA-based studies (in the manufacturing context) and this study (in the service context) has been mentioned before. Methodologically, this study is one of the few studies that explicitly aims to generalize results across a broad range of service industries. This was achieved by the use of a specific service classification framework — the Service Process Matrix — by Schmenner (1986) for choosing the sample service industries that formed part of the sampling frame. This was in direct response to the call for the need for more generalizable frameworks in services research, as opposed to testing frameworks in more limited contexts.

The managerial relevance of the current study is quite apparent in that most firms are engaged in or will be engaged in some form of outsourcing of service activities in their daily operations. The core vs. noncore distinction has been one decision rule that managers have used in deciding which activities to outsource. However, as highlighted in our study, while the core vs. noncore distinction may be relevant, other factors have a more significant impact on the decision to use outsourcing or in-house sourcing for a service activity. This study directly ascertains those factors and provides some useful insights to managers.

This study is a first attempt at developing a framework for understanding outsourcing of service activities. Based on this exploratory study, we hope that this study will encourage more researchers to further refine the framework and the measurement of constructs. There are various other issues relating to outsourcing of services that are also interesting areas for future research. First, the scope of the empirical part of this study was service firms. The same needs to be examined in the context of product manufacturing firms, that is, outsourcing of service activities by product manufacturing firms. Another area of future research is the need to examine the role of relationship management in outsourcing. The management of outsourcing relationships between service outsourcees and outsourcers is also an area that needs further examination. As more companies are engaging in outsourcing arrangements, management of outsourcing contracts is proving to be a challenge. There is the need to understand the mechanics and dynamics between firms to manage these relationships.

References

Adler, P. S., & Clark, K. B. (1991). Behind the learning curve: A sketch of the learning process. *Management Science, 37*(3), 267-281.

Afifi, A., & Clark, V. (1984). *Computer-aided multivariate analysis.* Belmont, CA: Lifetime Learning.

Anderson, E. (1985). The salesperson as outside agent or employee: A transaction cost analysis. *Marketing Science, 4*, 234-253.

Auguste, B. G., Hao, Y., Singer, M., & Wiegand, M. (2002). The other side of outsourcing. *McKinsey Quarterly, 1*, 52-63.

Balakrishnan, S., & Wernerfelt, B. (1986). Technical change, competition and vertical integration. *Strategic Management Journal, 7*(4), 347-359.

Bateson, J. E. G. (1989). *Managing services marketing.* Hinsdale, IL: Dryden Press.

Berry, L. L. (1980, May-June). Service marketing is different. *Business, 30,* 24-29.

Bettis, R. A., Bradley, S. P., & Hamel, G. (1992). Outsourcing and industrial decline. *Academy of Management Executive, 6*(1), 7-21.

Bharadwaj, S. G., Varadarajan, P. R. & Fahy, J. (1993, October). Sustainable competitive advantage in service industries: A conceptual model and research propositions. *Journal of Marketing, 57*, 83-99.

Bitner, M. J. (1990, April). Evaluating service encounters: The effects of physical surroundings and employee responses. *Journal of Marketing, 54*, 69-82.

Bitner, M. J., Brown, S. W., & Meuter, M. L. (2000). Technology infusion in service encounters. *Journal of the Academy of Marketing Science, 28*(1), 138-149.

Boone, T., & Ganeshan, R. (2001). The effect of information technology on learning in professional service organizations. *Journal of Operations Management, 19*, 485-495.

Bowen, D. E. (1990). Interdisciplinary study of service: Some progress, some prospects. *Journal of Business Research, 20*, 71-79.

Bowen, D. E., & Jones, G. R. (1986). Transaction cost analysis of service organization-customer exchange. *Academy of Management Review, 11*(2), 428-441.

Buckley, P. J., & Casson, M. (1976). *The future of the multinational enterprise.* Boston: Macmillan.

Cannon, J. P., & Perreault, W. D., Jr. (1999). Buyer-seller relationships in business markets. *Journal of Marketing Research, 36*(4), 439-460.

Carman, J., & Langeard, E. (1980). Growth strategies for service firms. *Strategic Management Journal, 1*, 7-22.

Caves, R. E., & Porter, M. E. (1977). From entry barriers to mobility barriers. *Quarterly Journal of Economics, 91*, 241-261.

Clark, T., Rajaratnam, D., & Smith, T. (1996). Toward a theory of international services: Marketing intangibles in a world of nations. *Journal of International Marketing, 4*(2), 9-28.

Contractor, F. K., & Lorange, P. (1988). *Cooperative strategies in international business.* Lexington, MA: Lexington Books.

Das, A., & Handfield, R. B. (1997). A meta-analysis of doctoral dissertations in purchasing. *Journal of Operations Management, 15*, 101-121.

Erramilli, M. K., & Rao, C. P. (1993, July). Service firms' international entry-mode choice: A modified transaction cost analysis approach. *Journal of Marketing, 57*, 19-38.

Fisk, R. P., Brown, S. W., & Bitner, M. J. (1993). Tracking the evolution of the services marketing literature. *Journal of Retailing, 69*(1), 61-103.

Fuchs, V. (1968). *The service economy.* New York: Columbia University Press.

Grant, R. M., & Baden-Fuller, C. (1995). A knowledge-based theory of inter-firm collaboration. *Academy of Management Journal, 20*, 17-21.

Greer, C. R., Youngblood, S. A., & Gray, D. A. (1999). Human resource management outsourcing: The make or buy decision. *Academy of Management Executive, 13*(3), 85-96.

Hakansson, H., & Snehota, I. (Eds.). (1995). *Developing relationships in business networks.* London: Routledge.

Hart, C., Heskett, J. L., & Sasser, W. E. (1990, July-August). The profitable art of service recovery. *Harvard Business Review, 68*, 148-156.

Heidi, J. B. (1994, January). Interorganizational governance in marketing channels. *Journal of Marketing, 58*, 71-85.

Heskett, J. L. (1986). *Managing in the service economy.* Boston: Harvard Business School Press.

Hoffman, K. D., Kelley, S. W., & Rotalsky, H. M. (1995). Tracking service failures and employee recovery efforts. *Journal of Services Marketing, 9*(2), 49-61.

Appendix: Measurement

Intangibility (Cronbach's α = .56) [26,34]

Based on your estimate:

the proportion of cost in the service attributable to the transfer of tangible objects or materials is very small

the service is highly intangible (tangibility of a service refers to the characteristic of not being seen, felt, tasted, or touched in the same manner in which goods can be sensed)

Customization (Cronbach's α = .87) [74]

the service requires significant adaptation to meet our firm's specific needs

the service is highly standardized (reverse coded)

Inseparability [40,58]

production and consumption of the service occur simultaneously

Demand Uncertainty (Cronbach's α = .67) [46]

the demand for the service fluctuates significantly

forecasts for the use of the service are likely to be inaccurate

Technological Uncertainty (Cronbach's α = .60) [46]

the process/es (or technology/ies) involved with the service change frequently

the process/es (or technology/ies) involved with the service are likely to improve significantly in the near future

it is difficult to forecast changes in the process and/or technology involved with the service

Complexity (Cronbach's α = .55) [75]

the service involves a large number of steps/sequences in order to be performed

the service involves tasks that are relatively simple to perform (reverse codes)

Hsieh, C. M., Lazzarini, S. G., & Nickerson, J. A. (2002). Outsourcing and the variability of product performance: Data from international courier services. *Academy of Management Proceedings*, G1-G6.

Huber, R. L. (1993, January-February). How continental bank outsourced its crown jewels. *Harvard Business Review, 71*, 121-129.

John, G., & Weitz, B. A. (1988). Forward integration into distribution: An empirical test of transaction cost analysis. *Journal of Law, Economics, and Organizations, 4*(2), 337-355.

Joskow, P. L. (1987). Contract duration and relation-specific investments: Empirical evidence from coal markets. *The American Economic Review, 77*(1), 168-185.

Kachigan, S. K. (1986). *Statistical analysis: An interdisciplinary introduction to univariate and multivariate methods.* New York: Radius Press.

Kelley, B. (1995). Outsourcing marches on. *Journal of Business Strategy, 16*(4), 38-42.

Klein, S., Frazier, G. L., & Roth, V. J. (1990, May). A transaction cost analysis model of channel integration in international markets. *Journal of Marketing Research, 27*, 196-208.

Kohnke, L. (1990, July). Designing a customer satisfaction measurement program. *Bank Marketing, 22*, 27-29.

Kotabe, M. (1990). The relationship between offshore sourcing and innovativeness of U.S. multinational firms: An empirical investigation. *Journal of International Business Studies, 21*(4), 623-639.

Kotabe, M. (1992). *Global sourcing strategy: R&D, manufacturing, and marketing interfaces.* New York: Quorum Books.

Kotabe, M., & Swan, S. (1994). Offshore sourcing: Reaction, maturation, and consolidation of U.S. multinationals. *Journal of International Business Studies, 25*, 115-140.

Lacity, M. C., Willcocks, L. P., & Feeny, D. F. (1995, May-June). IT outsourcing: Maximize flexibility and control. *Harvard Business Review, 73*, 84-93.

Larsson, R., & Bowen, D. E. (1989). Organization and customer: Managing design and coordination of services. *Academy of Management Review, 14*(2), 213-233.

Levitt, T. (1981, May-June). Marketing intangible products and product intangibles. *Harvard Business Review, 59*, 94-102.

Lovelock, C. H. (1983). Classifying services to gain strategic marketing insights. *Journal of Marketing, 47*, 9-20.

Maxham, J. G., III (2001). Service recovery's influence on consumer satisfaction, positive word-of-mouth, and purchase intentions. *Journal of Business Research, 54*, 11-24.

Mills, P. K., & Margulies, N. (1980). Toward a core typology of service organizations. *Academy of Management Review, 5*(2), 255-265.

Monteverde, K., & Teece, D. J. (1982). Supplier switching costs and vertical integration in the automobile industry. *Bell Journal of Economics, 13*, 206-213.

Mullin, R. (1996). Managing the outsourced enterprise. *Journal of Business Strategy, 17*(4), 28-32.

Murray, J. Y., & Kotabe, M. (1999, September). Sourcing strategies of U.S. service companies: A modified transaction-cost analysis. *Strategic Management Journal, 20*, 791-809.

Murray, J. Y., Kotabe, M., & Wildt, A. R. (1995). Strategic and financial performance implications of global sourcing strategy: A contingency analysis. *Journal of International Business Studies, 26*, 181-202.

Parasuraman, A., Zeithaml, V. A., & Berry, L. L. (1985). A conceptual model of service quality and its implications for future research. *Journal of Marketing, 49*, 41-50.

Patterson, P. G., & Cicic, M. (1995). A typology of service firms in international markets: An empirical investigation. *Journal of International Marketing, 3*(4), 57-83.

Piesch, R. (1995, May-June). When outsourcing goes awry. *Harvard Business Review, 73*, 24-37.

Poppo, L., & Zenger, T. (1998). Testing alternate theories of the firm: Transaction cost, knowledge-based, and measurement. *Strategic Management Journal, 19*(9), 853-877.

Porter, M. E. (1980). *Competitive strategy*. New York: The Free Press.

Prahalad, C. K., & Hamel, G. (1990, May-June). The core competence of the corporation. *Harvard Business Review, 68*, 79-91.

Regan, W. J. (1963, July). The service revolution. *Journal of Marketing, 27*, 57-62.

Rothery, B., & Robertson, I. (1995). *The truth about outsourcing*. Hampshire, UK: Gower Publishing.

Schmenner, R. W. (1986). How can service businesses survive and prosper? *Sloan Management Review, 27*, 21-32.

Sheth, J. N., Sisodia, R. S., & Sharma, A. (2000). The a consequences of customer-centric marketing. *Journal of Marketing Science, 28*(1), 55-66.

Shostack, G. L. (1977, April). Breaking free from product mar of Marketing, 41, 73-80.

Shostack, G. L. (1987, January). Service positioning through st *Journal of Marketing, 51*, 34-43.

Smith, A. K., Bolton, R. N., & Wagner, J. (1999). A mod satisfaction with service encounters involving failure and *nal of Marketing Research, 36*(3), 356-372.

Solomon, M. R., Surprenant, C., Czepiel, J. A., & Gutman, E. G theory perspective on dyadic interactions: The service enc of Marketing, 49, 99-111.

Sutcliffe, K. M., & Zaheer, A. (1998). Uncertainty in the trans ment: An empirical test. *Strategic Management Journal*

Tushman, M. L., & Nelson, R. R. (1990, March). Introductio organizations and innovation. *Administrative Science Qu*

Venkatraman, N. (1997). Beyond outsourcing: Managing IT value center. *Sloan Management Review, 38*, 51-76.

Walker, G., & Weber, D. (1984, September). A transaction c make-or-buy decisions. *Administrative Science Quarterl*

Webster, F. E., Jr. (1992, October). The changing role of m corporation. *Journal of Marketing, 56*, 1-17.

Williamson, O. E. (1975). *Markets and hierarchies: Analysi implications*. New York: The Free Press.

Williamson, O. E. (1985). *The economic institutions of capi markets, relational contracting*. New York: The Free P

Zeithaml, V. A. (1981). How consumer evaluation processes goods and services. In J. H. Donnelly & W. R. George (E of services (pp. 186-190). Chicago, IL: The American Mark tion.

Zeithaml, V. V., Parasuraman, A., & Berry, L. L. (1985). strategies in services marketing. *Journal of Marketing, 4*

Hsieh, C. M., Lazzarini, S. G., & Nickerson, J. A. (2002). Outsourcing and the variability of product performance: Data from international courier services. *Academy of Management Proceedings*, G1-G6.

Huber, R. L. (1993, January-February). How continental bank outsourced its crown jewels. *Harvard Business Review, 71*, 121-129.

John, G., & Weitz, B. A. (1988). Forward integration into distribution: An empirical test of transaction cost analysis. *Journal of Law, Economics, and Organizations, 4*(2), 337-355.

Joskow, P. L. (1987). Contract duration and relation-specific investments: Empirical evidence from coal markets. *The American Economic Review, 77*(1), 168-185.

Kachigan, S. K. (1986). *Statistical analysis: An interdisciplinary introduction to univariate and multivariate methods.* New York: Radius Press.

Kelley, B. (1995). Outsourcing marches on. *Journal of Business Strategy, 16*(4), 38-42.

Klein, S., Frazier, G. L., & Roth, V. J. (1990, May). A transaction cost analysis model of channel integration in international markets. *Journal of Marketing Research, 27*, 196-208.

Kohnke, L. (1990, July). Designing a customer satisfaction measurement program. *Bank Marketing, 22*, 27-29.

Kotabe, M. (1990). The relationship between offshore sourcing and innovativeness of U.S. multinational firms: An empirical investigation. *Journal of International Business Studies, 21*(4), 623-639.

Kotabe, M. (1992). *Global sourcing strategy: R&D, manufacturing, and marketing interfaces.* New York: Quorum Books.

Kotabe, M., & Swan, S. (1994). Offshore sourcing: Reaction, maturation, and consolidation of U.S. multinationals. *Journal of International Business Studies, 25*, 115-140.

Lacity, M. C., Willcocks, L. P., & Feeny, D. F. (1995, May-June). IT outsourcing: Maximize flexibility and control. *Harvard Business Review, 73*, 84-93.

Larsson, R., & Bowen, D. E. (1989). Organization and customer: Managing design and coordination of services. *Academy of Management Review, 14*(2), 213-233.

Levitt, T. (1981, May-June). Marketing intangible products and product intangibles. *Harvard Business Review, 59*, 94-102.

Lovelock, C. H. (1983). Classifying services to gain strategic marketing insights. *Journal of Marketing, 47*, 9-20.

Maxham, J. G., III (2001). Service recovery's influence on consumer satisfaction, positive word-of-mouth, and purchase intentions. *Journal of Business Research, 54*, 11-24.

Mills, P. K., & Margulies, N. (1980). Toward a core typology of service organizations. *Academy of Management Review, 5*(2), 255-265.

Monteverde, K., & Teece, D. J. (1982). Supplier switching costs and vertical integration in the automobile industry. *Bell Journal of Economics, 13*, 206-213.

Mullin, R. (1996). Managing the outsourced enterprise. *Journal of Business Strategy, 17*(4), 28-32.

Murray, J. Y., & Kotabe, M. (1999, September). Sourcing strategies of U.S. service companies: A modified transaction-cost analysis. *Strategic Management Journal, 20*, 791-809.

Murray, J. Y., Kotabe, M., & Wildt, A. R. (1995). Strategic and financial performance implications of global sourcing strategy: A contingency analysis. *Journal of International Business Studies, 26*, 181-202.

Parasuraman, A., Zeithaml, V. A., & Berry, L. L. (1985). A conceptual model of service quality and its implications for future research. *Journal of Marketing, 49*, 41-50.

Patterson, P. G., & Cicic, M. (1995). A typology of service firms in international markets: An empirical investigation. *Journal of International Marketing, 3*(4), 57-83.

Piesch, R. (1995, May-June). When outsourcing goes awry. *Harvard Business Review, 73*, 24-37.

Poppo, L., & Zenger, T. (1998). Testing alternate theories of the firm: Transaction cost, knowledge-based, and measurement. *Strategic Management Journal, 19*(9), 853-877.

Porter, M. E. (1980). *Competitive strategy.* New York: The Free Press.

Prahalad, C. K., & Hamel, G. (1990, May-June). The core competence of the corporation. *Harvard Business Review, 68*, 79-91.

Regan, W. J. (1963, July). The service revolution. *Journal of Marketing, 27*, 57-62.

Rothery, B., & Robertson, I. (1995). *The truth about outsourcing.* Hampshire, UK: Gower Publishing.

Schmenner, R. W. (1986). How can service businesses survive and prosper? *Sloan Management Review, 27*, 21-32.

Sheth, J. N., Sisodia, R. S., & Sharma, A. (2000). The antecedents and consequences of customer-centric marketing. *Journal of the Academy of Marketing Science, 28*(1), 55-66.

Shostack, G. L. (1977, April). Breaking free from product marketing. *Journal of Marketing, 41*, 73-80.

Shostack, G. L. (1987, January). Service positioning through structural change. *Journal of Marketing, 51*, 34-43.

Smith, A. K., Bolton, R. N., & Wagner, J. (1999). A model of customer satisfaction with service encounters involving failure and recovery. *Journal of Marketing Research, 36*(3), 356-372.

Solomon, M. R., Surprenant, C., Czepiel, J. A., & Gutman, E. G. (1985). A role theory perspective on dyadic interactions: The service encounter. *Journal of Marketing, 49*, 99-111.

Sutcliffe, K. M., & Zaheer, A. (1998). Uncertainty in the transaction environment: An empirical test. *Strategic Management Journal, 19*, 1-23.

Tushman, M. L., & Nelson, R. R. (1990, March). Introduction: Technology, organizations and innovation. *Administrative Science Quarterly, 35*, 1-8.

Venkatraman, N. (1997). Beyond outsourcing: Managing IT resources as a value center. *Sloan Management Review, 38*, 51-76.

Walker, G., & Weber, D. (1984, September). A transaction cost approach to make-or-buy decisions. *Administrative Science Quarterly, 29*, 373-391.

Webster, F. E., Jr. (1992, October). The changing role of marketing in the corporation. *Journal of Marketing, 56*, 1-17.

Williamson, O. E. (1975). *Markets and hierarchies: Analysis and antitrust implications*. New York: The Free Press.

Williamson, O. E. (1985). *The economic institutions of capitalism: Firms, markets, relational contracting*. New York: The Free Press.

Zeithaml, V. A. (1981). How consumer evaluation processes differ between goods and services. In J. H. Donnelly & W. R. George (Eds.), *Marketing of services* (pp. 186-190). Chicago, IL: The American Marketing Association.

Zeithaml, V. V., Parasuraman, A., & Berry, L. L. (1985). Problems and strategies in services marketing. *Journal of Marketing, 49*, 33-46.

Appendix: Measurement

Intangibility (Cronbach's α = .56) [26,34]

Based on your estimate:

- the proportion of cost in the service attributable to the transfer of tangible objects or materials is very small
- the service is highly intangible (tangibility of a service refers to the characteristic of not being seen, felt, tasted, or touched in the same manner in which goods can be sensed)

Customization (Cronbach's α = .87) [74]

- the service requires significant adaptation to meet our firm's specific needs
- the service is highly standardized (reverse coded)

Inseparability [40,58]

- production and consumption of the service occur simultaneously

Demand Uncertainty (Cronbach's α = .67) [46]

- the demand for the service fluctuates significantly
- forecasts for the use of the service are likely to be inaccurate

Technological Uncertainty (Cronbach's α = .60) [46]

- the process/es (or technology/ies) involved with the service change frequently
- the process/es (or technology/ies) involved with the service are likely to improve significantly in the near future
- it is difficult to forecast changes in the process and/or technology involved with the service

Complexity (Cronbach's α = .55) [75]

- the service involves a large number of steps/sequences in order to be performed
- the service involves tasks that are relatively simple to perform (reverse codes)

End-Customer Contact

• the service involves considerable contact with our end-customers

Type of Customer Contact

• the service involves direct (i.e., face-to-face) contact with our end-customers as opposed to indirect (i.e., distant form of, e.g., telephone) contact

Core vs. Noncore (Cronbach's α = .54) [43]

• the service aids considerably in formulating and implementing strategies that improve our firm's efficiency and/or effectiveness
• most of our competitors have access to the service (reverse coded)
• the service can easily be imitated by our competitors (reverse coded)

Number of Alternate Suppliers [46]

• there are many potential (alternate) suppliers for the service

Section III

Risk Issues in Management Information Systems Outsourcing

Chapter XII

Outsourcing and Information Systems Development:
How Complementary Corporate Cultures Minimize the Risks of Outsourced Systems Projects

Julie E. Kendall, Rutgers University, USA

Kenneth E. Kendall, Rutgers University, USA

Abstract

Many firms outsource creation of program code for management information systems, but not all experiences are successful. Although some researchers and practitioners are quick to blame failures on differing country cultures, this does not appear to be the reason. Rather it is the compatibility or differences in corporate cultures between the client company and the outsourcing partner that may help or hinder the development of quality systems. In this chapter we examine the metaphors found in the language of client corporations and outsourcing partners and explain how to look for compatibility when designing various types of information systems including traditional MIS, decision support systems, expert systems and AI, executive information systems, cooperative systems, and competitive systems. We explain how the development of certain types of systems can benefit from situations where more positive metaphors exist and offer some guidelines for the MIS practitioner, thereby minimizing risk and increasing the likelihood of a more successful client company-outsourcing partner relationship.

Introduction

"We will first crush our competition in the Northwest, then we'll annihilate them completely," is a quotation we heard not long ago from a company that wanted to stop at nothing short of "global domination" in their industry. They were building a new Web site and were determined to be the amazon.com of their field. It was clear to us that this company could and eventually would design a Web site that was innovative and customer-oriented to sufficiently reach premier, number one status in their industry.

If, however, they decided to outsource the design and construction of their Web site, would they still be able to speak successfully in those terms? Would their outsourcing partner need to adopt the same language and extreme philosophy? Would a more suitable metaphor be more appropriate for the outsourcing partner? Can we predict, encourage, and even change the probability of success of a client company-outsourcing partner relationship using metaphors? Those are the questions we examine in this chapter.

Corporate culture is defined as "The moral, social, and behavioral norms of an organization based on the beliefs, attitudes, and priorities of its members" (Corporate culture, 2005, p. 1). One manner in which we create, convey and maintain a corporate culture is through the shared use of metaphors. Metaphors are artifacts of culture that reflect the culture but also create the organization by giving voice to beliefs, attitudes, and priorities in a uniquely symbolic and meaningful manner.

One must be cognizant that organizations always support many diverse cultures (which are more appropriately called subcultures). Hence, organizations accommodate the use of multiple metaphors. However, there is usually a predominant metaphor that crystallizes the reality of the culture for its participants in such a profound way that it clarifies the underlying morals, social expectations, desired behaviors and more. We have found this to be true especially in the instance of metaphors and the creation of successful information systems.

The current thinking is that while culture is important, organizations do not design "personnel polices and reward systems" around cultural values because of a well-founded fear of stereotyping cultures in a superficial way. The concern is that such awkward and overbearing tactics will not help to deepen or inculcate the culture with organizational members, but will only serve to alienate employees because of the artifice of the approach and the clumsiness of the cultural views that is exhibited.

Metaphors are all around us. They are part of the artifacts of our society a well as our corporate cultures. We need to listen carefully to each person we meet on the client company's team as well as the outsourcing partner's team and hear what stories they tell. When someone uses a metaphor, they are saying that something *is* something else. If employees say that "We are a family" they do not mean they are like a family, they mean that they *are* one. This distinction is an important one to comprehend, because once you grasp it, you can then recognize that there is a father or mother who helps all of the other team members in completing the project.

In this chapter, we reflect on outsourcing, and where metaphors that create and sustain a corporate culture can help in minimizing the risks involved in choosing a partner. We look at nine key metaphors that are most common in business. Then we explain how the development of certain types of systems can benefit from situations where more positive metaphors exist. Finally we offer some guidelines and discuss whether it is possible or desirable to change a corporate culture's predominant metaphor into a more positive one, thereby increasing the likelihood of a more successful client company-outsourcing partner relationship.

Outsourcing and Risk

There was a time when outsourcing was an ill-regarded euphemism synonymous with corporate downsizing. Other authors hasten to point out that the number one problem associated with outsourcing is the fear of losing one's job or a change in the nature of the job (Elmuti & Kathawala, 2000).

Outsourcing in contemporary terms enjoys an improved connotation so companies now refer to the benefits the company receives form outsourcing rather than the problems encountered by the unfortunate employees who are targets of downsizing. With outsourcing, companies believed that they could make themselves more responsive to change and take advantage of lower costs.

Presently, we can view outsourcing as an intelligent business strategy, not a tactical move to save money. But as we know, anything that can be commoditized can be outsourced (Ochs, 2005). This includes software development.

A client company needs to handle every imaginable scenario in a spectrum of possibilities. It is not sufficient to write up goals and standards and then blithely let the outsourcing partner take over. Outsourcing involves:

- Evaluating the potential outsourcing partners
- Understanding the needs of the outsourcing partner
- Building relationships
- Understanding and resolving political issues

A publishing company, for example, agrees to publish a book written by a given author, but then proceeds to outsource all of the editing, proofreading, art, and printing to various outsourcing partners. If the art manuscript that accompanies the text material is drafted incorrectly, the outsourcing partner could argue with the publisher or hide their errors blaming the author, because the outsourcing partner was fearful of losing future jobs. Although this is considered to a dubious ethical practice in the United States, the outsourcing partner could ascribe to a different ethical code and feel that it is standard business practice.

 Of course this practice is short-term, because an outsourcing partner would not survive very long if too many complaints were lodged against their workers or regarding the goods or services they produced, that is, unless the outsourcing partner worked with different editors or different publishers and the problem was never caught. If the same errors were made by the publisher's own employee (as part of a non-outsourced, in-house project) it is much more likely that workers who are substandard would be revealed more quickly.

Some companies assert that outsourcing should be a relationship or partnership (Weston, 2002) rather than a temporary agreement that is required to get a project completed. This would build trust and avoid some of the problems of short-term thinking discussed earlier.

Schniederjans, Schniederjans, and Schniederjans (2005) identify other possible risks in the outsourcing process. Some of these risks include potential problems such as incorrectly identifying the outsource provider; failure to negotiate goals and measures of outsourcing performance; and evaluating the outsource provider and giving feedback to the provider. These risks can be minimized if one can match the provider with the company seeking an outsourcing partner.

Schniederjans, Schniederjans, and Schniederjans (2005, p. 41) point out that although researchers like Gouge (2003, pp. 149-154) claim that outsourcing transfers risk from the client company to the outsourcing partner, the outsourcing relationship invites new risks, many of which are substantial. These risks involve, labor, capital, infrastructure, instability, ideology, legalities, language, social names, gender roles, migration, urbanization, and population. The elements in this list can be gathered into four groups: economic, political, demographics, and culture. It is the culture group that we rely on as the organizing framework in this chapter.

There is the possibility that language, social norms, or gender roles may affect the success or failure of a client company-outsourcing partnership relationship. For example, differences in language may increase the risk of important instructions being misinterpreted.

Social norms can vary widely across cultures as well. This category includes the behavior and shared values of a group of people including, but not limited to political values, religious values, class divisions, and attitudes towards trust. Some of these social norms are explicitly expressed while others are part of the layers of culture, ready to be discovered by an outsider (in this case the client company).

Although languages and social norms were assumed be unique for different groups of people, we found that the same archetypal metaphors existed in every country and culture. Therefore, communicating through the use of metaphors can help companies and their outsourcing partner. Trust, for example, can become an international cultural issue and must be considered when determining the risk of a potential outsourcing failure (Alijifri, Pons, & Collins, 2003; Handby, 1996).

Considering risk factors is critical in assessing the potential success or failure of proposed outsourcing projects (Adeleye, Annansingh, Nunes, & Baptista, 2004; Sen, 2004). Meisler (2004) and Natovich (2003) point out some of the problems that arise when the outsourcing partner experiences cultural differences that separate it from the client company.

Metaphors, Corporate Culture, and IS

Metaphors and their application to business systems is a topic that has been explored before, albeit in a less formal way (Allen & Lientz, 1978; Lanzara, 1983; Madsen, 1989; Schon, 1979). The first researcher to write systematically and persuasively about business metaphors and their predominance in executive speech was Clancy (1989). He discussed six predominant metaphors that were used more often than others in business rhetoric. Boland (1989) went on to discuss metaphorical traps in designing new systems, and Kendall and Kendall

(1993) studied how systems were developed and how a specific metaphor was enacted during development of new systems or used by a project team who would design and develop a new information system.

Our approach is based on interviewing outsourcing providers and determining how best to characterize their organizations and employees. The next step is ensuring that the customer and the organization seeking help match with each other and ascertaining whether they belong together. Any company seeking outsourcing partners should ask themselves a series of basic questions that will increase their likelihood of success. Rather than concentrating solely on what the customer thinks, they should also focus on whether or not they are compatible with the outsourcing partner.

It has been shown that the success of new information systems development depends a great deal on the corporate culture. In particular, one of the variables that can transform success into failure is the use of a negative metaphor in the organization. There are adverse metaphors such as zoo, when it is used to state, "This place is a zoo when we have to handle a crisis," but even when positive metaphors exist, they don't always match with the objectives of the system under development.

For example, if a family metaphor is present, as was the case with the Egyptian cabinet in the 1990s, we found that the successful development of decision support systems was possible. However, even though the family metaphor is an excellent metaphor, creating a suitable climate for developing many types of systems, it was not helpful for the development of competitive systems. In that instance, the appropriate metaphor would be a competitive game, or even war. The same applies for companies seeking outsourcing partners. Partners, as is often proclaimed, need to be "on the same page" as the companies they are working with.

The next section will discuss all of these metaphors in order to provide definitions and context for the symbolic meaning of metaphors in corporate cultures.

Organizational Metaphors

Many authors have written about metaphors, but Clancy (1989) was the first to try to tie specific metaphors to business rhetoric. He identifies six main metaphors. Although Clancy was comprehensive with his research, it was somewhat constrained because it focused on the metaphors of executives or leaders. These executives use metaphors to describe, project, and even attempt to persuade individuals through the persuasive power of their rhetoric. The metaphors were: journey, game, war, machine, organism, and society.

Common Business Metaphors

Later on Kendall and Kendall (1993, 1994) built on Clancy's work by interviewing employees who were systems users, and determined that there were three additional metaphors not identified in Clancy's research. One metaphor (the family) was expressed quite often and always in a positive way. The two other "worker metaphors" were remarkably and undeniably negative. They were the zoo and the jungle. If employees were unhappy with how the organization was progressing, they would enact one of these two metaphors.

The Journey Metaphor

Imagine the journey metaphor as a sea voyage led by a captain and shared by the crew. Executives like to tell their employees (and often their stakeholders) that "We are all on this journey together." We can speculate that this is because times may be tough (there may be an impending storm or the waves appear dangerous). Journeys can be adventurous, too, but in all cases there seems to be an element of risk and potential reward. Companies like Vanguard Investments take the metaphor seriously. The executive usually likes to be pictured as the captain, a strong leader, one who can get the crew to perform cooperatively to reach its goal amid dangerous circumstances. Of course, some organizational members may speak of an unsuccessful endeavor as "sinking," "running aground," or "being stranded." Most of the time, however, the journey metaphor is a positive one.

The Game Metaphor

Teamwork is the key to the game. This metaphor has nothing to do with chess; instead it evokes a competitive game, sometimes a contact sport like football or basketball. There are some risks (players can get hurt) but they are mainly manageable. The leader is called a coach, and the coach needs to be strategic, tactical, supportive, and enthusiastic. In some games, winning is not everything, it is the only thing. Usually, the company team pits itself against an external competitor, but still plays by a set of rules.

The War Metaphor

War is certainly competitive, and warring parties may not always play by the rules. The goal is foremost in this metaphor. War is also risky, unpredictable, and much of the time, chaotic. In ancient history the leader physically went to war with the army, but in recent times the general often sits safely behind a desk. The general wants to obtain as much information about the enemy as possible. Orders are given from the top down. A war metaphor may be useful when a company is endangered or threatened by a competitor, but a company needs to be circumspect in their maneuvering when this metaphor is present. It is possible that a company will pay the ultimate price. Wars can mean that one company survives while the other does not.

The Machine Metaphor

Machines are usually designed to perform a single function, which is often a well-designed, albeit repetitive, task. Machines are expected to run all of the time and to run smoothly. Rationality and the predictability that accompanies it are the major entailments of the machine metaphor. Employees tend to not be creative or inspired when the machine metaphor is present, but employees do get the job done. Employees are considered as replaceable parts, and at first glance, someone contemplating outsourcing may want a group of replaceable employees to do the job. But this means that individuals are unimportant in their individual contributions and this is traditionally thought of as a very short-term approach. Note that neither the designer nor the machine itself are usually blamed for breaking down once in awhile. This is seen to be a normal occurrence.

The Organism Metaphor

An organism grows and even evolves. This metaphor is the opposite of the machine metaphor in numerous ways. If employees view the organization as an organism, they are realizing it was born and can mature, grow, and perhaps even die. There is some orderliness in this metaphor: a tomato plant cannot grow up to be a cactus. However, the quality of the system can be different, based on the leader (in this case, assume a gardener) who will nurture the plants by feeding and watering them, caring for them until they grow to maturity. Another interpretation of the leader in the organism metaphor is the innovator, someone who can envision a new garden, then proceed to plant and care for it.

The Society Metaphor

The society can be an organization that contains a population of employees that all possess different subgoals that will eventually coalesce to form the society. Picture a country or state as the society and a leader who is head-of-state. The society, over time, sets the rules of behavior within the society, and the head-of-state follows the rules and executes the decisions made by the members of society. This metaphor is useful in outsourcing, because the outsourcing partners need to develop the systems within the set of rules given to them.

The Family Metaphor

After imagining the perfect family for a minute or two, now imagine the animated cartoon family, *The Simpsons*. Families can mean many different things to different people, but they almost always have a positive outlook. A family may be chaotic; everyone may articulate their own wishes and desires, but in the end there is comfort in the family. "We know one another" is an expression one will hear if the employees think they are part of a family. In addition, the family members enacting this metaphor are always supportive of one another.

The Zoo Metaphor

"It's a zoo here" is often heard when things are so chaotic that employees feel everything is out of control. As we know, however, zoos are usually tightly controlled areas where many different animals live in cages, but do not cause a lot of trouble. The leader is the zoo keeper and they keep every animal in order. But when employees speak, the zoo metaphor portrays chaos and unpredictability. They are really describing a three-ring circus, not a zoo. There are different animals as well, but if the patrons attempt to focus on just one, they will not be able to. The zoo metaphor is a negative metaphor in almost every instance.

The Jungle Metaphor

When employees use a jungle metaphor, they want to be rescued. The jungle is chaos. It is also extremely dangerous. We could lose our lives if our guide (the leader for this metaphor) does not help us to find our way out of the jungle. The guide in this case can also be a savior. When people are thinking "Every man for himself" and "Survival of the fittest," it is a sign that new systems are not going to enjoy much of a chance of being developed for that organization. The jungle metaphor is almost always negative.

Systems Development and Positive Metaphors

Once positive metaphors (including journey, family, game, society, machine, society, and organism) are enacted by employees as part of the culture of the company, the successful development of systems can take place. Depending on the system that is commissioned for development, the right metaphors need to be present. Now that we have identified the major metaphors found in business, we can explain further how these will impact the outsourcing relationship.

Table 1. Systems and positive metaphors that would encourage their development

Type of System	Metaphors that encourage success in a client company	Metaphors that will encourage success in an outsourcing partner
Traditional MIS	Society Family	Society
Decision Support Systems	Family Society	Society
Expert Systems/AI	Machine Game Organism	Machine
Executive Systems	Organism Game	Game
Collaborative systems	Journey Game Organism	Game
Competitive systems	War Game Organism	Game

Although the success or failure of the development of information systems has been shown to be affected by the predominant metaphor within a company, outsourcing requires more. Not only does the positive metaphor need to be present in the organization, but a complementary or harmonizing metaphor must also present in the contracted outsourcing partner.

Table 1 illustrates which metaphors seem to be more conducive to successful working relationships between the company and its IT outsourcing partner. The complementary metaphors are ones that are part of the two or three metaphors that a company needs to foster the development of quality systems. In order for development to succeed, companies need to encourage their employees to adopt them (on a long-term basis). We mention long-term, of course, because, the encouragement of metaphors is not a superficial treatment that can be magically applied to an organization to transform culture overnight.

Systems that Keep Track of Internal Information

Traditional MIS tend to be internally-focused, so metaphors such as society (where rules are important) and family in which a traditional patriarch decides what is best for his family, encourage the development of these systems. MIS systems are aimed mainly at the middle manager and include routine reports like summary reports, error reports, and so on.

MIS are systems that keep the house orderly. When management information systems need to be outsourced, the outsourcing partner needs to have an appreciation for this. Because the outsourcing partner does not need to be creative, the society metaphor would suit this situation the best.

Systems that Support Decisions

Decision support systems (DSS) share many of the same properties as management information systems. Decision support systems are still aimed at internal problem-solving, but differ from traditional MIS in that they try to process many conflicting goals. A manager who depends on a DSS to aid and support their decision (not make it for them) can generate alternatives, assign them weights, and balance all of the factors during the DSS process.

The family metaphor appears to be the best for a client company that needs a decision support or business intelligence system. It seems that everyone in a family has a different set of goals, but in the end their defining characteristic is of staying together as a family. It would not be appropriate for the outsourcing partner to have a family metaphor, however. The outsourcing partner's goal should be well-defined when they sign the contract to develop the DSS. The society metaphor works the best in this case.

Systems that Perform Like Experts

Expert systems, just as DSS, are aids to help the decision maker solve a problem. The difference is that the process is more mechanical. Expert systems are rule-based and in order to develop an expert system, one needs to capture the knowledge and the rule execution behavior of the expert. Metaphors that are orderly and follow a set of rules work best.

The machine and game metaphors are preeminent when it comes to setting the environment to build expert systems. Systems that need to develop and grow, even evolve, would find an organism metaphor more useful. Although it has been shown that all three metaphors result in successful systems, the best metaphor for the outsourcing partner would be the game. The partner simply needs to follow all rules set forth by the systems designer and be made to feel as if they are part of the team.

Systems for Executives

Executive information systems (EIS) are those systems that are built for the CEO and other top executives, so that they know (1) what is happening within the company on a summary (not detailed) basis, (2) what they want (in great detail, if they ask), and (3) what the competition, government, and legal worlds are doing that may have an effect on the organization. Rockart and Treacy (1982) noted that EIS may require separate administration apart from traditional decision support systems. The gathering together of the information required for this system demands some manner of compatible metaphor.

In this case the game or organism metaphors work best. The organism metaphor allows the EIS to adapt, while the game is more structured and more strategically oriented. Can EIS systems be outsourced? Of, course. The outsourcing partner needs to try to present the information that executives want and need, all the while presenting them in the form requested. For example, some executives work best from information displayed in tables, others like to work with graphs. Although an organism metaphor would be ideal, asynchronous communication difficulties may make this type of metaphor unworkable. The client company should search for a partner expressing a game metaphor. That will work the best.

Systems that Aid Group Collaboration

While executive information systems are developed with information needs of executives in mind, collaborative systems are aimed at sharing information with everyone else in the organization. Cooperative systems are called group decision support systems (GDSS) or computer-supported collaborative work (CSCW). The distinctions between these systems have blurred over time and a variety of applications, but basically both are task oriented systems that make use of a computer for retrieving and storing information, calculation performance measures and summary information, and assisting a group of people to make a sound decision.

Cooperative systems are goal-oriented. The group needs to solve a problem and make a decision. The process is different from that of a physical meeting and supporters of GDSS claim that it is more democratic in allowing members who normally do not speak up at a meeting to be active online and even receive credit for their contribution.

Systems that Encourage Competitiveness

Competition means that the company wants to develop a system that goes beyond anything the competition has done and wants in the end to capture something that a competitor has. Competitive systems are the only systems that can benefit from an organization's use of the war metaphor.

War is the ultimate competition, after all. An organism metaphor can encourage innovation. A team can "take the ball away" from another team, but war really is the extreme metaphor a company can use to promote competitive systems (for example, the airline's system that became the first frequent-flyer program). A war metaphor is useful here, and the company can spirit away customers, but not land or treasure, like in a conventional war. One can clearly see why a war metaphor would not be useful for an outsourcing partner. War is uncertain. It can have disastrous results; the partner can turn out to be a spy or traitor.

The leader, in this case the general, may not be the ideal organizational member to manage both the client end and the outsourcing partner end of the relationship. Superior competitive metaphors are game and organism. Game is most obvious because one company is directly competing with another company. An alternative is the organism, where it is possible to grow things in an orderly manner and the leader is often more creative that the general or coach. When it comes to the outsourcing partner, however, creativity is not necessarily desirable. Neither is yet another general. Consequently, the game metaphor is likely to work best here.

Discussion

We can all agree that the process of outsourcing IT development demands a facilitative leader who is present in metaphors like the journey (the ship captain), the game (the coach), and the organism (the gardener who nurtures the garden). Part of the system can involve the computer (and can even be elementary, such as using basic email functions), but the entire system takes advantage of the facilitator. When systems like this are to be outsourced, look for a game metaphor in the organization. The outsourcing partner should not envision itself on a journey looking for land, nor should they see themselves as an organism, where the gardener tends the garden. The outsourcing partner must be goal-oriented, decisive, and dedicated to finishing the project. The coach is the best leader in this case.

Some authors, such as Marshall (1999) and Bracey (2003), have found that the process of building trust may require a long-term approach, but it starts with values such as honesty and shared interests. In this chapter we show that shared metaphors are not necessary; firms should strive to see that their metaphors are compatible however. We believe that members of client companies involved in creating, sharing and maintaining the culture (or even extending it to an outsourcing partner) will make much more rapid gains if they grasp the bigger picture of culture that a predominant metaphor offers.

For example, it is certainly acceptable for the client company to express themselves in terms of a family, but the outsourcing partner resembles a society. The metaphors do not need to be identical. Rather, they need only be compatible.

What if one cannot identify a single metaphor or even find more than one metaphor existing in the partner organization? Is it possible for a company to have a game metaphor and a journey metaphor at the same time? If some parts of a company are like a zoo, can the company ever hope to be a machine? The answers to these questions depend, we think, on how tightly or loosely organized a company is, how large it is, and how fervently it values a democratic approach. Good small projects are developed all of the time, but great projects occur less often. Really successful innovations are rare and those projects, certainly, need a single predominant metaphor, which understandably means that all employees of the organization must be thinking along the same lines.

Choosing an Outsourcing Partner

If we are a client company, we can use our knowledge of metaphors to bear on our choice of an outsourcing partner. In each of the above examples, we look for key metaphors that might show themselves when discussing future business relationships with an outsourcing partner. If one potential partner doesn't reveal a positive metaphor, it may be best to choose another.

Is it possible, however, to change a partner? A CEO or CIO cannot simply instruct an employee to behave in a certain way. For example, a boss can order an employee to be more aggressive in selling land in Florida but would have a difficult time telling the employee how to do it. Therefore, a CEO cannot simply harangue employees to "Be more war-like," or "Act like a family." These metaphors exist as a tapestry of culture and they need to be woven into the fabric of outsourcing partnerships over time.

Leadership and Outsourcing

There are some researchers who believe that an outsourcing team needs to be established. Greaver (1999, pp. 37-57) and Gouge (2003, pp. 162-166) surface the notion of what type of project manager is required on the client company side. What sort of qualities should this person possess? Metaphor analysis allows us to look at the role of the project leader and determine what it will take to lead, given the fact that the outsourcing contract could be finite or the relationship might evolve into a permanent one. The war metaphor gives us a leader who is a general, and the team metaphor provides us with a coach. The organism metaphor leaves us with a gardener, while the family pictures the idealistic father. The society is led by a head-of-state, while the jungle requires a guide to extricate us from the overgrowth of vegetation. The machine was created by a designer or engineer who assembles all of the parts and oils the machine once in awhile. If a journey metaphor is present, the leader is likely to be a ship's captain, while the zoo needs a keeper.

Summary

In this chapter we looked at outsourcing risks. We were most concerned with the risks associated with culture as manifested in metaphors, and explained how controlling risk would possibly solve some of the problems inherent in selecting an outsourcing partner. We examined nine metaphors that are most commonly found in business, expressed by both executives and employees. Then we looked at which systems could deliver more successful development provided the presence of certain metaphors was possible. Extending this to the outsourcing partner, we identified the metaphor most useful for each type of IS development project. To minimize risk, one should look for these metaphors when establishing a relationship with an outsourcing partner. This chapter is useful in amplifying our appreciation for the importance of corporate culture as well as serving as a guide to choosing outsourcing partners based on the metaphors that are enacted by each party to the outsourcing relationship.

References

Adeleye, B., Annansingh, C., Nunes, F., & Baptista, M. (2004). Risk management practices in IS outsourcing: An investigation into commercial banks in Nigeria. *International Journal of Information Management, 24*(2), 167-181.

Alijifri, H. A., Pons, A., & Collins, D. (2003). Global e-commerce: A framework for understanding and overcoming the trust barrier. *Information Management and Computer Security, 14*(3), 130-138.

Allen, J., & Lientz, B. P. (1978). *Systems in action.* Santa Monica: Goodyear Publishing.

Boland, R. J., Jr. (1989). Metaphorical traps in developing information systems for human progress. In H. K. Klein & K. Kumar (Eds.), *Systems development for human progress* (pp. 277-290). New York: North Holland.

Bracey, H. (2003). *Building trust: How to get it! How to keep it!* New York: HB Artworks.

Clancy, J. J. (1989). Th*e invisible powers: The language of business.* Lexington, MA: Lexington Books.

Corporate culture. (2005). Retrieved March 15, 2006, from http://www.AuxilliumWest.com/culture.shtml

Elmuti, D., & Kathawala, Y. (2000). The effects of global outsourcing strategies on participants' attitudes and organizational effectiveness. *International Journal of Manpower, 21*(1/2), 112-129.

Gouge, I. (2003). *Shaping the IT organization.* London: Springer.

Greaver, M. F. (1999). *Strategic outsourcing.* New York: American Management Association.

Handby, J. (1996). Outsourcing: Perfecting partnerships. *Management Consultancy, 11*, 11-20.

Kendall, J. E., & Kendall, K. E. (1993). Metaphors and methodologies: Living beyond the systems machine. *MIS Quarterly, 17*(2), 149-171.

Kendall, J. E., & Kendall, K. E. (1994). Metaphors and their meaning for information systems development. *European Journal of Information Systems, 3*(1), 37-47.

Lanzara, G. F. (1983). The design process: Frames, metaphors, and games. In C. Ciborra & L. Schneider (Eds.), *Systems for, with and by the users* (pp. 29-40). New York: North Holland.

Madsen, K. H. (1989). Breakthrough by breakdown: Metaphors and structured domains. In H. K. Klein & K. Kumar (Eds.), *Systems development for human progress* (pp. 41-53). New York: North Holland.

Marshall, E. M. (1999). *Building trust at the speed of change: The power of the relationship-based corporation.* New York: American Management Association.

Meisler, A. (2004). Think globally, act rationally. *Workforce Management, 83*(1), 40-45.

Natovich, J. (2003). Vendor related risks in IT development: A chronology of an outsourced project failure. *Technology Analysis and Strategic Management, 15*(4), 409-420.

Ochs, R. (2005, June). Value added services a must. *Accounting Technology, 21*(1), 10.

Rockart, J. F., & Treacy, M. E. (1982). The CEO goes on-line. *Harvard Business Review, 60*(1), 82-88.

Schniederjans, M., Schniederjans, A., & Schniederjans, D. (2005). *Outsourcing and insourcing in an international context.* New York: M. E. Sharpe.

Schon, D. (1979). Generative metaphor: A perspective on problem setting in social policy. In A. Ortony (Ed.), *Metaphor and thought* (pp. 254-283). Cambridge, UK: Cambridge University Press.

Sen, S. (2004). The new mantra: The rise of enterprise outsourcing management. *FSO Magazine,* p. Q1. Retrieved June 8, 2006, from http://www.fsoutsourcing.com

Weston, R. (2002). Methodology: Ask the users. *InformationWeek, 915*, 40.

Chapter XIII

Managing Risks of IT Outsourcing

Leonardo Legorreta, California State University, USA

Rajneesh Goyal, California State University, USA

Abstract

Outsourcing is one of the most talked about and widely debated topics. Over the past few years, firms have been outsourcing their IT operations at increasing rates. The fact that firms are turning to outside vendors in increasing numbers in order to meet their needs does not mean that outsourcing is without problems. Firms often enter outsourcing deals without considering risks or assuming that all risks lay with the external service provider. In this chapter, we provide an overview of IT outsourcing, its risks, and a model for managing those risks. We identify different firm-vendor configurations for sustaining long-term relationships aimed at diversifying risk over time and discuss the need for psychological contracts to manage such outsourcing relationships.

Introduction

Outsourcing is one of the most talked about and widely debated topics. Firms are outsourcing their IT operations at an increasing rate over the past years. Research by Gartner projects the worldwide IT outsourcing market to grow from $180.5 billion in revenue in 2003 to $253.1 billion in 2008 at a compound annual growth rate (CAGR) of 7.2% (Caldwell, Young, Goodness, & Souza, 2004). Some of the top reasons for outsourcing are cost reductions, the ability to focus on core competencies, access to specialized expertise, relief from resource constraints, and to eliminate problem areas.

The fact that firms in increasing numbers are turning to outside vendors in order to meet their needs does not mean that outsourcing is without problems. While outsourcing has helped organizations achieve major benefits such as cost savings, increased flexibility, higher quality services, and access to new technology, unsuccessful outsourcing experiences have also been reported in which

Figure 1. Metro-Pier case study

> **Case Study: Metropolitan Pier and Exposition Authority**
>
> Metropolitan Pier and Exposition Authority (MPEA) owns and manages the McCormick Convention center, a business gathering facility, and the Navy Pier, a popular tourist attraction. In early 1998, MPEA with limited capabilities did not consider itself to be a technical service provider. However, on occasions clients requested local area network and Internet services for their conventions. At that time, MPEA opted to outsource the Internet and network services to a third party. In January 1998, MPEA signed a three year revenue-sharing deal with RedSky Technologies for all the show-floor network services.
>
> Soon thereafter, MPEA's business requirements started changing. Increasingly customers were now requesting IT services - private virtual local area networks, firewall implementations, and high-speed bandwidth. MPEA sensed that offering such value-added services would add to their core competencies.
>
> RedSky chose not to expand to meet the demands of MPEA. They would only design and build a new network for each convention, leaving MPEA to tear it down after the show. At this point, MPEA decided to insource the IT services and did not renew the three year contract. MPEA spent $1.5 million initially to build the infrastructure and since then they have been successfully delivering all internet and network services requested by their convention clients.

suppliers have failed to meet expected service levels and deliver expected cost savings. IT outsourcing has thus become one of the most talked about and widely debated topics. Please see Figure 1.

In spite of outsourcing failures, IT outsourcing continues to grow and outsourcing options continue to expand. As the MPEA case study, above shows, it has become more important than ever to understand the risks associated with these different options. Enterprises often enter outsourcing deals without considering risks, assuming that all risks lay with the external service provider. A large number of studies show that the risks associated with various options need to be managed on IT outsourcing. In this chapter, we provide an overview of outsourcing risks, and a model for managing them. We identify different firm-vendor configurations for sustaining a long term relationship aimed at diversifying risk overtime and discuss the need for psychological contracts to manage outsourcing relationships.

The Monitoring Dashboard

IS outsourcing has been defined in many different ways by different researchers. Williamson (1985) defines it as a market vs. hierarchy decision, Rands (1992) defines it as a make or buy decision, while Gurbaxani and Whang (1991) and Porter (1980) define it as "vertical integration." In this chapter, IT outsourcing is broadly defined as a decision taken by an organization to contract-out or sell the organization's IT assets, people and/or activities to a third party supplier, who in exchange provides and manages assets and services for monetary returns over an agreed time period (Loh & Venkatraman, 1992). The definition is very broad and includes all types of outsourcing. The IT resources can either be transferred in part or in total. An external supplier can either own its own hardware or may provide the service on the organization's equipment. This creates different types of outsourcing and the need for rational decision making based on the risk for each option.

We introduce The Monitoring Dashboard (Figure 3) to manage the risks associated with the different types of outsourcing. The Monitoring Dashboard will help the organization selected and monitor the optional outsourcing strategy. First we need to carry out an overview of IT outsourcing practices. This overview exposes the dimensions or variables of outsourcing that need to be monitored and managed. The Monitoring Dashboard is the natural result of this analysis.

Overview of Outsourcing

IT outsourcing began to evolve in the early 1960s, largely in response to cost saving opportunities. In 1963, Electronic Data System (EDS) signed an agreement with Blue Cross of Pennsylvania for handling its data processing services. This was the first time a large business had turned over its entire data processing department to a third party (Dibbern, Goles, Hirschheim, & Jayatilaka, 2004). EDS continued to grow, increasing its customer base by signing contracts with Frito-Lay and General Motors in the 1970s and with Continental Airlines, First City Bank, and Enron in the 1980s (Dibbern et al., 2004). Please see Figure 2.

In 1989, Kodak followed the footsteps of General Motors and outsourced its mainframes, telecommunications, and personal computer maintenance and service to IBM. Never before had such a big company, in which information systems were considered to be a strategic asset, turned its assets over to a third party (Applegate, Austin, & McFarlan, 2003). IBM aimed to cut operating costs of Kodak's data center by 40% by consolidating the four existing data centers (Runnoe, 1989). Success of this deal fueled the growth of information systems outsourcing. More companies started outsourcing and many new players joined the business. In 1991, driven by growing customer demand and constrained by a 1956 U.S. Department of Justice Consent Decree (1991), IBM launched a new division called Integrated Systems Solution Corporation (ISSC) to provide a broader range of services. This new division later became IBM Global Services.

Outsourcing went on a global scale in 1994. Xerox turned over all its data operations, telecommunications, and network services in 19 countries to EDS. This global, $3.2 billion, 10-year contract was the largest outsourcing deal to date (Rifkin, 1994). Most of the deals formed in the early 1990s were single-vendor total outsourcing contracts. Since then other types of outsourcing arrangements have emerged.

Outsourcing arrangements evolved from simple transfer of control of information technology processes and infrastructure to complex cosourcing consortiums. Cosourcing is a collaborative and performance driven approach with complex arrangements involving multiple vendors and multiple clients. It shifted the emphasis from minimizing costs to maximizing benefits while sharing the risks and rewards. Teranet Land Information Services is an example of cosourcing. This was a company formed out of a partnership between the Government of Ontario and the private sector which included EDS, KPMG Peat Marwick Stevenson & Kellogg, Intergraph Canada, and SHL Systemhouse (1994).

In the last few years, many different forms of outsourcing have emerged such as business process outsourcing (BPO), application service provider (ASP), multisourcing, and net-sourcing. BPO involved the outsourcing of noncore business functions along with its IT to a third party. It enabled clients to focus on their primary business operations and to achieve a combination of lower costs, improved productivity, and flexible staffing options (1997). ASPs run enterprise applications on their own computers and provide access to those applications to their clients based on a service charge revenue model. Clients keep complete control of their data. The growth of the ASP option is due to the increasing cost of the software and evolution of the Internet (Taylor, 1999). A slight variation of the ASP model is net-sourcing. Net-sourcing provides a variety of service offerings, in addition to those offered by traditional ASPs. ASP suppliers realized that many other services can be bundled along with the stand-alone software (Kern, Lacity, & Willcocks, 2002). Multisourcing involves multiple suppliers so as to eliminate monopoly power and achieve advantages of "best of breed" (Lacity & Willcocks, 2001). There has also been growth in the areas of Web and e-business outsourcing (Dibbern et al., 2004). These are e-commerce instances of net-sourcing. Table 1 summarizes the IT outsourcing overview.

Table 1. IT outsourcing timeline

Year		
1963	EDS wins Blue Cross of Pennsylvania	(Dibbern et al., 2004)
1970s	EDS's signed deals with Frito-Lay and General Motors	(Dibbern et al., 2004)
Mid 1980's to late	EDS involved in financial outsourcing deals • Continental Airlines • First City Bank • Enron	(Dibbern et al., 2004)
1989	Kodak – IBM, Digital Equipment and BusinessLand ("Kodak Effect")	(Caldwell, 1995)
1991	IBM entered IS service business. ISSC was formed	(1991)
1994	$3.2 billion outsourcing deal between Xerox and EDS. As one of the first mega deal on a global scale	(Overby, 2003)
Mid 1990s	Co-sourcing evolved. A complex arrangement between multi-vendor and multiple clients.	(1994)
Late 1990s	New Outsourcing model BPO and ASP evolved	(Taylor, 1999)
Early 2000s	Net-Sourcing, Multi-Sourcing	

Figure 2. IT outsourcing timeline

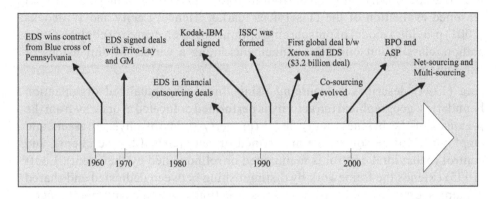

Having done an overview of IT outsourcing we are now able to distinguish the dimensions of outsourcing. These are independent variables or parameters within management's control that need to be monitored and assessed so as to manage risk and maximize benefits in the complex web of outsourcing options.

Dimensions of Outsourcing

There are different dimensions to IT outsourcing. First consider the "degree" of outsourcing. Lacity and Willcocks (1996) group the outsourcing decision into four categories: total outsourcing, total insourcing, selective sourcing, and de facto insourcing. Total outsourcing is the transfer of the IT assets, leases, staff, and management responsibility for delivery of IT services from internal IT functions to third-party vendors which represent at least 80% of the total outsourcing budget. Total insourcing retains the management and provision of at least 80% of the IT budget internally after evaluating the IT services market. The temporary buying-in of resources to meet temporary needs is included in this as long as the customer retains the responsibility of delivery of IT services. Selective sources transfers selected IT functions with external providers while still providing between 20 and 80% of the IT budget. The vendor is responsible for delivering the results of the selectively outsourced activities, and the customer is responsible for delivering the results of the retained IS activities. De facto insourcing uses internal IT departments that act like third parties to provide products and services that arise from historical precedent, rather than from a reasoned evaluation of the IT services market. Hence, Lacity and Willcocks (2001) provide a model of outsourcing options based on degree of control. Other authors classify outsourcing arrangements along a variety of dimensions or parameters.

Ang (1994) describes outsourcing using three conceptualized organization boundaries: geographical (an activity is performed or located at or away from the premises of the business unit), legal (property rights of physical assets and employment of personnel are maintained or relinquished by the client), and control (behavioral control is maintained or relinquished by the client). Looff (1995) extends the framework by distinguishing between dedicated and shared resources. Looff variables are as follows: location, ownership and employment, dedicated or shared use, and control. A dedicated and shared resource variable distinguishes if the resources are shared by suppliers among multiple clients or not to achieve economies of scale. The dedicated use is chosen for security reasons, to keep intellectual rights or to maintain competitive use of software (Looff, 1995).

Dibbern et al. (2004) defines four dimensions that determine the outsourcing arrangement a firm may enter into: degree (total, selective, and none), mode (single vendor/client or multiple vendors/clients), ownership (totally owned by the company or partially owned by the company), and timeframe (short term or long term).

Based on these research studies, we find that analyzing the risk of outsourcing involves five dimensions describing the different outsourcing arrangements: ownership of IT assets, degree, mode, timeframe, and location, as shown in Figure 3, The Monitoring Dashboard. Ownership is the percentage of IT assets owned by the client. Risk increases as more and more IT asset ownership is transferred to the suppliers. Ownership is classified into three categories: internal, partial, and external. Internal is when the client owns all IT assets, partial is when client and supplier both have investment in IT assets, and external is when supplier owns all the IT assets. Degree is classified based on the percentage of IT assets outsourced. The three options of degree are (1) total, when more than 80% of the assets will be transferred to the supplier, (2) selective, where 20% to 80% of the assets are transferred to the supplier, and (3) none, where less than 20% of the assets are transferred to the supplier. Risk increases with the increase in percentage of asset outsourced. Mode is the different client and supplier configurations. Possible options are single client — single vendor, multiple clients — single vendor, single client — multiple vendors, and multiple clients — multiple vendors. Each of these configurations have different associated levels of risks. Risk of lock-in due to single-vendor configu-

Figure 3. The Monitoring Dashboard

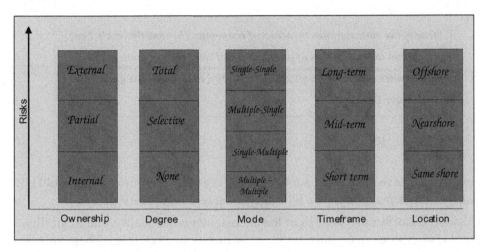

rations can be diversified by increasing the number of vendors, but at the same time transaction costs may increase. The fourth dimension is timeframe. IS outsourcing projects can be either short-term (1 year or 2 years), midterm (3 to 5 years), or long-term (10 years or longer). Clients are locked-in for the period of the contract. These contracts cannot be terminated without penalty. Risk increases with inflexible contracts which lock-in the client for longer periods of time. The final dimension is location. Location is the place where resources will be located. Resources include hardware, software, and people. The assets can be located at the client's location or the supplier's location. The recognized levels of location are off-shore, near-shore, and same shore.

The Monitoring Dashboard synthesizes the five dimensions. The risks associated with a given IT outsourcing configuration can be readily assessed and viewed with The Monitoring Dashboard. Moreover, the dashboard helps management stay alert to the sources of risk.

Next we review how the monitoring dashboard can be used to manage the risk of a given outsourcing configuration.

Risk Management

IS outsourcing, as a management strategy, entails both risks and benefits. It is impossible to run a business without taking risks. In order to obtain certain

Figure 4. Boehm-Bawerk's Law

> *"One of the most rigorous theorems of economics (Boehm-Bawerk's Law)*
> *proves that existing means of production will yield greater economic*
> *performance only through greater uncertainty, that is through greater*
> *risk"* **Peter Drucker**

benefits you have to expose yourself to risk. We seek, therefore, not to avoid all risks, but to manage those we willingly assume. Please see Figure 4.

Outsourcing offers the benefits of lower cost, increased quality, and flexibility, but it also exposes an organization to significant vulnerabilities. These vulnerabilities, if not managed properly, can eliminate the benefits partially or totally.

In the early 1990s, companies signing outsourcing contracts relied on total outsourcing with a single vendor. These early deals were fixed-price, exchange-based, long term contracts for a baseline set of services (Lacity et al., 2001). Very few of these deals were completely successful. Deals which made sense at the beginning of the contract did not make sense three years later. Many customers had to renegotiate and even terminate their contracts midstream (Lacity et al., 2001). The reasons for the failure of these deals were loss of power due to a monopoly supplier condition (lock-in), fixed prices that exceeded market value over the long term, hidden costs such as software license transfer fees, inability to adapt the market contract to even minor changes in business and technology, and excessive fees for service beyond the contract or excessive fees for services customers assumed were in the contract (Lacity et al., 2001).

Companies then pursued selective outsourcing with multiple vendors to mitigate the risk of total outsourcing. Success rate for this strategy was higher than that of total outsourcing as some of the risk of total outsourcing was mitigated or diversified across a portfolio of outsourcing arrangements. Selective outsourcing created an environment of competition and provided more flexibility for the customer. But the transaction cost associated with multiple evaluations, multiple vendors, multiple contract negotiations, and multiple suppliers needed to manage and coordinate activities also increased (Lacity et al., 2001). There are always risks. Hence, it becomes important to manage the risks no matter what kind of outsourcing configuration is used. Risk management is therefore an integral component of IT outsourcing. Please see Figure 5.

Risk management is a discipline in its own right. Here we focus on the application of risk management to outsourcing configurations. Boehm defines risk manage-

Figure 5. Peter Drucker Wisdom

> *"We must be able to choose rationally among risk-taking courses of action rather than plunge into uncertainty on the basis of hunch, hearsay, or experience, no matter how meticulously quantified."* **Peter Drucker**

ment to consist of identifying risks and controlling risks. Hence, we begin by identifying the top risks of outsourcing. Having identified the top risks of outsourcing, we break these into risk factors. This will be the basis for risk control. For example, having a small number of suppliers or insisting on asset specificity are risk factors for lock-in. Controlling risks involves steering clear from such identified risk factors and from the dangers they foretell. Lastly, as part of our suggestions for controlling risk, we identify different firm-vendor configurations for sustaining long-term relationships aimed at diversifying risk over time and discuss the need for psychological contracts to manage such outsourcing relationships.

Identifying Risks

The top risks need to be identified before we can develop meaningful risk control strategies. The relative importance of the risk will also be established along with some understanding as to why certain risks are perceived to be more important than others. This is necessary so that management attention can be focused on the areas that constitute the greatest threats. Finally, identified risks must be classified in a way that will help select the best sourcing option for the case in consideration and suggest meaningful risk control strategies (see Table 2).

Lock-in is one of the top risks of IT outsourcing. It refers to the situation where the client wants but cannot get out of a relationship except by incurring a loss or sacrificing part or all of its assets to the supplier (Aubert, Patry & Rivard, 1998). Some of the factors creating the lock-in situation are asset specificity (Williamson, 1985), small number of suppliers (Nam, Rajagopalan, Rao, & Chaudhury, 1996), and interdependence of activities (Aubert et al., 1998), among others. To perform a service, some assets used are common and some are dedicated to the particular use and are said to be specific. The specificity of an asset creates a lock-in situation where a party could extract a quasi-rent from the contracting party by threatening to withdraw from the transaction at a time when the specific asset is needed (Aubert et al., 1998).

Having a small number of suppliers may result in excessive fees for services and a lack of innovation. Excessive fees, in particular, is one of the top risks associated with outsourcing. In a survey of 50 companies, about 14% of outsourcing operations were deemed failures (Barthelemy, 2001). The major cause of these failures was hidden costs. They are also referred to as unexpected transaction and management costs (Bahli & Rivard, 2003). These costs are associated with vendor search and contracting, transitioning to the vendor, managing the effort, transitioning after outsourcing, and software license transfer fees (Barthelemy, 2001; Lacity et al., 2001). Most companies are outsourcing IT for the first time. They are not aware of these costs and fail to account for them, resulting in lower savings than expected. In addition, vendors may also charge excessive fees for services assumed to be included in the scope of the contract or excess fees for the additional services not included in the contract (Lacity et al., 2001).

Costly contractual amendments are also one of the threats to IT outsourcing. They are related to uncertainty. Contracting parties are rationally bounded and cannot foresee all eventualities, so writing a complete contract is impossible (Bahli & Rivard, 2003). Uncertainty can be linked to quantity, the exact nature of deliverables or evaluation of product and services being exchanged (Aubert, Rivard, & Patry, 2003). This problem increases with the increase in the number of teams or team members. Some of these changes have to be made in the normal course of business. Contracts have to be reopened and modified, resulting in premiums (Aubert et al., 1998).

Disputes and litigation are other major risks associated with IT outsourcing. They refer to any controversy concerning contracting parties (Bahli & Rivard, 2003). The disputes and litigation typically arise due to lack of experience of the client and supplier with outsourcing contract and measurement problems (Aubert et al., 1998). Earl (1996) points out that weak management is not an excuse for outsourcing but a recipe for conflicts and dissatisfaction. Outsourcing is not an option to fix the problem of weak management. The clients need strong internal management to manage contracts and relationships with suppliers. On the other hand, if suppliers have weak management, they may not be able to respond to a rapid change in business conditions, thereby causing disputes between the parties (Lacity et al., 2001). Improper or insufficient measurement techniques will result in accusations of declining services. Both parties need strong management and sound management techniques (Earl, 1996).

Service debasement and lack of innovations involve both the deterioration of service and the inability to evolve these services to meet the demands of the changing business and technology environment. As the MPEA case study shows, what was once not considered a core competency can readily become a strategic differentiator.

Table 2. Top risks of IT outsourcing

Top risks of IT outsourcing
1. Lock-in
2. Hidden cost/Excess cost
3. Costly contractual agreements
4. Disputes and Litigations
5. Vendor's inability to deliver/ Service debasement
6. Culture difference

Kliem (2004), in another study, examined the potential risk facing off-shore development projects. Most of the risks are associated with cultural differences. The risk factors identified because of culture differences are as follows: unclear responsibilities, no interaction among cross culture team members, conflicting development standards, widely divergent working styles, mistrust and miscommunication, poorly articulated requirements, inability to resolve time zone differences, poor communication of decisions, high turnover, and unwillingness to provide feedback. The risks associated with the sociopolitical and economic events are trade barriers, border tensions between two countries, political instability, and historical animosity between cultures.

Risk Factors

Lock-in

- Asset specificity
- Small number of suppliers
- Client's degree of expertise in outsourcing contracts
- Inability to adapt the contract to changing business and technology (Lacity et al., 2001)
- Inflexible contracting (Lacity et al., 2001)
- Treating IT as an undifferentiated commodity (Lacity & Willcocks, 2001)

Hidden/excess cost

- Uncertainty (Aubert et al., 2003)
- Opportunism (Aubert et al., 1998)
- Client's degree of expertise in IT operations
- Client's degree of expertise in outsourcing contracts
- Relatedness

- Fixed process that exceed market prices two to three years into the contract (Lacity et al., 2001)

Costly contractual amendments
- Uncertainty (Aubert et al., 2003)
- Technological discontinuity (Aubert et al., 1998)

Disputes and litigations
- Measurement problems
- Client's lack of experience in managing outsourcing project
- Supplier's degree of expertise in IT operations
- Supplier's degree of expertise in IT contracting

Service debasement
- Failure to retain requisite capabilities and skills
- Lack of innovation from supplier (Lacity et al., 2001)
- Deteriorating service in the face of patchy supplier staffing of the contract (Lacity et al., 2001)

Cultural differences
- Unclear responsibilities
- No interaction among cross-cultural team members
- Conflicting development standards
- Widely divergent working styles
- Mistrust and miscommunications
- Poorly articulated requirements
- Inability to resolve time zone differences
- Poor communication of decisions
- High turnover
- Unwillingness to provide feedback

Note that these are only the major risks and that there are many other outsourcing risks. Risk also varies based on the specific project. We will now develop a framework to assist managers in selecting the best option to meet their outsourcing requirements and manage their risks. We begin with an analysis of the top 10 risk mitigation strategies aimed at steering clear from known risk factors. Lastly, we identify different firm–vendor configurations for sustaining long-term relationships aimed at diversifying risk over time and discuss the need for psychological contracts to manage such outsourcing relationships.

Controlling Risks

There is no silver bullet, no step by step procedure for controlling risks over every outsourcing instance. Each outsourcing instance requires a mental predisposition to think things through and evaluate competing risk management strategies. General recommendations may not be ideally suited for all situations. In this section we identify the top practices to mitigate known risk factors and long-term strategies for diversifying risk over time.

Ten Best Practices to Mitigate Known Risk Factors

In the previous section we identified the top risks. Each of these risks has risk factors associated with them. Some risk factors are associated with more than one risk. But all risk factors do not lead to all undesirable outcomes. In Table 3, we identified the link between risks and risk factors. The risk factors, from our review of the literature, that appear to be most closely related to a given risk are only indicated in the table. Risk mitigation strategies are associated with each risk factor. Just as a single risk factor may be associated with many risks, similarly one risk mitigation strategy can mitigate one or more than one risk factor. Figure 6 shows how risk, risk factors, and risk mitigation are linked with each other. It can be seen that the framework is a complex web structure where many risks are associated with risk factors and many risk factors are associated with different risk mitigation strategies. Table 4, at the end of this section, shows the link between risk mitigation strategies and risk factors.

It is not enough to single-handedly execute the strategies. The best way to manage all risks is through firm-vendor partnerships and through so-called "psychological contracts." We identify seven structural models for such firm-vendor partnerships and we conclude our analysis of risk management with a discussion of psychological contracts. A summary of the literature yields the following list of best practices:

Table 3. Risk factors associated with current and emerging practices

Traditional Outsourcing	Selective Outsourcing
• Treating IT as undifferentiated commodity • Vendor lock-in • Inflexible contracting • Excess fees for services beyond the contract • Hidden costs • Fixed prices that exceeded market prices two to three years into the contract	• Management overhead cost *Not enough outsourcing experience. Risk yet to be fully identified.*
ASP/Net Sourcing (Kern, Lacity et al., 2002)	Spin-Offs
• Reliability and security of Internet • Application unavailability or slow response time • Unstable dot.com start-ups • Oversold supplier capability • Incomplete contracting • Customer's lack of experience with IT outsourcing • Unrealistic customer expectation • Idiosyncratic requirements which cannot be handles by generic systems • Risk of subcontracting	* Not enough outsourcing experience. Risk yet to be fully identified
Joint Venture	Business Process Outsourcing (BPO)
* Not enough outsourcing experience. Risk yet to be fully identified	* Not enough outsourcing experience. Risk yet to be fully identified

1. Negotiate short term contracts or renew contracts periodically to improve flexibility

2. Include a provision to terminate the contract with smooth transition

3. Use pilot project (start with pilot project to test supplier's capabilities)

4. Build experience by incremental outsourcing

5. Retain key capabilities in-house while outsourcing technology task

6. Establish a pricing strategy which encourages innovation (fixed price plus)

7. Hire an intermediary consulting firm

8. Manage performance through well constructed metrics (create balance scorecard metrics, frequent vendor reporting, and increase vendor oversight through project management)

9. Hire a legal expert to mitigate legal risks

10. Create a centralized program management office to consolidate management

We will now describe each of these best practices.

1. **Negotiate short term contracts or renew contracts periodically to improve flexibility:** Outsourcing contracts structured for very long periods of time have high risks, as discussed above. Contracts which make sense at the beginning of the period may make less economic sense three

Figure 6. Links between risks, risk factors, and risk mitigation strategies

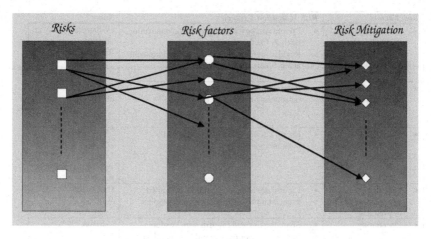

Table 4. Links between risk mitigation strategy and risk factors

Risk Factors	Risk Mitigation Strategies	Source
• Asset specificity • Small number of suppliers	• Short term contracts or renew contracts periodically to improve flexibility • Retain key capabilities in-house while outsourcing technology task	(Aubert, Patry et al.,1998; Bahli & Rivard,2003)
• Inflexible contracting	• Short term contracts or renew contracts periodically to improve flexibility • Provision to terminate the contract and smooth transition • Hire an intermediary consulting firm to serve as broker and guide	(Willcocks, Lacity et al.,1999)
• Client's degree of expertise in IT operations • Client's degree of expertise in outsourcing contracts	• Short term contracts or renew contracts periodically to improve flexibility • Build experience by incremental outsourcing • Retain key capabilities in-house while outsourcing technology task • Use Pilot project to mitigate business risk • Create a centralized program management office to consolidate management • Hire an intermediary consulting firm to serve as broker and guide • Hire a legal expert to mitigate legal risks	(Willcocks, Lacity et al.,1995; Rottman,2004)

Table 4. continued

Risk Factors	Risk Mitigation Strategies	Source
• Inability to adapt the contract to ng business and technology	• Pricing strategy which encourages innovation. Such as fixed price plus • Regular reviews of price/service/requirement against market	(Willcocks, Lacity et al.,1995; Rottman,2004)
• Vendor's failure to retain requisite capabilities and skills	• Retain key capabilities in-house while outsourcing technology task	(Willcocks, Lacity et al.,1999)
• Treating IT as an undifferentiated commodity	• Retain key capabilities in-house while outsourcing technology task	(Aubert, Patry et al.,1998; Willcocks, Lacity et al.,1999; Applegate, Austin et al.,2003)
• Unrealistic expectations of outsourcing	• Careful delineation in contract of limited expectations from both client and supplier	(Lacity & Willcocks,2001)
• Uncertainty	• Share the risk and rewards with vendors • Increase vendor oversight through project management • Manage performance through well constructed metrics	(Jurison,1995)
• Opportunism	• Share the risk and rewards with vendors • Manage performance through well constructed metrics • Hire an intermediary consulting firm to serve as broker and guide	(Jurison,1995)
• Relatedness	• Share the risk and rewards with vendors	(Jurison,1995)
• Measurement Problems	• Manage performance through well constructed metrics	(Rottman,2004)
• Technology discontinuity	• Short term contracts or renew contracts periodically to improve flexibility • Retain key capabilities in-house while outsourcing technology task	(Aubert, Patry et al.,1998)
• Supplier's degree of expertise in IT operations and outsourcing contracts	• Start with pilot projects to test supplier's capabilities • Customer feedback	(Lacity & Willcocks,2001)
• Deteriorating service in the face of patchy supplier staffing of the contract	• Well constructed and managed performance through SLAs • Supplier performance/reward mechanism	(Earl,1996; Lacity & Willcocks, 2001; Rottman,2004)
• Lack of innovation from supplier	• Pricing strategy which encourages innovation. Such as fixed price plus	(Earl,1996)
• Legal risks for offshore outsourcing	• Hire a legal expert to mitigate risk	(Rottman,2004)
• Company's ability to innovate may be impaired	• Retain key capabilities in-house while outsourcing technology task	(Lacity, Willcocks et al.,2004)

years later and require adjustments. Suppliers would like to have longer contracts. Their investments in the first year are high because of heavy capital made to purchase equipment and transitioning costs. This investment is made in expectation of a larger revenue stream in the later years (Applegate et al., 2003). So the longer the contract, the more beneficial it is for them. On the other hand, customers receive large benefits in the first couple of years. These benefits decline year after year because of changes in market pricing, technology, and business practices. Short term contracts or renewable contracts improve flexibility and reduce the risk associated with such environmental changes. It is highly recommended that customers don't lock themselves in a long term contract. They should sign either short term or renewable contracts.

2.   **Include a provision to terminate the contract with smooth transition:** A well drafted contract should enable its termination in a fair and reasonable manner prior to its end date. This reduces the risk of lock-in with a single vendor. In the event that the vendor's performance is not as expected, the contract can be transferred to another vendor or insourced, provided a smooth transition clause is in place. Hence, customers should ensure that the contract has a continuity clause requiring vendors to smoothly transition to any other preferred arrangement in case of termination of contract (Lacity et al., 2001).

3.   **Use pilot project (start with pilot project to test supplier's capabilities):** Pilot projects should be used to gain experience with outsourcing. They are a very useful tool in selecting suppliers. The supplier's capabilities can be tested on technology implementation and different sized projects (Rottman, 2004). The same project can be given to two different suppliers to compare their performance. Customers should use pilot projects for vendor selection to mitigate risks in the initial stages of the outsourcing project and to learn how best to configure the later stages of the outsourcing project.

4.   **Build experience by incremental outsourcing:** Companies can choose IT functions to be transferred to a vendor. The options of outsourcing are not limited to all-or-nothing. The transfer done incrementally rather than entirely does not have unnecessarily high economic stakes. The potential consequences of mismanagement will not be that far-reaching and can be controlled easily. Austin describes the levels of services offered by hosting providers for outsourcing data center as real estate services (suitable floor space and physical facilities), network services (connectivity within the facility and externally), platform services (support for hardware, operating system, and reboot services), application support services (support of software above the operating system level), and business operating ser-

vices (administering and operating an application level). It is apparent from this example of an outsourcing data center that there are a variety of alternatives from which customers can chose. It is not an all-or-nothing choice. Outsourcing services incrementally is a lower risk option.

5. **Retain key capabilities in-house while outsourcing technology task:** A low risk option is to retain the critical IT differentiators. Critical IT differentiators are the services which are unique to a company and provide it with significant advantages over competitors or are critical to achieving strategic advantages. These activities are so core to a company's business that an internal capability to manage and extend them must be maintained. They need to be monitored and controlled continuously for fast changes in the competitive environment. Customers will be well off by outsourcing commodity-like services, which have little to do with the key success factors of the company.

6. **Pricing strategy which encourages innovation (fixed price plus):** Customers often opt for fixed pricing. One of the problems with this option is the lack of incentives to the supplier for innovation. Suppliers maximize their economic returns by investing the minimum required to meet the service level agreements signed with the customer. Performance-based pricing would encourage suppliers to innovate and exceed customer expectations. In performance-based pricing structure the incentives are given to the supplier when performance exceeds an established criteria and a penalty is imposed when they fall short.

7. **Hire an intermediary consulting firm:** As Derek Bok said, "If you think education is expensive, try ignorance." It is always recommended to get advice from experts. More often than not the vendor has a lot more experience than the customer firm. The vendor has dealt with many situations and has worked through various difficulties, while the typical firm will be engaging in outsourcing for the first time. In order to balance the disparity in experience it behooves the customer firm to have an intermediary consulting firm. The probability of them winning without the third party support is very high. There are intermediary consulting firms such as NeoIT which specialize in information technology outsourcing and BPO. Intermediary consulting firms are advisory and management firms with a wide range of specialties and experience and offer independent point of view.

8. **Manage performance through well constructed metrics (create balance scorecard metrics, frequent vendor reporting, increase vendor oversight through project management):** The objectives of the outsourcing should be quantifiable. These criteria must be established at the beginning of the project and must be shared with the supplier. The current

performance can then be compared with the preestablished objectives to know if the benefits are being achieved or not. Detailed measurement and benchmarking are vital elements in the regulation of performance and relationships (Rottman, 2004). To monitor day-to-day performance, companies create a balance scorecard or dashboard. It measures costs, quality, timeliness, and risks. The data is analyzed monthly by management to monitor the real development cost and trends (Rottman, 2004).

9. **Hire a legal expert to mitigate legal risks:** Many companies have their own legal departments or are taking advice from a consulting firm to sign contracts. The need for legal expertise with off-shore or near-shore outsourcing is even more pronounced because customers abide by different legal systems and more regulatory requirements (Rottman, 2004). In-house legal staff may routinely draft domestic contracts but may lack the required knowledge to draft off-shore contracts. Existing legal advice must not be experienced in tax implications, protection of intellectual property, business continuity, regulatory compliance, visa formalities, governing law, and dispute resolution processes of other countries.

10. **Create a centralized program management office (PMO) to consolidate vendor management:** Customer firms should create an integrated PMO if they want business requirements to drive the supplier selection and if they want the suppliers to compete. PMO are ideal tools for assessing vendor suitability for a given project.

Each of these 10 risk mitigation strategies can be applied to control a series of risk factors. The next section links these strategies with the risk factors.

Risk Factors and Associated Risk Mitigation Strategies

- Asset Specificity/small number of suppliers (Aubert et al., 1998; Bahli & Rivard, 2003)
  - Negotiate short term contracts or renew contracts periodically to improve flexibility
  - Retain key capabilities in-house while outsourcing technology tasks
- Inflexible contracting (Willcocks, Lacity, & Kern, 1999)
  - Negotiate short term contracts or renew contracts periodically to improve flexibility
  - Include provision to terminate the contract with smooth transition
  - Hire an intermediary consulting firm to serve as broker and guide

- Client's degree of expertise in IT operations/client's degree of expertise in outsourcing contracts (Rottman, 2004; Willcocks, Lacity, & Fitzgerald, 1995)
  - Negotiate short term contracts or renew contracts periodically to improve flexibility
  - Build experience by incremental outsourcing
  - Retain key capabilities in-house while outsourcing technology task
  - Use a pilot project to mitigate business risk
  - Create a centralized program management office to consolidate management
  - Hire an intermediary consulting firm to serve as broker and guide
  - Hire a legal expert to mitigate legal risks
- Inability to adapt the contract to changing business and technology (Rottman, 2004; Willcocks et al., 1995)
  - Establish pricing strategy which encourages innovation, such as fixed price plus
  - Provide for regular reviews of price/service/requirement against market
- Vendor's failure to retain requisite capabilities and skills (Willcocks et al., 1999)
  - Retain key capabilities in-house while outsourcing technology task
- Treating IT as an undifferentiated commodity (Applegate et al., 2003; Aubert et al., 1998; Willcocks et al., 1999)
  - Retain key capabilities in-house while outsourcing technology task
- Unrealistic expectations of outsourcing (Lacity et al., 2001)
  - Careful delineation in contract of limited expectations from both client and supplier
- Uncertainty (Jurison, 1995)
  - Share the risk and rewards with vendors
  - Increase vendor oversight through project management
  - Manage performance through well constructed metrics
- Opportunism (Jurison, 1995)
  - Share the risk and rewards with vendors
  - Manage performance through well constructed metrics
  - Hire an intermediary consulting firm to serve as broker and guide

- Relatedness (Jurison, 1995)
  - Share the risk and rewards with vendors
- Measurement problems (Rottman, 2004)
  - Manage performance through well constructed metrics
- Technology discontinuity (Aubert et al., 1998)
  - Short term contracts or renew contracts periodically to improve flexibility
  - Retain key capabilities in-house while outsourcing technology task
- Uncertainty about supplier's degree of expertise in IT operations and outsourcing contracts (Lacity et al., 2001)
  - Start with pilot projects to test supplier's capabilities
  - Customer feedback
- Deteriorating service in the face of patchy supplier staffing of the contract (Earl, 1996; Lacity et al., 2001; Rottman, 2004)
  - Well constructed and managed performance through SLAs
  - Supplier performance/reward mechanism
- Lack of innovation from supplier (Earl, 1996)
  - Pricing strategy which encourages innovation such as fixed price plus
- Legal risks for off-shore outsourcing (Rottman, 2004)
  - Hire a legal expert to mitigate risk
- Loss of ability to innovate (Lacity, Willcocks, Hindle, & Feeny, 2004)
  - Retain key capabilities in-house while outsourcing technology task

It is not enough to single-handedly execute these strategies. Next we propose establishing long-term firm-vendor relationships and identify seven structural models aimed at diversifying risk over time.

Long-Term Strategies for Diversifying Risk Over Time

Perhaps the best approach to controlling outsourcing risk is to build long-term firm-vendor relationships. The prospect of being able to continue to do business has a psychological impact the benefits risk control. Researchers have found that so-called psychological contracts may be the best way to control for known and unknown risk factors. We review the psychological contract literature and provide seven models for long-term firm-vendor relationships.

Koh, Ang, and Straub (2004) introduced a psychological contract perspective to help understand the ongoing IT outsourcing relationship. Psychological contract refers to an individual's beliefs about his or her mutual obligations in a contractual relationship (Rousseau, 1995). It exists only if both parties believe that an agreement exists, that promises have been made.

The three distinctive principles of psychological contract theory leading to the success of an outsourcing relationship are mutual obligations, psychological obligations, and individual level of analysis. A mutual obligation is a belief that one is obliged to provide services based on the perceived promises of a reciprocal exchange. IT outsourcing involves a contract with a set of mutual obligations between customer and supplier. These mutual obligations should not be violated if the outsourcing project is to succeed. Moreover, there are implicit psychological obligations.

Psychological obligations are a kind of implied contract subject to interpretations. Legal contracts for IT outsourcing can never be complete and must be supplemented by unwritten promises and "understood" expectations. Successful IT outsourcing relies heavily on a psychological contract between the customer and supplier. These psychological contracts may be expressed partially in terms of a legal contract, or based simply on oral promises and other expression of commitment made by the parties. Failure to meet these obligations leads to mistrust between firms. One will view the "trespass" as a violation of the "spirit" of the contract. It is at this level where many of the risks can be mitigated.

An individual level of analysis means that a psychological contract applies at an individual level rather than the firm. In IT outsourcing relationships, project managers are typically viewed as representing their organizations. The contractual party views his or her actions as being those of the organization. They play a critical role in facilitating long term relationships and in assessing the outsourcing relationship. Hence, the psychological contract is derived from formal role relationship and interpersonal relationship among individuals.

Some of the customer's major obligations in an outsourcing project are clear specifications, prompt payment, close project monitoring, dedicated project staffing, knowledge sharing, and project ownership. Some of the major supplier's obligations are accurate project scoping, clear authority structures, taking charge, effective human capital management, effective knowledge transfer, and building effective organizational teams. In addition, outsourcing success requires that customers and suppliers understand and fulfill the impact psychological contract. Violation of the psychological contract would lead to significant negative effects for the parties involved. Hence parties are more likely than not to abide by such covenants.

Successful outsourcing requires a careful management of relationships. In this last section, we are going to describe a new perspective on managing outsourcing relationships by focusing on the best practices followed by university campuses and communities. Campuses and communities have successfully used seven structural models for managing their partnerships. These seven successful structural models can also be used for managing vendor-customer partnerships. This section will describe each of these models.

Communities and campuses establish partnerships to enhance experiential learning activities while addressing community needs. They have been successful in forming and managing partnerships between community organizations and their local institutions of higher education and have increased substantially during the 1990s. The community partners define the characteristics of good partnerships as effective in meeting short-term goals, contributing to long-term goals, and developing relationships with higher education institutions with the promise of benefits beyond the results of a given engagement activity. The seven structural models are centralized, cross-company collaborative, organizational-enhancement, vendor-enhancement, decentralized, issue focused, and vendor alliance.

Centralized Model

Centralized model focuses on building a centralized, enterprise-wide infrastructure for managing the outsourcing relationship as a means to transform the existing organizational culture. It brings together a variety of departmental initiatives to establish an enterprise-wide initiative. The projects are outsourced from a central place. Any department which wants to participate in outsourcing goes through this office. The central office offers different opportunities to fit the needs of all departments. It deals with multiple vendors and outsources the project to the vendor specializing in the area outsourced. The relationships are managed by experts, who are aware of the market changes because they are constantly involved in the marketplace. Money can be saved through careful negotiations and economies of scale.

Decentralized Model

Decentralized model focuses on letting all individual units manage their own outsourcing relationship. There is no central office to oversee the operations or to assist in forming vendor relations. The departments can form outsourcing arrangements in a way they prefer and approach vendors in ways that are most interesting and appealing to them. There are no controlling managers who approve or disapprove relationships to conform to specific policies. This model has little coordination and articulation among different departments in the organization that engage in an outsourcing relationship but is high flexible. In this model, there is a propensity for territorial issues and competition among departments to manifest.

Cross-Company Collaborative Model

Cross company collaborative model identifies and builds on the existing programs by bringing together a variety of existing organizational outsourcing programs through the application of enterprise-wide initiatives. It convenes departments that engage in outsourcing activities to collaborate with each other and interface with suppliers. Though the departments remains separate, the model places heavy emphasis on developing enterprise-wide policies and ensures that they are being followed across the company. It is a hybrid model of the centralized and decentralized models.

Organizational-Enhancement Model

Organizational enhancement model focuses on improving organizations practices by implementing the best practices recommended by vendors. It builds on existing partnerships that have developed over the years, placing heavy focus on developing best management practices. Vendors improve operation efficiencies by improving the existing processes. These processes can be implemented in the organization, too, by collaboration. It reduces the risk of process mismatch between vendor and client. This model uses vendor expertise to enhance the organization's business and outsourcing practices.

Vendor-Enhancement Model

Vendor-enhancement model focuses on improving the vendor's processes by implementing the best practices followed by the client. The vendor can effectively identify the culture and practices that need to be accommodated and implement them by successful collaboration. This will again reduce the risk of process mismatch. This model uses client expertise to enhance the organization's business and outsourcing practices.

Issue Focused Model

Issue focuses company partnership model focus on a particular issue, opportunity, or challenge they are facing. There are issues in the organization that can be addressed through a new partnership. The activities are focused on resolving the issue. Many such relationships, for example, have been formed to address the Sarbanes-Oxley issue. Vendors can provide the best solution, building a mutually beneficial partnership which focuses specifically on the issue.

Vendor Alliance Model

This model focuses on building a vendor coalition that works to improve the conditions of outsourcing. The coalition is composed of multiple vendor agencies to share experiences, create a learning environment, and share best practices and standards. Sourcing professionals collaborate with each other to continue improving management practices. One such example is Sourcing Interests Group (SIG), www.sourcinginterests.org. SIG has over 160 members, which includes 25 of the Fortune 100 companies. Members have all levels of sourcing experience and share noncompetitive information with each other to share best practices and their experiences.

To conclude our analysis of risk mitigation strategies, we must discuss psychological contracts as an emerging device for establishing outsourcing relationships.

Conclusion

Outsourcing will continue to grow despite the protests surrounding the loss of U.S. jobs. The types of outsourcing will evolve creating more options to meet the ever growing requirements of each organization. With the increase in outsourcing activities, the number of outsourcing failures unless more attention is placed on risk management. In this chapter, we highlighted the various types of IT outsourcing options existing today and the risks involved with these options. The risks were synthesized from our review of literature. We covered a new perspective on managing outsourcing relationships by focusing on the best practices followed by communities and campuses. Seven structural partnership models taken from the service literature were explained in detail and shown how they can be used for managing firm-vendor relationships. The importance of fulfilling psychological contracts for a successful outsourcing relationship was also discussed.

References

Ang, S. (1994). Business process re-engineering. *IFIP Transactions, A-54,* 113-126.

Applegate, L. M., Austin, R. D., & McFarlan, F. W. (2003). *Corporate information strategy and management* (6th ed.). New York: McGraw-Hill Higher Education.

Aubert, B. A., Patry, M., & Rivard, S. (1998). Assessing the risk of IT outsourcing. In *Proceedings of the 31st Hawaii International Conference on System Sciences.*

Aubert, B. A., Rivard, S., & Patry, M. (2003). A transaction cost model of IT outsourcing. *Information and Management, 41,* 921-932.

Bahli, B., & Rivard, S. (2003, September). The information technology outsourcing risk: A transaction cost and agency theory-based perspective. *Journal of Information Technology, 18,* 211-221.

Barthelemy, J. (2001). The hidden costs of IT outsourcing. *Sloan Management Review, 42*(3), 60-69.

Caldwell, B. (1995). Outsourcing megadeals: More than 60 huge contracts signed since 1989 prove they work. *InformationWeek, 34*(552).

Caldwell, B. M., Young, A., Goodness, E., & Souza, R. D. (2004). *Continued growth forecast for IT outsourcing segments: 3.* Gartner Research.

Dibbern, J., Goles, T., Hirschheim, R., & Jayatilaka, B. (2004). Information systems outsourcing: A survey and analysis of the literature. *Database for Advances in Information Systems, 35*(4), 6.

Earl, M. J. (1996). The risks of outsourcing IT. *Sloan Management Review, 37*(3), 26-32.

Gurbaxani, V., & Whang, S. (1991). The impact of information systems on organisations and markets. *Communications of the ACM, 34,* 59-73.

Jurison, J. (1995). The role of risk and return in information technology outsourcing decision. *Journal of Information Technology, 10*(4), 239-247.

Kern, T., Lacity, D. M. C., & Willcocks, D. L. P. (2002). Application service provision: Risk assessment and mitigation. *MIS Quarterly Executive, 1*(2), 113-126.

Lacity, D. M. C., & Willcocks, D. L. P. (2001). *Global information technology outsourcing.* New York: John Wiley & Sons.

Lacity, D. M. C., Willcocks, D. L. P., Hindle, J., & Feeny, D. (2004). IT and business process outsourcing: The knowledge potential. *Information Systems Management, 21*(3), 7-15.

Loh, L., & Venkatraman, N. (1992). Diffusion of information technology outsourcing: Influence sources and the Kodak effect. *Information Systems Research, 4*(3), 334-358.

Looff, L. A. D. (1995). Information systems outsourcing decision making: A framework, organizational theories and case studies. *Journal of Information Technology, 10*, 281-297.

Nam, K., Rajagopalan, S., Rao, H. R., & Chaudhury, A. (1996). A two-level investigation of information systems outsourcing. *Communications of the ACM, 39*(7), 36.

Overby, S. (2003, March 1). Bringing I.T. back home. *CIO.*

Porter, M. E. (1980). *Competitive strategy: Techniques for analysing industries and competitors.* New York: Free Press.

Rands, T. (1992). The key role of applications software make-or-buy decisions. *Journal of Strategic Information Systems, 1*, 215-223.

Rifkin, G. (1994). $3.2 billion Xerox-E.D.S. deal is set. *The New York Times,* Late Edition, 3.

Rottman, J. W. (2004). Twenty practices for offshore sourcing. *MIS Quarterly Executive, 3*(3), 117-130.

Rousseau, D. M. (1995). *Psychological contracts in organizations: Understanding written and unwritten agreements.* Thousand Oaks, CA: Sage Publications.

Runnoe, G. (1989, July 31). Kodak chooses IBM to run, upgrade its DP operations. *Network World, 46.*

Taylor, P. (1999). Internet provides a new market impetus: Web application hosting: Many companies find it too expensive to run their own IT systems, so farming them out to experts is an attractive option. *Financial Times,* 2nd ed., 2. London, England.

Willcocks, L., Lacity, M., & Fitzgerald, G. (1995). Information technology outsourcing in Europe and the USA: Assessment issues. *International Journal of Information Management, 15*(5), 333-351.

Willcocks, L. P., Lacity, M. C., & Kern, T. (1999). Risk mitigation in IT outsourcing strategy revisited: Longitudinal case research at LISA. *The Journal of Strategic Information Systems, 8*(3), 285-314.

Williamson, O. E. (1985). *The economic institutions of capitalism.* New York: Free Press.

Chapter XIV

A Framework
for Evaluating
Outsourcing Risk

Merrill Warkentin, Mississippi State University, USA

April M. Adams, Mississippi State University, USA

Abstract

This chapter provides a framework for evaluating and mitigating the risks associated with IT outsourcing projects. Outsourcing projects have been met with successes and many failures. The causes of such failures must be systematically investigated in order to provide managers guidance to avoid future risks from outsourcing projects. This chapter discusses the outsourcing relationship, highlighting the primary causes of project successes and failures, then offers a framework for evaluating vendor relationships to avoid contingencies that may lead to failure. The authors hope this framework will serve as a guide for managers of firms seeking to outsource various IT functions, as well as managers of vendor firms who seek success in these relationships.

Introduction

Outsourcing is the process of transferring or reassigning the operation and management of certain functions or activities from an internal group to an outside entity. Typically, the organization will delegate noncore operations to the external subcontractor or vendor, yet it often involves transferring a significant amount of management control to that vendor. Outsourcing goes beyond simple supply chain transactions in which a firm purchases products or services from an external vendor. It is a more closely coupled interaction in which the parties engage in extensive communication and coordination and which relies on an enormous amount of trust.

Any business function or activity can be outsourced, but most outsourcing experiences involve the transfer of design, production, and various services. It is unusual that a business will outsource all of its IT support, but it is not unheard of. Generally, businesses outsource IT projects that cannot be handled in-house. Most outsourcing relationships are between only two parties; in this chapter, we will call the company which outsources its work the *client,* and the one that does the work, the *vendor.*

Outsourcing has commanded extensive attention in the academic literature and the popular press over the last decade as many firms seek to benefit from hiring partner firms to provide certain nonmission critical products and services. Within the information technology (IT) arena, outsourcing has been particularly prominent as an issue for management consideration. IT managers have outsourced a variety of IT-related functions and activities, including development, maintenance, helpdesk activities, storage, database servers, data entry, and even strategic IT planning.

In the U.S., domestic outsourcing of IT related activities, which began as early as the 1960s, has focused on services and facility management and progressed to total solution in the 1990s (Lee, Huynh, Kwok, & Pi, 2003). The issue rose to prominence with the Kodak outsourcing deal with IBM, signed October 2, 1989, which permanently changed the rules of IT strategic management (Loh & Venkatraman, 1992). Before the Kodak project, large companies maintained their own IT support functions. It was unheard of to entrust IT to a vendor. Kodak changed all that to help legitimize outsourcing, and CIOs' attitudes changed as well. Miraculously, outsourcing became about core competencies, cost savings and strategic partnerships with IT service vendors. The precedence was set and within a decade, outsourcing has exploded into a global industry.

Was it all smooth sailing? Actually Kodak made some mistakes — its arrangement with DEC, for example, proved highly unsatisfactory. Kodak had to transfer to IBM as soon as contractual terms allowed. However, Kodak also did several things right. For one, it established at the start a relationship management group to foster good communication between Kodak and IBM. As we will discuss later in the chapter, good communication is paramount to outsourcing success.

Kodak led the field and created history by outsourcing their IT functions, but shortly after other big names followed suit, including Lloyds of London, Bank of America, and Barclays Bank. These firms decided to outsource their main IT functions with varying levels of success (Lacity, 2004). It is interesting to note that as larger firms began to feel more comfortable outsourcing their IT functions, midlevel firms followed. Because of the brave steps Kodak was willing to take, outsourcing was allowed to blossom and become a more mundane part of most firms' IT processes.

Almost all businesses outsource some aspect of their business. IT outsourcing has yielded both high expectations and catastrophic disappointments. However, despite outsourcing's reputation, the outsourcing industry has been growing at approximately 20% a year. Outsourcing spending is expected to grow to $17 billion by 2008 (Pfannenstein & Tsai, 2004). Companies have been using outsourcing as a source of system development because of the lower labor cost that outsourcing offers. In 2000, IT outsourcing represented almost 30% of IT budgets (Desouza, Awazu, & Mehling, 2004).

Many client organizations enter into outsourcing agreements in order to seek efficiencies or to achieve greater returns on their IS/IT investments. But this is typically only possible when the vendor firm is located in another nation with labor cost advantages. Thus, many vendors are located in foreign nations or off-shore. Ramarapu & Parzinger (1997, p. 27) define off-shore outsourcing as the sharing or transferring of responsibility for some or all IS services to a third-party vendor who operates from a foreign country, and other definitions imply that jobs are transferred to countries where labor is cheap. In 2003, the U.S. alone spent $10 billion in off-shore outsourcing, and this figure is expected to grow to $31 billion by 2008 (Thibodeau, 2004). Off-shoring (global outsourcing) of IT work, which started much later than domestic outsourcing, is driven by very different factors and circumstances. (Ramarapu & Parzinger, 1997). In these situations, managers must focus on issues related to separation between the client and vendor in the areas of geography, culture, language, laws, and technological infrastructure. For example, facilities management is easily domestically outsourced, but difficult to outsource to a company operating from an overseas destination. Other issues will be discussed below.

A significant portion of IT off-shoring includes systems development, or the utilization of developers in other countries to create programs or systems for a company from another country, usually a high-cost country such as the U.S. (McManus & Floyd, 2005). As companies move their off-shore efforts further and further away from the United States, they face more risks, more logistics costs, and more challenges in development (Maclellan, 2003). By outsourcing systems development projects, company executives are required to transfer intangible assets to the off-shore firm, which can include intellectual property, training, and other valuable information (Human, 2005).

Firms typically outsource to achieve one of the following goals: cost improvement, operations improvement, or business performance improvement. Cost improvement stems from lower cost labor and/or reduced overhead costs. In addition, competition may have driven the client's price down (Patterson, 2003). Operation improvement is expected because the vendor can specialize in one area, and can use its expertise in the area to help their client firm (Levina & Ross, 2003). This is common in specialty IT niches, such as Web hosting, ASP, ISP, ERP customization, and so forth. Business performance improvement, which focuses on improvement to supply chain or customer relationship management, is usually carried out prior to implementation of ERP/supply chain optimization/CRM product, and plays a key role in defining the business processes, performance metrics, business rules/policies and supporting organization structure (Lee, Miranda, & Kim, 2004). By outsourcing certain projects, a client firm seeks vendors that might contribute a comparative advantage in providing the required services, especially when the vendor is located in the same country and therefore offers no benefits from differential labor costs.

Success Factors and Sources of Outsourcing Project Risk

In order to ensure outsourcing and eventually off-shoring success, there are certain protocols that must be strictly followed (Greenemeier, 2001; Saunders, Gebelt, & Hu, 1997). Careful and consistent planning for off-shoring projects is one of the reasons most frequently cited for outsourcing and off-shoring success. Other items included in the list are business conditions, physical infrastructure, IT infrastructure, financial institution and government support, and various labor characteristics specific to a region (Davey & Allgood, 2002). All of these items must be carefully weighed and the best way to approach these possible opportunities must be determined. Finally, clear honest communication and trust between the vendor and client helps to add to the success of the project.

Failure to report bad news to the client has been consistently shown to contribute to the failure of the project (Smith & Keil, 2003; Wainwright, Reynolds, & Argument, 2003). Losses are sometimes increased by the reluctance of organizational members to transmit negative information concerning a project and its status. Thus, although evidence of a failing course of action may exist in the lower ranks of an organization, this information sometimes fails to be communicated up the hierarchy. This lack of communication results in a decision-maker lacking the authority to change the direction of the project or being unaware of its true status.

By analyzing the factors that contribute to outsourcing successes, we can then look at what contributes to the failures (Lyytinen & Robey, 1999). Outsourcing failures often result when the System Development Life Cycle is not followed to fruition (Trembly, 2003). When trusting the development of a system to an outside firm, the client firm needs to understand what their comfort level is, and how the communication of the project will be handled. Information technology outsourcing and off-shoring success requires careful management of customer-supplier relationships. By moving system development off-shore, it is more difficult for executives, users, and other IS staff to control the management of the relationship (Shamis, Green, Sorensen, & Kyle, 2005).

Other concerns are the theft or abuse of intangible assets like intellectual property given the lax enforcement of intellectual property laws in overseas locations. Domestic companies doing business overseas may have no legal recourse if problems arise. For example, in 2003, a Pakistani transcriptionist directly contacted a California hospital (Lazarus, 2003). She was a subcontractor hired to perform transcription work by a consulting firm doing transcriptions for the hospital. She threatened that if she was not paid for her transcription work that she would publish private health information from the hospital on the Internet. In her threatening email, she included patient data so that the hospital would know she had access to the sensitive information. The globalization of the healthcare industry has caused anxiety about the confidentiality of private health information fears that have been intensified by this single, highly publicized case. Unfortunately, legislation like the Health Insurance Portability and Accountability Act (HIPAA) has no teeth overseas. In fact, the Pakistani case caused California to pass legislation prohibiting health information from being shared abroad for any reason, including off-shoring of transcription services.

Perception of success or failure can vary by industry. It is often difficult to measure success or failure. Generally the vendors are measured on these three criteria: delivery competency, transformation competency, and relationship competency (Feeny, Lacity, & Willcocks, 2005). Evaluating a vendor prior to awarding a contract requires understanding the infrastructure, values and methodologies it brings to its area of expertise. Once the contract has been awarded, there must be stringent rules in place to evaluate the projects success or failure. Failed outsourcing projects can be costly mistakes for companies (Keil, Cule, Lyytinen, & Schmidt, 1998), but the perspective of vendors and clients may be very different.

In a study conducted by Koh, Soon, and Straub (2004), outsourcing success was shown to be achievable as long as clients perceive vendor obligations to include accurate project scoping, clear authority figures, effective human capital management, effective knowledge transfer, and effective inter-organizational teams. Vendors perceive client obligations to include clear specifications, prompt payment, close project monitoring, dedicated project staffing, knowledge sharing, and project ownership (Koh et al., 2004). Choosing the correct software tools when selecting an off-shoring vendor can also play a large role in the project's success (Human, 2005). In summary, a clear understanding of the specific nature of the vendor's activities is mission critical for project success (James, 2005).

Some cost-saving mirages have turned into costly mistakes for firms. Firms that do not understand one another well set themselves up for disasters in outsourcing projects (Desouza et al., 2004). Without a clear understanding of the risks involved with outsourcing, disastrous unfortunate and devastating consequences can result (Wallace, Keil, & Rai, 2004).

A Framework for Evaluating Outsourcing Risks

Numerous published studies have prescribed which functions should be outsourced and which should not. These normative approaches are based on theories such as resource based theory (Teng, Cheon & Grover, 1995), institutional theory (Ang & Cummings, 1997), and transaction cost economics (Ang & Straub, 1998). Further, Applegate, McFarlan, and McKenney (1998, pp. 458-459) recommend outsourcing noncore IT functions, while Lacity and Willcocks (2001) also recommend a selective sourcing strategy. Despite the plethora of success factors and risk factors which have been identified in the academic and practical literature (Carmel & Agarwal, 2002; Smith & McKeen, 2004), there is no widely recognized framework for IT outsourcing decisions. Fjermestad and Saitta (2005) presented a framework that comprises the following factors:

- Alignment to business strategy
- Management support
- Culture
- Infrastructure
- Contracts
- Strategic partnership
- Governance
- Economics

We suggest a framework that is based on the concept of proximity and distance. This framework is predicated on the premise that relationships between near neighbors are less risky than those between distant entities. In other words, risk increases as relative distance increases. The distance metric here applies not only to spatial or geographic space, but also to technological differences, legal barriers, national cultural divides (language, tradition, perspective, etc.), organizational cultural gaps, and other factors that contribute to the perceptual differences between two entities. For each dimension, proximity represents *low risk*, while distance represents *high risk*. This seems like common sense, but it is important to note that the more similar a vendor firm is to the client firm, the lower the risk factor the client firm faces.

To illustrate our conceptual framework, Figure 1 shows multiple axes of differences. Each axis on the diagram represents one dimension of inter-organizational outsourcing risk. Along any axis, the closer the vendor is to the hub (or origin) of the diagram, the less opportunities for risk in the relationship with that vendor.

Organizational culture is a system of collective meaning held by all the members of the organization that distinguish the organization or the company from other organizations. An organization's current customs, traditions, and general way of doing business are largely due to what has been done in the past. Organizational

Figure 1. Framework dimensions

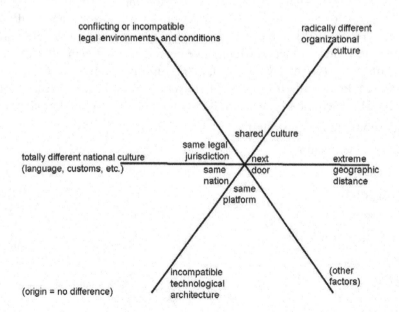

culture risk can be created when a client and vendor firm operate in a radically different cultural environment, exhibited by different norms, values, and standards of practice. What could be business as usual for one firm could be polar opposite to the processes of another firm. These types of obstacles could cause friction and cause the relationship to fail. An example of this is the relationship between General Motors (GM) and Electronic Data Systems (EDS), Ross Perot's old company.

Geographical distance uncertainties can include time zones, lack of rich face-to-face communication cues, technological advancement, political involvement, economic upheaval, and the possibility of a natural disaster. These can all add to risk for an outsourcing firm. Geographical distance uncertainty varies with location — there is certainly more uncertainty for a U.S. firm operating in India or Pakistan than for one operating in Dallas, Texas. To lessen location-induced uncertainty, client organizations can choose to outsource to vendor firms that are geographically closer.

Technological risk can be created when two firms engage in an exchange of electronic information, applications programming code, or other technological artifacts. The risk is especially significant when the vendor builds and delivers an application (system, program, etc.) for a client firm. It is imperative that the application is technologically compatible with the client's existing technology architecture. Though the system may be developed on a different platform, the resulting object code must be interoperable with the client's platform. When technological infrastructure is vastly different, there is greater risk for failure of the outsourced project.

National culture poses yet another type of outsourcing risk. National culture risks stem from different circumstances than organizational culture risk. National culture encompasses differences or similarities in language, business rituals, communication expectations, work ethic, trust, attitude towards intellectual property, and other perception differences. For example, a U.S. firm wishing to outsource its system development to India may address a myriad of cultural differences, though not nearly as many as would be encountered when outsourcing to a firm in a non-English speaking country. Even in countries that speak English there can still be a language barrier. All of these differences add to increased risk for the client firm.

The legal dimension is represented in the diagram by the legal risk continuum. Along this axis, a client firm can assess the proximity or distance of a potential vendor firm. For example, if two firms operate within the same legal jurisdiction, the distance is nearly zero, so there is little or no risk to the success of the outsourcing project posed by legal infrastructure differences. However, two firms in the same jurisdiction may operate in different industries and may be subject to somewhat different legal requirements. On the other hand, two firms may operate in disparate legal environments, such that the agreements and contracts between the two parties are difficult to negotiate and draft, and even more difficult to enforce (if necessary). A client firm may believe that a contract has been infringed, but may have no recourse due to legal restrictions based on jurisdictional issues. Tort laws, intellectual property protection laws, and even contract law vary widely from country to country around the globe. The client must evaluate each potential vendor firm along this dimension to assess the relative risk that is manifested by this factor.

In addition to the legal, cultural, technological, and geographic dimensions, other factors may also serve to generate proximity or distance between two outsourcing partners. A client or vendor seeking to evaluate a potential outsourcing relationship should consider all factors that may generate risk, and carefully select its outsourcing partners accordingly.

Figure 2 shows two relationship pairs in which the client and vendor organizations exhibit varying degrees of differences along the axes. The first client-vendor relationship in Figure 2 shows a highly cohesive relationship, while the one on the right shows how risk is increased as we move further away along many of the dimensional continua. The total area of the shape formed by connecting the points along each axis represents the total aggregate risks posed by a potential outsourcing relationship.

When any two organizations enter into an agreement to link their business activities in some way, it is essential that both parties have a clear and unambiguous understanding of the relationship. Who is responsible for what? What are the performance measures? What constitutes successful outcomes? What is the timetable? Many firms employ a carefully-drafted lengthy legal agreement, complete with sanctions for nonperformance, though the goal is to avoid resorting to the stipulations in the legal document.

Figure 2. Client-vendor relationships

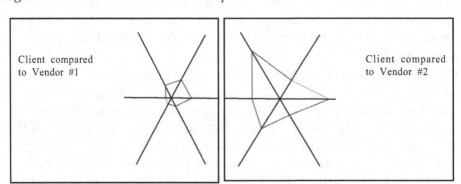

As has been noted above, clear concise and perpetual communication can mean success or failure for an outsourcing project. Some recurring themes from prior research include the impact of risk when outsourcing a project, imperative steps to take for a successful project, and the importance of realizing that outsourcing projects can fail. When the results of the project are not as expected, it can lead to disastrous consequences. The monetary investment alone can be crippling for an unsuccessful project.

In conclusion, this chapter seeks to introduce a model based on organizational propinquity and remoteness. The model addresses geography as playing a large part in the increase of risk for a client firm. However, it should be noted that geography is not the only factor, and that by looking beyond the geographic distance, we can estimate the virtual proximity of the client and vendor along various dimensions. If a client awards a contract to a vendor that is proximate in terms of culture, infrastructure, and other key factors, then the project will exhibit less risk. Additionally, the framework moves the focus from purely monetary concerns to other less expressed avenues. Though monetary concerns are paramount and though purely pecuniary measures are the industry standard, a firm must assess all relevant factors when evaluating a potential partner.

One proposal for future study would be an empirical investigation into the client and vendor perceptions of system development risk. An empirical study, based on survey data or in-depth structured interviews of outsourcing firms, might be pursued to find the perceptions of risk. Another study might ascertain if users at various levels in the managerial hierarchy perceive outsourcing risks differently. Applying the proposed model in comparative case studies could also generate practical knowledge.

References

Ang, S., & Cummings, L. L. (1997). Strategic response to institutional influences on information systems outsourcing. *Organization Science, 8*(3), 235-256.

Ang, S., & Straub, D. W. (1998). Production and transaction economies and IS outsourcing: A study of the US banking industry. *MIS Quarterly, 22*(4), 535-552.

Applegate, L. M., McFarlan, F. W., & McKenney, J. L. (1999). *Corporate information systems management* (5th ed.). Boston: Irwin/McGraw-Hill.

Carmel, E., & Agarwal, R. (2002). The maturation of offshore sourcing of IT work. *MISQ Executive, 1*(2), 65-77.

Davey, H., & Allgood, B. (2002) Offshore development, building relationships across international boundaries: A case study. *Information Strategy: The Executive's Journal, 18*(3), 13.

Desouza, K. C., Awazu, Y., & Mehling, J. (2004, October). The risks of outsourcing. *J@pan Inc., 60*, 32-37.

Feeny, D., Lacity, M., & Willcocks, L. P. (2005). Taking the measure of outsourcing providers. *MIT Sloan Management Review, 46*(3), 41-48.

Fjermestad, J., & Saitta, J. A. (2005). Strategic management framework for IT outsourcing: A review of the literature and the development of a success factors model. *Journal of Information Technology Cases and Applications Research, 7*(3), 43-56.

Greenemeier, L. (2001, December 10). A-B-Cs of outsourcing success. *InformationWeek, 867,* 77.

Human, C. (2005, September 13). Choose the right tools for offshore success. *Computer Weekly,* 26.

James, G. (2005). Success by design. *Electronic business, 31*(9), 54-58.

Keil, M., Cule, P. E., Lyytinen, K., & Schmidt, R. C. (1998) A framework for identifying software project risk. *Communications of the ACM, 41*(11), 76-83.

Koh, C., Soon, A., & Straub, D. (2004). IT outsourcing success: A psychological contract perspective. *Information Systems Research, 15*(4), 356-373.

Lacity, M. C., & Willcocks, L. P. (2001). *Global information technology outsourcing.* Chichester, UK: John Wiley & Sons.

Lacity, M., Willcocks, L., & Feeny, D. (2004). Commercializing the Back Office at Lloyds of London: Outsourcing and Strategic Partnerships Revisited. *European Management Journal, 22*(2), 127.

Lazarus, D. (2003, October 26). A politician who reads the papers. *San Francisco Chronicle,* I-1.

Lee, J. N., Huynh, M. Q., Kwok, R. C. W., & Pi, S. M. (2003). IT outsourcing evolution: Past, present and future. *Communications of the ACM, 46*(5), 84-89.

Lee, J. N., Miranda, S. M., & Kim, Y. (2004). IT outsourcing strategies: Universalistic, contingency, and configurational explanations of success. *Information Systems Research, 15*(2), 110-131.

Levina, N., & Ross, J. W. (2003). From the vendor's perspective: Exploring the value proposition in information technology outsourcing. *MIS Quarterly, 27*(3), 331-364.

Loh, L., & Venkatraman, N. (1992). Diffusion of information technology outsourcing: Influence sources and the Kodak effect. *Information Systems Research, 3*(4), 334-358.

Lyytinen, K., & Robey, D. (1999). Learning failure in information systems development. *Information Systems Journal, 9*(2), 85-101.

Maclellan, A. (2003, September 15). Mexico hangs tough as alternative to China. *Electronic Buyers' News,* (1380), 1-2.

McManus, J., & Floyd, D. (2005). The global software industry. *Management Services, 49*(2), 26-31.

Patterson, S. (2003). Who's outsourcing, why, and how are they making it work? *Human Resources Department Management Report, 3*(3), 1-4.

Pfannenstein, L. L., & Tsai, R. J. (2004). Offshore outsourcing: Current and future effects on American IT industry. *Information Systems Management, 21*(4), 72-80.

Ramarapu, N., & Parzinger, M. J. (1997). Issues in foreign outsourcing. *Information Systems Management, 14*(2), 27-31.

Saunders, C., Gebelt, M., & Hu, Q. (1997). Achieving success in information systems outsourcing. *California Management Review, 39*(2), 63-79.

Shamis, G. S., Green, M. C., Sorensen, S. M., & Kyle, D. L. (2005). Outsourcing, offshoring, nearshoring: What to do? *Journal of Accountancy, 199*(6), 57-61.

Smith, H., & McKeen, J. (2004). Developments in practice XIV: IT sourcing — how far can you go? *Communications of the Association for Information Systems, 14*, 508-520.

Smith, H. J., & Keil, M. (2003). The reluctance to report bad news on troubled software projects: A theoretical model. *Information Systems Journal, 13*(1), 69-95.

Teng, J. T. C., Cheon, M. J., & Grover, V. (1995). Decisions to outsource information-systems functions: Testing a strategy-theoretic discrepancy model. *Decision Sciences, 26*(1), 75-103.

Thibodeau, P. (2004). More IT jobs to go offshore, controversial ITAA report says. *Computerworld, 38*(14), 1-2.

Trembly, A. C. (2003). Outsourcing information technology: Cutting costs or cutting your throat? *National Underwriter/Life & Health Financial Services, 107*(27), 42.

Wainwright, C. E. R., Reynolds, K. A., & Argument, L. J. (2003). Optimising strategic information system development. *Journal of Business Research, 56*(2), 127-135.

Wallace, L., Keil, M., & Rai, A. (2004). Understanding software project risk: A cluster analysis. *Information & Management, 42*(1), 115-125.

Section IV

Quantitative Methods in Management Information System Outsourcing

Chapter XV

A Goal Programming Model for Evaluating Outsourcing Partners on a Global Scale

James J. Hoffman, Texas Tech University, USA

Eric Walden, Texas Tech University, USA

Francisco Delgadillo Jr., Texas Tech University, USA

Ronald Bremer, Texas Tech University, USA

Abstract

A critical concern for firms that decide to outsource their information technology (IT) functions (or other operational functions for that matter) is the evaluation on a global scale of potential outsourcing partners. In order for outsourcing to be successful, corporations must identify outsourcing partners that offer a good fit with the firm's overall outsourcing strategy. Unfortunately, little has been written to aid corporations in making complex decisions involving the evaluation of potential outsourcing partners. This chapter presents a goal programming model that combines the concepts of global outsourcing, the management science technique of goal programming, and microcomputer technology to provide managers with a more effective and efficient method for evaluating potential IT outsourcing partners. The chapter extends the existing literature on outsourcing by applying a computer optimization model to outsourcing partner selection in a way that has not been done before.

Introduction

Management of information technology (IT) has been, and continues to be, a complex task. Prior economics-based literature has focused primarily on understanding how IT can help business units generate value. This arises naturally from the need to justify, to senior managers, the large amounts spent on IT. However, by now we have moved beyond the *productivity paradox* and firmly believe that IT does generate value (Brynjolfsson & Hitt, 1998). In fact, a fundamental transformation of IT's place in the firm has occurred. Fueled by tremendous investment in the 1980s and 1990s, IT has become a business unit in need of management. Researchers need to recognize that the organization of IT work has important economic impacts on the ability of IT units to provide service (Bresnahan, Brynjolfsson & Hitt, 2002).

The ability to manage interorganizational relationships is one of the most valuable capabilities of a firm (Achrol, 1997; Bensaou, 1999; Dyer & Singh, 1998). Firms must not only execute tasks at a frenetic pace, they must also execute a greater number and variety of electronically enabled tasks. This obliges their IT infrastructure to be both highly reliable and extremely flexible. Success, and even survival, in such an environment, requires the ability to manage relationships between an organization and its partners. According to by Michael F. Corbett and associates, executives spend fully one-third of their budgets on the management of external relationships (Anonymous, 2005). This tremendous need to coordinate with outside entities prompted Frank Casale, CEO of the Outsourcing Institute, to propose a new executive officer — the chief relationship officer — whose sole job is to manage relationships with these outside entities (Mayor, 2001). As firms move away from simply outsourcing the development of software into multifaceted electronic business infrastructure projects, the nature of relationships become more complex. New outsourcing relationships include implementations of enterprise packages, such as SAP or PeopleSoft and exploitation of application service providers, such as Interelate (www.interelate.com) and SMS (www.sms.com). However, while popular opinion holds that outsourcing is an advantageous way to manage IT functions, the evidence on the value of outsourcing is far from equivocal (see Clemons, Reddi, & Row, 1993 for a moderating viewpoint). Many relationships end as failures, incurring huge costs for both firms. For example, a Deloitte and Touche survey indicated that 53% of firms attempt to renegotiate the original terms of the relationship with their partners, and one fourth of those renegotiations end in the termination of the relationship (Caldwell, 1997).

Though relationships are fraught with a number of potential problems, their use continues to grow. A rational firm would be more likely to institute a relationship with a partner who is more able to perform the task. This superior performance could manifest in the form of lower costs, higher quality, greater knowledge, or a myriad of other factors. While these performance results are widely described, the causal mechanism remains a mystery. What is the resource that the partner brings to the table that cannot be duplicated by the focal firm? It must be a very beneficial resource to overcome the tremendous obstacles involved. The contracting difficulties alone are enough to make firms quite weary. For example in IT outsourcing, estimates show that outsourcing clients spend 15% of their IT budget on litigation with erstwhile partners (Goodridge, 2001). Not only must the package of resources possessed by the IT partner be very valuable, but the package must also be quite unique because the focal firm cannot duplicate it and yet it is imitable by, literally, hundreds of other possible IT partners. Other research has found that, even at the height of dotcom mania, announcements of e-commerce relationships generated no significant returns for the participants (Subramnai & Walden, 2001).

Unfortunately, many firms that pursue outsourcing do not always select the best outsourcing partner. Often this is because they do not fully understand all the factors that should be taken into consideration when evaluating potential outsourcing partners. These factors can include things such as:

1. Commitment to quality
2. Price
3. References/reputation
4. Flexible contract terms
5. Scope of resources
6. Additional value-added capability
7. Cultural match
8. Location

This chapter focuses on the evaluation of outsourcing partners on a global scale and utilizes goal programming in order to provide managers with a computer based outsourcing partner selection model on which to base outsourcing decisions. The goal of this chapter is provide managers with a more effective and efficient model for making outsourcing decisions on a global scale. The specific objectives of the chapter are to:

1.   Develop a new outsourcing partner selection model that combines the concept of outsourcing strategy, the management science technique of goal programming, and micro computer technology to provide a more efficient and effective framework on which to base IT outsourcing decisions

2.   Apply the model to an example decision involving the selection of an IT outsourcing partner.

The Outsourcing Partner Selection Model

The concept of outsourcing deals with the process of matching or fitting the organization with an outsourcing partner in the most advantageous way. The outsourcing partner selection model, shown in Figure 1, uses goal programming

Figure 1. The IT outsourcing partner selection model

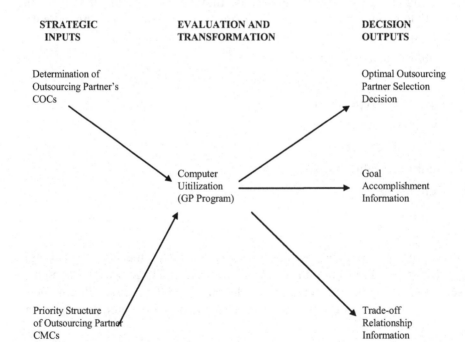

to help outsourcing firms select the outsourcing partner that best fits the outsourcing firm's needs.

Determination of Critical Outsourcing Characteristics

The outsourcing partner selection model has two steps. The purpose of step one is to determine what characteristics an outsourcing partner should have to fit most advantageously with the outsourcing firm's needs. These characteristics are referred to as the outsourcing partners' critical outsourcing characteristics (COCs) since they are critical to the chances the outsourcing relationship has of being successful. Literature dealing with factors in outsourcing partner selection has identified eight broad categories of outsourcing factors that are generally essential for outsourcing partner market selection. As mentioned above, these include factors such as commitment to quality, price, references/reputation, flexible contract terms, scope of references, additional value-added capability, cultural match, and location.

An outsourcing firm should only examine those critical outsourcing factors that are most important to the outsourcing relationship being successful. In the outsourcing partner selection model these factors are first ranked in order of importance. For example, if a high commitment to quality is a critical outsourcing partner characteristic, and a major goal of the outsourcing firm is to have as low costs as possible and flexible contract terms, then the outsourcing firm might rank quality as its highest critical outsourcing partner characteristic, then price, flexibility of contract terms, and so on until all the critical outsourcing partner characteristics have been included in the model.

Once the COCs are ranked, the next step is to weight them for each potential outsourcing partner that is examined. A weighting scale can be used to assign weights to those important COCs that cannot be precisely quantified. A rating scale allows those COCs that cannot be quantified with great precision to be rated relative to the same COCs of other outsourcing partners under consideration. For example, a potential outsourcing partner's commitment to quality cannot be quantified as easily or with the precision as price. Thus, a potential outsourcing partner's commitment to quality is rated relative to the commitment to quality of other potential outsourcing partners under consideration.

Evaluation and Outsourcing Partner Selection

During the second step of the model, several alternative outsourcing partners are identified. Relevant information about each potential outsourcing partner is then entered into the goal programming part of the model. The model will evaluate the information and determine which outsourcing partner best meets the needs of the outsourcing firm.

The goal programming (GP) formulation of the outsourcing partner selection model is shown in Appendix A. To use this model, a decision maker must decide the number of outsourcing partners (i.e., the alpha parameter in the model) with which the outsourcing firm wants to simultaneously have an outsourcing partnership for a particular task. While some outsourcing firms may want to have a relationship with only one outsourcing partner at a time for a particular task, this model can easily accommodate multiple outsourcing partner evaluation problems. In the outsourcing partner selection model, the variables or unknowns (i.e., x_j) that are being determined is (are) the outsourcing partner(s) with the best overall set of critical outsourcing characteristics. The strategic fit of a potential partner's critical outsourcing characteristics is described in the model as mathematical constraints, composed of the previously mentioned weighting scale values (i.e., a_{ij}) for each outsourcing partner's COC that management defines as desirable. Management must also define the relative importance, via a priority or ranking (i.e., P_i) for each of the COCs.

Once the model is formulated it can be computer loaded or the data for the model may be more easily obtained by merging files from data sources into a variety of Goal Programming software packages (see Bitran, 1979; Kiziltan & Yucaoglu, 1983). The use of computer technology allows decision makers to generate country selection solutions even when a substantial number of outsourcing partner's COCs are included in the model.

The informational output of the outsourcing partner selection model is quite extensive and goes far beyond any simple tabular solution. The model provides the best strategically fitting outsourcing partner for the outsourcing firm and also provides information on how well the choice satisfied the prioritized goals established by management on the COCs. In addition, the outsourcing partner selection model provides trade off information of the COCs that can help improve outsourcing partner selection decisions. For example, the model can define the exact trade off values for alternative outsourcing partners. These trade off values can be used to revise the priority structure to improve the outsourcing partner selection choice. In other words, the model offers information that can be used by managers to suggest refinements in the model for a better solution. Indeed, one real advantage of using the outsourcing partner selection model is that minor changes in the model's parameters can be easily made and a new solution can be quickly generated with the computer. Tabular methods, on the other hand, might require a substantial investment in time and effort for revision and recalculation of a new solution.

The trade off information generated from the goal programming step of the model also can reveal where subjective weighting scale values should be revised or reevaluated to improve the solution. By directing attention to the key solution determinates, management can focus their efforts and time more efficiently by evaluating the validity of the critically important and subjectively derived parameters in the model.

Application of the IT Outsourcing Partner Selection Model

To illustrate how the outsourcing partner selection model works, a case study is presented in which a U.S. firm wants to evaluate potential IT outsourcing partners from 20 different countries in order to determine which outsourcing partner (i.e., alpha = 1) offers the best outsourcing fit.

In Table 1 the assessment of each outsourcing partner's COCs is based either on objective dollar or percentage information, or is subjectively determined by senior management. A total of eight selection criteria are used. The eight selection criteria are structured in the IT outsourcing partner selection model as the parameters in the goal constraints. The actual desired goals (i.e., β_i) are usually set at an idealistic level of perfection that can rarely be achieved. The model will seek a solution that minimizes deviation from those impossible β_i goals by selecting the outsourcing partner whose selection criterion comes closest to the β_i. As shown in Table 1, the COCs for the potential outsourcing partners commitment to quality is set at 200 or more (commitment to quality examined is composed of five different quality dimensions and each dimension is rated on a 50 point scale). The point totals for the five dimensions are then added together), while the other factors such as price per IT resource is set at an ideal level of $20,000 or less. The ranked priorities (P_i) of the goals are based on the importance of each COC relative to the other COCs. While a single specific ranking is used in this example, it may be desirable to perform P_i sensitivity analysis (Anthony, Dearden, & Vancil, 1972) to see if other rankings will improve the resulting solution).

Based on the information in Table 1, the outsourcing partner selection model for the outsourcing partner selection problem can be formulated as presented in Appendix B. Each of the x_j decision variables in the model represents a different outsourcing partner from which one is to be selected. A computer that utilizes a FORTRAN program based on Bitran's zero one programming procedures (Bitran, 1979) can be used to solve the outsourcing selection problem.

Table 1. Data for IT outsourcing partner case study application

Alternative Outsourcing Partner Contribution toward Goal (a_{ij})

Critical Outsourcing Characteristics (COCs)	Unit of Measure	Desired Goal (β_i)	Ranked Priority (P_i)	Hungary (x_1)	India (x_2)	China (x_3)	...	Czech Republic (x_{20})
Commitment to Quality (Measured on three quality dimensions)	The sum of five 50 point quality scales	200 or more	8	250	200	150	...	165
Price per IT resource	Thousands of Dollars	20 or less	7	10	15	14	...	25
Reputation	1-5 Scale	4 or more	6	2	4	4	...	3
Flexibility of Contract Terms	1-25 point scale	20	5	12	8	15	...	9
Chance of Outsourcing Partner not having enough resources	0% - 100% Scale	2% or less	4	8	7	20	...	18
Additional Value Added Capability	1-10 Scale	4 or more	3	3	4	3	...	3
Differences in Culture	0-20 Scale with 0 being no difference	0	2	6	5	5	...	6
Location	0-100 Scale with 100 being an ideal location	100	1	70	95	80	...	91

Of the 20 outsourcing partners from which to select, the model selected the firm from India (i.e., x_2) as the best strategically fitting outsourcing partner. A complete break down of the goal accomplishment in this selection is presented in Table 2. The goal deviation and its interpretation in Table 2 are very useful post decision information. The solution generated deviation provides detailed information on how much deviation there will be between the needs of the outsourcing firm and the selected outsourcing partner's contribution to filling those needs.

The postsolution information provided by the model can also be extended by considering the dual solution to the problem and performing a sensitivity analysis on select desired goal parameters (β's). The selection of one outsourcing partner over another invariably involves trade-offs between the COCs. The dual variable values for each of the selection criteria provide very detailed trade-off information. A sensitivity analysis can be performed on each of the selection criteria goals that may be of special interest to the outsourcing firm's management.

In Table 3, the β's dual solution and sensitivity analysis values of the specific selection criteria objective of Commitment to Quality are presented. The dual

Table 2. IT outsourcing partner selection model solution for case study application

Critical Outsourcing Characteristics (COCs)	Ranked Priority (P_i)	Solution Generated (d_i^- d_i^+)	Goal Accomplishment and Interpretation on Model Selection of Outsourcing Partner's Country (x_n)
Commitment to Quality (Measured on three quality dimensions)	8	0	Selection fully satisfies the commitment to quality goal of 200 points
Price	7	0	Selection fully satisfies the goal of price being under $20,000
Reputation	6	0	Selection fully satisfies goal of reputation having a scaled measure of 4 or more
Flexibility of Contract Terms	5	-12	Selection does not fully satisfy flexibility of contract terms (12 points short of 20 point goal)
Chance of Outsourcing Partner not having enough resources	4	5	Selection does not fully satisfy the chance of outsourcing partner not having enough resources goal (5% higher than the goal of 2% or less)
Additional Value Added Capability	3	0	Selection fully satisfies additional value added capability goal of 4 or more
Differences in Culture	2	5	Selection does not fully satisfy differences in culture goal (5 points more than the goal of 0 point difference)
Location	1	-5	Selection does not fully satisfy location goal (5 points below the ideal goal of 100 points)

solution values provide trade-off information on the amount of deviation that can be reduced from the existing solution if a change in the 200 point commitment to quality goal is permitted. If the firm would be willing to decrease their commitment to quality goal of a minimum of 200 points to only 150 points, an alternative outsourcing partner selection is possible that would improve the outsourcing fit even better than the India selection. The dual value of 0.14 for the selection criteria of Flexibility of Contract Terms in Table 3 indicates that a 0.14 point increase in flexibility of contract terms is possible for each one point decrease in commitment to quality. The sensitivity analysis defines boundaries under which the changes can be made in the selection criteria. We can see in Table 3 that the quality point requirement for the selection criteria of Commitment to Quality can be decreased from 200 points to a boundary limit of 150 points (or a 50 point decrease). The result of such a decrease would be a new outsourcing partner selected that would reduce negative deviation (or increase the flexibility of contract terms) by seven points (i.e., 0.14 flexibility of contract points x 50 commitment to quality points).

Once this trade off information is identified, the next step of the model is to analyze it in the context of the specific firm that is under examination. In the IT outsourcing partner selection example it is assumed that the outsourcing firm (i.e., as opposed to the outsourcing partner) generates an additional 0.10% in profits from each additional commitment to quality point. If this is the case, the

Table 3. Dual solution values and sensitivity analysis of "Commitment to Quality" objective

Critical Outsourcing Characteristics (COCs)	Dual Variable Values	Sensitivity Analysis: Boundaries for Commitment to Quality Objective of 200 or more
Commitment to Quality (Measured on three quality dimensions)	0	-
Price	0	-
Reputation	0	-
Flexibility of Contract Terms	.14%	≥ 150
Chance of Outsourcing Partner not having enough resources	.20%	≥ 175
Additional Value Added Capability	0	-
Differences in Culture	1	≥ 195
Location	0	-

outsourcing firm would lose 5% in profits (0.10% in lost profits x 50) from the 50 point loss in commitment to quality. In return for losing the 50 commitment to quality points, the outsourcing firm would increase contract flexibility by 7 points.

If the increase in contract flexibility is more valuable than the lost profits from not having as high of number of commitment to quality points, then the model would have been rerun and the next set of trade off information would be analyzed using the same method as described above. It is important to note that the exact numbers and percentages used to put each of the trade off values into profit and loss terms will be contingent on the firm under study. But these calculations can easily be made once the model generates the exact trade off values that need to be evaluated.

After an outsourcing partner is selected, the dual solution values and sensitivity analysis can be performed for each of the eight selection criteria in this problem if desired. As can be seen from the Commitment to Quality criteria, this information would provide detailed trade-off values for any or all existing possible combinations of selection criteria.

Managerial Implications and Conclusions

The decision of where to introduce products into international markets is a critical and complex issue for the corporation that must be dealt with on a continuing basis by top managers. This chapter has presented a computer based model for introducing products into international markets that offers several benefits for marketing managers. These benefits include:

1. Provides trade off information revealing where subjective weighting scale values should be revised or reevaluated to improve the outsourcing partner selection

2. Simultaneously considers all decision making criteria to derive an optimal selection

3. Permits ordinary ranked prioritization of decision making criteria

4. Easy to change optimal performance factor and objective factor estimates (i.e., model parameters) and solve for a new solution with little or no effort from management

While the model presented in this chapter provides a powerful decision making tool for outsourcing partner selection on a global scale, the information it generates with duality and sensitivity analysis possesses some limitations. One of the limitations is that the dual solution values are limited to a single change. That is, multiple changes in selection criteria values will not necessarily result in desirable changes reflected in all of the dual decision values. A second limitation is that changes beyond the boundaries defined by sensitivity analysis cannot be interpreted from the dual solution values. Such changes can be determined by using the model as a simulation tool. That is, the change can be observed by making a parameter change in the model and resolving the problem to see the simulated effect of the change in the new solution. These limitations and others that are commonly discussed when using the methodologies presented in this chapter (see Schniederjans, 1984) limit the interpretation of the information from the model, but not its use in facility site selection. Despite these limitations, the careful application of the methodologies proposed in this chapter will reveal accurate and useful planning information that is not currently available to managers. Overall, it is hoped that the outsourcing partner selection model developed in this chapter provides managers with a tool that is helpful in reducing the risk of selecting outsourcing partners in the global market place. It is also hoped that this chapter serves as a point of reference for future research involving the evaluation of global outsourcing partners.

References

Achrol, R. S. (1997). Changes in the theory of interorganizational relations in marketing: Toward a network paradigm. *Journal of the Academy of Marketing Science, 25*, 56-71.

Anonymous. (2005, March 21). *Fortune, 151*(6), C1.

Anthony, R., Dearden, J., & Vancil, R. F. (1972). *Management control systems*. Homewood, IL: Irwin.

Bensaou, M. (1999). Portfolios of buyer-supplier relationships. *Sloan Management Review, 4*, 35-44.

Bitran, G. (1979). Theory and algorithm for linear multiple objective programs with zero one variables. *Mathematical Programming, 17*, 362 390.

Bresnahan, T., Brynjolfsson, E., & Hitt, L. (2002). Information technology, work organization and the demand for skilled labor: Firm-level evidence. *The Quarterly Journal of Economics, 117*, 339-376.

Brynjolfsson, E., & Hitt, L. M. (1998). Beyond the productivity paradox. *Communications of the ACM, 41*, 49-55.

Caldwell, B. (1997, September 29). Outsourcing backlash. *InformationWeek, 650*, 14-16.

Clemons, E. K., Reddi, S. P., & Row, M. C. (1993). The impact of information technology on the organization of economic activity: The "move to the middle" hypothesis. *Journal of Management Information Systems, 10*, 9-29.

Dyer, J. H., & Singh, H. (1998). The relational view: Cooperative strategy and sources of interorganizational competitive advantage. *Academy of Management Review, 23*, 660-679.

Goodridge, E. (2001, January 10). Outsourcing makes work for lawyers. *InformationWeek*. Retrieved March 16, 2006, from http://www.techweb.com/wire/story/TWB20010102S0004

Kiziltan, G., & Yucaoglu, E. (1983). An algorithm for multiobjective zero one linear programming. *Management Science, 29*, 1444 1453.

Mayor, T. (2001, November 1). Our vendors, ourselves. *CIO, 14*, 195-200.

Schniederjans, M. J. (1984). *Linear goal programming.* Princeton, NJ: Petrocelli Books.

Subramani, M. R., & Walden, E. A. (2001). The impact of e-commerce announcements on the market value of firms. *Information System Research, 12*, 135-154.

Appendix A:
IT Outsourcing Partner
Selection Model Formulation

minimize $Z = \sum_{i=1}^{m} P_i * (d_i^- + d_i^+)$

subject to: $\sum_{j=1}^{n} x_j = \alpha$

$\sum_{j=1}^{n} a_{ij} x_j + d_i^- - d_i^+ = \beta_i,$ for $i = 1, 2, \cdots, m.$

and $x_j = 0$ or 1; $d_i^-, d_i^+ \geq 0$

The following definitions hold:

n is the number of outsourcing locations (potential partners) being considered.

m is the number of targeted critical outsourcing characteristics.

x_j, j=1, 2, ..., n, are the decision variables, such that

$$x_j = \begin{bmatrix} 1, & \text{test in location j} \\ 0, & \text{do not test in location j} \end{bmatrix}$$

β_i, i=1, 2, ..., m are the targeted critical outsourcing characteristic objectives.

a_{ij}, i=1, 2, ..., m, j=1, 2, ..., n are the critical outsourcing characteristic weightings for the ith targeted location factor objective when the jth outsourcing location is selected.

d_i^-, d_i^+, i=1, 2, ..., m, are the underachievement and overachievements, respectively, from targeted critical outsourcing characteristics objectives. $d_i^-, d_i^+ \geq 0$.

P_i, i=1, 2, ...,m, are the rank priority (importance) of each critical outsourcing characteristic to the outsourcing company, where $P_1 > P_2 > ... > P_i$. If the critical outsourcing characteristics are listed by importance with the most important corresponding to i=1 then P_1=m, P_2=m-1 etc.

α is the number of outsourcing locations (partners) to be selected to perform the outsourcing task.

Appendix B:
Formulation of the IT Outsourcing Partner Selection Model for the Case

Study Application

Minimize $Z = P_1\ d_1^- + P_2\ d_2^+ + P_3\ d_3^- + P_4\ d_4^- + P_5\ d_5^+ + P_6\ d_6^- + P_7\ d_7^+ + P_8\ d_8^-$

Subject to: $x_1 + x_2 + x_3 ... + x_{20} = 1$

$250x_1 + 200x_2 + 150x_3 + ... + 165x_{20} + d_1^- - d_1^+ = 200$

$10x_1 + 15x_2 + 14x_3 + ... + 25x_{20} + d_2^- - d_2^+ = 20$

$2x_1 + 4x_2 + 4x_3 + ... 3x_{20} + d_3^- - d_3^+ = 4$

$12x_1 + 8x_2 + 15x_3 + ... + 9x_{20} + d_4^- - d_4^+ = 20$

$8x_1 + 7x_2 + 20x_3 + ... + 18x_{20} + d_5^- - d_5^+ = 2$

$$3x_1 + 4x_2 + 3x_3 + \ldots + 3x_{20} + d_6^- - d_6^+ = 4$$

$$6x_1 + 5x_2 + 5x_3 + \ldots + 6x_{20} + d_7^- - d_7^+ = 0$$

$$70x_1 + 95x_2 + 80x_3 + \ldots + 91x_{20} + d_8^- - d_8^+ = 100$$

and $x_j = 0$ or 1; $d_i^-, d_i^- \geq 0$.

Chapter XVI

Real Option Appraisal in R&D Outsourcing

Qing Cao, University of Missouri - Kansas City, USA

Karyl B. Leggio, University of Missouri - Kansas City, USA

Abstract

This chapter will stress MIS' strides in R&D outsourcing, and it will also detail the risks and uncertainty associated with the process of outsourcing core areas of the business such as R&D. Moreover, the chapter will propose the use of real option analysis to assist in the decisions of: "Why should a firm outsource R&D?" and "How does a company select a viable vendor using a two-stage process?" The purposes of this chapter include: a discussion of the cutting edge usage of outsourcing for R&D; and, to alleviate the R&D outsourcing risks, we will explore the two-stage vendor selection approach in information technology outsourcing using real options analysis.

Introduction

What began as a means of having routine processes completed by those external to the firm, has exploded into an industry that is on the frontier of product design and innovation. We are speaking, of course, of outsourcing, the reason for many corporate restructurings thus far in the 21st century. There does not appear to be abatement in this trend. Outsourcing offers firms the ability, in the face of limited resources, to attract specialized talent to rapidly solve a business issue. And, by outsourcing to several firms simultaneously, corporations are able to mitigate the risk of exposure to project failure by insourcing or single outsourcing.

Outsourcing offers a firm flexibility. By purchasing specialized knowledge through outsourcing agreements, firms no longer have to deploy internal re-sources to solve an array of problems. As circumstances change, firms that outsource have the ability to adjust and pursue different opportunities rapidly. In essence, outsourcing is a real option the firm acquires and exercises as warranted. This is particularly true in the area of R&D.

Rather than building an internal R&D program with the knowledge base to tackle a disparate series of issues, the firm can contract with external organizations with specialized research expertise. A technology manager study found that 90% of those surveyed expected to be involved in R&D partnerships within the next three years (Higginbotham, 1997). Additionally, the firm has the ability to hire two or more independent firms to address a business issue. At points in time during the development project, the firm can decide to continue to fund two independent firms working to solve a business problem or, if one firm appears to be progressing more rapidly, efficiently, and profitably towards a solution, can opt instead to fund only one firm to complete the project. This flexibility can often lead to a more rapid solution since the firm does not need to wait for one company to fail to develop a product before partnering with a second firm.

Outsourcing accounts for more than 20% of drug development expenditures (Malek, 2000). Consider a pharmaceutical firm. Rather than building an R&D department to solve a wealth of medical issues, the firm can outsource. For instance, the pharmaceutical firm may have no expertise in finding relief for arthritis sufferers. Rather than hiring researchers and building a lab, the firm can outsource to a research lab that specializes in arthritis research. Alternatively, the firm can hire two research labs to work independently on discovering new products for arthritis sufferers. At a predesignated point during the drug development process, the firm can then determine the success of each outsourcing firms' research and determine which outsourcing firm should continue to be funded. The same concept can be applied to the outsourcing of information technology research and development.

Information technology is in the forefront of the R&D outsourcing phenomenon. First, information technology has always been a part of the R&D process (Komninos, 2004). Take software engineering for instance. Changing from the awkward machine language to the "easy to use" fifth generation programming language is based on R&D efforts. Second, information technology also serves as an enabler for R&D (Nambisan, 2003). The aggressive implementation of information technology in the product development arena will reshape innovation. Unlike existing innovation processes which are passive, the IT enabled innovation processes are active, directly supporting innovation activities.

Real options is an alternative valuation method for capturing managerial flexibility that is inherent in R&D projects (Lewis, Enke, & Spurlock, 2004). In this study, we explore the multi-stage vendor selection issue in information technology outsourcing using real options analysis. We use the example of outsourcing the development of supply chain management information systems for a logistics firm. We find real options to be a viable project valuation technique for R&D outsourcing.

R&D Outsourcing

Outsourcing began as a means of having routine tasks completed inexpensively. Yet information technology outsourcing in India alone is forecasted to grow from a $1.3 billion business in 2003 to $9 billion in 2010. And this growth is not in low skill tasks. IT personnel in India will be engaged in encryption and network security, programming languages, and computing architectures (Highlands Ranch, 2004). R&D is, by its very nature, an uncertain undertaking. The firm faces an initial decision in determining if outsourcing of R&D is the correct decision, if the right vendor is selected, and if, once contracted, the research should continue to be funded. Over the past two decades, the speed of innovation and the quantity of new technologies has exploded. Innovation is being driven by a series of forces that are interacting.

Consumers are expecting, and demanding, new technologies at an increasing rate. The time between the introduction of new technologies and the adoption of these same technologies by consumers is shrinking. This causes firms to spend more on research and new product development (Chiesa, Manzini, & Pizzurno, 2004). In addition, globalization has increased the available supply of research-based workers, and new technologies improve the ability of these works to collaborate virtually.

To compete in this new frontier, many firms are choosing to outsource innovation (R&D). Firms have choices. They can choose not to innovate thus limiting future firm growth. They can choose to develop internal resources and employ a staff to innovate. Or the firm can choose to outsource its innovation needs. Many firms are choosing to outsource.

The reasons for making the choice to outsource the innovation function are numerous. Firms have limited resources and may not be able to employ an adequate number of specialists to allow the firm to innovate efficiently or may not be able to attract the talent to the firm. Being first to market often is valuable. The firm may not be able to develop a new technology internally in a timely manner. Finally, firms outsource to reduce exposure to research project failures. R&D is costly. By outsourcing, the firm is able to mitigate its risk exposure to projects that fail to result in marketable products.

There are, however, additional challenges associated with outsourcing core business functions such as R&D. Control for quality standards is difficult to manage when the R&D is being done by an external organization. Concern exists that the outsourcing organization may sell technologies developed to competitors if the contract is not structured properly. And there are uncertainties related to cost containment thus allowing the new technologies to be priced properly.

Information Technology Outsourcing: A Major R&D Outsourcing Application

The past decade has seen an explosion in information technology (IT) outsourcing for building basic computer applications, systems maintenance and support, routine process automation, and even strategic systems. Recent estimates suggest that this trend is likely to continue with projections of IT outsourcing contracts reaching $160 billion in 2005, up from $101 billion in 2000 (Vijayan, 2002). In transferring IT activities to outside suppliers, firms expect to reap various benefits, from cost savings to increased flexibility, and from improved quality of services to better access to state-of-the-art technology (McFarlan & Nolan, 1995). However, various undesirable results have also been associated with IT outsourcing including: service degradation, the absence of cost reduction (Scheier, 1996), and disagreement between the parties. In light of the high IT outsourcing failure rate, several researchers have argued for adopting a risk management approach to studying and managing IT outsourcing based on transaction cost theory (Kern, Willcocks, & van Heck, 2002; Willcocks, Lacity, & Kern, 1999). However, they neglect the vendor selection issue in managing the IT outsourcing risk.

Vendor Selection

Because IT is an intangible product that can be heavily customized for each company, it might be very difficult to accurately assess vendor quality during the bidding process. Moreover, even for situations where many aspects of performance can be measured, not all aspects of IT project outcome may be measurable to a degree where an outside party (vendor) can certify compliance (Grover, Cheon, & Teng, 1999). As such, the vendor selection problem with nonverifiable outcomes is an important issue in practice and has attracted attention in both the IT outsourcing literature (Lacity & Hirschheim, 1993) and practices.

A number of factors aggravate the vendor selection difficulties for IT projects. First, the unprecedented rate of technological change in IT makes it difficult at the outset to lock project specifications into an enforceable contract that can be externally monitored or verified. Second, project management of software development initiatives is much less predictable than project management for other engineering activities. Finally, the IT industry has a high degree of heterogeneity. Our two-stage vendor selection model is viable in IT outsourcing practices. First, IT contracts are increasingly structured as multistage agreements. Second, it might be that the early stages represent pilot projects to help resolve uncertainty in vendor quality. Pilot projects are regularly used in IT contracting for technology exploration and technical risk reduction, as they enable both clients and vendors to learn more about the needs of a project.

Vendor management involves both vendor selection and client-vendor relationship control. Many researchers have addressed the latter issue by the employment of transaction cost theory (Kern et al., 2002; Willcocks, 1999) or the analysis of incomplete contracts (Nam, Rajagopalan, Rao, & Chaudhury, 1996). The objective is for the client to induce the optimal performance from the vendors. It is equally important to select the right vendor for the task. As noted by Power, Bonifazi, and Desouza, (2004), one pitfall for outsourcing failure is the minimal knowledge of outsourcing methodologies, especially in the vendor selection process. This issue has been addressed by many, but the majority of the work focuses on the *single-stage* process; that is, to build mathematical models to help the client to choose one vendor from many *solely* based on the past performance data. Such approaches imply that vendors' past performance guarantees future results, an assumption which does not necessarily apply because of ever changing technology, a high degree of heterogeneity of outsourced projects, intrinsic variation, and low predictability in vendor performance (Snir & Hitt, 2004).

Two-Stage Vendor Selection

Recognizing the limitation of the single-stage approach, several researchers have discussed a two-stage process (DiRomualdo & Gurbaxani, 1998; Snir & Hitt, 2004). The first stage is a trial phase that helps the client to find the best match between the vendor and the outsourced project. In the second stage, the client employs the chosen vendor for the full implementation of the project. The dominant theme of the existing work is the dynamics of client-vendor interaction in the first stage, analyzed under the game theory framework.

In this chapter, we subscribe to the notion of the two-stage process, but try to answer a different question: Under resource constraints, how should the client determine the scope of the first-stage testing and decide which vendors should participate based on their prior performance information? The fundamental trade-off of this problem is embedded in the allocation of a fixed budget between the two stages. To improve its chance of getting a high-performing vendor for the task, the client would like to invite as many candidates to participate in the first-stage testing as possible. However, involving too many vendors depletes the client's budget and consequently, limits its ability to carry out the project to a full extent in the second stage. We argue that the first-stage testing is a process of gathering vendor information, so the investment in the process should depend on the value of the information to be gathered. These values depend on both the quality of information itself (by how much the client can expect to improve its knowledge about the vendors by the first stage testing), and the client's ability to act on that information. We also argue that choosing participating vendors in the first-stage testing resembles portfolio management; that is, vendors should be selected based on not only their own virtue, but also the complement of their performance profiles. Our two-stage vendor selection model is viable in IT outsourcing practices. First, IT contracts are increasingly structured as multi-stage agreements. Second, it might be that the early stages represent pilot projects to help resolve uncertainty in vendor quality. Pilot projects are regularly used in IT contracting for technology exploration and technical risk reduction, as they enable both clients and vendors to learn more about the needs of a project.

ROA or Not ROA

Firms consider the risk of new investments prior to undertaking a new project. The firm accounts for risk through the capital budgeting function. In capital budgeting decision-making, the goal is to identify those investment opportunities whose net value to the firm is positive. Discounted cash flow (DCF) analysis is the traditional capital budgeting decision model used (Mun, 2002.) It involves discounting the expected, time dependent cash flows for the time value of money and for risk via the calculation of a net present value (NPV).

$$NPV = -IO + \sum_{t=1}^{n} \frac{CF_t}{(1+r)^t} \tag{1}$$

Where IO equals the initial cash outlay for the project, CF is the cash flow, and r is the discount rate. The NPV represents the expected change in the value of the firm which will occur if the project is accepted. The decision rule is straightforward: accept all positive NPV projects and reject all negative NPV projects. A firm is indifferent to a zero NPV project as no change in current wealth is expected.

Today, most academic researchers, financial practitioners, corporate managers, and strategists realize that, when market conditions are highly uncertain, expenditures are at least partially "irreversible," and decision flexibility is present, the static, traditional DCF methodology alone fails to provide an adequate decision-making framework (Herath & Bremser, 2005). It has been suggested that current corporate investment practices have been characterized as myopic due, in large part, to their reliance on the traditional stand-alone DCF analysis (Pinches, 1982; Porter, 1992). An alternative project valuation method is real options analysis (ROA).

Real options are a type of option where the underlying asset is a real asset, not a financial asset (Copeland, & Antikarov, 2001). In general, real options exist when management has the opportunity, but not the requirement, to alter the existing strategic or the current operating investment strategy. Real option analysis allows firms to more accurately evaluate projects by explicitly valuing managerial flexibility. Managerial flexibility is valuable since it allows managers to continually gather information concerning uncertain project and market outcomes, and change the firm's course of action based on this information. Real option analysis is a dynamic means of adjusting corporate strategies with innovative product offerings (Barnett, 2005). The most general or all inclusive real option is the option to invest.

The analogy is to a financial call option: the firm has the right, but not the obligation, now or for some period of time to undertake the investment opportunity by paying an upfront fee. As with financial options, the option to invest is valuable due to the uncertainty relating to the underlying asset's future value where, in this case, the underlying asset is the investment opportunity. The investment rule is to invest when the present value of the benefits of the investment opportunity is greater than the present value of the direct cost of the investment opportunity *plus* the value of keeping the option to invest "alive":

$$PV(\text{Benefits}) > PV(\text{Cost}) + \text{Value of the Option to Invest} \qquad (2)$$

Outsourcing can be thought of as staged investment. A telecommunications firm chooses to fund two research labs to develop a new cell phone technology. The firm funds the research for a period of time. At the end of that time, both outsourcing firms present the results of their research to date. The funding firm then decides whether to continue funding one, both, or neither of the research labs. Suppose, at the first assessment stage, the telecommunications firm chooses to continue funding both research labs. As the research leads to the development of new technology, and the products work their way through the stages of development, the telecommunications company continues to assess whether to continue funding the research of the two firms.

ROA can lead to a change in decision-making. The traditional DCF analysis wants all point estimates to be as known and certain as possible, and in DCF models, an increase in risk is accounted for by increasing the discount rate, resulting in lower valuations. Thus, under traditional DCF reasoning, risk hurts. In comparison, option value is most often a positive function of the volatility of the underlying asset, as, generally, an increase in volatility leads to an increase in the range of possible future values for the underlying asset. As this line of reasoning quickly suggests, aggressive firms will seek projects with higher volatility because active management of those projects can create value for the firm. Under real options thinking, as long as management can control the downside risk of a project, firms should seek risk, at least to some degree. ROA also shows that sometimes negative NPV projects should be undertaken, given the upside potential embedded in the project (Alessandri, Ford, Lannder, Leggio, & Taylor, 2004).

The question we are concerned with is: how can the real options framework be used to improve the analyses of R&D outsourcing? The answer is that ROA can systematically organize the analysis and identify the uncertainties. ROA is, in essence, the quantification of the strategic premium — the gap between the economic value and the actual value of a firm as determined by the marketplace. It allows managers to formulate and implement strategic plans in high-commitment, high-uncertainty environments such as those found in R&D projects. The technique is often used at the firm level; however, more frequently what is needed is a project-level perspective.

Real Option Methodology

The generally accepted methodology for valuing a financial call option is the Black-Scholes (1973) formula as follows:

$$\text{Value of Call} = Se^{(b-r)T}N(d_1) - Xe^{-rT}N(d_2) \qquad (3)$$

where:

$$d_1 = \frac{\ln(S/X) + (b + \frac{\sigma^2}{2})T}{\sigma\sqrt{T}}$$

$$d_2 = d_1 - \sigma\sqrt{T}$$

S is the price of the underlying asset, X is the exercise price of the option, r is the risk free rate, b is the cost of carry, N(d1) and N(d2) represent the cumulative standard normal distribution, σ^2 is the volatility of the underlying asset, and T is the time until expiration of the option. The difficulty with using this closed-form solution for valuing real options is it is difficult to explain, is applicable in very specific situations, and limits the modeler's flexibility. On the other hand, the binomial lattice model, when used to price the movement in the asset value through time, is highly flexible. It is important to note the results are similar for the closed form Black-Scholes model and the binomial lattice approach. The more steps added to the binomial model, the better the approximation (Mun, 2002)

The binomial asset pricing model is based on a replicating portfolio that combines borrowing with ownership of the underlying asset to create a cash flow stream equivalent to that of the option. The model is created period by period with the asset value moving to one of two possible probabilistic outcomes each period. The asset has an initial value, and within the first time period, the asset value will either move up to an increased value, Su, or to a decreased value, Sd. In the second time period, the asset value can be any of the following: Su^2, Sud, Sd^2. The shorter the time interval, the smoother the distribution of outcomes (Amram & Kulatilaka, 1999).

The inputs for the binomial lattice model are equivalent to the inputs for the Black-Scholes model; namely, we need the present value of the underlying asset

Figure 1. Binomial lattice option model

						$S_o u^5$
				$S_o u^4$		
			$S_o u^3$		$S_o u^4 d$	
		$S_o u^2$		$S_o u^3 d$		
	$S_o u$		$S_o u^2 d$		$S_o u^3 d^2$	
S_o		$S_o ud$		$S_o u^2 d^2$		
	$S_o d$		$S_o d^2$		$S_o u^2 d^3$	
		$S_o d^2$		$S_o d^3 u$		
			$S_o d^3$		$S_o d^4 u$	
				$S_o d^4$		
					$S_o d^5$	

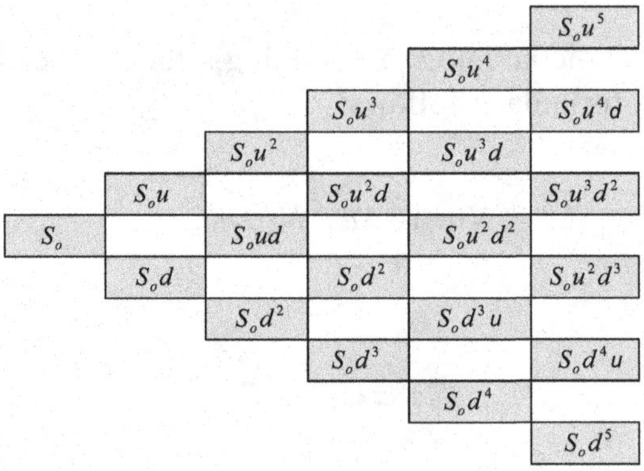

(S), the cost of exercising the option (X), the volatility of the cash flows (σ), the time until expiration (T), the risk free interest rate (r_f), and the dividend payout percentage (b). We use these inputs to calculate the up (u) and down (d) factors and the risk neutral probabilities (p).

$$u = e^{\sigma \sqrt{\delta t}} \tag{4}$$

$$d = e^{-\sigma \sqrt{\delta t}} = \frac{1}{u} \tag{5}$$

$$p = \frac{e^{(r_f - b)(\delta t)} - d}{u - d} \tag{6}$$

where p reflects the probable outcomes that determine the risk free rate of return. Figure one shows the binomial lattice option model.

Conclusion

In this chapter, we propose a two-stage vendor selection approach in R&D outsourcing using real options analysis. The conclusions from this study are much broader and have wider application. Without real options, traditional capital budgeting techniques such as net present value analysis cannot capture the potential upside potential of projects. Outsourcing information technology is an important opportunity for research firms to consider. The opportunity must be valued properly. Given the shortcomings of traditional methodologies to account for expansion options embedded in many R&D projects, firms may fail to pursue outsourcing ventures due to faulty valuation techniques. Real options analysis is a technique that needs to be used to value projects with growth opportunities. The chapter contributes to the outsourcing literature by providing a two-stage vendor selection framework employing real options analysis. It also extends the real options analysis applications to R&D outsourcing risk management arena, which has never been presented before, to the best of our knowledge.

In summary, this chapter drives home the reasons firms choose to outsource core functions such as R&D and provides firms with an analytical tool (real options) to evaluate the critical vendor selection process in R&D outsourcing.

References

Alessandri, T., Ford, D., Lander, D., Leggio, K., & Taylor, M. (2004). Managing risk and uncertainty in complex capital projects. *Quarterly Review of Economics and Finance, 44*(4), 751-767.

Amram, M., & Kulatilaka, N. (1999). *Real options: Managing strategic investment in an uncertain world.* Boston: Harvard Business School Press.

Barnett, M. L. (2005, January). Paying attention to real options. *R&D Management, 35*(1), 61-73.

Black, F., & Scholes, M. (1973). The pricing of options and corporate liabilities. *Journal of Political Economy, 81*(3), 637-659.

Chiesa, V., Manzini, R., & Pizzurno, E. (2004). The externalisation of R&D activities and the growing market of product development services. *R & D Management, 34*(1), 65-75.

Copeland, T., & Antikarov, V. (2001). *Real options: A practitioner's guide.* New York: Texere.

DiRomualdo, A., & Gurbaxani, V. (1998). Strategic intent for IT outsourcing. *Sloan Management Review, 39*(4), 67-80.

Grover, V., Cheon, M. J., & Teng, J. T. C. (1996). The effect of service quality and partnership on the outsourcing of information systems functions. *Journal of Management Information Systems, 12*(4), 89-116.

Herath, H. S. B., & Bremser, W. G. (2005). Real option valuation of research and development investments: Implications for performance measurement. *Managerial Auditing Journal, 20*(1), 55-73.

Higginbotham, J. S. (1997). Outsourcing R&D delivers results. *Research & Development, 39*(11), Q-S.

Highlands Ranch. (2004). R&D outsourcing to grow in India. *R&D, 46*(7), 19-20.

Kern, T., Willcocks, L., & van Heck, E. (2002). The winner's curse in IT outsourcing: Strategies for avoiding relational trauma. *California Management Review, 44*(2), 47–69.

Komninos, N. (2004). Regional intelligence: Distributed localized information systems for innovation and development. *International Journal of Technology Management, 28*(3-6), 483-506.

Lacity, M. C., & Hirschheim, R. (1993). *Information systems outsourcing, myths, metaphors, and realities.* Chichester, UK: Wiley.

Lewis, N., Enke, D., & Spurlock, D. (2004). Valuation for the strategic management of research and development projects: The deferral option. *Engineering Management Journal, 16*(4), 36-49.

Malek, J. (2000). R&D outsourcing that works. *Pharmaceutical Executive, 20*(3), 70-76.

McFarlan, F. W., & Nolan R. L. (1995). How to manage an IT outsourcing alliance. *Sloan Management Review, 36*(2), 9-23.

Mun, J. (2002). *Real options analysis: Tools and techniques for valuing strategic investments and decisions.* Hoboken, NJ: John Wiley & Sons.

Nam, K., Rajagopalan, S., Rao, H. R., & Chaudhury A. (1996). A two-level investigation of information systems outsourcing. *Communications of the ACM, 39*(7), 36-44.

Nambisan, S. (2003). Information systems as a reference discipline for new product development. *MIS Quarterly, 27*(1), 1-18.

Pinches, G. (1982). Myopia, capital budgeting and decision-making. *Financial Management, 11*(3), 6-20.

Porter, M. E. (1992). Capital disadvantage: America's failing capital investment system. *Harvard Business Review, 17*(5), 65-82.

Power, M., Bonifazi, C., & Desouza, K. C. (2004). The ten outsourcing traps to avoid. *The Journal of Business Strategy, 25*(2), 37-42.

Scheier, R. L. (1996). Outsourcing's fine print. *Computerworld, 30*(3), 70.

Snir, E. M., & Hitt, L. M. (2004). Vendor screening in information technology contracting with a pilot project. *Journal of Organizational Computing and Electronic Commerce, 14*(1), 61-88.

Vijayan, J. (2002). The outsourcing boom. *Computerworld, 36*(12), 42-43.

Willcocks, L., Lacity, M., & Kern, T. (1999). Risk mitigation in IT outsourcing strategy revisited: Longitudinal case research at LISA. *Journal of Strategic Information Systems, 8*, 285-314.

Chapter XVII

The Application of Real Options to the R&D Outsourcing Decision

Qing Cao, University of Missouri - Kansas City, USA

David N. Ford, Texas A&M University, USA

Karyl B. Leggio, University of Missouri - Kansas City, USA

Abstract

This chapter is a companion chapter to Chapter XVI, Real Option Appraisal in R&D Outsourcing. *We provide two real-world case studies of the application of real options to answer the question: "How do practicing planners and managers use and value flexibility in development projects?" The first case study we develop is based on the outsourcing decision-making process, more specifically, a two-stage vendor selection approach (applying real options theory) to adopting a supply chain management (SCM) system in a Shanghai-based transportation company — Chic Logistics. In the second case study, we use the example of the National Ignition Facility (NIF) to illustrate how decision-makers identify uncertainty and value flexibility in project analysis, and by deliberate decision, increase their options and thereby project value.*

Real Option Methodology

The generally accepted methodology for valuing a financial call option is the Black-Scholes (1973) model. The difficulty with using this closed-form solution for valuing real options is it is difficult to explain, is applicable only in very specific situations, and limits the analyst's ability to model. On the other hand, the binomial lattice model, when used to price the movement in the asset value through time, is highly flexible. It is important to note the results are similar for the closed form Black-Scholes model and the binomial lattice approach. The more steps added to the binomial model, the better the approximation (Mun, 2002).

The binomial asset pricing model is based on a replicating portfolio that combines borrowing with ownership of the underlying asset to create a cash flow stream equivalent to that of the option. The model is created period by period with the asset value moving to one of two possible probabilistic outcomes each period. The asset has an initial value and within the first time period, either moves up to Su or down to Sd. In the second time period, the asset value can be any of the following: Su^2, Sud, Sd^2. The shorter the time interval, the smoother the distribution of outcomes (Amram & Kulatilaka, 1999).

The inputs for the binomial lattice model are equivalent to the inputs for the Black-Scholes model; namely, we need the present value of the underlying asset (S), the cost of exercising the option (X), the volatility of the cash flows (σ), the time until expiration (T), the risk free interest rate (r_f), and the dividend payout percentage (b). We use these inputs to calculate the up (u) and down (d) factors that are then used to find the risk neutral probabilities (p) that adjust asset values each time step (δt).

$$u = e^{\sigma \sqrt{\delta t}} \tag{1}$$

$$d = e^{-\sigma \sqrt{\delta t}} = \frac{1}{u} \tag{2}$$

$$p = \frac{e^{(r_f - b)(\delta t)} - d}{u - d} \tag{3}$$

where p reflects the probable outcomes that determine the risk free rate of return. Figure 1 shows the binomial lattice option model.

Figure 1. Binomial lattice option model

					$S_o u^5$
				$S_o u^4$	
			$S_o u^3$		$S_o u^4 d$
		$S_o u^2$		$S_o u^3 d$	
	$S_o u$		$S_o u^2 d$		$S_o u^3 d^2$
S_o		$S_o ud$		$S_o u^2 d^2$	
	$S_o d$		$S_o d^2$		$S_o u^2 d^3$
		$S_o d^2$		$S_o d^3 u$	
			$S_o d^3$		$S_o d^4 u$
				$S_o d^4$	
					$S_o d^5$

Case 1: Chic Logistics

Chic Logistics Incorporated (CLI) is a $40 million Shanghai-based transportation company with funding from American Venture Capitals. Johnson Shen, CEO and the founder of the company, states "China's economy is growing in such a rapid pace that traditional transportation and warehousing systems have been unable to meet the increasingly sophisticated demands of the market. A modern approach to logistics management provides our customers with higher efficiency, more diversification of services, and above all, better technology." In 2004, CLI determined to make the transformation by adopting a supply chain management information system (SCMIS). Due to limited in-house IT capabilities, CLI decided to outsource the SCMIS project based on the rationale that purchasing IT components/services from external vendors would allow them to enjoy the benefits of specialization and lower costs. CLI faced two dilemmas of IT outsourcing. First, there are too many SCMIS vendors to choose from in China. Initially, they found 13 qualified SCMIS vendors in China and later they reduced the selection of vendors to 2 finalists (SSA Global and EXE Technologies) using a Delphi Method (a subjective selection approach).

However, CLI still needs to figure out an analytical screening approach in choosing the final vendor. Second, by its very nature, IT projects such as SCMIS are intangible products and, as such, it is difficult to identify vendor capabilities and assess vendor performance objectively. CLI decided to employ a two-stage outsourcing approach. In the first stage, namely, the prototype stage, CLI will invest $100,000 in both SSA Global and EXE Technologies. In the prototype stage, CLI engages each company for a pilot project and observes the outcome. Based on the outcome of the pilot projects, CLI decides whether to continue the project with one of these two companies to the second stage or to terminate the project.

Real option analysis (ROA) was chosen by CLI as the methodology for the vendor selection process. Using ROA, CLI was able to decide not only which vendor to select but also determine what is the optimal level of investment at each stage.

CLI Results

Presuming an initial firm value of $40 million, volatility of 15%, and a time period between steps of 0.20 years, the lattice for CLI if the firm were not to outsource to either firm appears below. In CLI's case, $u = e^{\sigma\sqrt{d_t}} = e^{0.15\sqrt{(0.20)}} = 1.055$ and $d = \frac{1}{u} = \frac{1}{1.055} = 0.95$. The volatility calculation is estimated by CLI based on historic volatility of previous IT R&D projects. The binomial tree indicates the R&D project value will vary from $52.31 million to $30.59 million at the end of five periods (Figure 2).

The projected future cash flows for CLI without an SCMIS range from a high of $52.3 million to a low of $30.58 million. CLI can alter these growth projections by choosing to outsource to one of two firms: SSA or EXE. Applying the same valuation approach as for CLI without outsourcing, CLI projects that if it outsources to SSA, the range of possible net present value cash flows due to outsourcing will vary between $5.3 million and $7.7 million with a probabilistic expected value of $6.54 million (Table 1). By running a Monte Carlo simulation,

Figure 2. CLI's underlying asset lattice

					52311.05
				49577.74	
			46987.25		46987.25
		44532.12		44532.12	
	42205.27		42205.27		42205.27
40000.00		40000.00		40000.00	
	37909.96		37909.96		37909.96
		35929.12		35929.12	
			34051.79		34051.79
				32272.55	
					30586.27

Table 1. Forecasted values before option valuation

	Forecasted Cash Flows ($1,000,000)			
	Minimum	Maximum	Present Expected Value ($1,000,000)	Volatility
CLI	30.6	52.3	40.0	15%
SSA	4.7	9.1	6.5	12%
EXE	2.3	10.3	4.8	34%

Figure 3. SSA's underlying asset lattice

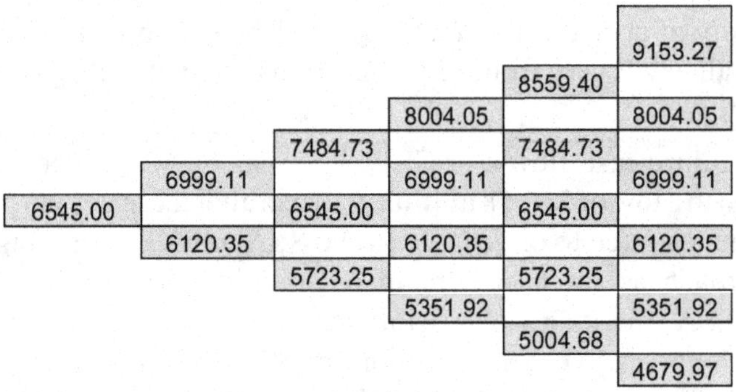

Figure 4. EXE's underlying asset lattice

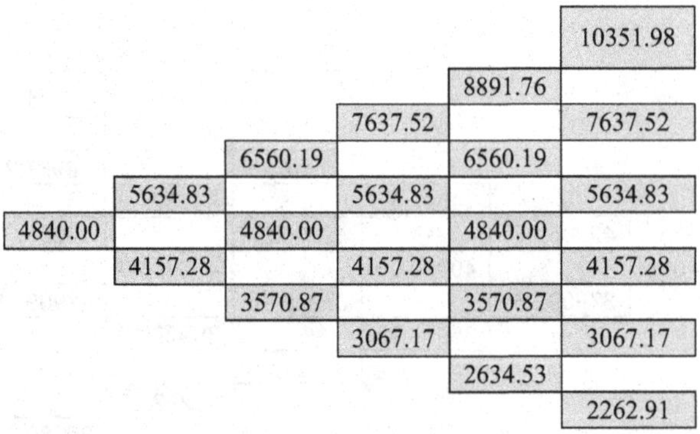

CLI derives a volatility estimate of 12% for SSA. On the other hand, the present value of the cash flows from partnering with EXE range from $3 million to $7 million with an expected value of $4.84 million and a volatility estimate of 34% when derived from the simulation. SSA's expected future cash flows range from $9.1 million to $4.68 million, while EXE has a larger upside potential with maximum expected cash flows of $10.3 million; however, on the downside, the lower expected cash flows for EXE are $2.26 million. The binomial lattices for SSA and for EXE appear in Figures 3 and 4.

To calculate the value of the option, ROA requires the future value of the projected cash flows be discounted back to the present. To calculate the value at each node, S, the present value is calculated as follows:

$$S = [Sup + Sd(1-p)]e^{-rt} \tag{4}$$

Figure 5. Option valuation lattice CLI and SSA

					61364.32
				58085.32	
			54981.87		54891.30
		52044.54		51959.24	
	49264.42		49184.07		49104.38
46633.08		46557.39		46482.31	
	44071.22		44000.48		43930.31
		41651.38		41585.25	
			39365.56		39303.71
				37206.22	
					35166.24

Figure 6. Option valuation lattice CLI and EXE

					62563.03
				58761.22	
			55212.89		54524.77
		51899.12		51281.83	
	48802.59		48248.81		47740.10
45907.38		45410.55		44954.12	
	42753.14		42343.59		41967.24
		39896.24		39558.49	
			37297.65		37018.96
				34924.53	
					32749.18

Table 2. Values of SCMIS development strategies with options

	Forecasted Cash Flows ($1,000,000)		Present Expected Value
	Minimum	Maximum	
CLI	30.6	52.3	40.0
CLI & SSA	35.2	61.4	46.6
CLI & EXE	32.7	62.6	45.9

Beginning at the far right side of the lattice, the nodes are calculated period by period and rolled back to arrive at the present value of the investment project. The expected future cash flows of the SCMIS strategy when partnering with SSA is $46,633.08 whereas the value of CLI partnering with EXE is $45,907.38. Table 2 presents a comparison of CLI's three options: to choose not to partner, to partner with SSA, or to partner with EXE.

Clearly, CLI should outsource. Both projects create value for the firm which far exceeds the $100,000 in prototype development costs. Whereas CLI has a present value of $40 million, with either an outsourcing venture with SSA or CLI, additional firm value is created. As the lattices show, despite the higher upside potential for a CLI/EXE outsourcing project ($62.563 million vs. $61.364 million), CLI realizes the greater value by outsourcing to SSA. Whereas a project to outsource to EXE yields an expected $45.907 million in present value (or, an additional $5.907 million incremental value), a venture with SSA leads to an expected value increase of $6.633 million due to options. CLI should choose to outsource to SSA.

For this particular project, we have consistency: both NPV and ROA lead to the conclusion that CLI should outsource to SSA. This is not surprising. For the same initial investment, SSA yields $6.54 million in present value whereas EXE only yields $4.84 million, a difference of 35%. Real option analysis adds real value to decision analysis when the outcome is not so clear-cut. With a vendor selection problem, it is more common to find a case where the expected cash flows are more similar. When this occurs, and the volatility of the cash flows for the two vendors is different, we typically see real option and NPV decisions that conflict. Although NPV and real option analysis led to the same decision in this case, for projects with growth opportunities, this frequently is not the case. For projects with growth options, the decision criterion should be to accept the project with the greatest real option value.

Not all projects are quantifiable like Chic Logistics. In some cases, managers cannot determine a point estimate of a future value. However, in these cases, real option analysis can be used to focus and improve managers' thinking. The National Ignition Facility case demonstrates this use of real option analysis.

Case 2: National Ignition Facility

The National Ignition Facility (NIF) is a nuclear explosion laboratory developed by the U.S. Department of Energy to create new means of stockpile testing and research (Lawrence Livermore National Laboratory, 2005). The facility exists largely due to the Comprehensive Nuclear Test-Ban Treaty signed by the United States in 2001, which banned the traditional ways of testing nuclear weapons.

NIF needed to develop slabs of laser glass blanks to be used in the testing of nuclear weapons and research. Laser glass procurement requires the production of high quality glass slabs called "blanks," the finishing of the blanks, and the coating of the blanks. Blanks for smaller lasers could be produced in batch processes. But the NIF project scaled up the laser size to about ten times that of the largest existing laser. No glass production technologies capable of producing the volume of glass blanks needed by NIF existed or were under development at the start of the project.

The ability of glass firms to develop feasible new glass production technologies and the quality of the glass produced if the production technologies were feasible were uncertain, as were costs and development schedules. NIF chose to hire two firms to begin initial research into the development of a technology to produce the blanks. At stages throughout the process, NIF had the ability to choose to (a) continue funding both companies and their technology development; (b) fund only one company going forward; or (c) discontinue funding both companies and explore alternative sources for the blank development. The choice at each step was based on the success of the outsourcing firms in meeting expectations and the cost of continuing to fund the research and development.

Through real option analysis, NIF was able to assess the cost effectiveness of its options at each stage. This analysis assisted managers in project management decision-making by providing a reliable decision tool.

Research and Development for Laser Glass Production Technology

NIF spent more than $350 million to produce over 3,000 pieces of laser glass. Laser glass begins as slabs of very high quality glass called "blanks." The large volume of blanks and project schedule and budget required a production rate 30 times larger and five times cheaper than was used on prototype lasers. This required the development of a new glass production technology. Glass vendors could not justify funding the development. Therefore, NIF invested in glass production technology R&D (Campbell, 2001). The R&D of a high-volume continuous-melting glass production process included two critical uncertainties: whether the technology could make the glass; and whether the quality of the glass would be acceptable. The threat posed by these uncertainties was that, if R&D efforts failed in either way, the project could be delayed too long to meet its deadline and would incur very high unbudgeted costs. Although NIF had relationships with experienced laser glass vendors, none could guarantee successful development within the required time a priori. NIF needed a higher likelihood of success than any one vendor could provide. Therefore, alternatives to a one-vendor strategy were considered during laser glass procurement planning.

In the laser glass case, the managed asset is the NIF project and the underlying uncertainty is the likelihood of a vendor successfully developing a feasible glass production technology with the required quality. NIF managers acquired several options to manage laser glass production technology R&D, including flexibility in funding, schedules, sharing of expertise and human resources, and other technologies. However, the most critical option was incorporated into the R&D procurement strategy (Ford & Ceylan, 2002). A base strategy would invest in a single production development effort, hoping for a successful development. An alternative strategy would simultaneously make initial investments in two phased independent R&D efforts by two glass producers. The latter strategy would provide two managerial options as well as increasing the likelihood that at least one effort would be successful. First, phased R&D would provide options for NIF to delay its decisions about the amount of support (if any) to provide each vendor until some technology feasibility uncertainty was resolved. Second, investing in two vendors would provide the following option based on the primary underlying uncertainty, what R&D effort or efforts would succeed. If only one effort succeeded, managers could abandon the failed effort, use the successful one, and avoid the consequences of having no successful glass production system. If both vendors succeeded, NIF could choose the better, or both.

The sequential investments in each vendor can be structured as a staged development process of options to extend support if adequate progress is demonstrated; or an option to abandon the vendor if adequate progress cannot be demonstrated. This flexibility initially would cost NIF approximately $12 million for either vendor. The flexibility provided by investing in multiple vendors can be structured as an option to choose the successful vendor (if only one succeeds), choose the more successful vendor (if both succeed), or retain both vendors (if both succeed). The cost of this flexibility is the funds required to invest in a second vendor (approximately $12 million). Given the uncertainties, potential costs, and benefits, the NIF managers had to assess whether the one-vendor or two-vendor strategy would best serve NIF and how to implement the chosen strategy.

Despite a plethora of factors that influenced strategy attractiveness, the option analysis centered on the comparison of scenario sets (Alessandri, Ford, Lander, Leggio, & Taylor, 2004). If a single vendor was selected, the development might succeed. But if the single vendor failed, the costs to the project in time, money, and political consequences would prevent the project from meeting its targets. Previous embarrassing and costly NIF failures to meet targets made this scenario tantamount to the death of the project to the NIF managers. In contrast, if two vendors were selected, none, one, or two could succeed. The likelihood of two failures was considered very low because of the many other project management tools and options available to managers (Moses, 2001). One or two successes would protect NIF from project failure. The avoided costs of project failure if investments were made in two vendors were (informally) estimated to greatly exceed the additional cost of investing in a second vendor (about 0.5% of the project budget), even if the avoided costs were discounted at any reasonable rate to account for the time value of money. Therefore, the option was considered more valuable than its cost. Based on this reasoning, NIF selected a two-vendor strategy and contracted with two vendors to initiate parallel R&D efforts.   The uncertainty about technology viability was resolved when both vendors successfully produced pilot runs of glass using continuous-melting processes. Due largely to the remaining uncertainties, NIF chose to continue investment in both vendors. Quality uncertainty was resolved when both vendors also demonstrated the ability to generate the required glass quality. NIF chose again to continue with both vendors to retain manufacturing and pricing flexibility. Each time NIF managers chose to support both vendors, NIF purchased quality, production, or pricing flexibility that they could use to manage other project uncertainties (e.g., funding profile changes). The costs avoided with these options were significant, albeit less than those saved in case of a development failure.

Conclusion

The Chic Logistics case illustrates how practicing mangers can use a formal (i.e., mathematical) model to estimate asset values with flexible strategies. These values were then used to improve strategic decision-making about outsourcing. The NIF laser glass production technology R&D case illustrates how practicing managers can use options to increase project value, even without formal valuation modeling. NIF managers included the monetary, schedule, and political consequences of strategy choices into their assessment of option values and thereby integrated the richness of the project into strategic decision-making.

A major challenge for corporate and project senior leaders is to more fully understand how to identify, evaluate, and manage the risks and uncertainties facing their organizations. Yet the complexity of many industries makes this task difficult. A thorough understanding of the risk factors that contribute to the variability in a firm's earnings and project values can determine the survivability of the firm, and will enhance the abilities of executives to anticipate competitive, environmental, regulatory, and legislative changes and their impacts. Executives are increasingly being called upon to meet financial expectations, manage risk to stabilizing earnings, and increase the firm's potential survivability. In this era, managing the firm's risk, and the firm, under conditions of uncertainty, becomes critical. Real options are a means to manage risk whether the analysis is in the traditional quantitative analysis demonstrated in the CLI case or in the strategic thinking used to make the NIF decision.

References

Alessandri, T., Ford, D., Lander, D., Leggio, K., & Taylor, M. (2004). Managing risk and uncertainty in complex capital projects. *Quarterly Review of Economics and Finance, 44*(5), 751-767.

Anram, M., & Kulatilaka, N. (1999). *Real options: Managing strategic investment in an uncertain world.* Boston: Harvard Business School Press.

Campbell, J. (2001). *Interview with author.* Livermore, CA: Lawrence Livermore National Laboratory.

Ford, D., & Ceylan, K. (2002). Using options to manage dynamic uncertainty in acquisition projects. *Acquisition Review Quarterly, 9*(4), 243-258.

Lawrence Livermore National Laboratory. (2005, June 14). *National Ignition Facility programs*. Retrieved March 16, 2006, from http://www.llnl.gov/nif

Moses, E. (2001, December 13). *Interview with author*. Livermore, CA: Lawrence Livermore National Laboratory.

Mun, J. (2002). *Real options analysis: Tools and techniques for valuing strategic investments and decisions*. Hoboken, NJ: John Wiley & Sons.

Chapter XVIII

An Application of Multi-Criteria Decision-Making Model to Strategic Outsourcing for Effective Supply-Chain Linkages

N. K. Kwak, Saint Louis University, USA

Chang Won Lee, Jinju National University, Korea

Abstract

An appropriate outsourcing and supply-chain planning strategy needs to be based on compromise and more objective decision-making procedures. Although factors affecting business performance in manufacturing firms have been explored in the past, focuses are on financial performance and measurement, neglecting intangible and nonfinancial factors in the decision-making planning process. This study presents development of an integrated multi-criteria decision-making (MCDM) model. This model aids in allocating outsourcing and supply-chain resources pertinent to strategic planning by providing a satisfying solution. The model was developed based on the data obtained from a business firm producing intelligent home system devices. This developed model will reinforce a firm's ongoing outsourcing strategies to meet defined requirements while positioning the supply-chain system to respond to a new growth and innovation.

Introduction

In today's global age, business firms are no longer able to manage all supply-chain processes from new product development to retailing. In order to obtain a successful business performance, appropriate outsourcing and supply-chain practices should be identified, established, and implemented within the firm. The growth of business scale and scope forces business decision-makers to resolve many of the challenges confronting business firms. These tasks and activities are often not well-defined and ill-structured. This new paradigm in business practices can deliver unprecedented opportunities to establish the strategic outsourcing and supply-chain planning in business firms (Heikkila, 2002; Li & O'Brien, 2001). Due to the technology and market paradigm shift, strategic outsourcing and supply-chain planning process in business firms may become more tightly coupled with new product research and development, capacity and financial planning, product launching, project management, strategic business alliances, and revenue planning.

Successful linkages of these complicated processes play a critical role affecting business performance in manufacturing settings (Cohen & Lee, 1988; Fisher, 1997; Min & Zhou, 2002; Quinn & Hilmer, 1994). Strategic outsourcing and supply-chain planning is a growing requirement for improving productivity and profitability. Many outsourcing studies have been conducted with supply-chain linkages directly and indirectly as follows: capacity planning (Lee & Hsu, 2004), downsizing (Schniederjans & Hoffman, 1999), dual sourcing (Klotz & Chatterjee, 1995), information system decision (Ngwenyama & Bryson, 1999), line balancing (Liu & Chen, 2002), service selection (Bertolini, Bevilacqua, Braglia, & Frosolini, 2004), transportation mode choice (Vannieuwenhuyse, Gelders, & Pintelon, 2003), and vendor selection (Karpak, Kumcu & Kasuganti, 1999).

In spite of a plethora of outsourcing studies in the existing literature, multi-criteria decision making (MCDM) applications are scarce and seldom identified as the best practice in business areas. Especially, an integrated MCDM model comprising goal programming (GP) and analytic hierarchy process (AHP) is rarely applied to manage an emerging outsourcing and supply-chain concern. This chapter has dual purposes: (1) to develop a decision-making model that aims at designing a strategic outsourcing and supply-chain plan, and (2) to provide the decision-makers with an implication for effectively managing strategic outsourcing and supply-chain planning in business firms and other similar settings.

The chapter is organized in the following manner. The "Introduction" section presents current research issues in both strategic outsourcing and supply-chain planning and MCDM in a business setting. The next section "Multicriteria Decision Making" provides a review of MCDM models. After that, a problem statement of the case study along with description of data collection is described. The model development to a real-world setting and the model results and a sensitivity analysis are provided, followed by concluding remarks.

Multi-Criteria Decision Making

Multi-criteria decision making (especially integrated MCDM) is defined as an applied linear programming model for a decision process that allows the decision-maker to evaluate various competing alternatives to achieve certain goals. Relative importance is assigned to the goal with respect to a set of chosen criteria. MCDM is appropriate for situations in which the decision-maker needs to consider multiple criteria in arriving at the best overall decisions. In MCDM, a decision-makers select the best strategy among a number of alternatives that they evaluate on the basis of two or more criteria. The alternatives can involve risks and uncertainties; they may require sequential actions at different times; and a set of alternatives might be either finite or infinite. A decision-maker acts to maximize a value or utility function that depends on the chosen criteria. Since MCDM assumes that a decision-maker is to select among a set of alternatives, its objective function values are known with certainty. Many MCDM problems are formulated as multiple objective linear, integer, nonlinear, and/or interactive mathematical programming problems.

One of the most widely used MCDM models is goal programming (GP). Charnes and Cooper (1961) conceptualized the GP technique and applied to an analytical process that solves multiple, conflicting, and noncommensurate problems. There are many different methods and models used to generate solutions for GP models. The natural decision-making heuristic is to concentrate initially on improving what appears to be the most critical problem area (criterion), until it has been improved to some satisfactory level of performance.

Classical GP assumes that there are some absolute target levels that can be specified. This means that any solution cannot always satisfy all the goals. Thus, the objective of GP is to find a solution which comes as close as possible to the target.

The formulation of a GP model assumes that all problem constraints become goals from which to determine the best possible solution. There are two types of constraints in GP: goal constraints and systems constraints. Goal constraints are called the goal equations or soft constraints. Systems constraints are called the ordinary linear programming constraints or hard constraints which cannot be violated.

One major limitation of GP is that the decision-makers must subjectively prioritize goals in advance. The concept of nondominated (noninferior) solutions for noncommensurable goals cannot make an improvement of one goal without degrading other conflicting goals. Regardless of the weighting structures and the goals, GP can lead to inefficient and suboptimal solutions. These solutions are not necessarily optimal for the decision-maker to acquire so that a satisfying solution is provided.

Among the MCDM models, the analytical hierarchy process (AHP) is another popular decision-making tool for multi-criteria decision-making problems. AHP provides a method to assess goals and objectives by decomposing the problem into measurable pieces for evaluation using a hierarchical structure. The procedure requires the decision-maker to provide judgments about the relative importance of each criterion and then specify a preference on each criterion for decision alternatives. The output of AHP is a prioritized ranking indicating the overall preference for each of the decision alternatives. An advantage of AHP is that it enables the decision-maker to handle problems in which the subjective judgment of an individual decision-maker constitutes an important role of the decision-making process (see Saaty, 1980 for a detailed analysis).

Problem Background

Problem Statement

A consortium of seven different firms developing and manufacturing the related products of the smart home system for home security was established in Korea. The consortium firm has recently released the smart home system to the general public.

The consortium firm secured $20 million for new product development in the 5-year period (2004-2008). It currently possesses a world-class frontier for developing a smart home system. Each member company has its own unique, special knowledge and human resources to carry on required manufacturing. There are five primary systems for making a smart home system: (1) multifunction home server with an Internet gateway function, (2) intelligent context awareness-based agent system, (3) digital video recorder for home security and applications, (4) biokey system with fingerprint access control solution, and (5) wireless digital home controller functions. It is intended to support a further growth and innovation in home security, home automation, remote controlling, and mobile multimedia functions. The infusion of additional information technology must be consistent with the business mission, strategic direction, business plans, and priorities of the consortium firm.

This special project for an integrated intelligent information technology is intended to address the dramatic growth in information technology use, to foster continued innovation and adoption of new technologies, and to expand information technology foundation for the next-generation smart home system. Thus, the consortium's information technology investment strategies throughout the next five years have been developed.

Data Collection

The data utilized to formulate this MCDM model was collected from the consortium of business firms developing and manufacturing the smart home system for home security. All the necessary data on budget, technical services, and personnel resources was gathered through the consortium's strategic business units. Additional data for establishing the consortium's resource allocation model was collected through the consortium's international business development directors who are in charge of outsourcing and supply-chain

Figure 1. Strategic goals and criteria

Vision		Strategic Outsourcing Goals		Criteria
Becoming the industry leader in smart home systems	→	Quality Improvement (G_1) Cost Effectiveness (G_2) Customer Satisfaction (G_3) Customizing Services (G_4) Manpower Quality (G_5) Supplier Competency (G_6) Strategic Partnership (G_7)	→	Financial Criteria (C_1) Customer Criteria (C_2) Internal Business Criteria (C_3) Innovation and Learning Criteria (C_4)

management. Project managers participated in the strategic planning process and identified the necessary goals and criteria derived from the proposal for strategic outsourcing and supply-chain planning.

The data was validated by the consortium decision-makers in the outsourcing and supply-chain planning process. The validation of the consortium's resource allocation model is critical to accept the model solutions and to implement the result. The validation process provides the management with a meaningful source to ensure the input, decision-making process, and the outcomes.

The success of the model is based on the accurate measurement of the established goals and criteria. Decision-makers involved in the current outsourcing and supply-chain planning process to complete the validation reviewed the results of both prioritization of the goals, as well as the related projects/ alternatives. Figure 1 presents a framework for strategic goals and related criteria.

Model Development

Goal Decomposition and Prioritization

In the MCDM model development of outsourcing and supply-chain planning process, the AHP has been utilized for establishing goal decomposition and prioritization. In order to obtain the overall relative importance of the seven goals, a synthesized priority is calculated for each goal. The proposed model requires the evaluation of goals with respect to how much these goals affect the overall effectiveness of strategic outsourcing and supply-chain planning for resource allocation in the consortium firm. Since no prior quantitative data exists for each goal combination, the decision-maker will make pairwise comparisons of each goal with all others, using the AHP judgment scale.

The AHP values for goal prioritization provide their eigenvalue and consistency ratio. There are four derived criteria, such as financial (C_1), customer (C_2), internal business (C_3), and innovation and learning criteria (C_4).

Strategic outsourcing and supply-chain management is prioritized with AHP weights as follows: quality improvement (G_1), cost effectiveness (G_2), customer satisfaction (G_3), customizing services (G_4), manpower quality (G_5), supplier competency (G_6), and strategic partnership (G_7).

Table 1. AHP results for goal prioritization

Criteria	Goal Decomposition								GEV	CEV	CR
		G_1	G_2	G_3	G_4	G_5	G_6	G_7			
C_1										.165	.083
	G_1		4	3	4	6	8	8	.352		
	G_2			2	2	4	6	7	.218		
	G_3				3	3	5	6	.144		
	G_4					3	4	5	.139		
	G_5						2	3	.070		
	G_6							2	.044		
	G_7								.032		
C_2										.620	.046
	G_1		4	3	4	6	8	8	.404		
	G_2			2	2	4	6	7	.200		
	G_3				3	3	5	6	.168		
	G_4					3	4	5	.110		
	G_5						2	3	.056		
	G_6							2	.035		
	G_7								.026		
C_3										.142	.086
	G_1		4	3	4	6	8	8	.342		
	G_2			2	2	4	6	7	.238		
	G_3				3	3	5	6	.158		
	G_4					3	4	5	.116		
	G_5						2	3	.078		
	G_6							2	.034		
	G_7								.034		
C_4										.073	.059
	G_1		4	3	4	6	8	8	.334		
	G_2			2	2	4	6	7	.258		
	G_3				3	3	5	6	.174		
	G_4					3	4	5	.099		
	G_5						2	3	.067		
	G_6							2	.041		
	G_7								.026		
Goal Priority		.347	.244	.168	.106	.068	.040	.028			

GEV: Goal Eigenvalue, CEV: Criteria Eigenvalue, CR: Consistency Ratio

Decision Variables

The integrated GP problem consists of two types of decision variables in this study. The consortium firm wants to contract for the supply of five different smart home system components. Five outsourcing suppliers are being considered

Table 2. Estimated price ($) per system component in each supplier group

System Component	Outsourcing Supplier Group					Monthly Demand Level (00 units)
	1	2	3	4	5	
Home server	80	75	90	90	85	144
Awareness agent	90	85	75	80	90	360
Recorder database	75	90	80	90	75	380
Biokey	85	80	90	75	90	420
Controller box	90	85	75	80	90	320
Monthly Supply Level (00 units)	300	300	300	300	300	

Table 3. Project categories and available budgets for three stages

Project Category	Product Development			Available Project Budget ($000)
	Stage 1	Stage 2	Stage 3	
Security	150	100	130	380
Automation	120	200	130	450
Remote control	100	60	70	230
Mobile multimedia	150	110	100	360
Total	520	470	430	1,420

for contracting on the system components. Tables 2 and 3 present the necessary information for decision variables and constraints. The decision variables are:

$X^s_{ij} =$ decision variables for demand levels assigned to different types of component i (i =1,2,..,5) to be selected with various suppliers j (j =1,2,..,5) in demand capacity

where $X^s_i \geq 0$

$X^p_{ij} =$ decision variables for project i (1, 2, 3, and 4) to which available amounts can be allocated over three-stage period j (1,2 and 3) where:

$$X^p_{ij} = \begin{cases} 1 & \text{if ith project is selected} \\ \\ 0 & \text{otherwise} \end{cases}$$

Constraints

The MCDM model has 37 constraints: 14 systems constraints and 23 goal constraints. Systems constraints for this consortium firm's outsourcing and supply-chain planning are (1) demand-supply constraints for each system component, and (2) supply-chain linkages on the number of certain projects development.

Systems constraint 1: Set the demand-supply constraints for five components. 14,400 units [displayed as 144(00)].

$$X^s_{11} + X^s_{12} + X^s_{13} + X^s_{14} + X^s_{15} \leq 144(00) \tag{1}$$

$$X^s_{21} + X^s_{22} + X^s_{23} + X^s_{24} + X^s_{25} \leq 360 \tag{2}$$

$$X^s_{31} + X^s_{32} + X^s_{33} + X^s_{34} + X^s_{35} \leq 380 \tag{3}$$

$$X^s_{41} + X^s_{42} + X^s_{43} + X^s_{44} + X^s_{45} \leq 420 \tag{4}$$

$$X^s_{51} + X^s_{52} + X^s_{53} + X^s_{54} + X^s_{55} \leq 320 \tag{5}$$

$$X^s_{11} + X^s_{21} + X^s_{31} + X^s_{41} + X^s_{51} = 300 \tag{6}$$

$$X^s_{12} + X^s_{22} + X^s_{32} + X^s_{42} + X^s_{52} = 300 \tag{7}$$

$$X^s_{13} + X^s_{23} + X^s_{33} + X^s_{43} + X^s_{53} = 300 \qquad (8)$$

$$X^s_{14} + X^s_{24} + X^s_{34} + X^s_{44} + X^s_{54} = 300 \qquad (9)$$

$$X^s_{15} + X^s_{25} + X^s_{35} + X^s_{45} + X^s_{55} = 300 \qquad (10)$$

Systems constraint 2: Select one project for supply-chain management perspectives in each development stage.

$$X^P_{11} + X^P_{12} + X^P_{13} = 1 \qquad (11)$$

$$X^P_{21} + X^P_{22} + X^P_{23} = 1 \qquad (12)$$

$$X^P_{31} + X^P_{32} + X^P_{33} = 1 \qquad (13)$$

$$X^P_{41} + X^P_{42} + X^P_{43} = 1 \qquad (14)$$

There are seven goals to achieve in this study. Necessary goal priorities are presented next.

Priority 1 (P_1): Avoid overachievement of the financial resource level by providing appropriate system resources in terms of a continuous quality improvement goal (G_1), (See Table 3).

$$150X^P_{11} + 120X^P_{21} + 100X^P_{31} + 150X^P_{41} + 100X^P_{12} + 200X^P_{22} + 60X^P_{32} + 110X^P_{42}$$
$$+ 130X^P_{13} + 130X^P_{23} + 70X^P_{33} + 100X^P_{43} - d^+_1 = 1,420$$

$$(15)$$

Priority 2 (P_2): Avoid underachievement of the budget level meeting to all outsourcing suppliers of $138(00,000) in terms of cost effectiveness goal (G_2), (See Table 2).

$$80X^s_{11} + 75X^s_{12} + 90X^s_{13} + 90X^s_{14} + 85X^s_{15} + 90X^s_{21} + 85X^s_{22} + 75X^s_{23} + 80X^s_{24} +$$
$$90X^s_{25} + 75X^s_{31} + 90X^s_{32} + 80X^s_{33} + 90X^s_{34} + 75X^s_{35} + 85X^s_{41} + 80X^s_{42} + 90X^s_{43} +$$
$$75X^s_{44} + 90X^s_{45} + 90X^s_{51} + 85X^s_{52} + 75X^s_{53} + 80X^s_{54} + 90X^s_{55} + d^-_2 = 138$$

$$(16)$$

Priority 3 (P_3): Do not overutilize the available market resource level for each product development stage in terms of customer satisfaction goal (G_3), (See Table 3).

$$150X^P_{11} + 120X^P_{21} + 100X^P_{31} + 150X^P_{41} - d^+_3 = 520 \qquad (17)$$

$$100X^P_{12} + 200X^P_{22} + 60X^P_{32} + 110X^P_{42} - d^+_4 = 470 \qquad (18)$$

$$130X^P_{13} + 130X^P_{23} + 70X^P_{33} + 100X^P_{43} - d^+_5 = 430 \qquad (19)$$

Priority 4 (P_4): In terms of customizing services goal (G_4), avoid underachievement of resources to select an outsourcing supplier by using a total budget amount ($000) for (1) a home server outsourcing of $1,200; (2) an awareness agent component outsourcing of $3,060; (3) a digital recorder database component outsourcing of $3,200; (4) a biokey component outsourcing of $3,500; and (5) a controller box component outsourcing of $2,700 (see Table 2).

$$80X^s_{11} + 90X^s_{21} + 75X^s_{31} + 85X^s_{41} + 90X^s_{51} + d^-_6 = 1,200 \qquad (20)$$

$$75X^s_{12} + 85X^s_{22} + 90X^s_{32} + 80X^s_{42} + 85X^s_{52} + d^-_7 = 3,060 \qquad (21)$$

$$90X^s_{13} + 75X^s_{23} + 80X^s_{33} + 90X^s_{43} + 75X^s_{53} + d^-_8 = 3,200 \qquad (22)$$

$$90X^s_{14} + 80X^s_{24} + 90X^s_{34} + 75X^s_{44} + 80X^s_{54} + d^-_9 = 3,500 \qquad (23)$$

$$85X^s_{15} + 90X^s_{25} + 75X^s_{35} + 90X^s_{45} + 90X^s_{55} + d^-_{10} = 2,700 \qquad (24)$$

Priority 5 (P_5): Implement projects in the three product development stages in terms of manpower balancing goal (G_5).

$$X^P_{11} + X^P_{12} + X^P_{13} + X^P_{14} + d^-_{11} - d^+_{11} = 1 \qquad (25)$$

$$X^P_{21} + X^P_{22} + X^P_{23} + X^P_{24} + d^-_{12} - d^+_{12} = 1 \qquad (26)$$

$$X^P_{31} + X^P_{32} + X^P_{33} + X^P_{34} + d^-_{13} - d^+_{13} = 1 \qquad (27)$$

Priority 6 (P_6): Determine the demand capacity in each supplier to assign an appropriate outsourcing supplier group in terms of supplier competency goal (G_6).

$$X^s_{11} + X^s_{12} + X^s_{13} + X^s_{14} + X^s_{15} + d^-_{14} - d^+_{14} = 1 \qquad (28)$$

$$X^s_{21} + X^s_{22} + X^s_{23} + X^s_{24} + X^s_{25} + d^-_{15} - d^+_{15} = 1 \qquad (29)$$

$$X^s_{31} + X^s_{32} + X^s_{33} + X^s_{34} + X^s_{35} + d^-_{16} - d^+_{16} = 1 \qquad (30)$$

$$X^s_{41} + X^s_{42} + X^s_{43} + X^s_{44} + X^s_{45} + d^-_{17} - d^+_{17} = 1 \qquad (31)$$

$$X^s_{51} + X^s_{52} + X^s_{53} + X^s_{54} + X^s_{55} + d^-_{18} - d^+_{18} = 1 \qquad (32)$$

Priority 7 (P_7): In terms of strategic supplier partnership goal (G_7), decision-makers in the consortium firm decide that all suppliers are assigned to supply a certain component.

$$X^s_{11} + X^s_{21} + X^s_{31} + X^s_{41} + X^s_{51} + d^-_{19} - d^+_{19} = 1 \qquad (33)$$

$$X^s_{12} + X^s_{22} + X^s_{32} + X^s_{42} + X^s_{52} + d^-_{20} - d^+_{20} = 1 \qquad (34)$$

$$X^s_{13} + X^s_{23} + X^s_{33} + X^s_{43} + X^s_{53} + d^-_{21} - d^+_{21} = 1 \qquad (35)$$

$$X^s_{14} + X^s_{24} + X^s_{34} + X^s_{44} + X^s_{54} + d^-_{22} - d^+_{22} = 1 \qquad (36)$$

$$X^s_{15} + X^s_{25} + X^s_{35} + X^s_{45} + X^s_{55} + d^-_{23} - d^+_{23} = 1 \qquad (37)$$

Objective Function

The objective of this MCDM problem is to minimize the sum of the deviational variable values subject to constraints (1)-(37), satisfying the preemptive priority rules. The objective function depends on the preemptive priority sequence of the goals that have seven priorities.

$$\text{Minimize: } Z = P_1 d^+_1 + P_2 d^-_2 + P_3 \sum_{i=3}^{5} d^+_i + P_4 \sum_{i=6}^{10} d^-_i + P_5 \sum_{i=11}^{13} (d^+_i + d^-_i)$$

$$+ P_6 \sum_{i=14}^{18} (d^+_i + d^-_i) + P_7 \sum_{i=19}^{23} (d^+_i + d^-_i)$$

Model Analysis

Model Solution and Discussion

In this MCDM model, decision-makers seek a solution that satisfies as close as possible a set of goals. Thus, GP requires the concept of measuring discrepancy from the goals. The concept of nondominated solutions for noncommensurable goals cannot make an improvement of one goal without a trade-off of other conflicting goals. In the GP problem, a nondominated solution is examined. A nondominated solution is defined in the following manner: a feasible solution to an MCDM problem which is efficient, if no other feasible solutions yield an improvement in one goal, without sacrificing another goal. This MCDM model was solved using AB: QM system software (Lee, 1996). Table 4 presents an analysis of the objective function. Table 5 exhibits the results of both decision and deviational variables.

Priority 1 (P_1) is to avoid overachievement of the financial resource level for continuous quality improvement (i.e., G_1). Priority 1 is fully satisfied ($P_1 = 0$). The related deviational variable (d^+_1) is zero.

Table 4. Analysis of the objective function

Priority	Goal Achievement	Values
P_1	Satisfied	0
P_2	Satisfied	0
P_3	Satisfied	0
P_4	Satisfied	0
P_5	Partially satisfied	1
P_6	Partially satisfied	1,495
P_7	Partially satisfied	1,495

Table 5. Analysis of decision and deviational variables

Decision Variable (supplier)	Solution Value	Decision Variable (project)	Solution Value	Deviational Variable*
X^s_{11}	0	X^P_{11}	0	$d^-_1 = $ 1,030
X^s_{12}	0	X^P_{12}	0	$d^+_2 = $ 125,102
X^s_{13}	0	X^P_{13}	1	$d^-_3 = $ 420
X^s_{14}	144	X^P_{21}	0	$d^-_4 = $ 310
X^s_{15}	0	X^P_{22}	1	$d^-_5 = $ 300
X^s_{21}	0	X^P_{23}	0	$d^+_6 = $ 24,300
X^s_{22}	0	X^P_{31}	1	$d^+_7 = $ 23,840
X^s_{23}	0	X^P_{32}	0	$d^+_8 = $ 19,300
X^s_{24}	36	X^P_{33}	0	$d^+_9 = $ 21,340
X^s_{25}	200	X^s_{41}	1	$d^+_{10} = $ 22,800
X^s_{31}	0	X^s_{42}	0	$d^+_{11} = $ 1
X^s_{32}	280	X^s_{43}	0	$d^+_{14} = $ 143
X^s_{33}	0	X^s_{44}	0	$d^+_{15} = $ 235
X^s_{34}	0			$d^+_{16} = $ 379
X^s_{35}	100			$d^+_{17} = $ 419
X^s_{41}	300			$d^+_{18} = $ 319
X^s_{42}	0			$d^+_{19} = $ 299
X^s_{43}	0			$d^+_{20} = $ 299
X^s_{44}	120			$d^+_{21} = $ 299
X^s_{45}	0			$d^+_{22} = $ 299
X^s_{51}	0			$d^+_{23} = $ 299
X^s_{52}	20			
X^s_{53}	300			* All other
X^s_{54}	0			deviational
X^s_{55}	0			variables are zero.

Priority 2 (P_2) is to avoid underutilization of the budget level for cost effectiveness. Priority 2 is fully satisfied ($P_2 = 0$). The related deviational variable (d^-_2) is zero.

Priority 3 (P_3) is to not overutilize the available market resource level in each product development period for customer satisfaction. The management desires that their market resource of outsourcing should not be overutilized in each development stage 1 (d^+_3), stage 2 (d^+_4), and stage 3 (d^+_5). This third priority goal is fully satisfied ($P_3 = 0$), and its related deviational variables (d^+_3, d^+_4 and d^+_5) are zero.

Priority 4 (P_4) is to avoid underachievement of resources to select outsourcing suppliers who have the industrial leading knowledge in five different smart home system components, since the management considers that all five technology resources are highly unattainable. This priority goal is fully satisfied ($P_4 = 0$). Its related deviational variables are all zero: underachievement in home server technology outsourcing resources ($d^-_6 = 0$); underachievement in awareness agent technology outsourcing resources ($d^-_7 = 0$); underachievement in recorder database technology outsourcing resources ($d^-_8 = 0$); underachievement in biokey technology outsourcing resources ($d^-_9 = 0$); and underachievement in controller box technology outsourcing resources ($d^-_{10} = 0$).

Priority 5 (P_5) is to implement appropriately four projects in the three product development periods for securing outsourcing manpower balancing. This priority goal is partially satisfied ($P_5 = 1$). Its related deviational variables are not all zero ($d^+_{11} = 1$, $d^+_{12} = 0$, $d^+_{13} = 0$, $d^-_{11} = 0$, $d^-_{12} = 0$, $d^-_{13} = 0$). There is one project with overachievement. However, this does not mean that the goal is not achieved because four projects should be assigned in any product development stage.

Priority 6 (P_6) is to meet the demand-supply level to select an appropriate outsourcing supplier group for a supplier competency goal. This priority goal is partially satisfied ($P_6 = 1,495$). Its related deviational variables are not all zero ($d^+_{14} = 143$, $d^+_{15} = 235$, $d^+_{16} = 379$, $d^+_{17} = 419$, $d^+_{18} = 319$, $d^-_{14} = 0$, $d^-_{15} = 0$, $d^-_{16} = 0$, $d^-_{17} = 0$, $d^-_{18} = 0$). Table 6 indicates demand levels that are assigned to supplier groups for each system component. Supplier 1 is assigned to a demand level of 300 biokey components. Likewise, supplier 2 has demand levels of 280 recorder database and 20 control box components; supplier 3 for a demand level of 300 control box components; supplier 4 for demand levels of 144 home server, 36 awareness, and 120 biokey components; and supplier 5 for demand levels of 200 awareness agent and 100 recorder database components.

Table 6. Demand level assigned supplier groups to system components

System Component	Outsourcing Supplier Group				
	1	2	3	4	5
Home server				144	
Awareness agent				36	200
Recorder database		280			100
Biokey	300			120	
Controller box		20	300		

Table 7. Assigned projects in each development stage

Project Category	Product Development		
	Stage 1	Stage 2	Stage 3
Security			X
Automation		X	
Remote control	X		
Mobile multimedia	X		

Priority 7 (P_7) is to assign certain contracts to supplier groups to achieve a strategic partnership goal. This priority goal is partially satisfied ($P_6 = 1,495$). Its related deviational variables are not all zero ($d^+_{19} = 299, d^+_{20} = 299, d^+_{21} = 299, d^+_{22} = 299, d^+_{23} = 299, d^-_{19} = 0, d^-_{20} = 0, d^-_{21} = 0, d^-_{22} = 0, d^-_{23} = 0$). Table 7 presents the selected projects assigned to each development stage. In stage 1, remote control function and mobile multimedia function will be recommended to develop. Home automation function will be developed in stage 2 and home security function in stage 3.

Outsourcing and supply-chain planning in supply-chain management perspective has become a significant and integral activity of strategic planning in a firm. The goals surrounding outsourcing and supply-chain planning decisions are complex and conflicting. Like other business decision making problems, outsourcing problems cannot derive a single optimal solution. Most top decision-makers agree that this planning process ultimately depends on a firm's business strategies, competitiveness roadmap, and business value and mission. In order to improve the system's overall effectiveness, decision-makers should recognize the ways to improve product quality, to enhance the internal and external customer satisfaction, to provide more strong commitment to manpower management, and to establish a sound alliance and collaboration with other business partners.

Sensitivity Analysis

Sensitivity analysis is an evaluation tool that is used once a satisfying solution has been found. It provides an insight into how satisfying solutions are affected by changes in the input data. Sensitivity analysis is performed with two scenarios. The management considers three goals (G_1, G_6, and G_7) to be evaluated. Quality improvement goal (G_1) and supplier competency goal (G_6) are changed (i.e., $P_6 \rightarrow P_1$ and $P_1 \rightarrow P_6$); and quality improvement goal (G_1) and strategic partnership goal (G_7) are changed (i.e., $P_7 \rightarrow P_1$ and $P_1 \rightarrow P_7$).

With sensitivity analysis available for the management, various scenarios can be evaluated more easily at less cost. Table 8 presents the results of two scenarios. It shows an important implication for strategic planning considering effective outsourcing and supplier management. Solution values of supplier decision variables in the original option and the revised scenarios indicate the new demand levels that are assigned to the supplier groups.

The top decision-makers in the consortium firm have accepted the final results as valid and feasible for implementing the outsourcing planning in their real business setting. The consortium firm has started its strategic outsourcing and

Table 8. Sensitivity analysis with two scenarios

Original Option		Revised Scenario 1		Revised Scenario 2	
Decision Variables	Solution Value	Decision Variables	Solution Value	Decision Variables	Solution Value
X^s_{11}	0	X^s_{11}	144	X^s_{11}	0
X^s_{12}	0	X^s_{12}	0	X^s_{12}	64
X^s_{13}	0	X^s_{13}	0	X^s_{13}	0
X^s_{14}	144	X^s_{14}	0	X^s_{14}	0
X^s_{15}	0	X^s_{15}	0	X^s_{15}	80
X^s_{21}	0	X^s_{21}	0	X^s_{21}	0
X^s_{22}	0	X^s_{22}	256	X^s_{22}	236
X^s_{23}	0	X^s_{23}	0	X^s_{23}	0
X^s_{24}	36	X^s_{24}	0	X^s_{24}	0
X^s_{25}	200	X^s_{25}	0	X^s_{25}	0
X^s_{31}	0	X^s_{31}	80	X^s_{31}	0
X^s_{32}	280	X^s_{32}	0	X^s_{32}	0
X^s_{33}	0	X^s_{33}	0	X^s_{33}	0
X^s_{34}	0	X^s_{34}	0	X^s_{34}	180
X^s_{35}	100	X^s_{35}	300	X^s_{35}	200
X^s_{41}	300	X^s_{41}	76	X^s_{41}	300
X^s_{42}	0	X^s_{42}	44	X^s_{42}	0
X^s_{43}	0	X^s_{43}	0	X^s_{43}	0
X^s_{44}	120	X^s_{44}	300	X^s_{44}	120
X^s_{45}	0	X^s_{45}	0	X^s_{45}	0
X^s_{51}	0	X^s_{51}	0	X^s_{51}	0
X^s_{52}	20	X^s_{52}	0	X^s_{52}	0
X^s_{53}	300	X^s_{53}	300	X^s_{53}	300
X^s_{54}	0	X^s_{54}	0	X^s_{54}	0
X^s_{55}	0	X^s_{55}	0	X^s_{55}	0
X^p_{11}	0	X^p_{11}	0	X^p_{11}	0
X^p_{12}	0	X^p_{12}	0	X^p_{12}	0
X^p_{13}	1	X^p_{13}	1	X^p_{13}	1
X^p_{21}	0	X^p_{21}	0	X^p_{21}	0
X^p_{22}	1	X^p_{22}	1	X^p_{22}	1
X^p_{23}	0	X^p_{23}	0	X^p_{23}	0
X^p_{31}	1	X^p_{31}	1	X^p_{31}	1
X^p_{32}	0	X^p_{32}	0	X^p_{32}	0
X^p_{33}	0	X^p_{33}	0	X^p_{33}	0
X^s_{41}	1	X^s_{41}	1	X^s_{41}	1
X^s_{42}	0	X^s_{42}	0	X^s_{42}	0
X^s_{43}	0	X^s_{43}	0	X^s_{43}	0

supplier-customer management planning with ongoing base. The effects from these model outputs will be evaluated in the next fiscal year or two. The future outsourcing and supplier management planning agenda will be identified to compare with this proposed MCDM model for the strategic outsourcing planning. The strategic outsourcing planning based on the proposed MCDM model will provide the management with a significant insight to set an appropriate outsourcing strategy, while enhancing customer satisfaction and relationship management, and improving the firm's global competitiveness. Thus, the consortium firm currently reviews all these alternatives as possible outsourcing strategies.

Conclusion

This study presents an MCDM model for outsourcing and supply-chain planning in a smart home system components manufacturing industry in Korea. The proposed MCDM model will provide the management with better understanding of outsourcing and supply-chain planning. This proposed model would give a practical decision-making way for analyzing the outsourcing resource planning. This study indicates that the effective decision-making process in outsourcing and supply-chain planning can enforce the firm's competitive advantages and improve the firm's business performance. It is necessary to be able to assess the relative contribution of the individual member organizations within the supply chain. This requires a performance measurement system that can not only operate at several different levels but also link or integrate the efforts of these different levels to meeting the objectives of the supply chain.

When management considers several conflicting goals to achieve, subject to a set of constraints, MCDM models can provide effective decision-making results for strategic outsourcing and supply-chain planning in business operational environments. Subjective decision-making processes can make the multiple and complicated business problems into the worst situation of both business performance and business partnership due to the potential irrational decision-making. Thus, an appropriate use of MCDM models for effective decision-making is essential to create a long-term strategic plan for a competitive advantage and survival of any business organization in challenging environments.

Acknowledgment

This work was supported by the Korea Research Foundation Grant (KRF 2003-041-B20171).

References

Bertolini, M., Bevilacqua, M., Braglia, M., & Frosolini, M. (2004). An analytical method for maintenance outsourcing service selection. *International Journal of Quality & Reliability Management, 21*(7), 772-788.

Charnes, A., & Cooper, W. W. (1961). *Management models and the industrial applications of linear programming.* New York: Wiley.

Cohen, M., & Lee, H. (1988). Strategic analysis of integrated production-distribution systems: Models and methods. *Operations Research, 36*(2), 216-228.

Fisher, M. L. (1997). What is right supply chain for your product? *Harvard Business Review, 75*(2), 105-116.

Heikkila, J. (2002). From supply to demand chain management: Efficiency and customer satisfaction. *Journal of Operations Management, 20*(6), 747-767.

Karpak, B., Kumcu, E., & Kasuganti, R. (1999). An application of visual interactive goal programming: A case in vendor selection decisions. *Journal of Multi-Criteria Decision Analysis, 8*(2), 93-105.

Klotz, D., & Chatterjee, K. (1995). Dual sourcing in repeated procurement competition. *Management Science, 41*(8), 1317-1327.

Lee, C.-E., & Hsu, S.-C. (2004). Outsourcing capacity planning for an IC design house. *The International Journal of Advanced Manufacturing Technology, 24*(3-4), 306-320.

Lee, S. M. (1996). *AB:QM system software.* Englewood Cliffs, NJ: Prentice Hall.

Li, D., & O'Brien, C. (2001). A quantitative analysis of relationships between product types and supply chain strategies. *International Journal of Production Economics, 73*(1), 29-39.

Liu, C.-M., & Chen, C.-H. (2002). Multi-section electronic assembly line balancing problems: A case study. *Production Planning & Control, 13*(5), 451-461.

Min, H., & Zhou, G. (2002). Supply chain modeling: Past, present, and future. *Computers and Industrial Engineering, 4*, 231-249.

Ngwenyama, O. K., & Bryson, N. (1999). Making the information systems outsourcing decision: A transaction cost approach to analyzing outsourcing decision problems. *European Journal of Operational Research, 115*, 351-367.

Quinn, J. B., & Hilmer, F. G. (1994). Strategic outsourcing. *Sloan Management Review, 35*(4), 43-55.

Saaty, T. L. (1980). *The analytic hierarchy process.* New York: McGraw-Hill.

Schniederjans, M. J., & Hoffman, J. J. (1999). Downsizing production/operations with multi-objective programming. *International Journal of Operations & Production Management, 19*(1), 79-91.

Vannieuwenhuyse, B., Gelders, G., & Pintelon, L. (2003). An online decision support system for transportation mode choice. *Journal of Enterprise Information Management, 16*(2), 125-133.

Chapter XIX

Is the Business Model Broken?
A Model of the Difference Between Pay-Now and Pay-Later Contracts in IT Outsourcing

Eric Walden, Texas Tech University, USA

Param Vir Singh, University of Washington, USA

Abstract

This chapter seeks to evaluate the dominant IT outsourcing contracts model (pay-later) as compared to an alternative model (pay-now) in light of changing economic conditions. We integrate practitioner observations in the spirit of mathematical transaction cost problems to develop a conceptual economic model to compare these two types of contracts. We uncover three very important facts which suggest that pay-now contracts are always at least as good as pay-later contracts, and pay-now contracts are better than pay-later contracts when economy is volatile. These findings provide a rich insight into the problem of failing IT outsourcing contracts since the prevailing poor state of economy. We further discuss the implications of our findings and suggest that simply shifting the contract from a pay-later to a pay-now will fix the IT outsourcing business model.

Introduction

In a recent Fortune magazine article, one of the interviewees, William Nygen of Oakmark funds, comments on outsourcer EDS's business model. He brings up the possibility that "the business model is worse than we thought it was" (Loomis, 2003, p. 74). This chapter is an investigation of the business model not just of EDS, but of information technology (IT) outsourcers across the board.

For a decade or more outsourcing has been hailed as the panacea for IT problems (Lacity & Hirschheim, 1993). Some industry observers go so far as to claim that outsourcing is *the* payoff from IT (Kirkpatrick, 2002). However, the analysis provided in this work shows that there are fundamental problems with the traditional IT outsourcing arrangement. In short, the business model is broken. Fortuitously, the analysis also suggests an easy way to fix the problem.

This work shows that the back-end loading of IT contracts results in misalignment between clients and vendors. This misalignment results in transactions, which should take place, failing to transpire, resulting in losses to both client and vendor. The findings presented here help explain why more than half of IT outsourcing contracts must be renegotiated (Caldwell, 1997; Lacity & Willcocks, 2001). The model also suggests that simply moving from a back loaded to a front loaded contract will fix the business model.

The rest of the chapter is organized as follows. In the next section we briefly review the relevant literature on IT outsourcing. Following that, we present two models of how to structure an IT outsourcing contract and show how they result in different levels of value. We then derive three propositions for IT outsourcing based on these two models. Finally, we conclude with a discussion of the implications of this work and directions for future research.

Literature Review

Our background literature is a combination of practitioner observations and economic modeling. From the practitioner side we find three stylized facts. First, IT outsourcing contracts are typically back-loaded, with the vendor offering discounts early in the contract and receiving profits in the later periods of the contract. Second, a majority of IT outsourcing contracts have to be renegotiated before conclusion. Lastly, the cost for the baseline services is very close to the vendor's cost, but additional services command considerable margins.

IT outsourcing contracts, and here we are speaking of the *total* outsourcing deals, usually begin with the vendor purchasing the assets of the client and hiring all of the client's employees. Frequently, the vendor will overpay for the assets and in some cases offer loans to the client (Lacity, Willcocks, & Feeny, 1995). In fact, in a study of the top reasons for outsourcing, The Outsourcing Institute (1998) found that number ten was the *cash infusion* offered from vendor to client. However, like any pay-later deal, the bill eventually comes due and the vendor recaps the initial capital outlay by charging more in later periods.

Interestingly, practitioner research indicates that more than half — 53% to be exact — of outsourcing contracts are renegotiated before running their full term (James, 2000). For example, less than two years after signing an IT outsourcing agreement with Computer Sciences Corp., health maintenance organization Oxford Health Plans Inc. canceled the deal (Rosencrance, 2002). Halifax bank of Scotland abruptly ended a 10-year contract with IBM after only two years (Arminas, 2002). Mony Insurance of New York canceled a $210 million contract with Computer Sciences Corp. less than half way through it (Caldwell, 1997). Chase Manhattan Bank paid $15 million to terminate its contract with Fiserv, and Zale Corporation terminated a 10-year contract with ISSC after only 5 years (Lacity & Willcocks, 2001).

Why must so many contracts be renegotiated? One standard complaint is that the contract performs well for some time and then the costs of add-ons and additional services begin to overwhelm the client (Barthelemy, 2001). Even academic research shows that lack of flexibility, as defined by the cost of reacting to changes, is the prime source of contract failure in IT outsourcing (Lacity et al., 1995).

The vendor essentially covers all of the transition costs up front, then to make up profit in later periods, charges a great deal for additional services. This frequently leads to contract failure. For example, in August of 2002, EDS reassured investors that earnings guidance was correct. Then in September, they revised guidance down by 80% (Loomis, 2003). The claimed reason for this miscalculation was that the bulk of profits were made from discretionary spending on additional services, which have much higher margins than baseline spending, and that discretionary spending failed to appear at the end of the quarter. Essentially, EDS's (and most other vendors') profit comes not from the contracted services, but from additional add-on services, which are overpriced in order to allow the vendor to recoup the transition costs.

This discussion of practitioner observations suggests that problems in the original contract lead to outsourcing failures later in the relationship. Specifically, there are significant transition costs involved in moving control of IT services from the client to the vendor. The parties are faced with a decision on how to pay for these costs and usually decide to have the vendor pay for them. However, the vendor must recoup these costs in order to make a profit. This is accomplished by charging high margins for optional add-on services. Early in the relationship, when the client's needs are very close to the baseline, the costs are well below what it costs the client to achieve internally and the bulk of the value from the relationship goes to the client. However, as the relationship develops and the client's needs expand beyond the baseline services, more and more high margin add-ons are needed and the majority of the value then goes to the vendor. While the timing of payments is not a problem, it does create an imbalance in the relationship that results in loss to both client and vendor.

To these stylized facts we add economic modeling. There is a class of economic problems including incomplete contract theory (Bakos & Brynjolfsson, 1993; Grossman & Hart, 1986; Hart & Moore, 1988), agency theory (Arrow, 1985; Eisenhardt, 1989) and double marginalization (Spengler, 1950; Tirole, 1990) that deals with failures of dyads. The goal of a dyad should be to maximize *joint* surplus first, then decide how to divide that surplus. However, problems arise because each economic agent maximizes, not the joint surplus, but the individual surplus. These can be classed as transaction cost problems.

We model these practitioner observations in the spirit of mathematical transaction cost problems. We show that the traditional back-loaded outsourcing model results in significant transaction cost problems, when the demand for IT services is elastic. This elasticity issue is very important, because it explains why this problem has not been detected earlier. For the past decade or more, the demand for IT services has been very inelastic. IT has been a must-have and has been perceived as the driver of innovation. However, since the dotcom crash in 2000 and the slow economy of 2001 and beyond, IT expenditures have been more closely scrutinized. Thus, the expected discretionary spending does not occur and the model shows its weakness.

Model

Practitioner observations suggests that IT outsourcing contracts can be broadly classified as pay-now or pay-later contracts based on the way transactions are conducted through the life of the contract. A pay-now contract is defined as an arrangement between the client and the vendor in which the client pays the vendor a lump-sum amount at contract inception and then all the IT needs of the client are provided at vendor's marginal cost. A pay-later contract is defined as an arrangement between the client and the vendor in which the vendor pays the client a lump-sum amount at contract inception (usually to cover transition costs) and then all the IT needs of the client are provided at client's marginal cost. Practitioner research suggests that most of the contracts in practice today are pay-later contracts where the vendor initially buys the assets of the client and later charges him a higher price for service demanded.

We develop a two period model to analyze the value of pay-now contract over pay-later contract and the effect of changes in economy over these contracts. We analyze this by deriving the lost joint surplus which could have occurred if a pay-now contract were signed over a pay-later contract. This lost surplus is called dead weight loss. Dead weight loss is the value of the transactions that are worth more to the client than they cost to the vendor, but that do not get executed because the contract price is too high.

Assumptions

We describe a two period game with two risk neutral firms — a client and a vendor. The firms wish to formalize an agreement in which the vendor supplies IT services to the client. In order to keep the model simple, we characterize IT outsourcing services as being described only by a single service. Clearly, in a real outsourcing arrangement, quantity would be a vector of various services, but the model is not significantly enhanced by considering multiple services.

The client has a random demand curve depending upon a variety of exogenous factors. In the interest of parsimony we characterize this demand curve as $D(q) = b_d + m_d q$, where b_d is distributed uniformly over the interval $[b_{ds}, b_{df}]$. Thus, the demand curve is linear and demand shocks shift the curve, without changing the slope.

The vendor's cost curve is given by $C_v(q) = b_v + m_v q$ and the client's by $C_c(q) = b_c + m_c q$. We assume $b_v < b_c$ and $m_v < m_c$. Thus, the vendor has lower cost and greater economies of scale at all positive values of quantity. Note that we have assumed the marginal cost curves to be linear functions of quantity q but in reality they may be better depicted by quadratic curves. However, using quadratic curves makes the calculations cumbersome without significantly enhancing our model.

Period One

In period one, client and vendor negotiate for signing a pay-now or pay-later contract. If they sign the pay-later contract then vendor makes a lump-sum payment to the client in period 1, and the services demanded by client are provided at client's marginal cost. If, instead, they sign a pay-now contract the client makes a lump-sum to the vendor in period 1, and the services demanded are provided at vendor's marginal cost. We further assume no discount rate as it does not enhance the meaning of the model or change its outcomes.

The exact size of the lump-sum distribution depends upon the model of bargaining used. In a one-to-one bargaining situation, the Nash solution would be for firms to set a lump-sum that splits the joint surplus equally (Grossman & Hart, 1986). A competitive bargaining model would suggest that the share of the lump-sum given to the vendor would be infinitesimally less than the minimum size of a side payment the second best competitor could accept and still make a profit (Snir & Hitt, 2001). A variety of other bargaining mechanisms are possible. However, the nature of the bargaining and the size of the lump-sum distribution are not important to our outcomes and hence we do not delve into the question of how the bargaining proceeds. While the bargaining method is important to how the joint surplus is divided, it does not play a role in our model, which examines the size of the joint surplus. Thus, we leave bargaining considerations for future research and other scholars.

Note that this scenario is a simplified explanation of pay-now and pay-later contracts but captures their essence. In actuality, in pay-later contracts, the services are provided at a higher price than the price in a pay-now contract. This higher price can be anything, but for keeping calculations simple we define these prices as client's marginal cost and vendor's marginal cost, respectively.

To summarize, in period one the parties to the contract decide on contract type — pay-now or pay-later — and negotiated the appropriate side payment.

Period Two

In period two, b_d is realized, determining the client's demand curve. The client chooses the quantity of IT services to purchase based on the contract price and pays the vendor the appropriate price. The model can be illustrated graphically as in Figure 1.

Figure 1. Comparison of pay-now and pay-later contracts

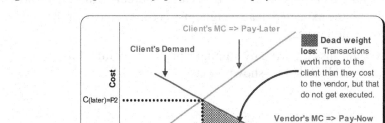

Quantity demanded by the client depends upon the type of contract signed as well as the demand curve. As is shown in the figure the client pays price $C_{(later)}$ for quantity $Q_{(later)}$ in the case of a pay-later contract whereas the client pays price $C_{(now)}$ for quantity $Q_{(now)}$ in the case of a pay-now contract. Note that $C_{(later)}$ is more than $C_{(now)}$ and $Q_{(later)}$ is less than $Q_{(now)}$. That is, in the case of the pay-later contract, client pays more per unit for fewer units as compared to a pay-now contract.

Calculating the Expected Dead Weight Loss

Ideally, any contractual arrangement should aim at maximizing the joint surplus (Williamson, 1985). Joint surplus is the combined profit made from the arrangement by the client and the vendor. Though the client receives a number of benefits like economic gains, expertise in IT, and more concentration on core-capabilities, research suggests that economic benefits are the most important reason for any client firm to consider outsourcing IT (Loh & Venkatraman, 1992; McFarlan & Nolan, 1995; Smith, Mitra, & Narsimhan, 1998). Benefits for the vendor are mainly economic (Chaudhary, Nam, & Rao, 1995). Since our model discusses the pay-later contract and the pay-now contract from an economic viewpoint, we will consider joint surplus in terms of economic benefits obtained by the vendor and the client.

To compare a pay-now contract with a pay-later contract we compare the joint surplus in two cases. As shown in the figure, the difference between the joint surplus in pay-now and pay-later contracts is the dead weight loss. Dead weight loss incurred by signing a pay-later contract over a pay-now contract for a given demand curve is the area given by the shaded triangle in Figure 1. Because the intercept b_d of the demand curve is distributed uniformly, there are infinite numbers of demand curves possible. For every demand curve there will be a different triangle. So the expected dead weight loss is calculated over the entire possible set of demand curves.

Expected dead weight loss incurred by signing a pay-later contract over a pay-now contract can be calculated as shown next.

$$E(DW_{n-l}) = E(\text{Joint Surplus}_{now} - \text{Joint Surplus}_{later})$$

$$= \int_{Demand} prob(\text{Demand Realization}) \times (\text{Joint Surplus}_{now} - \text{Joint Surplus}_{later}) dDemand$$

$$= \int_{b_{ds}}^{b_{df}} pdf(b_d) \times \left(\frac{1}{2} base \times height \right) db_d$$

$$= \frac{1}{2} \frac{1}{\Delta b_d} \left[\left(\frac{1}{m_v - m_d} \right) \left(b_c \frac{\Delta b_d (b_{df} + b_{ds})}{2} - b_c b_v \Delta b_d - b_v \frac{\Delta b_d (b_{df} + b_{ds})}{2} + b_v{}^2 \Delta b_d \right) \right.$$

$$- \left(\frac{1}{m_c - m_d} \right) \left(b_c \frac{\Delta b_d (b_{df} + b_{ds})}{2} - b_c{}^2 \Delta b_d - b_v \frac{\Delta b_d (b_{df} + b_{ds})}{2} + b_v b_c \Delta b_d \right)$$

$$+ \left(\frac{m_c - m_v}{(m_c - m_d)(m_v - m_d)} \right) \left(\frac{\Delta b_d (b_{df}^2 + b_{ds}^2 + b_{df} b_{ds})}{3} - \frac{\Delta b_d (b_{df} + b_{ds})}{2} b_v - b_c \frac{\Delta b_d (b_{df} + b_{ds})}{2} + b_c b_v \Delta b_d \right)$$

$$\left. - \left(\frac{m_c - m_v}{(m_c - m_d)^2} \right) \left(\frac{\Delta b_d (b_{df}^2 + b_{ds}^2 + b_{df} b_{ds})}{3} - b^2{}_c \Delta b_d - \frac{\Delta b_d (b_{df} + b_{ds})}{2} b_c \right) \right]$$

(1)

where $\Delta b_d = b_{df} - b_{ds}$

Evaluating the Expected Dead Weight Loss Incurred by Signing a Pay-Later Contract over a Pay-Now Contract

The first question we address is to determine if the assumptions given above allow us to unambiguously determine which type of contract performs better.

To evaluate (1) for finding the sign of $E(DW_{n-l})$ we need to reiterate the underlying assumptions of the model.

$$b_d > b_c > b_v > 0, \tag{2}$$

$$m_d < 0, \text{ and} \tag{3}$$

$$m_c > m_v > 0 \tag{4}$$

We now evaluate (2) based on the assumptions of the model. We find that:

$$E(DW_{n-l}) > 0. \tag{5}$$

This means that the expected dead weight loss of signing a pay-now contract over a pay-later contract is positive. That is, the difference between the expected joint surplus of a pay-now contract and a pay-later contract is positive. This is expressed in Proposition 1.

Proposition 1: *The expected joint surplus achieved in a pay-now contract is greater than the expected joint surplus achieved in a pay-later contract.*

The pay-now contract enables additional transactions to occurs, which would not have occurred if it were a pay-later contract. In the real world, this would mean that in the case of a pay-now contract, the client would be able to obtain more services at a lower per-unit cost compared to what it receives in a pay-later contract. Thus, we see that the fundamental problem with the pay-later contract is not the timing of the payment, but rather the way the pricing must be structured to allow the vendor to recoup the upfront costs of transition.

Evaluating the Impact of Changes in Demand Elasticity

Services demanded by the client depend upon the IT demand curve of the client. During the long running, technology driven bull market of the 1990's, firms tended to have very inelastic demand curves. That is to say, that the quantity of IT demanded was not very sensitive to the price of IT. However, after the dotcom crash and subsequent cool economy, firms became more sensitive to the price of IT. Again, citing the Fortune article on EDS, we find that EDS is currently suffering because clients are curbing discretionary spending more than they had in the past. Thus, it is interesting to examine the effect of changes in demand elasticity on the difference in joint surplus between the traditional pay-later contract and the pay-now contract.

The elasticity of demand can be measured by $dq/dp \times p/q$. For a given price and quantity, dq/dp is measured by the slope, m_d, of the demand curve. If demand becomes more elastic in response to environmental conditions, the effect of the change in elasticity is proportional to the effect of a change in m_d. To determine the effect of changes in demand elasticity we differentiate (1) with respect to m_d which yields:

$$
\begin{aligned}
\frac{\partial E(DW_{l-n})}{\partial m_d} = \frac{1}{2} \bigg[& b_c \frac{(b_{df} + b_{ds})}{2} \left(\frac{2(m_c - m_v)}{(m_c - m_d)^3} \right) + \left(\frac{2(m_c - m_v)}{(m_c - m_d)^3} \right) b_c^2 \\
& + \frac{(b_{df}^2 + b_{ds}^2 + b_{df}b_{ds})}{3} \left(\frac{(m_c - m_v)^2 (2(m_c - m_d)(m_v - m_d) + (m_c - m_d)^2)}{(m_c - m_d)^4 (m_v - m_d)^2} \right) \\
& + \left(\frac{(b_v - b_c)^2 ((m_v - m_d) + (m_c - m_d))}{(m_v - m_d)^2 (m_c - m_d)^2} \right) + \left(\frac{(m_c - m_v)((m_c - m_d) + (m_v - m_d))}{(m_c - m_d)^2 (m_v - m_d)^2} \right) b_c b \bigg].
\end{aligned}
$$

$$(6)$$

From this, it can be shown that:

$$
\frac{\partial E(DW_{l-n})}{\partial m_d} > 0. \tag{7}
$$

This is an important implication of the model. It explains the fact that dead weight loss incurred by signing a pay-later contract over a pay-now contract increases as the client's demand for IT services becomes more elastic. IT demand over the last decade has been very inelastic and hence the dead weight loss was negligible. Thus, it did not matter if the client and vendor signed a pay-now contract or a pay-later contract. On the contrary, since the dotcom crash and the poor state of the economy, the demand for IT has become more elastic, and, hence the dead weight loss problem has surfaced. This logic yields our Proposition 2.

Proposition 2: *As the client's demand for IT services becomes more elastic, the pay-later contract becomes worse as compared to a pay-now contract.*

Evaluating the Impact of Demand Shifts

IT has a fluid environment where changes occur each day. IT is considered essential for strategic advantage and receives a major share of financial resources when the economy is strong but is first to face budget cuts when economy is poor. The demand for IT tends to vary over time. Firms in different industries and firms outsourcing different facets of their IT services are likely to face very different demand variability. Therefore, it is interesting to ask how the variability of demand influences the value of contractual choice.

We measure the realized level of demand as a function of the intercept, b_{df}, of the demand curve. The greater the intercept the greater the increase in demand for IT services at all prices. To determine the effects of changes in the variability of demand we note that the variance of the uniform distribution is $1/12*(b_{df} - b_{ds})^2$. By increasing the distance between the endpoints, we increase the possible range of demand realizations and the variance of demand. Thus, to examine the impact of demand variability on the value of contractual choice we differentiate (1) with respect to b_{df}. This yields:

$$\frac{\partial E(DW_{n-1})}{\partial b_{df}} = \frac{1}{2}\left[\frac{b_c}{2}\left(\frac{m_c - m_v}{(m_c - m_d)^2}\right) + \frac{(2b_{df} + b_{ds})}{3}\left(\frac{(m_c - m_v)^2}{(m_c - m_d)^2(m_v - m_d)}\right)\right]. \qquad (8)$$

Given the assumptions it can be shown that:

$$\frac{\partial E(DW_{l-n})}{\partial b_{df}} > 0. \qquad (9)$$

This gives us our third proposition.

Proposition 3: *As the variance of demand for IT services increases, the pay-later contract becomes worse as compared to a pay-now contract.*

This shows us that the greater the variance in demand the larger the difference between the pay-now and pay-later contracts. In other words, as the potential change in IT demand increases, the dead weight loss associated with the pay-later contract increases. This occurs because the relative difference between vendor and client capabilities increases as quantity increases. The vendor is more flexible and more able to respond to changing IT needs. Thus, if IT needs change dramatically, the loss associated with failing to take advantage of the vendor's advantage increases. This is particularly problematic for rapidly growing, or rapidly technologizing firms.

Discussion

The work presented here compared pay-now and pay-later contracts with an aim to figure out if one has any advantage over the other. The model compares the two types of contracts by evaluating (1) dead weight loss incurred by choosing one contract over other, (2) impact of changes in demand elasticity, and (3) impact of demand shifts. The general propositions are summarized in Table 1.

Our first proposition is that if a pay-later contract is selected over a pay-now contract, dead weight loss is incurred. If a pay-later contract is selected over a pay-now contract, fewer transactions take place, which leads to less joint surplus. This point is extremely important here because the aim of any outsourcing arrangement is to increase the joint surplus. This implies that signing a pay-now contract is beneficial for both the client and the vendor.

However, very few large-scale outsourcing projects will actually save money in the first year because of significant transitions costs. The employees of the client must be shifted to the vendor, and these employees need to be retrained in the procedures of the vendor. Similarly, the vendor's employees must be trained in the systems and processes of the client. Leases for both software and hardware must be transferred, and perhaps renegotiated. Significant legal and managerial fees in structuring the contract must be paid. Finally, some learning curve and adjustment to the new procedures must be overcome. All of this creates great expense that overshadows the benefits to outsourcing for the first year.

Table 1. Implications of contractual choice

	Summary	Logic
Proposition 1	A pay-now contract generates greater surplus than a pay-later contract.	In order to recoup the upfront payment to the client, the vendor must charge a higher per unit price for IT services. This higher per unit charge means that some transactions in which the vendor's cost to perform the duties is less than the clients value of having the duties performed will NOT take place.
Proposition 2	The greater the client's elasticity of demand, the more pronounced the difference between the pay-now and pay-later contracts	If a client is not sensitive to the cost of IT then the client will demand transactions even when the price is higher.
Proposition 3	The greater the variability of demand the more pronounced the difference between the pay-now and pay-later contract	Because the vendor has economies of scale over the client, the larger the quantity of IT services the more cost advantage the vendor has. Thus, more transactions meet the criteria of being between the vendor's cost and the client's valuation.

Convincing clients to adopt a pay-now contract may be very difficult. In general, clients outsource to reduce costs and they expect clear cost savings immediately. Rather than offer a contract that increases IT costs, for instance, 10% in the first year and then saves 20% per year, vendors offer a contract that saves 30% the first year, then 20% the second year, then breaks even in the third year and actually costs in the forth year. This sort of contract is certainly appealing for a variety of psychological reasons, particularly if the people responsible for the outsourcing arrangement expect to be in different positions in a few years. Sadly, it comes at significant economic cost.

Our second and third propositions are driven by the fluid nature of the IT environment, the changes in the state of economy over the past few years, and their effect on the attitude of firms towards spending on IT. To understand the difference between pay-now and pay-later contracts in regard to a changing economy, it is important to first understand how changes in the economy affect the attitude of a firm towards IT. Changes in economy combined with the fluid environment of IT affect the attitude of firms towards spending on IT in two ways: (1) overall spending on IT and (2) sensitivity towards spending on IT. Throughout the 1990s, the economy was growing and firms were spending on resources of strategic advantage. IT was considered extremely important for strategic advantage, so IT gained a tremendous share of capital budgets during the past decade. During that phase, demand of IT was very inelastic. That is, firms wanted to gain all the IT resources available and at the same time remained insensitive to price. For example, to gain strategic advantage brick and mortar firms wanted to become click and mortar firms and spent millions of dollars to do so. Nonetheless, since the dotcom burst in 2000 and the prevailing poor state of the economy since 2001, firms' overall attitude has changed from growth to survival. This shift in attitude has hit IT expenditures particularly hard. IT expenditures have been more closely scrutinized, and hence, the overall spending on IT has declined and the sensitivity towards spending on IT has increased. Now firms want to get only those IT resources or services that are essential. Consequently, spending on IT has declined considerably and now firms are less willing to devote large amounts of capital to IT than they were in the 1990s.

Proposition two states that as the demand curve shifts from inelastic to elastic behavior, the pay-later contract becomes worse as compared to a pay-now contract. This point is of consequence, because during the last couple of years the demand of IT has shifted from inelastic to elastic, but a shift in contracts has not yet been observed. As long as the client is insensitive to price, pay-later contracts work as good as pay-now, but as soon as the sensitivity towards price changes, the joint surplus in pay-later contract lags the joint surplus in pay-now contract. Earlier, clients considered IT as a must have and were not very considerate about the price, but now they are very considerate about the price. Slowing down of the economy has dried up the funds for IT spending. Therefore,

Table 2. How changes in elasticity interact with contractual choice

	Inelastic Demand	Elastic Demand
Pay-later	No Problem	BIG Problem
Pay-now	No Problem	Small Problem

fewer and fewer transactions are taking place and hence, less and less joint surplus is being achieved. This means lesser individual surplus for both client and vendor. As a result, arrangements that follow pay-later contracts for IT outsourcing do not seem to be a profitable strategy anymore to both the parties. This is possibly one of the explanations as to why outsourcing contracts are failing with alarming regularity. This is depicted in Table 2.

Proposition three states that as the variance of demand for IT increases, the pay-later contract becomes worse as compared to a pay-now contract. It should be noted that this phenomenon does not occur if the demand of IT is perfectly inelastic. If the demand of IT is perfectly inelastic then increase in demand has the same effect on a pay-later contract as on a pay-now contract. One of the chief forces that would tend to increase the variance of IT demand is the rate of technology innovation. This finding is particularly interesting for IS scholars, because it suggests that IT outsourcing contractual choice is sensitive to the rate of technological change.

This is also an important finding for practitioners for two reasons. First, as the rate of technological advancement seems to increase over time, it suggests that the value of making the correct contractual choice will increase over time. Second, one of the often cited reasons for outsourcing is to be able to make changes quickly (Lacity et al., 1995). This implies that those firms that are outsourcing are specifically the firms with greater demand variability. Hence, the firms that are exploring outsourcing options are those that suffer the most from improper contractual choice. Therefore, special effort should be made in contract selection.

Changes in the IT environment and the state of the overall economy suggest the necessity of shifting IT outsourcing contracts from a pay-later to pay-now. As shown by the model, under the prevailing state of the economy, a pay-now contract is better than a pay-later contract for both the vendor and the client. We showed that by just changing the type of contract from a front loaded one to a back loaded one, additional joint surplus can be generated. Such a shift in the type of contracts requires a shift in the thinking of the management, but the benefits are worth it.

References

Arminas, D. (2002). Bringing it all back home. *Supply Management, 7*(12), 16.

Arrow, K. J. (1985). The economics of agency. In J. W. Pratt & R. J. Zeckhause (Eds.), *Principals and agents: The structure of business* (pp. 37-55). Boston: Harvard Business School Press.

Bakos, J. Y., & Brynjolfsson, E. (1993). Information technology, incentives, and the optimal number of suppliers. *Journal of Management Information Systems, 10*(2), 37-53.

Barthelemy, J. (2001). The hidden costs of IT outsourcing. *MIT Sloan Management Review, 27*(3), 60-69.

Caldwell, B. (1997, September 29). Outsourcing backlash. *InformationWeek, 650*, 14-16.

Chaudhary, A., Nam, K., & Rao, R. (1995). Management of information systems outsourcing: A bidding perspective. *Journal of Management Information Systems, 12*(2), 131-159.

Eisenhardt, K. M. (1989). Agency theory: An assessment and review. *Academy of Management Review, 14*(1), 57-74.

Grossman, S. J., & Hart, O. D. (1986). The costs and benefits of ownership: A theory of vertical and lateral integration. *The Journal of Political Economy, 94*(4), 691-719.

Hart, O., & Moore, J. (1988). Incomplete contracts and renegotiation. *Econometrica, 56*(4), 755-785.

James, G. (2000, October 30). How companies court disaster in outsourcing deals. *Computerworld, 34*(44), 41.

Kirkpatrick, D. (2002, December 27). Finally a productivity payoff from IT? *Fortune.com*. Retrieved May 30, 2006, from http://archives.cnn.com/2002/TECH/ptech/12/18/fortune.ff.it.productivity/index.html

Lacity, M. C., & Hirschheim, R. (1993). The information systems outsourcing bandwagon. *Sloan Management Review, 35*(1), 73-86.

Lacity, M., & Willcocks, L. (2001). *Global information technology outsourcing*. New York: John Wiley & Sons.

Lacity, M., Willcocks, L., & Feeny, D. (1995). IT outsourcing: Maximizing flexibility and control. *Harvard Business Review, 73*(3), 84-93.

Loh, L., & Venkatraman, N. (1992). Determinants of information technology outsourcing: A cross-sectional analysis. *Journal of Management Infor-*

mation Systems, 9(1), 7-24.

Loomis, C. J. (2003, February 17). I own this problem. *Fortune, 147*(3), 72-76.

McFarlan, F. W., & Nolan, R. L. (1995). How to manage an IT outsourcing alliance. *Sloan Management Review, 36*(2), 9-23.

Outsourcing Institute, The. (2003, April 30). *Executive survey: The Outsourcing Institute's annual survey of outsourcing end users.* Jericho, NY. Retrieved May 30, 2006, from http://www.outsourcing.com/content.asp?page=01b/articles/intelligence/oi_top_ten_survey.html

Rosencrance, L. (2002, May 13). Oxford health pulls plug on pact, will move IT in-house. *Computer World, 36*(20), 14.

Smith, M., Mitra, S., & Narsimhan, S. (1998). Information technology outsourcing: A study of pre-event firm characteristics. *Journal of Management Information Systems, 15*(2), 61-93.

Snir, E. M., & Hitt, L. M. (2001). Vendor screening in information technology contracting with a pilot project. *Journal of Organizational Computing and Electronic Commerce, 14*(1), 61-88.

Spengler, J. J. (1950). Vertical integrations and anti-trust policy. *Journal of Political Economy, 58*(2), 347-352.

Tirole, J. (1990). *The theory of industrial organization.* Cambridge, MA: MIT Press.

Williamson, O. (1985). *The economic institutions of capitalism.* New York: Free Press.

Appendix

Calculations for the Expected Surplus Benefits of Signing a Pay-Now Contract over a Pay-Later Contract

Client marginal cost curve:

$$C_c = b_c + m_c q \qquad (1)$$

Vendor marginal cost curve:

$$C_v = b_v + m_v q \qquad (2)$$

Demand curve:

$$D = b_d + m_d q \qquad (3)$$

The expected surplus of signing a pay now contract over a pay later contract for a given demand curve is the area given by the shaded triangle above. There are infinite numbers of demand curves. For every demand curve there will be a different triangle. So the expected surplus benefit (difference in surplus of signing a pay now contract over a pay later contract) over the entire possible set of demand curves will be the sum of areas of all such triangles multiplied by their probabilities.

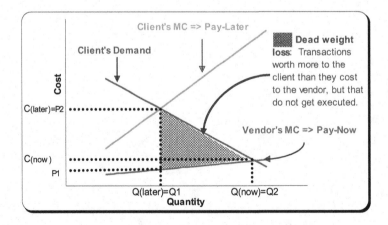

In the Appendix figure,

$$\text{Area of triangle} = (1/2)\,\text{Base} * \text{Height} = (1/2)(P_2 - P_1)(Q_2 - Q_1) \tag{4}$$

Q_1 is quantity where demand curve and client cost curve intersect.

$$Q_1 = \frac{b_d - b_c}{m_c - m_d} \tag{5}$$

Similarly, Q_2 is the quantity where the demand curve and the vendor curve intersect.

$$Q_2 = \frac{b_d - b_v}{m_v - m_d} \tag{6}$$

P_1 is the price given by the vendor curve corresponding to quantity Q_1

$$P_1 = b_v + m_v Q_1 = b_v + m_v \frac{b_d - b_c}{m_c - m_d} \tag{7}$$

P_2 is the price given by the client curve corresponding to quantity Q_1

$$P_2 = b_c + m_c Q_1 = b_c + m_c \frac{b_d - b_c}{m_c - m_d} \tag{8}$$

$$\text{Area of triangle} = \frac{1}{2}(P_2 - P_1)(Q_2 - Q_1) \tag{9}$$

$$\text{Area} = \frac{1}{2}\left(b_c + m_c \frac{b_d - b_c}{m_c - m_d} - b_v - m_v \frac{b_d - b_c}{m_c - m_d} \right)\left(\frac{b_d - b_v}{m_v - m_d} - \frac{b_d - b_c}{m_c - m_d} \right) \tag{10}$$

Area =

$$\frac{1}{2}\left((b_c - b_v)\left(\frac{b_d - b_v}{m_v - m_d}\right) - (b_c - b_v)\left(\frac{b_d - b_c}{m_c - m_d}\right) + (m_c - m_v)\left(\frac{b_d - b_c}{m_c - m_d}\right)\left(\frac{b_d - b_v}{m_v - m_d}\right) - (m_c - m_v)\left(\frac{b_d - b_c}{m_c - m_d}\right)\left(\frac{b_d - b_c}{m_c - m_d}\right) \right)$$

(11)

$$\text{Area} = \frac{1}{2}(A - B + C - D)$$

(12)

$$A = (b_c - b_v)\left(\frac{b_d - b_v}{m_v - m_d}\right) = \left(\frac{1}{m_v - m_d}\right)\left(b_c b_d - b_c b_v - b_v b_d + b_v^2\right)$$

(13)

$$B = (b_c - b_v)\left(\frac{b_d - b_c}{m_c - m_d}\right) = \left(\frac{1}{m_c - m_d}\right)\left(b_c b_d - b_c^2 - b_v b_d + b_v b_c\right)$$

(14)

$$C = (m_c - m_v)\left(\frac{b_d - b_c}{m_c - m_d}\right)\left(\frac{b_d - b_v}{m_v - m_d}\right) = \left(\frac{m_c - m_v}{(m_c - m_d)(m_v - m_d)}\right)\left(b_d^2 - b_d b_v - b_c b_d + b_c b_v\right)$$

(15)

$$D = (m_c - m_v)\left(\frac{b_d - b_c}{m_c - m_d}\right)\left(\frac{b_d - b_c}{m_c - m_d}\right) = \left(\frac{m_c - m_v}{(m_c - m_d)^2}\right)\left(b_d - b_c\right)^2$$

(16)

Expected surplus benefit over the entire range of possible is given by:

$$E(DW_{l-n}) = \frac{1}{b_{df} - b_{ds}} \int_{b_{ds}}^{b_{df}} \frac{1}{2}(A - B + C - D)db_d = \frac{1}{2(b_{df} - b_{ds})}\left[\int_{b_{ds}}^{b_{df}} A db_d - \int_{b_{ds}}^{b_{df}} B db_d + \int_{b_{ds}}^{b_{df}} C db_d - \int_{b_{ds}}^{b_{df}} D db_d \right]$$

(17)

Solving the previous equation.

$$\int_{b_{ds}}^{b_{df}} A db_d = \int_{b_{ds}}^{b_{df}}\left(\frac{1}{m_v - m_d}\right)\left(b_c b_d - b_c b_v - b_v b_d + b_v^2\right)db_d$$

(18)

$$\int_{b_{ds}}^{b_{df}} A\,db_d = \left(\frac{1}{m_v - m_d}\right)\left[b_c\frac{b_d^2}{2} - b_c b_v b_d - b_v\frac{b_d^2}{2} + b_v^{\;2}b_d\right]_{b_{ds}}^{b_{df}} \tag{19}$$

$$\int_{b_{ds}}^{b_{df}} B\,db_d = \int_{b_{ds}}^{b_{df}}\left(\frac{1}{m_c - m_d}\right)\left(b_c b_d - b_c^{\;2} - b_v b_d + b_v b_c\right)db_d \tag{20}$$

$$\int_{b_{ds}}^{b_{df}} B\,db_d = \left(\frac{1}{m_c - m_d}\right)\left[b_c\frac{b_d^2}{2} - b_c^{\;2}b_d - b_v\frac{b_d^2}{2} + b_v b_c b_d\right]_{b_{ds}}^{b_{df}} \tag{21}$$

$$\int_{b_{ds}}^{b_{df}} C\,db_d = \int_{b_{ds}}^{b_{df}}\left(\frac{m_c - m_v}{(m_c - m_d)(m_v - m_d)}\right)\left(b_d^{\;2} - b_d b_v - b_c b_d + b_c b_v\right)db_d \tag{22}$$

$$\int_{b_{ds}}^{b_{df}} C\,db_d = \left(\frac{m_c - m_v}{(m_c - m_d)(m_v - m_d)}\right)\left[\frac{b_d^{\;3}}{3} - \frac{b_d^2}{2}b_v - b_c\frac{b_d^2}{2} + b_c b_v b_d\right]_{b_{ds}}^{b_{df}} \tag{23}$$

$$\int_{b_{ds}}^{b_{df}} D\,db_d = \int_{b_{ds}}^{b_{df}}\left(\frac{m_c - m_v}{(m_c - m_d)^2}\right)\left(b_d - b_c\right)^2 db_d \tag{24}$$

$$\int_{b_{ds}}^{b_{df}} D\,db_d = \left(\frac{m_c - m_v}{(m_c - m_d)(m_c - m_d)}\right)\left[\frac{b_{\;d}^3}{3} - b_{\;c}^2 b_d - b_d^2 b_c\right]_{b_{ds}}^{b_{df}} \tag{25}$$

$$E(DW_{l-n}) = \frac{1}{b_{df} - b_{ds}}\int_{b_{ds}}^{b_{df}}\frac{1}{2}(A - B + C - D)db_d$$

$$\frac{1}{2}\frac{1}{b_{df} - b_{ds}}\left[\left(\frac{1}{m_v - m_d}\right)\left(b_c\frac{b_d^2}{2} - b_c b_v b_d - b_v\frac{b_d^2}{2} + b_v^{\;2}b_d\right)_{b_{ds}}^{b_{df}}\right.$$

$$-\left(\frac{1}{m_c - m_d}\right)\left(b_c\frac{b_d^2}{2} - b_c^{\;2}b_d - b_v\frac{b_d^2}{2} + b_v b_c b_d\right)_{b_{ds}}^{b_{df}}$$

$$+\left(\frac{m_c - m_v}{(m_c - m_d)(m_v - m_d)}\right)\left(\frac{b_d^{\;3}}{3} - \frac{b_d^2}{2}b_v - b_c\frac{b_d^2}{2} + b_c b_v b_d\right)_{b_{ds}}^{b_{df}}$$

$$-\left(\frac{m_c - m_v}{(m_c - m_d)(m_c - m_d)}\right)\left(\frac{b^3_d}{3} - b^2_c b_d - b^2_d b_c\right)\Big|_{b_{ds}}^{b_{df}}\,\Bigg]\,\Bigg]$$

(26)

Let us denote $b_{df} - b_{ds} = \Delta b_d$

(27)

$$E(DW_{l-n}) = \frac{1}{2}\frac{1}{\Delta b_d}\Bigg[\left(\frac{1}{m_v - m_d}\right)\left(b_c\frac{\Delta b_d(b_{df} + b_{ds})}{2} - b_c b_v \Delta b_d - b_v\frac{\Delta b_d(b_{df} + b_{ds})}{2} + b_v^2 \Delta b_d\right)$$

$$-\left(\frac{1}{m_c - m_d}\right)\left(b_c\frac{\Delta b_d(b_{df} + b_{ds})}{2} - b_c^2\Delta b_d - b_v\frac{\Delta b_d(b_{df} + b_{ds})}{2} + b_v b_c \Delta b_d\right)$$

$$+\left(\frac{m_c - m_v}{(m_c - m_d)(m_v - m_d)}\right)\left(\frac{\Delta b_d(b_{df}^2 + b_{ds}^2 + b_{df}b_{ds})}{3} - \frac{\Delta b_d(b_{df} + b_{ds})}{2}b_v - b_c\frac{\Delta b_d(b_{df} + b_{ds})}{2}\right)$$

$$+b_c b_v \Delta b_d\Bigg) - \left(\frac{m_c - m_v}{(m_c - m_d)^2}\right)\left(\frac{\Delta b_d(b_{df}^2 + b_{ds}^2 + b_{df}b_{ds})}{3} - b^2{}_c\Delta b_d - \frac{\Delta b_d(b_{df} + b_{ds})}{2}b_c\right)\Bigg]$$

(28)

Finding the Sign of the Expected Surplus

Taking out Δb_d from the entire factor and dividing by denominator we get:

$$E(DW_{l-n}) = \frac{1}{2}\Bigg[\left(\frac{1}{m_v - m_d}\right)\left(b_c\frac{(b_{df} + b_{ds})}{2} - b_c b_v - b_v\frac{(b_{df} + b_{ds})}{2} + b_v^2\right)$$

$$-\left(\frac{1}{m_c - m_d}\right)\left(b_c\frac{(b_{df} + b_{ds})}{2} - b_c^2 - b_v\frac{(b_{df} + b_{ds})}{2} + b_v b_c\right)$$

$$+\left(\frac{m_c - m_v}{(m_c - m_d)(m_v - m_d)}\right)\left(\frac{(b_{df}^2 + b_{ds}^2 + b_{df}b_{ds})}{3} - \frac{(b_{df} + b_{ds})}{2}b_v - b_c\frac{(b_{df} + b_{ds})}{2} + b_c b_v\right)$$

$$-\left(\frac{m_c - m_v}{(m_c - m_d)^2}\right)\left(\frac{(b_{df}^2 + b_{ds}^2 + b_{df}b_{ds})}{3} - b^2{}_c - \frac{(b_{df} + b_{ds})}{2}b_c\right)\Bigg]$$

(29)

$$2E(DW_{l-n}) = \left[b_c \frac{(b_{df} + b_{ds})}{2} \left(\left(\frac{1}{m_v - m_d} \right) - \left(\frac{1}{m_c - m_d} \right) - \left(\frac{m_c - m_v}{(m_c - m_d)(m_v - m_d)} \right) + \left(\frac{m_c - m_v}{(m_c - m_d)^2} \right) \right) \right.$$

$$- b_v \frac{(b_{df} + b_{ds})}{2} \left(\left(\frac{1}{m_v - m_d} \right) - \left(\frac{1}{m_c - m_d} \right) - \left(\frac{m_c - m_v}{(m_c - m_d)(m_v - m_d)} \right) \right)$$

$$+ \frac{(b_{df}^2 + b_{ds}^2 + b_{df}b_{ds})}{3} \left(\left(\frac{m_c - m_v}{(m_c - m_d)(m_v - m_d)} \right) - \left(\frac{m_c - m_v}{(m_c - m_d)^2} \right) \right) + \frac{b_v}{m_v - m_d} (b_v - b_c)$$

$$\left. - \frac{b_c}{m_c - m_d} (b_v - b_c) + \left(\frac{m_c - m_v}{(m_c - m_d)(m_v - m_d)} \right) b_c b_v + \left(\frac{m_c - m_v}{(m_c - m_d)^2} \right) b_c^2 \right] \qquad (30)$$

$$2 E (DW_{l-n}) S1 + S2 + S3 + S4 + S5 + S6 \qquad (31)$$

$$S1 = b_c \frac{(b_{df} + b_{ds})}{2} \left(\left(\frac{1}{m_v - m_d} \right) - \left(\frac{1}{m_c - m_d} \right) + \left(\frac{m_c - m_v}{(m_c - m_d)(m_v - m_d)} \right) + \left(\frac{m_c - m_v}{(m_c - m_d)^2} \right) \right)$$

$$= b_c \frac{(b_{df} + b_{ds})}{2} \left(\frac{m_c - m_v}{(m_c - m_d)^2} \right) \qquad (32)$$

$$S2 = -b_v \frac{(b_{df} + b_{ds})}{2} \left(\left(\frac{1}{m_v - m_d} \right) - \left(\frac{1}{m_c - m_d} \right) - \left(\frac{m_c - m_v}{(m_c - m_d)(m_v - m_d)} \right) \right) = 0 \, (33)$$

$$S3 = \frac{(b_{df}^2 + b_{ds}^2 + b_{df}b_{ds})}{3} \left(\left(\frac{m_c - m_v}{(m_c - m_d)(m_v - m_d)} \right) - \left(\frac{m_c - m_v}{(m_c - m_d)^2} \right) \right)$$

$$= \frac{(b_{df}^2 + b_{ds}^2 + b_{df}b_{ds})}{3} \left(\frac{(m_c - m_v)^2}{(m_c - m_d)^2 (m_v - m_d)} \right) \qquad (34)$$

$$S4 = \frac{b_v}{m_v - m_d} (b_v - b_c) - \frac{b_c}{m_c - m_d} (b_v - b_c) = \left(\frac{(b_v - b_c)^2}{(m_v - m_d)(m_c - m_d)} \right) \qquad (35)$$

$$S5 = \left(\frac{m_c - m_v}{(m_c - m_d)(m_v - m_d)} \right) b_c b_v \qquad (36)$$

$$S6 = \left(\frac{m_c - m_v}{(m_c - m_d)^2} \right) b_c^2 \qquad (37)$$

To find out the sign of $E(DW_{n-l})$ we have to follow these underlying assumptions of the model:

$$b_d > b_c > b_v > 0 \qquad (38)$$

$$m_d < 0 \qquad (39)$$

$$m_c > m_v > 0 \qquad (40)$$

Following the assumptions:

$$S1 > 0 \qquad (41)$$

$$S2 = 0 \qquad (42)$$

$$S3 > 0 \qquad (43)$$

$$S4 > 0 \qquad (44)$$

$$S5 > 0 \qquad (45)$$

$$S6 > 0 \qquad (46)$$

Putting these values in Equation 31 we get,

$$E(DW_{l-n}) > 0 \tag{47}$$

Following Equations 31-37, we have:

$$E(DW_{l-n}) = \frac{1}{2}\left[b_c \frac{(b_{df} + b_{ds})}{2}\left(\frac{m_c - m_v}{(m_c - m_d)^2} \right) + \frac{(b_{df}^2 + b_{ds}^2 + b_{df}b_{ds})}{3}\left(\frac{(m_c - m_v)^2}{(m_c - m_d)^2(m_v - m_d)} \right) \right.$$

$$\left. + \left(\frac{(b_v - b_c)^2}{(m_v - m_d)(m_c - m_d)} \right) + \left(\frac{m_c - m_v}{(m_c - m_d)(m_v - m_d)} \right)b_c b_v + \left(\frac{m_c - m_v}{(m_c - m_d)^2} \right)b_c^2 \right] \tag{48}$$

Differentiating Equation 48 wrt m_d

$$\frac{\partial E(DW_{l-n})}{\partial m_d} = \frac{1}{2}\left[b_c \frac{(b_{df} + b_{ds})}{2}\left(\frac{2(m_c - m_v)}{(m_c - m_d)^3} \right) + \right.$$

$$+ \frac{(b_{df}^2 + b_{ds}^2 + b_{df}b_{ds})}{3}\left(\frac{(m_c - m_v)^2(2(m_c - m_d)(m_v - m_d) + (m_c - m_d)^2)}{(m_c - m_d)^4(m_v - m_d)^2} \right)$$

$$+ \left(\frac{(b_v - b_c)^2((m_v - m_d) + (m_c - m_d))}{(m_v - m_d)^2(m_c - m_d)^2} \right) + \left(\frac{(m_c - m_v)((m_c - m_d) + (m_v - m_d))}{(m_c - m_d)^2(m_v - m_d)^2} \right)b_c b_v$$

$$\left. + \left(\frac{2(m_c - m_v)}{(m_c - m_d)^3} \right)b_c^2 \right] \tag{49}$$

Following the underlying assumptions of the model (Equations 38, 39, 40) we find that:

$$\frac{\partial E(DW_{l-n})}{\partial m_d} > 0 \tag{50}$$

Differentiating Equation 48 wrt b_{df}

$$\frac{\partial E(DW_{l-n})}{\partial b_{df}} = \frac{1}{2}\left[\frac{b_c}{2}\left(\frac{m_c - m_v}{(m_c - m_d)^2}\right) + \frac{(2b_{df} + b_{ds})}{3}\left(\frac{(m_c - m_v)^2}{(m_c - m_d)^2(m_v - m_d)}\right)\right] \quad (51)$$

Following the underlying assumptions of the model (Equations 38, 39, 40) we find that:

$$\frac{\partial E(DW_{l-n})}{\partial b_{df}} > 0 \quad (52)$$

About the Authors

Marc J. Schniederjans is the C. Wheaton Battey distinguished professor of business in the College of Business Administration at the University of Nebraska - Lincoln. He teaches classes in operations management, decision sciences, and management information systems. Dr. Schniederjans has won several distinguished teaching awards and has edited, co-edited, authored or co-authored 15 books in the field of management. He has published more than 90 articles, appearing in journals such as *Operations Research, Decision Sciences, Decision Support Systems, Communications of the ACM, Computers and Operations Research, Information and Management, Information Processing and Management*, and *Interfaces*. Professor Schniederjans is serving on various journal editorial review or advisory boards, and has served as a journal editor. He has been an active member of the Decision Sciences Institute for more than 20 years and has served as a consultant and trainer to a variety of business and government agencies.

Ashlyn M. Schniederjans is currently a student at Johns Hopkins University, USA, majoring in economics. She previously worked for the Gallup Organization and Morgan Stanley. In 2002 she received the Woodrow Wilson Research Fellowship grant to do research on decision making. In 2005 she co-authored the textbook, *Outsourcing and Insourcing in an International Context* and 2004 she co-authored the textbook, *Information Technology Investment: Decision Making Methodology*. She has also contributed research article chapters to other decision making books.

Dara G. Schniederjans is currently a student in the Carlson School of Management at the University of Minnesota - Twin Cities, USA. In 2005 she co-authored the textbook, *Outsourcing and Insourcing in an International Context*. She has also co-authored chapters in reading books such as in *Advanced in Mathematical Programming* and *Financial Planning* and *Applications in Management Science*.

*   *   *   *

April M. Adams is a doctoral student in information systems at Mississippi State University, USA. Her research interests include outsourcing, privacy issues, security management, and systems analysis and design. Adams has served as a consultant to numerous organizations including the State of Georgia, Tenet Hospitals, and the Alzheimer's Association of Texas. She also has several years teaching experience at University of West Georgia and New Mexico State University. Adams holds a BS and MS in MIS from Auburn University.

Vijay K. Agrawal is an associate professor of MIS at University of Nebraska - Kearney, USA. He received his BS in mechanical engineering from University of Indore, an MBA from University of Toledo, an MS in computer science from Bowling Green State University, and a PhD from University of Millia Islamia. He has taught at Bowling Green, University of North Carolina - Greensboro, University of Missouri - Kansas City, and Apeejay School of Management. He has 18 years of experience as head of information systems and as an engineer. He has published in *Production and Operations Management, National Social Science Journal, Global Journal of Flexible Systems Management,* and *Encyclopedia of Operations Research and Management Science.*

Joaquin Alegre is an assistant professor of management at the University Jaume I, Castellón, Spain, where he teaches subjects related to operations and innovation management. In 2002, he was a visiting researcher at INSEAD, Fontainebleau, France. His research interests are in knowledge management and technological innovation from a strategic perspective. Dr. Alegre has participated in several research projects dealing with local firms' competitiveness and with ceramic tile producers.

Ronald Bremer is an associate professor in information systems and quantitative sciences at Texas Tech University, USA. He received his PhD in statistics from Texas A&M University. Areas of research are linear statistical models, finance statistical methodology, econometric methodology and statistical quality control.

Anthony (Tony) Briggs is a business information officer in the Best Buy Technology Group, Best Buy Stores, USA. Tony has the executive responsibility of overseeing Best Buy's information systems in support of finance, human resources, legal, and IT security, reporting to the CIO. His duties also include IT responsibility for holiday operational readiness, Sarbanes-Oxley and Data Privacy compliance, and other mandates. Tony is a graduate of the United States Military Academy - West Point, and served as an officer in the Infantry, as well as in Operations and Logistics assignments. He has been an independent consultant, a MIS director for many small firms, and was an instructor at Johnson County Community College, Kansas. He is the author of text books on topics such as advanced programming.

Qing Cao is an assistant professor of MIS at the H.W. Bloch School of Business, University of Missouri - Kansas City, USA. He holds an MBA from University of Wisconsin and a PhD from the College of Business Administration at the University of Nebraska. Dr. Cao has combined eight years of industrial experiences in engineering, operations management and IT consulting before entering the academic field. His research focuses on e-commerce, systems analysis and design, and artificial intelligent. His work on these topics has been published or forthcoming in journals such as: *Journal of Operations Management, Decision Sciences, Communications of ACM, IEEE Transactions on Systems, Man, and Cybernetics, European Journal of Operational Research, Journal of Database Management,* and others.

Donald A. Carpenter is an associate professor of computer information systems at Mesa State College, USA. He holds a BS from Kearney State College, an MBA from the University of Colorado - Colorado Springs, and a PhD from University of Nebraska - Lincoln. Prior to starting his teaching career, he accumulated 10 years experience in the information technology industry. Carpenter's teaching and research interests are in CIS education, DSS, IRD, ERP and meaningfulness of IS work. He has published in *Journal of Computer Information Systems, Journal of Computer Science Education, International Journal of Decision Support Systems,* and others.

Maneesh Chandra is a manager at ZS Associates, USA, a global management consulting firm specializing in sales and marketing issues. He has had academic research interests in outsourcing of services and global strategy issues. His

consulting experience has including working with various Fortune 500 pharmaceutical companies in the U.S., Canada, Latin America, and Japan on sales and
marketing strategy issues. These issues include brand planning, segmentation
and targeting strategy, promotional mix, sales force strategy, sales organization
design, sales force alignment, and sales incentive compensation programs.
Maneesh holds a BTech from IT-BHU, a PGDM (MBA) from IIM - Bangalore,
and a PhD from the University of Texas - Austin.

Ricardo Chiva is an assistant professor of management at the University Jaume
I, Spain. He holds a PhD in management from the Universitat Jaume I and an
International MBA from the European School of Management (EAP), taken in
Oxford, Paris, and Berlin. His areas of interest are organizational learning,
innovation management and complexity theory.

Francisco Delgadillo Jr. is an assistant professor in the Department of ISQS
in the College of Business Administration, Texas Tech University, USA. He
received his BS in electrical engineering from the University of Notre Dame and
completed his MBA and PhD in production/operations management from TTU.
He has served as an electrical-aerospace engineer for T.R.W. Space and
Technology Group in Redondo Beach, California, a business consultant for
Arthur Andersen, and a lecturer at UTEP.

David N. Ford, PE, is an assistant professor in the Construction Engineering and
Management Program in the Department of Civil Engineering, Texas A&M
University, USA. Prior this position, Dr. Ford was on faculty in the Department
of Information Science at the University of Bergen, Norway, where he re-
searched and taught in the System Dynamics Program. For over 14 years he
designed and managed the development of constructed facilities in industry and
government. He received his PhD from the Massachusetts Institute of Technology and his master's and bachelor's degrees from Tulane University. His current
research interests include strategic managerial flexibility, the dynamics of
development supply chains, and resource allocation policies.

Rajneesh Goyal currently works for a boutique consulting firm in New York as
a business analyst in the medical and financial industries. He is a graduate of the
MIS graduate program at California State University - Sacramento, USA. He
has a BS in electronics and communication from Bangalore University, India. On
graduation from Bangalore University, Rajneesh went to work as a software
engineer for Metamor Global Solutions India and eventually was recruited by
IBM Global Services.

Mark Hoelscher is an assistant professor of entrepreneurship in the Department of Management and Quantitative Methods in the College of Business, Illinois State University, USA. He graduated from Texas Tech University with a PhD in strategy and entrepreneurship. His research interests include the measurement of social capital in family businesses as well as the development of a new construct, family capital. Hoelscher is also an active researcher in the study of nascent entrepreneurs and their use as proxies in understanding the entrepreneurial personality.

James J. Hoffman is the Rawls professor of operations management in the Rawls College of Business at Texas Tech University, USA. He holds a PhD from the College of Business Administration at the University of Nebraska - Lincoln. His research interests are in operations management and business strategy. His research has appeared in journals such as *Information Systems & Operational Research Journal, Journal of Engineering and Technology Management, International Journal of Operations and Production Management, Systems Research,* and the *Strategic Management Journal.*

Julie E. Kendall, PhD, is an associate professor of e-commerce and information technology in the School of Business - Camden, Rutgers University, USA. Dr. Kendall is the chair of IFIP Working Group 8.2. She was awarded the Silver Core from IFIP. Dr. Kendall's research has been published in *MIS Quarterly, Decision Sciences, Information & Management, Organization Studies* and many other journals. Additionally, Dr. Kendall has recently co-authored a college textbook with Kenneth E. Kendall, *Systems Analysis and Design,* 6th Edition. She is a senior editor for *JITTA,* and Dr. Kendall is on the editorial review boards of the *International Journal of e-Collaboration;* the *Decision Sciences Journal of Innovative Education;* the *Journal of Database Management;* the *Journal of Cases on Information Technology* and the *Information Resource Management Journal.* She served on the inaugural editorial board of the *Journal of AIS* and as an associate editor for *MIS Quarterly.* Julie served as treasurer and vice president for the Decision Sciences Institute.

Kenneth E. Kendall, PhD, is a professor of e-commerce and information technology in the School of Business - Camden, Rutgers University, USA. He is one of the founders of the International Conference on Information Systems (ICIS) and a fellow of the Decision Sciences Institute. He is an associate editor for the *International Journal of Intelligent Information Technologies,* and he is on the senior advisory board of *JITTA;* a member of the editorial board of *Journal of IT for Development* and is on the editorial review board of the *Decision Sciences Journal of Innovative Education.* Dr. Kendall has been named as one of the top 60 most productive MIS researchers in the world, and he was awarded the Silver Core from IFIP. He recently co-authored a text, *Systems Analysis and Design*, 6th Edition, published by Prentice Hall and *Project Planning and Requirements Analysis for IT Systems Development*, second edition *and* edited *Emerging Information Technologies: Improving Decisions, Cooperation, and Infrastructure.*

Masaaki "Mike" Kotabe holds the Washburn Chair professorship in international business and marketing, and is director of research at the Institute of Global Management Studies at the Fox School of Business and Management, Temple University, USA. Dr. Kotabe currently serves as the editor of the *Journal of International Management* and prior to joining Temple University in 1998, he was Ambassador Edward Clark Centennial endowed fellow and professor of marketing and international business at the University of Texas at Austin. Dr. Kotabe served as the vice president of the Academy of International Business in 1997-98. In 1998, he was elected a fellow of the Academy of International Business for his significant contribution to international business research and education. He is the recipient of the 2002 Musser Award for Excellence in Research at Temple University. He has written over 100 scholarly articles and over a dozen books, including *Global Sourcing Strategy: R&D, Manufacturing, Marketing Interfaces* (1992), *Anticompetitive Practices in Japan* (1996), *Market Revolution in Latin America: Beyond Mexico* (2001), *Global Marketing Management*, 3rd Ed. (2004), *Marketing Management* (2005), and *Global Supply Chain Management* (2006).

N. K. Kwak is a professor of decision sciences in the John Cook School of Business, Saint Louis University, USA. He received his BA from Seoul National University, MA from the University of California - Berkeley, and PhD from University of Southern California, all in economics, and a certificate in advanced management studies from Carnegie-Mellon University. He was a senior Fulbright scholar. He has authored/co-authored 14 books, five monographs, and over 130 papers. His publications have appeared in *Computers & Operations Research, Decision Sciences, European Journal of Operational Research, Journal of the Operational Research Society, Management Science, Omega, Operations Research,* and others.

Rafael Lapiedra is a lecturer in management at the University Jaume I of Castellón, Spain. He holds a PhD in business administration and a master in European business management and information systems from Anglia Polytechnic University. He has been a visiting professor at the Universidad Tecnológica

Metropolitana of Santiago in Chile and at the London School of Economics and Political Science. His research interests lie in information systems management, strategic alliances and inter-organizational systems.

Chang Won Lee is an associate professor of business administration in the Department of Venture Management, Jinju National University in Korea. He received his MS and PhD degrees from Saint Louis University. His publications have appeared in *Advances in Mathematical Programming, European Journal of Operational Research, Journal of Medical Systems,* and others. He is a member of the editorial advisory boards of the *Journal of Strategic e-Commerce, Journal of Systematics, Cybernetics, and Informatics,* and others. His research interests are in the areas of entrepreneurial studies with innovation, ERP-SCM linkages, information and technology management, and multi-criteria decision-making modeling.

Karyl B. Leggio is chair of the Department of Finance, Information Management and Strategy and an associate professor of finance at the Henry W. Bloch School of Business and Public Administration, University of Missouri - Kansas City, USA. She also serves as the executive director of Bloch's EMBA program. She received a BS with majors in finance and management from Virginia Tech and an MBA from East Tennessee State University. She received a PhD in business with a concentration in finance from the University of Kansas. Dr. Leggio's primary area of research is in deregulating industries, specifically in the area of risk management. Additional avenues of active research for her are in the areas of real options, corporate restructuring, mergers, and individual risk management.

Leonardo Legorreta is an assistant professor of MIS at the California State University, Sacramento, USA. His research interests lie in studying the impact of IT on organizations. His postdoctoral work at the University of Utah centered on developing metrics for measuring IT architectural flexibility. His interests now include organizational agility. Leo teaches graduate MIS courses in IT strategy and undergraduate courses in business software development. Prior to becoming an MIS professor, Leo trained and worked as a research mathematician.

Jeanette Nasem Morgan was recently technical director and principal consultant for PricewaterhouseCoopers, LLP, where clients included the FAA, the U.S. Department of Defense, and the U.S. Postal Service on a variety of software engineering and information management projects. She was also formerly division manager for the Boeing Company where she worked on numerous multi-million dollar projects for NASA, the Pentagon, NIMA, and the Department of Defense. Her early career was in regional and international banking. Dr. Morgan is currently an assistant professor of information systems management at Duquesne University, Pittsburgh, Pennsylvania, USA.

Janet Y. Murray is E. Desmond Lee professor for developing women leaders and entrepreneurs in international business at the Department of Marketing, University of Missouri - St. Louis, USA. Dr. Murray received her PhD in marketing from the University of Missouri - Columbia. She has previously held faculty positions in marketing and international business at Saint Louis University, Cleveland State University, and City University of Hong Kong. Dr. Murray's publications have appeared in journals such as the *Journal of Marketing, Strategic Management Journal, Journal of International Business Studies, Industrial Marketing Management, Management International Review, International Marketing Review*, and others. She has consulted with Fortune 500 and other firms in the areas of marketing and international business strategies. Dr. Murray serves on the editorial review boards for several journals. In October 2005, researchers at Michigan State University identified 89 most prolific researchers in International Business, among whom Dr. Murray was ranked #21.

Param Vir Singh is a doctoral student in the Management Science Department at UW Business School, University of Washington, Seattle, USA. He holds a BE in chemical engineering from Panjab University, Chandigarh and an MA in interdisciplinary studies from Texas Tech University. Param's research interests include inter and intra-organizational issues in systems development and procurement. Param has presented his work at leading conferences and workshops such as Workshop on Information Technology and Systems (WITS), Seattle Innovation Symposium and Informs Annual meet.

Steve Smithson is a senior lecturer in IS at the London School of Economics and Political Science, UK, with a PhD in IS from the same institution. He was editor of the *European Journal of Information Systems* from its inception in 1991 until the end of December 1999. He is currently president of the UK Academy for Information Systems. His research interests lie in information systems management, the evaluation of information systems, and developments in e-business. He has published numerous journal articles and conference papers, as well as four books.

Eric Walden is currently an assistant professor at the Rawls College of Business at Texas Tech University, USA. His research interests focus on developing a greater understanding of information systems in the organizational context. This includes issues within and among organizations combining a strong theory from industrial organization in economics, with empirical validation within an organizational context. Eric received his PhD from The University of Minnesota, and his prior research has appeared in *Information Systems Research*, *MIS Quarterly*, *Harvard Business Review*, *The International Journal of Electronic Commerce* and *Electronic Markets*.

Merrill Warkentin is a professor of MIS at Mississippi State University, USA. He has published over 125 research manuscripts, primarily in computer security management, e-commerce, and virtual collaborative teams, which have appeared in books, proceedings, and journals such as *MIS Quarterly*, *Decision Sciences*, *Communications of the AIS*, *Information Systems Journal*, *Journal of End User Computing*, *Journal of Global Information Management*, and others. Professor Warkentin is the co-author or editor of four books, and is currently an associate editor of *Information Resources Management Journal* and *Journal of Information Systems Security*. Dr. Warkentin has served as a consultant to numerous organizations and has served as national distinguished lecturer for the Association for Computing Machinery (ACM). Previously, Dr. Warkentin held the Reisman Research Professorship at Northeastern University - Boston, where he was also director of MIS and e-commerce programs. Professor Warkentin holds BA, MA, and PhD degrees from the University of Nebraska - Lincoln.

Kathryn M. Zuckweiler is an assistant professor in the College of Business and Technology, University of Nebraska at Kearney, USA. She teaches classes and conducts research in the fields of operations management, strategic management, and management information systems. Her research has appeared in the *International Journal of Production Research*, *Management Decision*, the *International Journal of Human Computer Interaction*, and the *International Journal of Distance Education Technologies*. She is a member of the Decision Sciences Institute.

Index

A

ABC 71, 80, 137, 149
ABC analysis 140
access control 119
activity based costing (ABC) 71, 80, 137
AHP (see analytical hierarchy process)
alliance 2, 13
analytical hierarchy process (AHP)
    321, 323
application service provider (ASP) 32,
    243
application SLA 102
architecture 117
architectures 109
Artemis 80
ASP (see application service provider)

B

B2B 46
balanced scorecard 99, 106, 107, 111
Balanced Scorecard Institute 107
benchmarking 103, 120
benchmarks 2
best-of-breed outsourcing 45
binomial model 304, 309
Black-Scholes formula (1973) 303
Black-Scholes model 309
boilerplate 102
bona fide tools 71
BPO (see business process outsourcing)
budgets 80, 141
business intelligence 138, 144, 147
business process 94

business process outsourcing (BPO)
    3, 97, 148, 243
business strategies 47

C

CAGR (see compound annual growth
    rate)
capability maturity model (CMM) 101
capacity 98
capital costs 136
causes 17
centralization 123, 124, 126
centralized contracting 130
centralized IT procurement 127
CFO 5
change control 99
change management 120
changing workforce 23
chic logistics 315
Chic Logistics Incorporated (CLI) 310
CIO 6
CLI (see Chic Logistics Incorporated)
client 269, 270, 271, 275
client organizations 270
client-vendor relationships 276
CMM (see capability maturity model)
CMMi (see integration capability maturity
    model)
CMO (see contract manufacturing
    organization)
COCs 285
commercial off the shelf (COTS) 79
competencies 176
competency-critical success factor 29

competition 23
complexity 205, 209
compound annual growth rate (CAGR)
    241
Computer Sciences Corporation (CSC)
    136
computer-supported collaborative work
critical success factors 17, 27, 28, 47,
    58, 99, 107
CRM 22
CROs (see Contract Research Organiza-
    tions)
CSC (see Computer Sciences Corpora-
    tion)
CSCW (see computer-supported collabo-
    rative work)
CSF 77, 107
cultural attitudes 71
cultural feasibility 141
cultural norms 71
cultural practices 109
culture
    70, 111, 227, 237, 270, 273, 275
culture, national 275
customer focus 21, 22
customer relationship management
    (CRM) 22
customization 202, 209

D

data mining 132, 138, 144
data warehouses 132, 138, 144
DataMirror 143
DCF (see discounted cash flow)
dead weight loss 343, 345
decentralization 125
decentralized 124
decision model 83, 136, 138, 140, 146
decision model 62, 71, 79, 135, 138,
    145
decision model criteria 135
decision support system (DSS) 144, 233
decision support tools 138
degraded performance 121
degree 245, 246
Demand uncertainty 203
demand uncertainty 203, 209
descriptive decision model 145
differentiated oligopoly 3
disaster recovery 137
disaster-recovery plan 103

discounted cash flow (DCF) 301
DSS (see decision support system)

E

earned value analysis (EVA) 71, 137
ED 242
EDS (see Electronic Data System)
EIS (see executive information system)
Electronic Data System (EDS) 44, 97,
    242
encrypted 102
encryption 102, 121
environmental uncertainty 205
ethics 62, 74
EVA (see earned value analysis)
evaluating 58
evaluation 141
evolution of information system 44
executive information system (EIS) 234
external relationship 282
extranet Web site 110

F

feasibility 114, 134, 141
feasibility analysis 76, 140
feasibility study 140
First American 143
fixed costs 134
formalization 124
functional aspect 48
future of the IS department 48

G

GDSS (see group decision support
    systems)
GE (see General Electric)
General Electric (GE) 9
global activity 20
global competition 23
global economy 22, 23
global industry value chain 20
global outsourcing 292
global scale 283, 284, 291
globalization 23, 74, 104
goal programming (GP) 286, 321, 322
goal programming software 286
goals 47
goals and strategies 47
government 72, 97, 100, 133
government decision-making 132

governmental agency 74
GP (see goal programming)
group decision support systems (GDSS) 235

H

help desk 70, 73, 134, 144
heuristic 142
heuristical bias 142
heuristical processes 132
hierarchical business organization 5
HIPAA 272
historical perspective 19, 34, 42
hosting SLA 102, 103
human resource management 73

I

improvement 58, 67, 97, 100, 133
in-house sourcing 199, 201
information systems outsourcing 44
information security 109, 117
information systems processes 47
information technology (IT) 46, 124, 269, 282
infrastructure 70, 71, 82, 94, 101, 141
infrastructure weaknesses 118
inseparability 209
insource 71
insourcing 69, 70, 245
intangibility 201, 209
Integrated Systems Solution Corporation (ISSC) 243
integration capability maturity model (CMMi) 101
intercultural teamwork 114
International Organization for Standardization 101
International Trade Agreement (ITO) 31
international transactions 84
Internet 135, 142
Internet service provider 78
Internet software application 73
interorganizational relationships 282
intranet Web sites 110
IR 97
IS outsourcing 152
ISO 9000 101
ISSC (see Integrated Systems Solution Corporation)
IT (see information technology)
IT processes 46

IT-based business processes 46
ITO (see International Trade Agreement)

J

JIT (see just-in-time management)
job loss 23
just-in-time management (JIT) 14

K

knowledge base 96, 138
knowledge management 192
knowledge transfer 137, 141
knowledge-based model 146

L

likelihood 225
local government 95
Logitech 105
long-term strategic alliance 2
LotusNotes 110

M

maintenance contracts 134
make-or-buy 200, 205, 212
Malcolm Baldrige 100
Malcolm Baldrige National Quality Award 100
management heuristics 138
management-by-objectives (MBO) 14
managing outsourcing 53
matrix organizations 13
maturity 99, 140
MBO (see management-by-objectives)
MCDM (see multicriteria decision making)
measurement 80, 107
medium category of service 139
metaphor, the family 231
metaphor, the game 229
metaphor, the journey 229
metaphor, the jungle 231
metaphor, the machine 230
metaphor, the organism 230
metaphor, the society 231
metaphor, the war 230
metaphor, the zoo 231
metaphors 224
metaphors, business 229
metaphors, organizational 228
metrics 74, 82, 93, 99, 102, 103, 139, 149

MIS 62, 296
MiTAK-SYNNEX Group 31
MLS 71
mode 246
modification 97
monitoring 58
monitoring dashboard 242
monitoring performance and controlling
 102
motivation 123, 126, 128
multicriteria decision making (MCDM)
 321, 322
multisourcing 243, 244

N

NAFTA (see North American Free Trade
 Agreement)
Nash solution 344
National Ignition Facility (NIF) 308, 315,
 316
National Institute of Standards in Technology (NIST) 100
near-shore outsourcing 18
near-shoring 69
net present value (NPV) 301
net-sourcing 243, 244
network infrastructure 102
network SLA 102
NIF (see National Ignition Facility)
NIST (see National Institute of Standards
 in Technology)
noncore activity 203
noncore competitive business activity 6
noncore service activity 209
norms 112, 189
North American Free Trade Agreement
 (NAFTA) 29
NPV (see net present value)

O

obsolescence 24
off-shore outsourcing 18
off-shoring 18, 69
online (video) meetings 114
operational feasibility 141
opportunism 123, 126, 127
option analysis 317
organization structure 27
organizational culture 274
outsource partner 83, 99
outsource service provider 83

outsource vendor 84
outsourced project 58
outsourcee 199
outsourcer 199, 201
outsourcer, selecting an 100
outsourcing 70, 94, 175, 176, 178, 199,
 201, 296
outsourcing as a natural evolutionary step
 43
outsourcing contract 42, 52, 56, 58
outsourcing contracts model (pay-later)
 339
outsourcing, critical factors 285
outsourcing failures 152
outsourcing finance and accounting (F&A)
 functions 33
outsourcing level 154, 161, 162
outsourcing MIS 62, 73, 83, 104, 135
outsourcing of customer care functions
 33
outsourcing of human resource (HR)
 functions 33
outsourcing of information technology
 functions 31
outsourcing of pharmaceutical functions
 32
outsourcing outcomes 152
outsourcing partner 85, 224, 225, 236
outsourcing partner selection 291
outsourcing partner selection model 283
outsourcing partners, selecting 136
outsourcing, project risk 271
outsourcing, R&D 298
outsourcing risks 237, 273
outsourcing, selection of services 138
outsourcing software development 104
outsourcing, sources of 271
outsourcing, strategic 322
outsourcing success 152, 156, 167
outsourcing-insourcing alliance network
 2, 5, 13
ownership 246

P

partner selection model 283
pay-later 341, 342
pay-now 339, 342
payroll 73
PDA (see personal digital assistant) 114
Peregrine 97
performance 79, 82, 93, 99, 144

performance criteria and metrics 94
performance levels 102
performance measurement 70
performance metrics 93, 137
performance specifications 94
personal digital assistant (PDA) 114
PMIS (see project management informa-
    tion system)
Primavera 80
productivity 69, 71, 99, 110, 135, 136
productivity levels 75
productivity paradox 282
profitability 82
project 178
project evaluation 77
project feasibility 138
project management 154, 170
project management and monitoring 167
project management information system
    (PMIS) 111
project management, success 168
project management tool 114
project proposal 140
project renewal 155, 169
project risk 271
project selection 140
project termination 155, 169
project 175
proposal 82
psychological contract 242, 249, 253

Q

quality 71, 94, 99, 100, 133, 134, 136
quality model 100
quality process 101

R

R&D 4, 297
R&D outsourcing 298
real option 297, 302
real option analysis (ROA) 302, 311, 314
reasons 47
recovery 94, 142, 143
remedy 97
remote control and virtual management
    119
renewing 58
request for proposal (RFP) 55
response times 94, 103
return on investment 81
RFP 55

risk 4, 84, 98, 99
risk factors 116
risk management 107, 118, 249
risks 4, 10, 141, 225
risks of outsourcing 27
ritical success factors (CSFs) 77
ROA (see real option analysis)
ROA, not 301
rural sourcing 69

S

SCM (see supply chain management)
SCMIS (see supply chain management
    information system)
security 80, 93, 102, 104, 137
security architecture 120
security breaches 117
security consultants 118
security framework 120
security procedures 120
security staff 137
security systems 70
SEI (see Software Engineering Institute)
select specific projects 67
select the projects 80
select the right candidate 77
selected outsourcing partnerships 112
selecting a provider 99
selecting an outsourcer 100, 101
selecting viable projects 139
selection of outsource partners 99
selection of services to be outsourced
    138
service activity 201
service level agreement (SLA) 94, 99,
    103, 138
service life cycles 22
services 203
services, additional 340
services, essential 203
shrinkage in product 22
single, multiprocess outsource provider 7
SLA 54, 94, 95, 102, 105, 107, 138,
    149
SLA model 138
social capital 190, 192
social norms 190
societal, political, and ethical factors 25
software 178
software development 70, 83, 84, 114
software development toolset 77

Software Engineering Institute (SEI) 101
software tool 119, 144
spillover risk 9
spot checks 97
strategic intent 153, 159, 160, 162, 167
strategic outsourcing 321
strategic planning 63, 65, 69, 71, 73, 80
strategic vision 63
strategy 62, 63, 74, 107, 136, 175
subcultures 224
success 160
success factors 271, 273
successful contract negotiations 166
successful project management 168
supplier source selection 101
supply chain 321
supply chain management (SCM) 308, 324
supply chain management information system (SCMIS) 310
support costs 136
systems life cycle 22

T

TCA (see transaction cost analysis)
team 66, 73, 79, 94, 107, 111, 140
technical feasibility 140
technological innovations 24
technological uncertainty 204, 209
technology transfer 116
technology transfer block exemption (TTBE) 116
telecommunications 70, 71, 74, 84, 104, 136
telecommunications network 70, 84
ttelephone answering service 78
third party logistics (3PL) 30
timeframe 246, 248
tools 69, 97, 120, 147
transaction cost 204
transaction cost analysis (TCA) 198, 200, 203, 212
transference of the contract 115

trust 189, 190
TTBE (see technology transfer block exemption)
type of service provider 83

U

U.S. Congress 100
U.S. Department of Defense 117
U.S. Government 101
UCTA (see Unfair Contract Trams Act 1977)
uncertainty 203
uncertainty, demand 203
uncertainty, environmental 205
uncertainty, technological 204
Unfair Contract Trams Act 1977 (UCTA) 115
unforeseen costs 69, 71
unpredictability 203
users 175, 178

V

value chain 20
various alliances 13
vendor 170, 269, 270, 271, 342
vendor evaluation 105
vendor quality 299
vendor selection 154, 163, 165, 299
vendor selection criteria 54
vendor selection, two-stage 300
vendors 270
virtual teams 109, 110

W

Web site hosting 78
why, when, and what to outsource 17, 27
work ethic 71, 72

X

Xerox Corporation 159

Y

Y2K 29

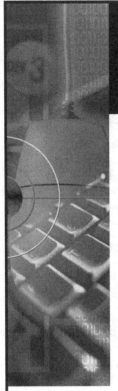